Books from

THE COUNCIL FOR BASIC EDUCATION

THE CASE FOR BASIC EDUCATION,
edited by James D. Koerner

TOMORROW'S ILLITERATES: THE STATE OF
READING INSTRUCTION TODAY,
edited by Charles C. Walcutt

SWISS SCHOOLS AND OURS: WHY THEIRS ARE BETTER,
by H. G. Rickover

HIGH SCHOOL ENGLISH TEXTBOOKS:
A CRITICAL EXAMINATION,
by James J. Lynch and Bertrand Evans

Books from

THE COUNCIL FOR BASIC EDUCATION

High
School
English
Textbooks

High School English

Textbooks: *A Critical Examination*

◇◇

BY JAMES J. LYNCH
AND BERTRAND EVANS

PROFESSORS OF ENGLISH,
UNIVERSITY OF CALIFORNIA, BERKELEY

An Atlantic Monthly Press Book

LITTLE, BROWN AND COMPANY · BOSTON · TORONTO

ATLANTIC–LITTLE, BROWN BOOKS
ARE PUBLISHED BY
LITTLE, BROWN AND COMPANY
IN ASSOCIATION WITH
THE ATLANTIC MONTHLY PRESS

Published simultaneously in Canada
by Little, Brown & Company (Canada) Limited

PRINTED IN THE UNITED STATES OF AMERICA

Dedicated to the memory of my colleague, James J. Lynch.

Bertrand Evans

THE COUNCIL FOR BASIC EDUCATION

THIS VOLUME was produced under the sponsorship of the Council for Basic Education, 725 Fifteenth Street N.W., Washington, D.C. The Council is a nonprofit, lay-oriented group devoted to the maintenance of quality in American education; it is financed by foundation grants and by the dues and payments of its members and subscribers. As explained in its original statement of purpose in 1956:

The Council for Basic Education was established in the belief that the purpose of education is the harmonious development of the mind, the will, and the conscience of each individual so that he may use to the full his intrinsic powers and shoulder the responsibilities of citizenship. It believes in the principle of universal education and in the tax-supported public school system. It insists that only by the maintenance of high academic standards can the ideal of democratic education be realized — the ideal of offering to all the children of all the people of the United States not merely an opportunity to attend school, but the privilege of receiving there the soundest education that is afforded any place in the world.

Among the Council's regular activities in support of these ideals are the publication of a monthly newsletter, the CBE *Bulletin*, and the organization of research and publication projects of special significance to the strengthening of basic education.

Acknowledgments

THE COUNCIL FOR BASIC EDUCATION wishes to thank the Old Dominion Foundation for its support of the project that produced this book. Thanks are also extended to several specialists who read the manuscript and made helpful suggestions. Special thanks are due Irving Gersten who, with the cooperation of the surviving author, Professor Evans, has done extensive editorial work in making the manuscript ready for the printer, and who wrote the Introduction, summing up the findings and recommendations of the authors.

Preface

WE ATTEMPT in the following pages to present a faithful report on the textbooks currently in use in high school English classes throughout the United States. Although we have not ignored other kinds of books — "teen-age tales," special editions of high school "classics," reading handbooks, collections of readings by genres, handbooks of grammar and composition, spelling and vocabulary booklets, workbooks, peripheral materials on the language arts, and so forth — we concentrate on the two principal kinds of textbooks that continue to be most influential in determining the organization and content of high school English courses; namely, the series of anthologies of literature, and the series of grammar and composition books.

The selection of textbooks to be examined was accomplished by a variety of means. Our first correspondence was with publishers, from whom we received catalogues and often very helpful information on the use of particular textbooks. We next requested from all state departments of education throughout the United States adoption lists, adoption practices, and available lists of criteria used in the selection of books. In addition, we selected some two hundred cities and towns, representing every state, and addressed letters to the superintendent of schools, in each case asking for information on books in use, criteria for selection, etc. From these superintendents we received also names of a very considerable number of classroom teachers to whom we might turn for more specific help. In these ways we drew together at last the body of materials on which our examination concentrated and which formed the center of the following report.

In the course of a very considerable correspondence with classroom teachers we accumulated much comment and criticism, some of which is represented in the body of the report, with additional examples appended. Our later corespondence with teachers failed to discover titles of series not already identified and ordered from publishers; hence we assume that all series in significant use are covered in the report. We are aware that some of the volumes examined in this study no longer are vigorously promoted by their publishers and, in a few instances, are no longer in the active market; however, they continue to be used in the schools, and teachers and state departments of education continue to list them. Furthermore, even if the books were no longer in use in a single classroom, the criteria by which they were evaluated and the recommendations we have made for the improvement of English textbooks would remain unaffected.*

It has proved impossible to include in this report all the interesting and often revealing details disclosed by our close examination of the books. We have been content, therefore, to let the tables and summaries present the mass of evidence accumulated and beyond these to limit ourselves to the discussion of representative details to indicate the books' tendencies and characteristics.

---

* EDITOR'S NOTE: Since the writing of this section, and the subsequent untimely death of Professor Lynch in May, 1962, at least two more anthologies of literature, Harcourt, Brace's Laureate edition and American Book Company's *Worlds of Literature,* as well as McGraw-Hill's volume *Literature of the World,* have been or are about to be published. The present study does not include data from these new texts, but presumably the evaluations and conclusions here included will be as pertinent to them as to the many others which are so painstakingly analyzed.

These tables and summaries, which include all the relevant factual and descriptive data, can be used, if it is so desired, without reference to other parts of the report. Most of the tables and summaries are intended to be purely quantitative rather than evaluative; their figures are, we believe, as accurate as repeated thumbing of pages and counting could make them.

The prose elaborating upon the tables records both our interpretation and evaluation of the data. Our evaluation consists of comments on the validity and relevance of the criteria used by editors in selecting and organizing their materials, the relationship of these criteria to the purposes of teaching (and studying) literature and composition, and the role of the textbooks in this relationship. We have tried to make the evaluative comments of such a nature that they will be useful, at least in stimulating relevant questions, to anyone charged with the responsibility of selecting or evaluating textbooks, whether or not those available to him are the same ones as those examined in this study. We have hoped to suggest the kind of questions that will enable him to draw his own conclusions about the shortcomings, strengths, and relative merits of the textbooks.

We undertook this study because of our personal conviction that the study of English is of quintessential importance in American high schools, now more than ever before. We are pleased to note that this conviction is shared by others. We have in mind recent activities of the National Council of Teachers of English (NCTE), including the publishing of the important document, *The National Interest and the Teaching of English;* "Project English," sponsored by the United States Office of Education; the cooperative English Program under the auspices of the Modern Language Assocation of America, the NCTE, the College English Association, and the American Studies Association; the Summer Institutes of the Commission on English of the College Entrance Examination Board; and, finally, the recent statement of President

Kennedy: "If, in the effective use of language, style is the man, style is the nation too; men, countries, and even entire civilizations have been tested and judged by their literary tone."

Clearly, a study of such importance requires textbooks of a very high order, for, in an overwhelming number of instances, it is undoubtedly true that the textbook literally is the course. It is solely in the hope that our effort will contribute to the preparation of more adequate textbooks for high school English classes that we submit the following report for the consideration of classroom teachers, administrators, textbook commissions, state departments of education, instructors in teachers' colleges and schools of education, authors and publishers of textbooks, and those members of the general public who are interested in the quality of America's schools.

A survey of this magnitude could not have been completed without the cooperation of many persons. We should like to acknowledge, in a less impersonal way, the help we have received from them, but their very number precludes our doing so. We wish to thank the publishers for copies of textbooks, for information about their use, and in general for the courteous treatment we have received; and the officials in the various state departments of education, superintendents, principals, and curriculum coordinators in local districts for information about book adoption and criteria of selection. We especially thank the numerous teachers who have responded to our requests, many of whom took the time from their own busy schedules to write long comments on the books they are using and even to canvass their departments in order to obtain a fuller reflection of teachers' judgments; to these we cannot adequately express our gratitude. We also thank the many present and past officials of the National Council of Teachers of English whose advice has been steadily helpful, and especially, for favors too numerous to mention, its Executive Secretary, Dr. James R. Squire. We owe a special debt to the Council for Basic Education and its staff for negotiating the grant that made this study possible and for their unfailing counsel all along the way. To the Old Dominion Foundation we are indebted for the grant itself. The University of California and its Department of English gave indispensable assistance, including leaves of absence and office space on the campus. A very special word of thanks we convey to our secretary and "staff," Mrs. Margaret B. Ackerman. Finally, to our families we are grateful for their patient endurance during a very bookish time.

Berkeley, California   J. J. L.
                                                  B. E.

Contents

High
School
English
Textbooks

Introduction and Summation

TEACHERS OF high school English do not need to be convinced of the importance of anthologies of literature and composition textbooks. Whatever innovations have come into our classrooms in recent years — one thinks immediately of team-teaching, programed instruction, advanced placement classes, paperback books and a host of audio-visual aids — it remains a fact for the present and for the foreseeable future that such textbooks must continue to be the foundations upon which most high school programs in English will be built. Certainly textbook publishers still seem to be operating on this premise. Each school year, the mail of an English teacher (and more especially that of a chairman of an English department) is filled with decorative brochures announcing the newest and obviously the best editions of anthologies and composition series, all of them almost guaranteeing to achieve what their predecessors — once new and best — somehow failed to accomplish: the enjoyment of literature, and the mastery of writing skills. These textbooks pour forth in such cornucopic abundance that anyone charged, as I have sometimes been, with reviewing them for possible adoption, might do well to recall the plaint in Ecclesiastes: "Of making many books there is no end; and much study is a weariness of the flesh." (xii:12)

A forthright investigation of anthologies and composition textbooks has long been needed. Until now, however, volunteers to engage in this hazardous pursuit have not stepped forward. Teachers of English will therefore find it easy to applaud the sense of mission which compelled Professor Evans and the late Professor Lynch to undertake, through a period of many months, the survey which this chapter is privileged to introduce. Their book, I believe, is a tribute to their zeal, energy, and candor. It cannot be denied that what these seemingly indefatigable scholars found among the anthologies and composition textbooks they so painstakingly studied was, both in quantity and quality, seldom to their liking — and they have said so with unmistakable clarity. Conceivably their labors may even strike some readers as an example of supererogation. These readers may carp at what they consider excessive (and ironical) repetition, especially since the authors have challenged this very characteristic in the textbooks under review. At the risk of seeming to engage in a semantic quibble, I would accept the authors' marshaling of cumulative evidence — so granitic in its solidity — and the judgments deriving from such evidence, not as the kind of repetition which might have been avoided, but rather as the presentation through necessary reiteration of an incontestable case. And powerful indeed is the case which results from such an exercise in fastidious documentation.

Readers would be wrong to infer from the authors' vigorous criticisms that they consider all anthologies and textbooks utterly beyond repair and therefore to be judged completely useless in the high school program. Such a conclusion would do injustice to the intent of the authors, as it would misrepresent the nature of their recommendations. Quite on the contrary, one must emphasize, the basic purpose of the Lynch-Evans survey from its inception was corrective, not destructive. It is thus to be hoped that its effect will be to meliorate, not merely palliate, certain widespread deficiencies in the basic matter of our English programs.

Since it is the primary function of this chapter to summarize the main findings and recommendations to be discovered in much greater detail in the mother lode of the book itself, I would first direct attention to the anthologies of literature and to the position from which the authors chose to examine them. Briefly stated, their bias (or value system) was that anthologies should be the repositories of the very best ever thought and written in the spirit of the humanistic tradition and the Anglo-American heritage; whatever does not fulfill these criteria has no place in an anthology, regardless of grade level or the kind of reader to whom it might be directed.

Although, as the authors indicate in Part III of the book, variations among the anthologies (or indeed among their several parts) are so great as to preclude the possibility of generalizing about them, they still find it reasonable to indict many of the series for falling far short of their test of ultimate excellence. On the face of the evidence so compendiously offered to the reader, few people will want to contest the indictment. By their own overwhelming testimony, the anthologies do manifest, in the authors' judgment, a number of common enough and serious enough defects, the correction of only a portion of which would go far to improve them both in quantity and quality.

For example, one such basic inadequacy, especially noticeable in textbooks designed for the ninth and tenth grades and in second-track readers for all grades, is the excessive reliance upon a spate of nonliterary, nonfictional, "informational" materials more suitable at their best to the daily newspaper than to a hard-covered, sturdily constructed anthology with a presumed claim to longevity exceeding twenty-four hours. The effect of such selections, according to the authors, has been to cheapen the text. That the anthologies also deign to include examples of "literature" is no assured guaranty of their quality, for, as the authors declared (a study of the book itself will bear them out), where such "literature" has been selected as a sampling of the work of distinguished authors, it has all too often represented these authors at their second- or third-best. By one device or another, therefore, significant literature has gone by default.

Another chronic defect, in the authors' view, has resulted from the solicitous urge to make anthologies "easier" and thus more palatable to "reluctant" and other readers who otherwise might shy away from more substantial challenges to their intelligence, sensitivity, and endurance, and give up reading altogether. Such an urge, no matter how humanitarian it may be, has brought about the wholesale, almost capricious abridgement of selections, to the point where works of literature that might have had merit are reduced to snippets and swatches, and where emendations, omissions, simplifications, and other acts of more or less ruthless editorial surgery, rather than sharpening the meanings of the selections, have often distorted them instead.

Much of the failure of the anthologies, according to Professors Lynch and Evans, is so basic as to be structural, in that it resides in the very organization of the books. The reader will perhaps see in this failure the well-known error of putting the cart before the horse. It is the authors' thesis that anthologists, again more often for the ninth and tenth grades and the second-track readers, determine first upon the organization of their books (topical, chronological, etc.) and then choose, regardless of lasting literary value, those selections which would best (or at least most easily) fit into the subdivisions or units of the texts. As a result, many anthologies seem depressingly contrived.

Not only are they pre-organized, but — as the authors prodigiously demonstrate — they are also over-organized, and to a flagrant extreme. In topically and chronologically arranged anthologies, especially, the extensive introductions and other editorial machinery, sometimes directed at one short poem, an ephemeral essay, or a cursory abridgement of a novel, serve only to overwhelm to the point of obliteration the puny examples to which they address themselves.

The desire to entice the student's interest by showing him that "literature," after all, can be both timely and relevant would seem to have influenced the choice of numerous selections, the questions asked about these selections, and the activities developed around them. Generally speaking, timeliness and relevance are, in the anthologies, often made the characteristics of selections more closely related to the social, physical, and natural sciences than to fiction, poetry, and drama. "Literature" in too many anthologies, according to the authors, is chosen to "socialize" rather than "humanize" the student, as if the first goal of literary study is to learn to live in a group instead of with oneself. To this end, committee reports, panel discussions, notebooks put together by entire classes, and other group ventures are directed, at the inevitable expense of concentration upon the individual mastery of subject matter, the close, intent, arduous, meaningful study of distinguished examples of unalloyed and unapologetic literature.

In their eagerness to keep their anthologies timely and presumably, therefore, more interesting, the anthologists have blurred the distinction between untimeliness and timelessness, or have forgotten the intimate and unseverable connection between "past" and "prologue." The investigation of Professors Lynch and Evans demonstrates clearly to what extent, especially in anthologies for the ninth and tenth grades, literature written before 1930, to say nothing of before 1900, has become conspicuous by its absence. Although the restriction in time is not so stringent in anthologies for the eleventh grade, dealing as they traditionally do with surveys of American literature, or in those of the twelfth grade, concentrating upon English literature in similar survey fashion, even in these the authors have been able to detect two unfortunate trends: with subsequent revisions, earlier literary periods tend to be given less space; or else newer editions tend to replace earlier American or English literature with examples of contemporary literature of the Western hemisphere or the world. The result of these trends has meant, in the authors' phrase, "the dismissal of the past," the denial of those sources from which the humanities draw their sustenance.

It cannot be gainsaid, as one reads of the various activities suggested for students (but never really required of them), that the anthologists have manifested a desire to keep young people busy, if not necessarily to get them thinking. The authors' trenchant analysis of this tendency would suggest that here certainly is an instance of a virtue becoming a vice, that in the greater number of anthologies there is too much of almost everything, too much of a sense of hustle and bustle, too much vitiating of what should be the central energy of all such texts: the single-minded, undistracted focusing upon the universal values of literature, the age-old questions involving man's condition to which great, free minds working within the Anglo-American tradition have directed themselves throughout the centuries.

Too much of *almost* everything, Professors Lynch and Evans conclude. But not nearly enough of one essential thing — composition. Writing, the authors' investigation would seem to show, is all too seldom required, although it may permissively be suggested. Furthermore, even when a writing assignment happens to be a definite one, it may only remotely — if at all — require that a student write of what he understood of a specific selection in the anthology. Although literature, as the authors cannot stress strongly enough, is the ideal subject for composition because it is humane and therefore most relevant to all human beings, all too frequently it gets short shrift from anthology editors who find in the student's everyday experiences, his contacts with relatives, friends, and neighbors, a preferred reservoir for reflections on the nature of man and things. If the student's writing is then desultory, reluctant, shamefaced, or narcissistic, the authors would insist it is so because the student himself — at least as of now — is too squirming and evasive a target for significant self-analysis. And while he toys at writing, like a child dawdling over unpalatable food he is being made to eat by duress, unconvinced that what he has been invited or forced to do counts at all, that definite body of nutritive subject matter traditionally called literature goes by the board. Teachers might regard as a truism the authors' contention that theme assignments based upon literature, regularly assigned, patiently explained, and diligently read by a competent instructor can lead to a most meaningful experience — the deeper understanding of literature. Anthologists seem yet to be convinced.

The editorial tone which Professors Lynch and Evans find offensive in so many of the anthologies and which they sum up as "catering" would seem to derive from the commonly held conviction that anthologists, like teachers, must take students as they find them, namely, as adolescents, with undiscriminating teen-age drives, aspirations, points of view, and even vocabulary. To a reasonable degree, perhaps, no one can argue against the notion that dealing with teen-agers involves a realistic appraisal of where one must start with them. But the authors' distress resulted from the belief, fortified by the numerous examples they cite, that the anthologies have gone one perilous step farther, leaving students at the end of the journey no more mature than at the beginning, in effect abdicating all responsibility for helping them grow toward the deeper, subtler insight. Stated somewhat differently, the editorial tone of many anthologies pampers adolescent minds, rather than prods them; restricts the gaze of teen-agers to themselves; is chatty, juvenile, and intellectually arid.

In the light of the above findings, it is easy to concur in the authors' two general and related recommendations and their suggestions dealing with particular literary genres. Bulk in itself being no assurance of excellence, the first basic recommendation is to reduce drastically the size of the anthologies, limiting their contents to a central core of important readings which all students would truly *study*, not merely skim, and which, furthermore, all teachers would actively teach. Then, too, each work in every anthology, regardless of grade level, should be one of high literary distinction, chosen not because it is "easy" or "hard," but only because it is good for the student to know, because it says something so important and so well that knowing it will make a student grow in heart and mind and spirit.

The authors' recommendations dealing with the particular genres and with the organization of anthologies follow below:

1. *Short stories.* Inasmuch as there are far too many short stories at all grade levels, their number should be rigorously reduced, especially in anthologies for the eleventh and twelfth grades. Only those short stories which honestly and artistically examine the human condition should be retained, and these in their full text. By application of such a yardstick, popular or "slick" stories, whose only merit is their ability to entertain momentarily, would be eliminated, as would those selections from novels or other longer, nonfiction works which have been mislabeled short stories.

2. *Novels.* It would be preferable to omit the novel entirely from the anthologies, thus by one stroke reducing their size appreciably. Such omission cannot be considered unjustified, since well-edited novels in paperback, suited for each grade level, have become increasingly available. However, when it is felt that excerpts from novels must be used, these should be represented as the abridgements which they are, not as the entire works, and should be so distinguished in quality as to be worth including, even in truncated form.

3. *Essays*. Short, self-contained, rich in intellectual and literary values, the essay should be an indispensable part in every anthology, regardless of grade level. It should, therefore, be represented in considerable number and variety and deal with subjects important to man because he is human. All miscellaneous nonfiction which now serves to clutter up so many anthologies — articles, sketches, "informational" selections, quick-interest pieces — and which obviously cannot be justified on artistic grounds should be completely eliminated. Timeliness and fashion should be disregarded as bases for selection. Use of excerpts and abridgements of longer nonfiction works should be reduced, if not omitted entirely. By such rigorous pruning, anthologists would insure room for those other essays, representative of significant authors throughout the centuries, which in their original form retain permanent value. In brief, all nonfiction should be worthy, not merely of reading, but indeed of keen and diligent study.

4. *Drama*. It is cause for deep concern that Shakespeare, except for anthologies designed for the twelfth grade, has so little place in the anthologies, having made way for ephemeral television plays, Broadway musicals, or one-act plays by writers of dubious talent. The first play and probably even the second play studied in *each* of the four years of high school should be by Shakespeare. In any case, all plays included in the anthologies, whether they are modern or not, should be chosen by the sole test of their literary merit. Their texts should be treated with utmost respect. The editorial equipment which presently overwhelms so many plays, reducing to spoon-feeding what should require study, should be limited only to the most essential clarification. Glossing should be accurate and done in moderation.

5. *Poetry*. Too many anthologies have flung a wide net to gather in a haul of poems almost beyond number. Many of these are nondescript ventures in versification by poets whose names today are barely remembered. Editors would do well to reduce

the number of poems, retaining only those which represent the best efforts of the more important poets. In addition to limiting selections to poems of proven literary merit, anthologists should concentrate on poems central to the Anglo-American tradition, instead of wandering into more exotic areas, apparently only to be different. Considerable improvement could be effected easily if about one-third of the contents of anthologies henceforth were given over to poetry; and if the poetry, by way of its subjects and forms, made progressively greater demands, grade by grade, upon young but maturing readers. Finally, a noticeable advance would result from the editors' resolutions *never* to abridge, simplify, adapt, or alter a poem.

6. *Organization.* Instead of organization by topical units, which lends itself to disregarding the literary value of selections chosen primarily to fill in various units, arrangement of contents by genres, a more flexible plan applicable to all four grades, would focus primary attention upon poems as poems, essays as essays, plays as plays. To be sure, such arrangement would mean discarding the traditional assignment of American literature to the eleventh grade and English literature to the twelfth. However, if the basic purpose of the high school program is to help students understand and react sensitively to literature as such, and not necessarily to acquaint them with the facts of literary history, then the eleventh and twelfth grade anthologies as they now stand can justifiably be considered as unduly restrictive. For those eleventh- and twelfth-grade English courses in which a knowledge of literary history is presumed important, it may be possible to supplement the anthologies with separate short histories, or to prepare relevant mimeographed materials. In any case, tradition for its own sake should not be permitted to restrict the choice of the best literature in the Anglo-American tradition.

Whatever virtues Professors Lynch and Evans have been able to discover in the grammar and composition series they have so assiduously examined must, in the total view, be set down as minor ones. In all fairness, they have credited many of the textbooks with covering the details of grammar, usage, and mechanics adequately. They have also concluded that the texts treat satisfactorily the principles and techniques of writing, especially in regard to the sentence and paragraph. Finally, they would not deny (indeed, they would strongly insist) that the books offer the student an overabundance of exercises, activities, and topics for writing.

These several assets, however, are overshadowed, in the authors' opinion, by a number of basic liabilities so prevalent in the textbooks as to detract generally from their value.

The first defect, so obvious as to be oppressive, is that of the repetition which pervades the series. Any reader who wishes evidence of this contention can find it distributed profusely in Part II of the book. By way of summary, let it suffice here to say that, according to Professors Lynch and Evans, all principal matters of grammar, usage, mechanics, rhetoric, and composition are treated in essentially the same way for all grade levels, so much so that most of the texts, regardless of the grade numbers on their covers, sound distressingly alike.

Another fault, equally widespread, results from the inclusion of a great number of topics whose relevance to the fundamental concern of grammar and composition is minimal at best, and of "motivational" material attempting so strenuously to be helpful that it seems to recognize no limits. Such alien topics and extravagant motivational contributions appear everywhere in the series, in those parts given over to grammar and composition, which might have benefited from a more straightforward handbook-type of presentation, as well as in those numerous sections which the reader will find designated in Part II as "Other" or "Miscellaneous."

Much as the authors have found composition neglected in the anthologies of literature, so they have discovered that literature has suffered a similar oversight in the composition texts. Activities involving writing, speaking, listening, thinking, and library research abound in the grammar and composition series, but seldom if ever do they go for their subject matter to the literature which, it is not unreasonable to expect, students might be reading at the same time. It is as if the anthologist and the author of the composition textbook were determined to live in peaceful non-awareness of the other's existence, as if, to be sure, East were East and West were West.

Because literature has been so cavalierly neglected as the source of activity, what passes for "progression" — the orderly movement from simpler to more difficult tasks in all the areas of the "language arts" — has become an anxious scrambling after anything at all for students to write or speak about, as long as they do write and speak. In the ensuing confusion, according to the authors, teachers with a liberal education, whose inclinations are toward literature, can only feel themselves at a loss in attempting to supervise these multifarious and sterile nonliterary activities.

Again like the anthologies, too many grammar and composition series must stand guilty of the charge of "catering." Having eschewed literature as the focus of their attention, the texts invite the student to exploit himself, his family, and his friends, his interests, tastes, and attitudes; but the invitations, for all their insistence, are curiously apologetic, "as though (as the authors comment) it were an imposition to ask students to indulge themselves in what it is assumed they should be most eager to indulge themselves."

Composition series, Professors Lynch and Evans observe, go to considerable pains to devise "real" situations and settings, removed from the classroom, wherein students, who must look upon their classrooms as unreal, can more naturally demonstrate their speaking, reporting, telephoning, listening, and writing skills. By so doing, such texts strive to deny the undeniable; namely, that the real situation of students at that particular time can only be their situation in the classroom. Contrivances, however ingenious they may be, which are designed to remove students to habitats more natural and more congenial than the classroom, are thus so palpably artificial as to result, understandably, in self-conscious and often contemptuous performances.

Even more frequent and, to the authors, more serious than the use of the ironically artificial "real" situation is the "mere exercise" character of the various activities suggested to students. Many of these activities are found to be altogether unrelated to the students' work in literature or composition at the time. In such circumstances, it is understandable why library assignments, oral reports, vocabulary study, sentence analysis, and a score of other activities accepted within the province of "language arts" should be dismissed as "dry runs" rather than as the significant contributions to enduring learning, which they might have been.

As Professors Lynch and Evans show, the often adolescent prose style of the composition series does not vary appreciably from grade to grade. Definitions and explanations are repeated in almost the same breezy language in four successive years. In this connection, the authors have commented about the texts: "though not at all difficult to read in, they are most difficult to learn from." In the hope of making the lot of students easier, the series have dispersed and diffused their topics over pages, chapters, and sections, when such topics could have been more effectively treated in a page or two. Whatever the motive, spreading material throughout a text in this way can only make mastery of such material extremely difficult, if not virtually impossible.

Neither the writers nor the publishers of grammar and composition textbooks, in the opinions of Professor Lynch and Professor Evans, are really to be blamed for the deficiencies noted above. At fault, rather, are "two potent conventions": that of the four-volume series, and of the separate series for literature and composition. The first of these, by its very nature, encourages the kind of repetition and diffusion so markedly present in the texts and so thoroughly documented in this study. The second, as Professor Lynch and Professor Evans have shown, invites an arbitrary and often crippling division in the English program.

The solution of the problem, in the authors' view, is simple enough. They advocate the abandonment of the four-volume series, and the substitution of a single (and, hopefully) short handbook dealing with grammar, usage, mechanics, and principles of rhetoric and composition, to be used through all four years of high school. As for the activities of speaking, listening, thinking, and writing, they recommend that these be incorporated into the anthologies of literature, where they can be put to use more properly in an integrated and effective English program.

I would not be so rash as to suggest that this summary introduction can do more than the slightest justice to the important study which follows it. If anything, it will, I hope, serve as a key to open the door of the house which two dedicated scholars, with such painstaking attention to detail, have built. The reader, let me be the first to say, can be assured of an informative and a rewarding tour.

Irving Gersten
Chairman of the English Department
Horton Watkins High School
Ladue, Missouri

PART I

The Anthologies

CHAPTER 1

The Anthologies of Literature

THE STUDY of literature virtually means, in a large number of America's high schools, the use of a series of anthologies, often the only textbooks available in sufficient quantity for a class of any size — and some schools provide even the anthology on a basis of only one book for every two members of a class. Although schools of more than average means stock class-size complements of additional texts (for example, collections of short stories and of poems, separately bound novels and plays), and although the rapid growth of the paperback book industry promises to revolutionize the textbook situation in literature, for some time to come the anthology will continue to provide almost all the literature that many high school students meet, and will continue to influence — if not determine — the internal organization of many literary curricula.[1]

---

[1] There are few useful statistics on this subject. A survey of about four thousand teachers in California revealed that 25 per cent checked "Follow textbook" as a preferred method of organizing their courses in literature for the eleventh and twelfth grades (*English Language Arts in California Public High Schools*, Bulletin of the California State Department of Education, Vol. XXVI, No. 7, September, 1957, p. 32). A recent study sponsored by the National Council of Teachers of English disclosed that even in those high schools consistently producing the nation's award-winning students in English, nearly 10 per cent of the teachers responding said they organize their courses "however the text is arranged." (*The National Interest and the*

At the same time it should be emphasized that the picture of literary study in the high schools to be derived from an examination of the anthologies and other books is not necessarily the same as that to be obtained from observation of actual classroom practices. The descriptions, analyses, and evaluations contained in this report relate to the textbooks rather than to the classroom, as our primary purpose is to comment upon the materials available rather than the individual use that is made of them. The two of course are often closely related, for materials tend to set limits beyond which it is difficult to proceed, and their very organization and manner of presentation tend to prescribe method, approach, tone, attitude, and even purpose. To be sure, we know of teachers who leave the adopted anthology on the shelf, or at most make a token use of it to satisfy legal requirements. On the other hand, we know of other teachers who follow the anthology slavishly. Most teachers having an anthology as the adopted text probably fall somewhere between these extremes. In any case, where we are critical it is to be understood that the criticism is directed at the textbooks and not at the classroom teacher.

Because our investigations show that, whatever the range of variations in degree of use, the anthology is still the most widely

---

Teaching of English, 1961, p. 124.) Our own correspondence with several hundred selected English teachers throughout the United States suggests that actually the influence of the textbook on the organization of English courses is considerably greater than these percentages indicate; many of the teachers expressing a preference for chronological, typological, or topical organization, implement their preference by proceeding through an anthology organized in one of these ways. This matter has recently been called to the attention of the profession by the editor of one of the NCTE's official journals. In an "Editorialette" in *The English Journal* he asks, "Are we teaching literature or are we teaching anthologies?" (December, 1961, p. 638). At least one publisher appears to agree with this view: Harcourt, Brace says that its eleventh-grade anthology has, "perhaps more than any other textbook . . . helped to establish *the content and organization*" of the eleventh-grade course in (American) literature in the nation's high schools (*Adventures in American Literature*, Mercury Edition, p. 765; emphasis added).

used and the most influential kind of high school textbook in literature, it is necessary that we make a detailed inquiry into the nature of anthologies: their contents, their organization, their pedagogical usefulness, and their philosophical bases. These four topics are the concerns of the report that follows.[2] Before coming to them, however, we shall attempt to describe the anthologies in a more general way.

The most immediately apparent properties of the anthologies are their color, their titles, and their size. Not only are their bindings gay, but also many of them have colorful illustrations. This fashion, which seems to have grown in recent years, we cannot but regard as more expensive than useful. Furthermore, the relevance of many of the cover pictures for literary textbooks, dealing as such pictures do with parties and sports, we are unable to determine. The members of a group of practicing and prospective high school teachers, to whom we showed a representative selection of currently used anthologies, visibly cringed at sight of some of the grosser specimens. We conclude that too much attention is now given to the exteriors of many of the anthologies.

We have also observed that the cover often provides a clue to the tone struck by the editors within the book. For example, the ninth-grade volume of one of the Harcourt, Brace series, after the cover illustration showing a winter sports scene, continues by its internal illustrations to make "extra-curricular activities" central: young people are shown dancing, eating ice cream, applying eye makeup, petting the family dog — almost anything except reading books and using their minds. It seems to us that books of this kind deliberately glorify the ephemeral, making of adolescence a state rather than a stage, and tend to prolong mental immaturity.

---

2 Although the anthologies have been our principal interest for the reason stated above, we have also examined supplemental volumes of various kinds, some of which are discussed below. We have found that many of our observations about the anthologies apply with equal force to the supplementary books.

The titles of some of the volumes also show a lack of emphasis upon literature that is in keeping with their garish bindings. Of the seventy-two anthologies examined (the titles are listed at the end of this chapter), exactly one-third do not use "literature" or a synonym for it in their titles: nine use the inadequate substitute "reading" or "readings"; and six de-emphasize "literature." Volumes titled, for example, *Worlds to Explore*, *All Around the Land*, *Adventures in Living*, *Exploring Life*, *This Is America*, *Flights in Friendship*, *From Here On*, *Interesting Friends*, and *To Be an American* might more appropriately deal with geography, psychology, history, anthropology, or civics, than with literature — as indeed much of their contents also suggests. The substitution of "reading" for "literature," as we shall have occasion to say again in the following chapters, points to a misconception of what we believe is the high school English teacher's proper and unique role, which is not the teaching of reading but the teaching of the reading of literature. The de-emphasis results from the use of literature for nonliterary ends, as is indicated by such titles as *People in Literature*, *America Through Literature*, *Exploring Life Through Literature*, *The United States in Literature*, and *England in Literature* — titles that suggest by their reversal of emphasis the exploitation of literature rather than the study of it for its own sake. In short, more than half the volumes examined show, even in their titles, an apparent lack of confidence in literature. This lack is also demonstrated in the titles of several of the remaining volumes, for the vocabulary upon which they draw runs heavily to "adventures," "explorations," "flights," "journeys," and "trails" — as if literature must be vigorously pursued instead of quietly pondered. And to title volumes *Good Times Through Literature* and *Prose and Poetry for Enjoyment* is, we believe, to insist upon reversing the educative process: "good times" and "enjoyment" are among the end-products of literature, but to be successfully gained they must be preceded by careful study. In short, both bindings and titles show the influence of the market place and the heavy hand of the adman, an influence to which, unfortunately, some teachers contribute by speaking of "selling" literature to their students.

After more than a year of living on intimate terms with seventy-two of these books, and now and then carrying armloads between office and home, we continue, however, most of all to be impressed by their sheer bulk — two hundred pounds and forty-nine thousand pages of it! These figures average out to about three pounds and six hundred and eighty pages per volume. We can sympathize with the teacher who wrote us, "The paperback will help to eliminate big, fat anthologies, I hope." Another teacher commented in the same vein: "Textbooks are getting too large. Soon our students will have to drive to school to get the textbooks back and forth."

Anthologies under investigation show an average of about one hundred and twenty selections per volume, written by about ninety different authors — a remarkable fact itself. The typical anthology also contains well over one hundred pages of editorial apparatus.[3]

The sad fact is that, although all devoted English teachers fondly hope their students will develop a taste for literature and will continue to read it throughout their lives, the bulky and often garish volumes with which they must contend are uninviting. Why should the student, who has met literature only in the chaos

---

[3] The use of the page as a unit of measurement, although frequently necessary, is not always, we must admit, an adequate standard, for the anthologies vary widely in the amount of letterpress per page. Some series, for example those published by Lippincott, Prentice-Hall, Scott, Foresman, and Harcourt, Brace (Olympic), often print very little text on a page, whereas those published by Macmillan, Rand McNally, Singer, and Harcourt, Brace (1949) regularly print many solid pages of text. The number of illustrations, especially those inserted within selections, also influences size of book and quantity of content. For these reasons we have frequently expressed our findings in percentages rather than pages.

and clutter of the ponderous anthology, feel inclined ever to seek it again?

By any standard, to deal with the anthologies is to confront literature — and nonliterature — en masse. The anthologies are so large, in fact, that they contain more than high school classes can adequately and thoughtfully cover. Their size suggests a number of questions. Do the editors assume that students will make use, in some fashion, of *all* the contents? If so, are some selections to be given class time during which the teacher will help the students to understand and experience them? Are some to be assigned but left undiscussed? In short, is it assumed that only a part of the textbook will actually be *taught* and *studied*? It would seem that only by some such division could enough of the contents be used to justify the existence of these large books. And is this division to be left to the discretion of the teacher? Two important documents show that many persons now teaching English in the schools are unprepared to do so.[4] These teachers need all the help that the textbook can give them. Is it not possible — indeed likely — that an inadequately prepared English teacher might be encouraged to select from its multitudinous contents the least literary and the second-rate and to let those pieces remain unread, or at least untaught, that are more challenging and potentially more rewarding? In short, may not the bulk itself perform an actual disservice for many students?

Or do editors assume that their function is to provide a large quantity of material, only a part of which will be used in any given class? Again we ask, will all teachers choose with equal wisdom and taste? Or will some students be deprived of an acquaintance with important literature because the anthology provides

---

[4] See *The National Interest and the Teaching of English,* pp. 39-87, and *Preparation in English for College-Bound Students* (1960), p. 4. According to the latter, prepared by the Commission on English of the College Entrance Examination Board, only half of those now teaching English in secondary schools "have had adequate formal preparation for their duties."

much that is mediocre alongside the excellent, both equally available? Is it, after all, the anthologist's function to provide "something for everybody"? Or have the anthologists a responsibility to encourage the improvement of literary taste, to help to define the literary heritage, and to implement the judgments of sound literary criticism? And if editors assume that, in order to provide something for everybody, they must include many selections that in some classes will be read by nobody, then what happens to the anthology's organization? All of the volumes we have examined show that their editors have labored diligently to construct a framework to contain the selections. Many of these are highly ingenious, and most of them strive for coherence and a unifying principle. If the organization of an anthology is as important as editors evidently believe it to be, what happens to it when much content must be omitted for lack of time?

These are some of the questions that would occur at the outset to any objective observer. These are questions that have ramifications reaching far beyond mere size and quantity, for they involve criteria of selection, rationale of arrangement, reliability of text, and effect of editorial treatment; and they must be answered if the anthologies are to be adequately evaluated.

We have tried to answer them in the following chapters. Our procedure has been, first, to analyze the contents quantitatively; second, to interpret and comment upon the results of the analysis; and third, to evaluate the findings according to appropriate norms. The burden of the analysis is carried by the numerous tables throughout the text or in the appendices. In the interpretation and comment we have attempted to assess the relationships, whether explicit or implicit, between content and such matters as arrangement and organization, the excerpting and abridging of texts, the study questions and suggested activities that accompany selections, and the possible general effect upon students of the manner in which the material is presented. Our evaluation of the anthologies is twofold: it measures the books against each other in various ways and thus results in comparative judgments; and it measures them against what we advocate as the proper function of literary anthologies in American high schools.

The analysis and comment are self-explanatory, but the basis of evaluation may require further statement. We believe that the function of the anthology is to make available — *for teaching by the teacher and for study by the students* — accurate texts of suitable literary pieces. These may be organized in various ways and accompanied by various editorial aids, but neither the organization nor the aids should detract from the *literary character* of the books. In short, the books for classes in literature must be just as obviously literary as those for classes in biology are obviously biological. It is on this basis that our final evaluations are made.

The seventy-two volumes that we have examined were selected according to the best evidence we could obtain. We wished to include in our study all anthologies used in a significant number of the nation's high schools, grades nine through twelve. To determine which ones should be included we sought information from the sources mentioned in the Preface. To the basic list of anthologies thus compiled, we have added a few others for special reasons: two volumes of world literature (Harcourt, Brace and L. W. Singer) that are used in some schools as supplementary or alternate textbooks for the twelfth grade; one complete "second-track" series (Harcourt, Brace) and the one volume of another (Scott, Foresman) that had appeared in time for our study; the tenth- and eleventh-grade volumes of an alternate series ("Living Literature" from Harcourt, Brace) that turned up with some frequency in our correspondence with teachers; and, to represent for comparative purposes the "developmental readers," the "Let's Read" series (Holt).

In general we have confined our examination to the latest edition of each publisher's series of anthologies, for we found that few schools are using the earlier editions. There are two notable exceptions, however, both, as it happens, concerning books from the same publisher. We discovered that not only Harcourt, Brace's most recent edition (Olympic) but also the 1952 (Mercury) and the 1949 editions are still in use. A considerable number of schools continue to use the Mercury edition, and several teachers remarked that they so much prefer the 1949 to either of the later editions that they are attempting to make it last as long as possible. Consequently, we have included both the Mercury and the 1949 editions in our survey. That no anthology of importance to our purpose has been omitted from our list is attested by the fact that the later questionnaires and letters from teachers failed to turn up a title which we had not already included. To these we have also added a representative sampling of textbooks of other kinds.

The anthologies upon which this survey is based are listed at the end of this chapter. This list includes books from two principal kinds of series: all the volumes in four-book series prepared for grades nine through twelve, and the third volume in three-book series prepared for grades seven through nine. These total more than three-fourths of the anthologies examined. Most of the remaining volumes either are published outside the series arrangement or are the most widely used volumes within series not generally adopted *in toto* by the schools.

For the sake of brevity in the following chapters, we have referred to these volumes by symbols, which also appear at the end of the chapter. We have tried to keep the symbols as nearly self-evident as possible: initials or a contraction standing for the publisher's name, an additional letter (L, M, O) or year numerals (49) when more than one series by a publisher is included, 2 and D standing respectively for "second-track" and "developmental" series, and after the hyphen a number standing for the grade to which the volume is assigned. Thus, HBM-11 stands for the eleventh-grade volume in Harcourt, Brace's Mercury series, SF2-9 stands for the ninth-grade volume in Scott, Foresman's "second-track," series, and Sgr-12a stands for the alternate twelfth-grade (world literature) volume in the Singer series.

LIST OF LITERATURE ANTHOLOGIES USED IN STUDY

ABC-9   Matilda Bailey and Ullin W. Leavell, eds. *Worlds to Explore.* Revised and enlarged edition. New York: American Book Company, 1956.

ABC-10   Matilda Bailey and Ullin W. Leavell, eds. *The World of Endless Horizons.* Revised and enlarged edition. New York: American Book Company, 1956.

ABC-11   Matilda Bailey and Ullin W. Leavell, eds. *The World of America.* Revised and enlarged edition. New York: American Book Company, 1956.

ABC-12   Matilda Bailey and Ullin W. Leavell, eds. *The World and Our English Heritage.* Revised and enlarged edition. New York: American Book Company, 1956.

Gn-9   J. N. Hook, Vesta M. Parsons, Blanche E. Peavey, and Frank M. Rice, eds. *Literature of Adventure.* Boston: Ginn and Company, 1957.

Gn-10   J. N. Hook, Vesta M. Parsons, Blanche E. Peavey, Frank M. Rice, and Miriam H. Thompson, eds. *Literature of Achievement.* Boston: Ginn and Company, 1957.

Gn-11   J. N. Hook, Mildred Foster, Nell M. Robinson, Miriam H. Thompson, and Charles F. Webb, eds. *Literature of America.* Boston: Ginn and Company, 1957.

Gn-12   J. N. Hook, Mildred Foster, Nell M. Robinson, and Charles F. Webb, eds. *Literature of England.* Boston: Ginn and Company, 1957.

Glb-11[5]   Glenn Holder, Olive Eckerson, Erwin H. Schubert, and Ruby Withers, eds. *Journeys in American Literature: An An-*

---

[5] This volume is in use in both tenth and eleventh grades: because it is restricted to American Literature, it seems appropriate to class it with the eleventh-grade volumes.

thology for Secondary Schools. New York: Globe Book Company, 1958.

HB49-9 Jacob M. Ross and Blanche Jennings Thompson, eds. *Adventures in Reading.* Third edition. New York: Harcourt, Brace and Company, 1949.

HB49-10 Luella B. Cook, H. A. Miller, Jr., and Walter Loban, eds. *Adventures in Appreciation.* Third edition. New York: Harcourt, Brace and Company, 1949.

HB49-11 Rewey Belle Inglis, Mary Rives Bowman, John Gehlmann, and Wilbur Schramm, eds. *Adventures in American Literature.* Fourth edition. New York: Harcourt, Brace and Company, 1949.

HB49-12 Rewey Belle Inglis, Alice Cecilia Cooper, Celia Oppenheimer, and William Rose Benét, eds. *Adventures in English Literature.* Fourth edition. New York: Harcourt, Brace and Company, 1949.

HBM-9 Jacob M. Ross, Blanche Jennings Thompson, and Evan Lodge, eds. *Adventures in Reading.* Mercury Edition. New York: Harcourt, Brace and Company, 1952.

HBM-10 Luella B. Cook, Walter Loban, and Susanna Baxter, eds. *Adventures in Appreciation.* Mercury Edition. New York: Harcourt, Brace and Company, 1952.

HBM-11 Rewey Belle Inglis, John Gehlmann, Mary Rives Bowman, and Wilbur Schramm, eds. *Adventures in American Literature.* Mercury Edition. Harcourt, Brace and Company, 1952.

HBM-12 Rewey Belle Inglis, Donald A. Stauffer, and Cecil Evva Larsen, eds. *Adventures in English Literature.* Mercury Edition. New York: Harcourt, Brace and Company, 1952.

HBO-9 Evan Lodge and Marjorie Braymer, eds. *Adventures in Reading.* Olympic Edition. New York: Harcourt, Brace and Company, 1958.

HBO-10 Walter Loban, Dorothy Holmstrom, and Luella B. Cook, eds. *Adventures in Appreciation.* Olympic Edition. New York: Harcourt, Brace and Company, 1958.

HBO-11 John Gehlmann and Mary Rives Bowman, eds. *Adventures in American Literature.* Olympic Edition. New York: Harcourt, Brace and Company, 1958.

HBO-12 Rewey Belle Inglis and Josephine Spear, eds. *Adventures in English Literature.* Olympic Edition. New York: Harcourt, Brace and Company, 1958.

HB2-9   Herbert Potell, Marian Levrien, and Prudence Bostwick, eds. *Adventures for Today.* New York: Harcourt, Brace and Company, 1955.

HB2-10   Martin Levrien, Herbert Potell, and Prudence Bostwick, eds. *Adventures in Living.* New York: Harcourt, Brace and Company, 1955.

HB2-11   Wilbur Schramm, Virginia Cestadasi, John K. Dunn, and Melissa Miner, eds. *Adventures for Americans.* New York: Harcourt, Brace and Company, 1956.

HB2-12   Robert Freier, Arnold Leslie Lazarus, and Herbert Potell, eds. *Adventures in Modern Literature.* Fourth Edition. New York: Harcourt, Brace and Company, 1956.

HBL-10   Luella B. Cook, Walter Loban, Ruth M. Stauffer, and Robert Freier, eds. *People in Literature.* Living Literature Series. Revised Edition. New York: Harcourt, Brace and Company, 1957.

HBL-11   Luella B. Cook, Walter Loban, Tremaine McDowell, and Ruth Stauffer, eds. *America Through Literature.* Living Literature Series. New York: Harcourt, Brace and Company, 1948.

HB-12a   Rewey Belle Inglis, William K. Stewart, Oscar James Campbell, and Eunice Chappell Stearn, eds. *Adventures in World Literature.* Revised Edition. Living Literature Series. New York: Harcourt, Brace and Company, 1958.

Hth-9   Paul Witty, Miriam E. Peterson, and Kathryn P. Welsh, eds. *Reading Roundup, Book Three.* Boston: D. C. Heath and Company, 1958.

Hlt-9   Harold H. Wagenheim, Elizabeth Veris Brattig, and Matthew Dolkey, eds. *Exploring Life.* New York: Henry Holt and Company, 1956.

Hlt-10   Harold H. Wagenheim, Elizabeth Veris Brattig, and Matthew Dolkey, eds. *Ourselves and Others.* New York: Henry Holt and Company, 1956.

Hlt-11   Harold H. Wagenheim, Matthew Dolkey, and Donald G. Kobler, eds. *This is America.* New York: Henry Holt and Company, 1956.

Hlt-12   Harold H. Wagenheim, Donald G. Kobler, and Matthew Dolkey, eds. *England and the World.* New York: Henry Holt and Company, 1956.

HltD-9   George Murphy, Helen Rand Miller, and Nell Appy Murphy, eds. *Reading for Fun.* Book 1, The Emerald Book. New York: Henry Holt and Company, 1953.

HltD-10   George E. Murphy, Emma Lundgren, and Helen Rand Miller, eds. *Reading for Experience.* Book 2, The Steel-Blue Book. New York: Henry Holt and Company, 1953.

HltD-11   George E. Murphy, Helen Rand Miller, and Nell Appy Murphy, eds. *Growing Up in Reading.* Book 3, The Silver Book. New York: Holt, Rinehart, and Winston, 1955.

HltD-12   George E. Murphy, Helen Rand Miller, and Thomas J. Quinn, eds. *Reading for Life.* Book 4, The Bronze Book. New York: Holt, Rinehart and Winston, 1955.

HM-9   Arno Jewett, A. H. Lass, and Margaret Early, eds. *Literature for Life.* Boston: Houghton Mifflin Company, 1958.

Irq-9   Georgia Gantt Winn, Rudolph W. Chamberlain, and Robert L. Chamberlain, eds. *Action!* Syracuse: Iroquois Publishing Company, 1953.

Irq-10   Georgia Gantt Winn, Rudolph W. Chamberlain, and Robert L. Chamberlain, eds. *Flights in Friendship.* Syracuse, Iroquois Publishing Company, 1953.

Ldw-9   John E. Brewton, Babette Lemon, Blanche Wellons, and Louise Abney, eds. *Expanding Literary Interests.* River Forest: Laidlaw Brothers, 1957.

Ldw-10   John E. Brewton, Babette Lemon, Russell A. Sharp, and Louise Abney, eds. *Exploring Literary Trails.* River Forest: Laidlaw Brothers, 1957.

Ldw-11   John E. Brewton, Babette Lemon, Russell A. Sharp, and Louise Abney, eds. *Literature of the Americas.* River Forest: Laidlaw Brothers, 1950.

Ldw-12   John E. Brewton, Babette Lemon, Russell A. Sharp, and Louise Abney, eds. *English and Continental Literature.* River Forest: Laidlaw Brothers, 1950.

Lipp-9   John D. Husband and Frank F. Bright, eds. *From Here On.* Chicago: J. B. Lippincott Company, 1954.

Lipp-10   Dorothy J. Colburn, ed. *All Around the Land.* Chicago: J. B. Lippincott Company, 1954.

Lipp-11   Frank F. Bright and Ralph Potter, eds. *To Be an American.* Chicago: J. B. Lippincott Company, 1957.

Lipp-12   Charlotte C. Whittaker, ed. *Youth and the World.* Chicago: J. B. Lippincott Company, 1954.

McM-9   E. A. Cross, Florence M. Meyer, and Emma L. Reppert, eds. *Interpreting Literature.* Revised Edition. New York: The Macmillan Company, 1955.

McM-10   E. A. Cross and Neal M. Cross, eds. *Types of Literature.* Revised Edition. New York: The Macmillan Company, 1954.

McM-11   E. A. Cross, Grace A. Benscoter, and William A. Meacham, eds. *Heritage of American Literature.* Revised Edition. New York: The Macmillan Company, 1954.

McM-12   E. A. Cross and Helen Fern Daringer, eds. *Heritage of British Literature.* Revised Edition. New York: The Macmillan Company, 1954.

MGH-9   Thelma G. James, Walter R. Northcott, and Marquis E. Shattuck, eds. *World Neighbors: A Book of Readings of Many Countries.* New York: McGraw-Hill Book Company, 1950.

PH-9   Charles H. Carver, Harold G. Sliker, Morris H. Ball, and Lois M. Grese, eds. *They Found Adventure.* Engelwood Cliffs: Prentice-Hall, 1960.

PH-10   Charles H. Carver, Harold G. Sliker, and Elizabeth J. Herbert, eds. *Youth and the Future.* Engelwood Cliffs: Prentice-Hall, 1959.

PH-11   Charles H. Carver, Harold G. Sliker, and Morris H. Ball, eds. *America Today.* Englewood Cliffs: Prentice-Hall, 1959.

PH-12   Charles H. Carver and Harold G. Sliker, eds. *Literature of the World Around Us.* Englewood Cliffs: Prentice-Hall, 1957.

RM-10   Mark A. Neville, ed. *Interesting Friends.* Chicago: Rand McNally & Company, 1958.

RM-11   Mark A. Neville and Max J. Herzberg, eds. *Literature in America.* Chicago: Rand McNally & Company, 1958.

RM-12   Mark A. Neville and Max J. Herzberg, eds. *This England.* Chicago: Rand McNally & Company, 1956.

RP-9   Wilfred Eberhart, Irma Dick Swearingen, and Bernice E. Leary, eds. *Reading-Literature, Book Three, Revised.* Evanston: Row, Peterson and Company, 1955.

SF-9   Robert C. Pooley, Irvin C. Poley, Joan Cravens Leyda, and Lillian J. Zellhoofer, eds. *Good Times Through Literature.* Chicago: Scott, Foresman and Company, 1957.

SF-10   Robert C. Pooley, Irvin C. Poley, Joan Cravens Leyda, and Lillian J. Zellhoofer, eds. *Exploring Life Through Literature.* Chicago: Scott, Foresman and Company, 1957.

SF-11   Robert C. Pooley, Walter Blair, Theodore Hornberger, and

Paul Farmer, eds. *The United States in Literature*. Chicago: Scott, Foresman and Company, 1957.

SF-12   Robert C. Pooley, Paul Farmer, Helen Thornton, and George K. Anderson, eds. *England in Literature*. Chicago: Scott, Foresman and Company, 1957.

SF2-9   Robert C. Pooley, Virginia Belle Lowers, Frances Magdanz, and Olive S. Niles, eds. *Vanguard*. Chicago: Scott, Foresman and Company, 1961.

Scb-9   Ethel M. Orr, Evelyn T. Holsten, and Stella S. Center, eds. *Exploring Literature Old and New*. New York: Charles Scribner's Sons, 1953.

Sgr-9   J. Kenner Agnew and Agnes L. McCarthy, eds. *Prose and Poetry for Enjoyment*. Fifth Edition. Syracuse: The L. W. Singer Company, 1955.

Sgr-10   J. Kenner Agnew and Agnes L. McCarthy, eds. *Prose and Poetry for Appreciation*. Fifth Edition. Syracuse: The L. W. Singer Company, 1955.

Sgr-11   Agnes L. McCarthy and Delmer Rodabaugh, eds. *Prose and Poetry of America*. Fifth Edition. Syracuse: The L. W. Singer Company, 1955.

Sgr-12   Delmer Rodabaugh and Agnes L. McCarthy, eds. *Prose and Poetry of England*. Fifth Edition. Syracuse: The L. W. Singer Company, 1955.

Sgr-12a   J. Kenner Agnew and Agnes L. McCarthy, eds. *Prose and Poetry of the World*. Syracuse: The L. W. Singer Company, 1954.

CHAPTER 2

Contents

1. THE SHORT STORY

OF ALL THE genres represented in the anthologies, the short story receives most attention, a circumstance that is hardly surprising since it is the genre that is easiest for most students to read and since editors have a vast quantity of short stories in magazines and collections from which to choose. The quality of short stories varies widely, ranging from the most ephemeral to those generally regarded as permanent additions to our literary heritage, and raises an initial problem of selection. There is also the problem of placement of the stories by grade level, of determining which are most suitable for ninth-grade students, which for tenth-grade students, and so forth. Editorial decisions about the necessity or advisability of abridgement pose still another problem, although it occurs less frequently for the short story than for most other genres.

In the following pages we have considered the editors' various solutions to these problems of quantity, quality, placement, and abridgement, and, more briefly, that of classification, which arises from the definition of the short story itself. At the same time we have attempted to describe the anthologies in terms of their short stories, so that the particulars of their representation of this genre can be readily seen.

QUANTITY

The anthologies examined contain over seven hundred and fifty different short stories; however, since some stories appear in more than one anthology, the total number of selections in this genre is upwards of twelve hundred. These are the work of nearly five hundred different authors. Table I of Appendix A shows the attention given the short story by the various series and by the volumes within series. For each volume and for each series the first figure given is the percentage of selections that are short stories and the second is the percentage of pages given to short stories in the entire volume of series. It will thus be seen that 57 per cent of the selections in HltD-9 are short stories, and that 68 per cent of the pages in that volume are devoted to short stories.

It will also be apparent from Table I that a very large part of the typical anthology is devoted to the short story, on the average about one-sixth of the selections and about one-third of the pages. The range is great: in proportion to the number of short stories from 78 per cent (HltD-11) to 2 per cent (RM-12) and of pages devoted to short stories from 87 per cent to 8 per cent for the same two volumes. Although anthologists seem to regard the short story as the easiest of the genres, there is no apparent pattern in amount of attention given the short story in the various series. The pattern that might be expected to appear, namely, a progressive lessening of attention through the four years as the short story is to some degree displaced by the more demanding genres, is found only in Hlt, Sgr, and HB49, and in the first two of these the changing emphasis is slight.

The somewhat smaller percentages of pages devoted to the short story in the tenth- and twelfth-grade volumes than in the other two is an interesting phenomenon for two reason: (1) the ninth- and eleventh-grade volumes are those that typically give the least space to the drama, including Shakespeare's, thereby suggesting that there is a kind of automatic compensation of genres among the volumes, and (2) editors seem to be unable to agree upon short stories for the tenth and twelfth grades as readily as for the other two.

Attention given to the short story can also be measured by comparing it with that given to other genres. In number of selections the short story ranks third in most volumes, behind poetry and miscellaneous nonfiction. In number of pages, however, it ranks first in ninth-, tenth-, and eleventh-grade volumes, second in twelfth-grade volumes, and first in all volumes regardless of grade. In all ninth-grade anthologies taken together, the short stories occupy approximately as much space as all the poetry, novels, drama, and essays; in tenth-grade volumes as much space as all the poetry, novels, and essays; in the eleventh-grade volumes as much space as all the poetry, novels, and dramas; in the twelfth-grade volumes as much space as all the essays, novels, and miscellaneous nonfiction and almost as much space as all the poetry; in all volumes as much space as all the poetry and dramas.

The Holt developmental series, which heads Table I, Appendix A, devotes almost three-quarters of its pages to the short story. This emphasis is probably not surprising in view of both the purpose of the series (to stimulate "non-readers") and the lesser abilities of the readers for whom it is intended. It is more surprising to discover that some of the series intended for first-track and heterogeneous classes (Lipp, Hlt, PH) give almost as much space to the short story as to *all* other types — poetry, drama, novel, essay, and miscellaneous nonfiction, and that some single volumes actually give *more* attention to the short story than to all other kinds of literature (Lipp-9, Lipp-11, Hlt-9, PH-12, RP-9). No one is likely to accuse the anthologies of failing to give adequate representation to the short story.

A question on the other side might, however, be asked: is too much space devoted to the short story? The answer to this question is by no means simple. Because most of the editors stress "enjoyment" or "entertainment" as a principal criterion in determining the contents of their anthologies, and because the short story is probably the most readily entertaining and the most easily accessible of all genres, by including large numbers of stories they have perhaps insured for their textbooks a willing, or at least a not unfavorably disposed, audience of readers. But this question cannot be answered in quantitative terms alone, for much depends upon the quality of the stories included, and perhaps even more depends upon the relationship of the short story as a genre to the function of textbooks and, beyond that, upon its relationship to the purpose of literary study in the classroom. In any event, the temptation to include a large and sometimes excessive number of short stories is one that some editors have apparently found difficult to resist.

QUALITY

Howard Baker in a classic essay on the short story has remarked:

> Since the form is peculiarly suited to commercial exploitation, it tends constantly to adapt itself to the processes of commerce — that is, to a formula necessary for mass production and to the cultivation of a standard effect of widest popular appeal. The hackneyed example of this hackneyed truth is, of course, the O. Henry product, the sad memorial to a man who, damned with cleverness and undeveloped conscience, was content with cranking a mill for lazy Sunday-morning customers.[1]

It must be admitted that a great number of the seven hundred fifty stories included in the anthologies are little more than for-

---

[1] Howard Baker, "The Contemporary Short Story," originally published in *The Southern Review*, and reprinted in Herbert Gold and David L. Stevenson, eds., *Stories of Modern America* (New York: St. Martin's Press, 1961). The quotation above is from the latter, p. 446.

mulas filled out with interchangeable characters, dialogues, and settings.

Baker asks "only that the short story be taken seriously, that it should be granted a wholeness in itself, an indestructible, unparaphrasable, and essentially unanalyzable character like that of a good poem." [2] Relatively few of the stories included meet this requirement. That the two chief sources of the anthologists' short stories are popular mass magazines, *Saturday Evening Post* and the late *Colliers*, from which nearly every series borrows and upon which the Lipp and PH series lean very heavily, is a kind of evidence that most of the selections are decidedly lightweight, for, although notably literary and durable stories have occasionally appeared in popular magazines, including the *Post* and *Colliers*, the more characteristic story found there is ephemeral and slight, ideally suited to, in Baker's phrases, "lazy Sunday-morning customers." [3] That the editors of the anthologies also find their stories in Sunday newspaper supplements (*This Week* is a leading source), chain grocery publications (for example, *Woman's Day, the A & P Magazine*), and magazines deliberately aimed at children and adolescents (for example, *St. Nicholas, Seventeen, Boy's Life, Calling All Girls, American Girl*) suggests that the short story is not commonly regarded as a serious literary genre, but rather as an attractive short piece easily handled by the teacher and "appreciated" by students with a minimum of teaching.

Here, as with some of the other genres discussed below, the principal criticism to be made is not that such stories are not

[2] *Ibid.*, p. 447.
[3] Herschel Brickell, "What Happened to the Short Story?" originally published in the *Atlantic Monthly* and reprinted in Eugene Current-Garcia and Walter R. Patrick, eds., *What Is the Short Story?* (New York: Scott, Foresman and Company, 1961). "The 'bigslicks' talk glibly about printing the best stories they can, and I have heard some of their editors say they avoided formula stories when possible, but patient reading of what they print convinced me that most of them are kidding themselves." (p. 121.)

worth reading but that as entertainment they do not deserve a place in the textbooks prepared at considerable expense for high school classrooms. To give such stories as much space as more enduring works of genuine literature, is at once to blur distinctions between the great and the mediocre (thereby frustrating the development of taste).

As a matter of interest, the magazines upon which the anthologists draw most frequently are here listed in order of use: *Saturday Evening Post, Colliers, The New Yorker, Scholastic Magazines, Atlantic Monthly, Esquire, Cosmopolitan, This Week, Story, Boy's Life, Seventeen, Harper's, American Girl, Ladies' Home Journal.* Others laid under contribution include such varied publications as *Fantasy and Science Fiction, Good Housekeeping, Outdoor Life, Weekend Picture Magazine, American Legion, Farm Journal, Hearst's International, Life,* and *Today's Woman.*

Of all the short stories in the anthologies, 558, or 73 per cent, appear in a single volume each. These are, with some exceptions, ephemeral pieces, properly classified as "commercial" or "formulary." On the other hand, some of the stories anthologized are drawn from collections or from the "quality" magazines and are among those most frequently included. These give several of the anthologies a more literary character than they might otherwise have.

Table II of Appendix A lists the stories most frequently printed and shows the grade level to which they are assigned. In our opinion many of these frequently printed stories are of respectable quality and are of a kind likely to broaden, deepen, or sensitize the students' interests. All the stories in Table I represent, however, only 4 per cent of the total number appearing in the anthologies.

Table III lists in order the authors having the greatest numbers of short stories anthologized and the number of appearances of them. The authors listed in Table III are responsible for about 22 per cent of all the stories anthologized and for 31 per cent of all appearances of the short story.

The most notable characteristic of the anthologies in their choice of short stories is that there is so little agreement among the editors on what constitutes a short story worthy of inclusion. A relatively small number are found in several anthologies, but beyond these there is almost no agreement. The result is that there is little beyond this handful of frequently anthologized stories that could be thought of as part of a more or less well-defined heritage of short stories which students can share, a result that is not surprising when it is remembered that these seventy-two volumes offer more than seven hundred and fifty different stories by almost five hundred different authors. In the light of the evidence it is difficult to believe that quality has been the overriding criterion in the selection of short stories.

ABRIDGEMENT

The problem of abridgement, important for several of the literary genres, arises somewhat less frequently with the short story. However, short stories are often abbreviated or simplified in anthologies prepared for second-track classes; for example, Kantor's "That Greek Dog" and Addington's "Clodhopper" appear in adapted versions in HB2-10, and O'Rourke's "Flashing Spikes" and Mercer's "The Only Way to Win" in SF2-9.

The purpose of altering stories in books intended for readers of lesser ability is primarily to shorten them and to make them easier. The following passages will illustrate how such alteration may occur.

It hovered like a hawk, soaring on outstretched wings; yet it was much too big for a hawk. As the bird came nearer, Harry was astonished at its size. Once or twice it approached and then went soaring and floating away again.

It hovered like a hawk, yet it was much too big for a hawk.

As the bird came nearer, Harry was surprised at its size. Once or twice it came close and then went floating away again.

The first passage is from Beachcroft's "The Erne from the Coast" as it appears in Hlt-10, and the second, from the same story, though now titled "Eagle from the Sea," as it appears in HltD-10. In every respect — vocabulary, syntax, paragraphing, and even punctuation — the passage has been simplified. In the process it has, unfortunately, lost much of its vigor. It is possible to see also, even in a passage this short, how the reader of lesser ability is deliberately prevented from meeting words like *soaring, outstretched, astonished,* and *approached.* The systematic emasculation of texts, undertaken in the belief that only thus can the "slow reader" be accommodated, might well be subjected to re-evaluation; it may be that texts from which the interest and challenge have been removed are not those that, however easy, are best suited to the development of reading ability.

In volumes intended for first-track and heterogeneous classes the editing of short stories is generally less frequent than in second-track volumes.

Abridging or otherwise altering literary texts, a practice that is almost always regrettable, is impossible to condone (1) when it is done silently, that is, when there is inadequate or no indication that the text is not printed as the author wrote it, or (2) when the deletions or changes in language result in changes of tone, theme, purpose, atmosphere, characterization, setting, plot, or other essential components. Because the majority of the short stories anthologized are recent enough to be protected by copyright, they are usually supplied with a footnote indicating whether they have been "adapted," "shortened," "condensed," "simplified," or otherwise edited. Silent editing is more likely to occur in stories of the nineteenth century and earlier, and since these are the "classical" stories in the English curriculum the teacher must be on his guard if he wishes to teach stories by Poe, Hawthorne, and Irving, for example, in the form in which these authors wrote their stories.

Even when a story is still protected by copyright, however, it is necessary that the teacher be circumspect. As an example of editing that consists of both silent abridgement and alteration, we may note the treatment of Doyle's "The Adventure of the Speckled Band" in HM-9 and SF-9. Both volumes acknowledge the 1892 copyright by Harper and Brothers and the author's copyright of 1920. However, neither mentions that the text has been abridged or altered in any way. Yet the two are not identical. Whereas HM-9 prints a text that is virtually complete, SF-9 makes deletions at twenty-five points in the story, ranging in length from one word to one hundred and twenty-three words and totaling about six hundred words. There are no indications to show where the deletions occur or what they contain. There are also changes in wording, made necessary by the deletions. Among passages omitted in the SF-9 version are some that help to characterize Sherlock Holmes, refer to earlier cases he has solved (a kind of omission that no Holmes enthusiast would countenance), motivate the later actions of the villain, and help to establish the tone. Some of the deletions seem merely arbitrary, and several of the alterations are superfluous and perhaps patronizing. The two following passages will illustrate:

In glancing over my notes of the seventy-odd cases in which I have during the last eight years studied the methods of my friend Sherlock Holmes, I find *many tragic, some comic, a large number merely strange, but none commonplace. For working as he did, rather for the love of his art than for the acquirement of wealth, he refused to associate himself with any investigation which did not tend toward the unusual, and even the fantastic. Of all these varied cases, however, I cannot recall any* which presented more singular features than that which was associated with the well-known Surrey family of the Royletts of Stoke Moran.

The italicized words in this passage, which opens the story, add an essential detail to the character of Holmes; however, they are omitted in SF-9. It then becomes necessary to add, without textual authority, the word *none* after *find* in order to make the single remaining sentence readable.

At dusk we saw Dr. Grimesby Roylett drive past, *his huge form looming up beside the little figure of the lad who drove him. The boy had some slight difficulty in undoing the heavy iron gates, and we heard the hoarse roar of the doctor's voice and saw the fury with which he shook his clenched fists at him. The trap drove on,* and a few minutes later we saw a sudden light spring up among the trees as the lamp was lit in one of the sitting rooms.

The italicized words, again deleted by SF-9, help to characterize the villain and in some measure lessen our disbelief in his potential for evil. Because the indication of place has also disappeared with the omitted words, it was found necessary to supply the lack by inserting *at the manor house* after *spring up.*

The anthology used here to illustrate abridgement is no worse than others in this respect. It has been cited only because the story concerned is widely known. On the whole, however, the texts of short stories are treated with proper respect in the anthologies.

GRADE PLACEMENT

The placement of short stories by grades raises a question of a different kind, which can be considered by reference to Table II of Appendix A. There it will be seen that editors' judgments about the proper placing of works often do not coincide. That some editors place a certain short story in the ninth grade and others in the tenth is hardly a matter for comment, but that the choice is often two years apart between the ninth and the eleventh grades (for example, "The Split Cherry Tree," "The Tell-tale Heart") or even three years apart, between the ninth and twelfth (for example, "The Open Window," "Quality") may seem strange. And that a short story can be assigned to all four grade levels by different editors (for example, Callaghan's "The Snob") would seem further to belittle the significance of two of the criteria most widely used and highly regarded by professional curriculum makers — level of difficulty and suitability to "developmental" stages.

Besides the examples of disagreement about placement that can be seen in Table II, the following, among numerous others, can also be noted: Chekhov's "The Bet" placed in the tenth grade by ABC, Ldw, and HB49, but in the twelfth by Hlt; Lagerlof's "The Christmas Guest" in SF-9, ABC-10, and Ldw-12; Saroyan's "The Summer of the Beautiful White Horse" in Gn-9 and Lipp-11; Ullman's "Top Man" in Gn-9, PH-10, and Lipp-11; Stevenson's "Sire de Maletroit's Door" in Irq-9 and Gn-12; Katkov's "The Torn Invitation" in HM-9, Gn-10, and HltD-12; Payne's "Prelude" in Hth-9, Sgr-10, and RM-11. There is even greater disagreement about placement when the earlier book is for the second-track (for example, Gale's "Bill" in SF2-9 and ABC-11, Lardner's "I Can't Breathe" and Lewis's "The Hack Driver" in HB2-9 and Sgr-11), for in these instances the assignment involves not only differences between grade levels but also those between students of widely varying abilities.

One may reasonably conclude that the reasons for discrepant placements of short stories (as well as works in some other genres), in spite of assertions to the contrary, are not so much the editors' varying decisions about their difficulty and about their appropriateness to stages of adolescent development as the organization of the typical series of anthologies. Although some series place a certain short story in the ninth grade because it is relatively easy to read, others place it in the eleventh grade apparently because it was written by an American author or in the twelfth grade because it was written by an English author. This practice raises an interesting question: Is the best way of organizing a series one that allows pieces easy enough for ninth-graders to turn up in the later years simply because of the nationality of the authors? To us this criterion seems irrelevant.

A second principle seems also to be at work. The most common kind of organization of ninth- and tenth-grade volumes is the topical, and some of the stories seem to have been assigned to these grades because of their relevance to the topics predetermined as suitable for these years. This is a potentially dangerous criterion to use, for it not only confines the stories that can be included in a given volume to certain subject matters (sports, animals, science fiction, mystery, adventure, etc.), thus determining placement by restrictive means that do not arise from the literature itself, but also it may allow the inclusion of much writing that is not literature. Literature *can*, of course, treat these topics (and much else besides), but all pieces of writing that treat them are not thereby literature.

RECOMMENDATIONS

We find the treatment of the short story in the anthologies examined better than that accorded most other genres, in spite of the fact that many decidedly inferior stories have been admitted. At the same time, however, most of the anthologies do contain at least a few stories of distinction and the stories most frequently included, with notable exceptions, do have some degree of literary merit. We believe that there is room for improvement and therefore offer the following recommendations.

1. We recommend that the number of short stories in the ninth- and tenth-grade volumes be held to not more than one-sixth of the total selections and that they take up not more than one-fourth of the pages. In the eleventh and twelfth grades, the number of short stories and the pages devoted to them should be

restricted still further. More attention than this is likely to reduce unduly the space available for other, and in many ways more important, literary genres. Indeed, since there are now on the market many well-edited collections of short stories, there is today much less reason than formerly for devoting a large section of the anthology to this genre.

2. We recommend further that no short story be admitted that is not distinguished: the role of the English teacher at this point would seem to be not to prepare a student to read "popular" literature (for which he requires little or no preparation) but to show him how to read and to prefer something better. The role of the anthology is to supply the best short stories — those that confront and examine human life with honesty and artistic skill and without oversimplification. It follows also that such criteria as mere topicality, timeliness, and nationality of author are distinctly secondary.

3. We recommend that the full text of a short story as the author wrote it be printed. This recommendation should cause editors little or no hardship since so many distinguished stories are available that range through various levels of difficulty. As most of the anthologists point out, accepting the doctrine of Poe, a good short story has unity of effect. To alter a good story is almost surely to vitiate its unity and destroy its effect.

4. We recommend that the word "story" be used with care by the editors and that every selection they admit as a short story be one in fact. We have found many selections from novels and books of nonfiction placed among the short stories or identified as short stories by the editorial apparatus. We believe that such classification misrepresents literature and can only add to the sense of its vagueness or "scientific" inexactness.

5. The short story is a genre so intrinsically valuable and so pedagogically useful for the English class that its resources should be explored to the fullest. It can make a significant contribution

to the study of literature. But to do so, those who are responsible for compiling anthologies as well as those who use them might well look further into the theory of the short story as a genre and read what critics and short-story writers have had to say about it. We recommend, therefore, that editors and teachers familiarize themselves with the considerable body of criticism that has grown up around the short story. In particular, we recommend acquaintance with the following: Mark Schorer, ed., *The Story, A Critical Anthology* (Prentice-Hall, Inc., 1950); "Notes on Fictional Techniques," in Caroline Gordon and Allen Tate, eds., *The House of Fiction, An Anthology of the Short Story* (Charles Scribner's Sons, 1960); the essays by Howard Baker, Robert Penn Warren, and Lionel Trilling in Herbert Gold and David L. Stevenson, eds., *Stories of Modern America* (St. Martin's Press, 1961); and the twenty-seven essays in Eugene Current-Garcia and Walton R. Patrick, eds., *What Is the Short Story?* (Scott, Foresman and Company, 1961).

2. THE NOVEL

THE NOVEL, chiefly because of its length, presents a special problem for the anthologists, which they have attempted to solve in a variety of ways. We have gathered anthologies into three groups on the basis of how they deal with the novel. About one-fourth of the volumes examined, designated as Group I, include a novel or novelette, either with the full text or in a lengthy abridgement or condensation, and present it as a representative of the genre. Another one-fourth (Group III) include only short excerpts from novels, often several in one volume; many of these, however, do not identify the excerpts as parts of novels and sometimes treat them as if they are short stories or other self-contained pieces.[1] A few of the anthologies in Group II contain

---

[1] The practice of presenting an excerpt as if it were a short story, a sketch,

discussions of the novel, especially the history of its development, even though the genre is not represented by examples. Discussions and historical sketches of the novel are also found in some volumes of Groups I and III. Particularly noteworthy are those in HB49-11, HB49-12, Ldw-10, and Ldw-11. Most of the anthologies include titles of novels, often along with other kinds of books, as "Suggested Readings" or under a similar rubric. The volumes belonging to each of the three groups are indicated below, and some of them, particularly those in Group I, are discussed in some detail.

Table IV of Appendix A indicates the space given to the novel in the anthologies in Group I. The percentage represents the relative attention which the novel receives in each volume and includes the number of pages given to the complete novel or abridgement listed, as well as those pages devoted to any shorter excerpts that the anthology may contain. Thus, the first anthology listed, Glb-11, devotes 13 per cent of its pages to the novel, which are apportioned among the complete novelette, *The Voice of Bugle Ann,* and the three short excerpts from novels (*The Deerslayer, Moby Dick,* and *Tom Sawyer*) that it contains. (The excerpts are identified in Table VI.)

Table IV indicates that the space given to the novel ranges widely, from about one-eighth of an anthology's pages (Glb-11, HM-9, McM-11) to almost one-half (Irq-9). Also, except for the Macmillan series and Glb-11 (which is used at least as often for the tenth grade as for the eleventh), it is obvious the incorporat-

---

or an essay is often difficult to detect. Unless the teacher is well acquainted with the work, he may not be able to determine from the footnotes, customary in some of the anthologies, whether the book identified as that from which the selection is taken is a novel, a collection of short stories, or something else. The student is also at a loss, for he is deprived of a lead to the complete text of the novel if he should find the excerpt interesting enough to cause him to pursue it.

ing of a novel in the anthology is exclusively a practice of the volumes for the first two years.

The novels that are included in the anthologies of Group I fall into two classes: the "classic" novels of nineteenth-century England, and contemporary novels and novelettes mostly by American authors. The former are limited to four novels by three authors, Scott, Eliot, and Dickens, whereas the latter show a greater variety. At least three of the "classic" novels are long-familiar titles in English curricula, but most of the contemporary novels are relatively new to the classroom. Finally, there is another difference between the novels of the two classes, one that has important consequence. Almost all the newer novels are short and thus can be printed in their entirety without greatly enlarging the size of the anthology. Most of these texts are therefore unabridged. The older novels are much longer and pose a problem because of their size. If, for example, SF-9 had included all of *David Copperfield*, using the same lavish format throughout, the volume would have been about 25 per cent larger than it is just to include the novel. The problem has been solved in each instance by abridging the novel. Because the versions appearing in the anthologies are all that a great many students know of these famous novels of another day, each of the four novels is discussed below in some detail.

The version of *David Copperfield* that appears in SF-9 consists of the novel's first fourteen chapters or about 22 per cent of the original. These chapters constitute one of the anthology's topical units, titled "One Boy's Life" although they follow David only to the point where he begins his studies under Dr. Strong. He has not yet met Uriah Heap, Agnes Wickfield, and her father, and a score or so of other interesting characters who appear later in the novel. This version is, however, not only an excerpt but an abridged excerpt, for passages have been deleted from the fourteen chapters printed. The first page, for example, contains six paragraphs in contrast to Dickens's original ten, omitting those in which David recounts the circumstances of his birth, the neighbors' predictions of an unlucky future for him, and the history of the caul with which he was born. The next deletion occurs at the end of the second (Dickens's sixth) paragraph: five lines are omitted in which David reveals his sensitivity about his father's gravestone "lying out alone there in the dark night, when our little parlour was warm and bright with fire and candle, and the doors of our house were — almost cruelly, it seemed to me sometimes — bolted and locked against it." The final paragraph on this page is a condensation of the original which reduces Dickens's 113 words to 49. Many of the characteristic Dickensian touches — for which one reads Dickens — are thus omitted in the interests of speeding up the plot, and, perhaps, of conserving space (although, of the 119 pages given to the novel, 11.5 are devoted to pictures and 10 to editorial equipment). In the interest of accuracy, it must be said that many of the following pages do not have as many alterations as does the first page, but there are also some pages that have more.

Although it is impossible to justify the deletions, particularly because they are made silently, it would seem possible to justify a long excerpt from such an important novel as *David Copperfield* on the grounds that by the classroom discussion of the fourteen chapters and the enthusiasm of the teacher, students would be impelled to read the rest of the novel. We are, therefore, surprised to find that neither in headnote nor in the following comments do the editors suggest to the student that he might finish the novel on his own. In fact, the editorial insistence on its length, its "slowness" in getting started, and the multiplicity of its characters might be thought rather to discourage the reader from continuing unaided.

Great Expectations, an ideal novel for high school classes because of both its artistry and its theme, was included in HBM-9 and was retained when the anthology was revised six years later as HBO-9. In the earlier edition the statement was made that the novel was abridged but had not been rewritten. This statement does not appear in the later edition. Its removal was well-advised, for a close examination of the text shows that there has been rewriting as well as abridgement. In the first 43 pages of the adaptation (which correspond to the first 118 pages of the original) there are, for example, sixty-four changes in the vocabulary. There are also many shortened sentences, sentences or parts of sentences of the adapter's own substituted for the originals, and deletions of metaphors, similes, and modifiers. The adaptation is about three-sevenths the length of the original. Although the anthology is intended for students of average and superior ability, some of the alterations seem to belie the intention; for example, Dickens's own words, some of which rank as sixth-grade words on the Thorndike lists, are sometimes replaced by what Thorndike classed as third-grade words, although the volume is intended for the ninth grade. Even on pedagogical grounds this adaptation would therefore appear to be unacceptable. On literary grounds it is even more so, for much of the color, the humor, and the humaneness with which Dickens endowed his novel have vanished, leaving a "melancholy mutilation" (not our phrase, but that of a high school teacher) of a great book. The results suggest that the adapter set out to make *Great Expectations* more nearly conform with the factual, informational, fast-moving, and often unimaginative prose pieces that have become such a ubiquitous element in high school anthologies.

Although the attempt to pass this version off as merely an abridgement and not as a simplified alteration cannot be justified, and although the abridging itself has been done silently, this version is by no means the worst example of the *"eviscerated classics"* that we have seen. Some of the separately printed editions of famous novels especially edited for high school use, a number of which are discussed below, are even more successful in removing the marks of greatness. Nevertheless, the widespread use of the adapted version in HBM-9 and HBO-9 is cause for consternation, for it is the only version that thousands of students have ever read. Its influence should therefore not be underestimated. Because it illuminates in several ways the whole vexing issue of "adapted classics," we quote at length the comment made by a teacher who was well acquainted with the original, after she had, perforce, used this version in her classroom.

I am resentful at having been duped when my editors avow that the [Dickens] novel is abridged but neglect to add that it is also simplified. I am downcast when I discover changes in vocabulary which show two-thirds of the words reduced to third-grade level. I am dismayed when I view opportunities for predicting outcomes, drawing conclusions, and making inferences swept away either by deletion or, still worse, by the editor's insertions. I am depressed when I find the challenge gone and with it the process of thinking and subsequent satisfaction of solution, all of which are important factors in learning to read. At a time when reading is being called upon to make its greatest contribution to personal development and social progress, I am sorry to see our reading made simple instead of increasingly difficult. . . . I am chagrined when I discover someone tampering with a work of art. . . . Can I with a clear conscience invite my ninth graders to partake of a meager meal as represented by the adapted version when they might rather be enjoying from the original the aperitif of Dickens' implications, the flavor of his comparisons, the spice of his humor, the bittersweet quality of his pathos and sentiment, and the nourishment of his vocabulary? [2]

The text of *Ivanhoe* in Irq-9 consists of about 59 per cent of the original. The editors remark that because the complete novel "would be long, dull reading" they have deleted the "dull pas-

---

[2] The quotation and the summary of some details that precedes it are from an unpublished essay, "Abridged *vs.* Original: a Revelation," by the late Mignon L. Erickson.

sages that do nothing toward furthering the action." It is enlightening to discover what in this novel the editors regard as unnecessary. The first five paragraphs, for example, contain twelve separate deletions (none of which is indicated), ranging in length from 5 to 216 words, and together accounting for 64.3 per cent of the original text. The matter thus deleted includes three passages that help to set the story in its historical context by referring to earlier (Druidical and Roman) days in England and to the reader's own present moment, a comment on the revival of baronial strife and feudal power that is helpful for an understanding of the plot. It would seem that a careful teacher, sensitive to the historical context and wishing to make the novel come alive for his students, would be handicapped by such omissions, to offset which he would have to provide, outside the literary context and without the novelist's help, much of the very same material.

Silas Marner, the novel appearing most frequently at length in the anthologies, is variously treated, but none of the abridgements is so drastic as those of *Great Expectations, David Copperfield,* and *Ivanhoe.* An examination of six representative and crucial passages in *Silas Marner,* in the five anthologies that include the novel, reveals the extent of the abridgements. The relevant details are set down in Table V of Appendix A.

The selected passages amount to approximately one-tenth of the novel. From Table V it can be seen that of this tenth Irq-10 omits 2.5 per cent, SF-10 omits about 5.6 per cent, and HBO-10 omits 22.0 per cent. It is also interesting to note that as the illustrations and editorial apparatus come to bulk larger in the latest (Olympic) revision of the Harcourt, Brace anthology than in the two earlier ones, the deletions become more numerous and more extensive. Whether line drawings, lengthy headnotes to chapters, and other devices are a fair exchange for the words of George Eliot that have been omitted is hardly a plausible question when the nature of the omitted passages is considered. The lines omitted from the Irq-10 text give further description and motivation of character. Most of those omitted from the SF-10 text are of the same kind. The more extensive deletions in the HBO-10 text include lines developing character, similes, corroborative evidence, local color, authorial generalizations, and revelations of Silas Marner's train of thought. At least one deletion in the HBO-10 text is striking enough to be worthy of special comment. We refer to a silent emendation in Chapter 7. From Eliot's sentence, "By this pregnant speech the farrier had re-established his self-complacency. . . ." the word "pregnant" is removed. Since the word is now used in polite conversation even in its primary sense, and since here it is used only in a secondary meaning, one is led to wonder by what standards of prudery the editors have been guided. Such an emendation is not only deceptive but impoverishing of the language. Furthermore, what a refined mid-Victorian lady could write, surely a mid-twentieth century tenth-grader can read!

The remaining anthologies in Group I solve the problem of including the novel by printing a shorter, contemporary novel or novelette — which may or may not be complete (*The Ox-Bow Incident* is abridged). The question to be raised about these "modern" books is not so much concerned with abridgement, alteration, and silent editing as with the justification of choice. Why, for example, should a novel that is deliberately adolescent (like *Johnny Tremaine,* which won for its author the Newberry Award given for children's books) or one that has not yet stood the test of time be given so much space in an already bulky anthology? These seem more appropriate for supplementary, "outside," or "free" reading than for class study. The weakness of several of them for use — that is, *study* — in the classroom is primarily that there is little to *teach* because they hardly need to be taught.

The anthologies in Group II contain neither whole novels (whether the full text or an abridgement) nor short excerpts from novels.

The anthologies in Group III are the most numerous. Table VI of Appendix A indicates the extent of attention given to the novel in these volumes.

As Table VI indicates, most of the excerpts are short, some only two or three pages long. It is doubtful that pieces of this length provide much inducement for the student to read the entire novel. To be sure, many of them are included because they "fit" into topical units, but there are numerous short complete works — poems, short stories, essays — that can serve this purpose just as well without having to be tampered with. Also, the presence of excerpts, particularly the shorter ones, further augments that characteristic of the anthologies that many teachers are deploring when they speak of the anthologies as "made up of snippets." If excerpts from novels are included, they should be long enough and representative enough to give the reader some sense of the whole and the desire to read it. We have found in the anthologies only a few excerpts that are successful in this respect: 25 pages of *Arrowsmith* in HBL-11, 21 pages of *Twenty Thousand Leagues Under the Sea* in Hth-9, and 27 pages of *Moby Dick* in Sgr-11.

An excerpt that is both discontinuous and altered, a twenty-page passage from *Huckleberry Finn* in Sgr-11, will serve to illustrate a defect of abridgement. This excerpt is really two, taken from different sections of the novel. From the first are omitted two passages of eighty-five and twenty lines respectively, which together contain the whole point of the episode — Huck's reasons for calling upon Mrs. Loftus while he is disguised as a girl and for his uneasiness when he hears that Mr. Loftus has set out to capture Jim for the reward money. The deletions have apparently been made to avoid Twain's frequently used word, "nigger."

That this is the motive is clearly indicated by the second fragment, in which various euphemisms are employed: "a nigger
woman" becomes "one of the servants"; "nigger" and "niggers"
become "boy" and "hands" or are simply deleted; "a young white
gentleman" becomes "a young gentleman." Apparently it has been
the intention to remove all traces of the racial difference between
Huck and Jim, a change that of course completely vitiates the
novel. Since much of the effectiveness of the novel is produced
by Twain's use of dialect and vulgate speech, the linguistic realism is also partially destroyed. One supposes that the purpose
in expurgating the text is to avoid offending a minority group:
yet in attempting to do so the editors have made it impossible for
the reader to see that the novel is not just an adventure story but
the account of a genuine and self-sacrificing mutual affection between a Negro slave and a white boy. The emasculated version is
thus basically dishonest for it "solves" the racial problem by pre-
tending that there is none. Admittedly, dealing with racial questions poses difficulties, but literature, by and large, attempts to
treat them honestly and, above all, *in context;* and effective teachers can treat them with tact and skill. To ignore one of America's
greatest novels because of this difficulty is, it seems to us, to adopt
the psychology of the ostrich. This course of action is really unnecessary, we are happy to learn, for a number of schools use the
complete text of the novel for classroom reading even with racially
mixed groups.

Ten of the anthologies in Group I contain excerpts as well as
complete novels or long abridgements. These are the anthologies
marked by an asterisk in Table IV of Appendix A. The number
and length of these excerpts are shown in Table VII. Since many
of the excerpts are short, as was indicated in Tables IV and VII,
the actual percentage of pages devoted to the novel is relatively
small. This situation is shown in Table IV.

The higher percentage of pages devoted to the novel in ninth-

and tenth-grade volumes reflects the practice in several of them (those in Group I) of printing complete texts or long abridgements. The sharp drop after the tenth grade accords with the regular practice thereafter of representing the novel only by short excerpts. In all the anthologies examined, the novel ranks last of all the genres in the percentage of selections and next-to-last in percentage of pages devoted to it; however, the ranking varies by grade levels. In ninth-grade volumes the novel is given about as much space as poetry, and more than the drama and the essay combined. In tenth-, eleventh-, and twelfth-grade volumes it outranks only the essay. For the anthologies of Group I the percentage of pages given to the novel is obviously higher than it is for those in Group III.

We have already remarked, in our discussion of the short story, that some editors are rather lax in their regard for genre classifications. Such laxity is also exercised in regard to the novel. The result is that some excerpts from novels are to be found among a group of short stories and may actually be regarded as belonging to that genre. Occasionally, excerpts from novels are classified in still other ways. In ABC-11, for example, a short excerpt from Dos Passos's *U.S.A.* is called a biographical sketch and one from Steinbeck's *Grapes of Wrath* is called an essay. Although such matters may at first seem rather trivial, we believe that enough is at stake to warrant greater care in distinguishing among the literary genres. While critical terminology is wont to shift its ground, there are occasions when exactness is possible. The terms of literary typology, if they are not to be deprived of all usefulness, should be applied with some care. In short, an excerpt should be identified as taken from a novel, if that is its source, and should not be called something else as if it were a complete literary piece. We see no legitimate purpose served by a blurring of the distinctions among genres. Indeed, the careless treatment of literary genres is akin to the cavalier treatment of literary texts and the frequent oversimplifications of literary history.

Table IX lists all the novels that are excerpted in the anthologies, shows where they can be found, and indicates their length. It thus serves two purposes: it provides a bibliography for the teacher who wishes to locate a sample of a particular novel, and it provides the basis for further comments on the anthologists' treatment of the novel.

When the novels in Table IV and those in Table IX are considered together, we can see that the novelist most frequently anthologized is Dickens: six of his books are represented by eleven appearances in the anthologies — two long abridgements, one long and eight short excerpts. The single novel most often included, although only in short excerpts, is *Moby Dick*, which makes nine appearances. This novel is followed by Rölvaag's *Giants in the Earth* (seven short excerpts), Eliot's *Silas Marner* (five long abridgements or full texts), and Twain's *Huckleberry Finn* (five short excerpts). Beyond these there is little agreement among editors in their choice of novels to include, whether in full or by excerpt. The conclusions are self-evident: the novels most frequently anthologized do have literary respectability and are important components of the Anglo-American literary heritage, but they are presented in abridged form or only in excerpts. Beyond these there is so little agreement that alongside novels of great distinction are found others that have little or none. Like the short stories, the excerpts of some novels have been included, we strongly suspect, not because they are great, but because they fit into the predetermined organization.

For an evaluation of the anthologies' treatment of the novel it is helpful to note what has been omitted as well as what has been included. Some authors (for example, Hawthorne and Orwell) are not represented by their best work. The omission of *The Scarlet Letter*, thought by many to be America's greatest novel, is especially noteworthy. None of the great eighteenth-century novelists is represented even by excerpts. Few of the Nobel and Pulitzer prize-winning novelists are represented. Only one French and one Russian novel are included, in spite of the large contribution that France and Russia have made in this genre. Among American and English novelists unrepresented are such important novelists as Jane Austen, Charlotte Brontë, Henry Fielding, Henry James, and from more recent times, William Faulkner, Ernest Hemingway, Aldous Huxley, James Joyce. The omissions can also be noted in other ways. Of the ten novels recently called the world's greatest by Somerset Maugham only four are included and those only by excerpts. Of the twenty-eight novels among the "100 Significant Books" listed in *Good Reading*, a bibliography sponsored by the College English Association and endorsed by, among others, the National Council of Teachers of English, twenty are unrepresented in the anthologies. And of the forty-two novels on the list of "Books the World Cherishes" in *Books for You*, a publication of the NCTE, twenty-four are omitted and seventeen others are represented only by short excerpts. It is clear that, whether one considers what is included or what is omitted, the anthologies cannot be given high marks for their treatment of the novel.

In defense of the anthologies, however, it can be said that teachers customarily supplement them with separate editions of one or more novels and that the anthologists are not, therefore, primarily responsible for representing the genre. This defense does not hold, of course, for the twenty volumes which do attempt to represent it and devote from about one-eighth to almost one-half their space to the novel (see Table IV). It should also be noted that some of the anthologies, especially those for the twelfth grade, include long prose fiction of other types: for example, *Gulliver's Travels, Pilgrim's Progress,* and *Morte D'Arthur.* Also, some ninth- and tenth-grade volumes include prose reductions of myths, epics, and legends. Among these are to be commended especially ABC-10, Irq-9, RM-10, and SF-9.

The choice of a novel to include in an anthology, because of the space it occupies and the time it demands of both teacher and student, is surely one of the most important decisions that the editors must make. It is therefore necessary that the choice be made with the greatest possible care and according to the most relevant criteria. There seems to us no excuse for printing anything less than the best — the best being those novels that inevitably appeal to thoughtful readers, that confront life honestly, and that are rendered with artistry.

The editors' dilemma is a real one, which is illustrated by the contrasting solutions in Hth and HBM-9. The editors of the former chose to print *Winter Thunder*, a novelette that could be contained in thirty pages, which, they said, "has many of the characteristics of the novel," thereby suggesting that their choice was dictated by length rather than by literary criteria. The editors of HBM-9 took a different course. They chose *Great Expectations*, a decision that can be defended on the strictest literary grounds; however, in order to print the novel they chose to cut away more than half the text. As we have seen, what remains is a frail shadow of the original. Neither practice is defensible.

There is, we believe, a better solution than either of these. We suggest that anthologies should not attempt to include the whole or a large part of a novel. Since most suitable first-rate novels are too long to be included in their entirety, and since the anthologies would still tend toward ponderosity even if they contained no more than their present array of poems, short stories, essays, and dramas, omitting the novel entirely seems the best solution to the problem. In an earlier day we would not have made this suggestion, but there are now available inexpensive, attractive, well-edited, unabridged, and unadapted paperback editions of almost any novel that a teacher may wish to use. If the legal and budgetary regulations of the school district permit, this is far and away the most satisfactory means of representing the novel in the classroom. We suggest that the teacher or textbook committee obtain a copy of *Paperbound Books in Print,* copyrighted by the R. R. Bowker Company (62 West 45th Street, New York 26, N.Y.), which lists the paperbacks of more than one hundred publishers, conveniently classified by genres.

There are two other possible solutions of this problem, one of them, at least, better than settling for an anthologized novel chosen by the editors simply because it is short enough to print or cut to fit the available space. These are the multi-novel volumes and the clothbound separate editions prepared for high school use. The former is a recent innovation, best known from the four-novel volumes published by Harcourt, Brace and Company; the latter have been with us at least since the nineteenth century. Each has its advantages and disadvantages, which should be carefully weighed.

The multi-novel volumes tend to commit a school to all the novels included, even though they are often uneven in quality and distinction. Also, it is a common practice to abridge one of the novels, sometimes the most important one in the volume. It is well to remember, therefore, that even the most careful abridgement may cause significant changes. In the version of *Jane Eyre* that appears in *Four Novels for Appreciation* (Harcourt, Brace and Company), for example, the ninth paragraph in Chapter 1 begins, "I returned to my book. Each picture told a story . . . ," but between those two sentences there are 308 additional words and a stanza of poetry in the original. The deleted passage helps to establish at the outset the image of Jane as an imaginative girl, highly sensitive to suggestion and to the subtle nuances of language. Because this passage also names (and describes in considerable detail) the book she is reading, the omission necessitates a slight alteration a paragraph later: of "With Bewick on my knee . . . ," a reference plain enough in the complete text, to "With my book on my knee. . . ." On the whole this is a successful abridgement, and the reader will be deprived of very little; whether he should be deprived of *any* of the text the teacher must decide. The important point is that he and his students should be aware that the text is abridged.

As advantages can be counted the convenience of the multi-novel volumes, the implicit encouragement they give the student to read beyond the novel assigned, and not least (in the Harcourt, Brace volumes) editorial comments and relevant study questions that are superior to the run of those found in anthologies. Questions in the anthologies, on the other hand, are as often as not irrelevant, trivial, and patronizing. Frequently they seem quite oblivious to the developments in literary criticism of the past several decades. Nevertheless, in spite of the shortcomings mentioned above, as long as the multi-novel volumes continue to maintain their present standards, we recommend them as an alternative solution to the problem of presenting the novel in the classroom.

The other possible solution, using separately printed high school editions of famous novels, must be approached with great caution, for they differ widely in quality, in textual responsibility, and in editorial equipment.

RECOMMENDATIONS

1. Our first recommendation is that the novel be entirely omitted from the anthology and that it be presented in the classroom by means of a well-edited paperback, a multi-novel volume such as those by Harcourt, Brace and Company, or a special high school edition of superior quality.

2. We also recommend that short excerpts of novels be omitted from anthologies. Their value is dubious, and the space they occupy could be better used for something else that is complete. If,

however, excerpts are included, they should be chosen to represent the novel fairly, be clearly identified as coming from the novel, and be presented for the primary purpose of inducing students to read the complete work. In any case, only the most distinguished novels should be thus sampled.

3. We recommend further that anthologies for all grades include a discussion of the novel as a literary genre. This discussion should be designed primarily to prepare the student to read novels thoughtfully. Its emphasis should therefore be upon the characteristics of the novel rather than upon its history. The discussion should be followed by a highly selective list of novels (preferably with the best editions of each carefully specified), from which the teacher may choose one *for classroom study*. The novels on the list should have been chosen, first, for their unquestioned permanent value as literature, and second, for their suitability to the program of reading that is worked out in the anthology. This solution to the problem of including a novel would seem desirable because it allows for greater flexibility and the exercise of the individual teacher's taste and judgment, and because at the same time it provides for the integration of the novel into the course of reading so that it is not merely an obtrusive and unrelated part.

4. Finally, we recommend that the novels suggested in the lists of supplementary, "outside," or "free" reading also be chosen with a careful eye to their literary quality and their possible relationships to the in-class readings. In short, by this means the whole body of reading undertaken by the students, both in and out of class, assuming that equal care has been taken in the choice of all selections, can be combined into what is a real *program*, marked by both its literary quality and its unity.

3. PROSE NONFICTION

THE CHIEF PROBLEMS raised by the nonfictional prose contents of the anthologies concern classification, literary merit, and the abridging and excerpting of the selections. The kinds of selections falling into this general category are so numerous and so varied that their classification is difficult. At the same time, it has seemed to us that many of the kinds are probably inappropriate for anthologies because of their nature, which is more factual and informational than literary and humanistic. We have therefore discussed the first two problems together. In order to view this large body of material (27.2 per cent of the total contents) from a perspective that makes discussion possible, we have singled out the one genre that we think has an indisputable right to be included — the essay — and have treated it separately. Then follow our comments on all the rest of the prose nonfiction, which is chiefly characterized by its miscellaneousness and by what we conclude to be its general unsuitability as a substitute for more distinctively literary selections.

We begin with a consideration of the third problem. Excerpting and abridging are at least as commonly practiced with the nonfiction contents as with the novel: and, because nonfictional pieces are numerous, they, more than the selections in any other genre, are responsible for the kind of anthology that teachers describe as "a collection of bits and pieces." The extent of excerpting, abridging, adapting, or otherwise altering the selections in the anthologies is indicated in Table X, Appendix A, which lists all volumes examined in which one-fifth or more of the selections are excerpts, abridgements, etc.

Table XI shows the extent of the practice of altering selections in all the anthologies examined.

Although Tables X and XI record the alterations of all genres, it is the prose nonfiction more than any other single genre that causes the percentages to be so high. This conclusion is substantiated by a comparison of the above tables with Table XII, which indicates the amount of space given to miscellaneous nonfiction. The comparison shows a high correlation between percentage of excerpts and percentage of nonfictional selections.

The alteration may take one of several forms. The commonest practice is to select an excerpt from a book, often an autobiographical account of some adventure: for example, *Kon-Tiki, North to the Orient, Strangest Creatures on Earth,* and *Across the Space Frontier.* Although the language of the original (the material from which editors choose is so abundant that prose negotiable by students at any ability level can be found), is usually retained, some of the excerpts are subjected to further alteration: adaptation by simplifying the language, abridgement and condensation, or expurgation. The following instances will illustrate: ABC-10 prints a brief biographical sketch of Grandma Moses that is an abridgement of an article in *Time;* the selection in Gn-9 from Stewart's *Names on the Land* is both an excerpt and an adaptation. Occasionally the author's language goes through several dilutions before it reaches the student; for example, SF-9 prints a selection by Jacqueline Cochran that is an adaptation of an article in *Life,* which was a condensation of her book *Stars at Noon.* Because most of this kind of nonfiction is recent and therefore protected by copyright, the anthologists regularly identify the sources of their selections and indicate whether or not they have been altered.

Other kinds of alterations, especially in older writings, are not always acknowledged and sometimes they are difficult for the teacher to detect, so that he may be teaching something less than what he thinks. A curious example of expurgation is found in ABC-11, HB49-11, HBM-11, HBO-11, and SF-11. Each prints the famous passage on "the bold and arduous project of arriving at moral perfection" from Franklin's *Autobiography*. Franklin there lists the thirteen virtues that he hopes to develop in himself, and for each he sets down a "precept" for his own guidance. All of these save the precept for chastity are printed in the anthologies, but after the word "Chastity" appears only a blank space. A student with any curiosity will ask if Franklin had nothing to say about chastity. The answer, of course, is that he had: "Rarely use venery but for health or offspring, never to dullness, weakness, or the injury of your own or another's peace or reputation." Ironically, by expurgating at this point the editors have called attention to a topic which they apparently are trying to avoid.

The excerpts from nonfictional works vary greatly in length. Hlt-12 prints a two-page excerpt from a very long and important biography, Boswell's *Life of Johnson*. On the other hand, RM-10 devotes 110 pages (almost 20 per cent of its space) to a long abridgement of a popular but hardly distinguished book, *Kon-Tiki*. Indeed, the disparity between importance of the book excerpted and length of excerpt is an odd feature of some of the anthologies. Apparently in the interests of "covering" a large number of works that have a secure place in the Anglo-American literary heritage, they include numerous short excerpts of famous pieces — often too short to be of any use beyond bringing to the attention of the students a number of titles and authors' names; but there is little text to which the reader can attach this newly acquired information.

The problem of abridging and excerpting nonfictional works is actually twofold. There are pieces that because of their importance and literary quality should not be altered or shortened; for example, Washington's *Farewell Address* and Emerson's *Self-Reliance* (the latter is shortened in almost all eleventh-grade volumes). There are other works whose abridging and excerpting we consider a matter of indifference. To excerpt and abridge many of either kind results in an anthology that is miscellaneous and fragmentary. The proper solution would seem to be the inclusion of works of the former kind in their full texts and more careful discrimination among works of the latter kind, with many or even most of them removed from the anthology. The result would be a volume representing far fewer authors, a substantial amount of whose work could be read and studied with care.

Although the altering of nonfictional texts is not as harmful as is the tampering with fiction, and certainly not as harmful as the abridging of poetry, since with fiction and poetry their artistic unity is violated, nevertheless we are distressed to observe that as anthologies go through their periodic revisions they accumulate an increasing number of nonfictional works, many of which are ephemeral. These we discuss below as "miscellaneous nonfiction." But before we turn to them we shall consider one kind of prose that we believe is unduly neglected, namely, the essay.

THE ESSAY

Defining the essay may seem to be undertaking the impossible. It has been observed that one writer spends forty-three pages attempting to define it.[1] "Yet," as Christopher Morley, himself an essayist of stature, has remarked, "it is a mere quibble to pretend that the essay does not have easily recognizable manners." [2] The essay, most critics agree, must be prose nonfiction and have some or all of the following qualities: brevity, unity, a graceful style, freshness, vivacity, freedom from stiffness and affectation, and a lack of restriction on subject matter.[3]

---

[1] William Flint Thrall and Addison Hibbard, *A Handbook to Literature* (New York: The Odyssey Press, 1936), p. 163.

[2] Christopher Morley, ed., *Modern Essays* (New York: Harcourt, Brace and Company, 1921), p. v.

[3] Besides the works of Thrall and Hibbard and Morley cited above, see, for example, John L. Stewart, ed., *The Essay: A Critical Anthology* (New York: Prentice-Hall, 1952), p. xiii; Houston Peterson, ed., *Great Essays* (New York: Pocket Books, 1956), p. xiv; Stanley V. Makewer and Basil H.

Even by such a broad definition as this, many of the selections in the anthologies, although called essays, clearly do not belong in this genre. As an example, we may note that of the ten pieces in RM-10 classified as essays not more than half — probably fewer — would be regarded as essays by most literary critics. An even more remarkable use of the term is made in PH-12. Of the twenty-two pieces called essays, ten are newspaper or magazine articles, eight are excerpts from books of various kinds, one is a poem, and one is a series of discrete aphorisms. Not more than two could properly be classed as essays. There are two chief reasons why many of the works called essays do not deserve the classification: because they are parts of longer works, they lack the essential unity demanded of the essay; because they are largely factual or informational in content and purpose, they lack the stylistic qualities of the essay form.

Not all the anthologies use the term "essay" in the same fashion. Some are meticulous in their classification of essays (for example, Hlt-9). Some avoid the problem of completely defining the genre by including essays along with other prose types (for example, Sgr-9 and HBO-10, which include essays under the large heading "Nonfiction"). Others distinguish between the essay and some other forms but combine it with certain related genres such as the "article" or the "sketch" (for example, ABC-10, HBM-11, HBO-11). A large number, by using a topical arrangement and by not including a typological index, avoid the problem of classification entirely (for example, Ldw-9, McM-9). An examination of all the anthologies shows that the majority practice tends to blur distinctions or even to equate the essay with other forms. We believe it is of some importance that a volume of literary selections attempt to use the critical terminology of literature with as much precision as possible.

Blackwell, eds., *A Book of English Essays,* 1600-1900 (London: Oxford University Press, 1927), pp. v-vii, for definitions of the essay as a literary genre.

The essay is the most neglected of the principal literary genres. Table XIII reveals its sparse representation in the anthologies examined.

Only five anthologies devote as much as one page in ten to the essay, and all of these are for the junior and senior years. The volumes for the first two years represent the essay even less adequately. The difference is the result of one of the commonest practices of the anthologies: making the volumes for the first two years into miscellaneous readers and reserving much of the best American and English literature for the eleventh and twelfth grades. Hence, the essays of Emerson and Thoreau, of Bacon, Addison, and Lamb, for example, are normally found in the anthologies for the two upper grades and consequently increase the attention given the essay in those years. The common practice in the ninth- and tenth-grade volumes, on the other hand, is to substitute for the essay other kinds of prose nonfiction, particularly the true-adventure narrative.

If the essay content is measured by number of selections rather than by pages, similar results are obtained. The volume with the greatest number of essays (26) is RM-12, and only seven others have as many as ten essays. The series with the greatest number of essays are Ldw (32), HB49 (26), Gn (25), HBO (24), Sgr (23), and HBM (21); however, in terms of percentage of essays among all selections the leading series are Ldw (6.9 per cent), RM (6.6 per cent), PH (5.7 per cent), and Sgr (5.4 per cent). From any of these sets of statistics, it is clearly evident that the essay is only slightly represented.

That the anthologists pay so little attention to the essay may be a cause for wonder. If, as many of the editors assert, one of the purposes of the anthology is to acquaint the student with the major literary genres, this genre, so widely practiced that the student will be likely to meet it throughout his adult life, would seem to be unduly neglected. Furthermore, because of all genres this one probably comes closest to the kind that all students, whatever their academic and vocational plans, will be called upon to practice, the essay might be thought to be particularly useful in teaching writing and composition. (It is so regarded by the typical freshman English course at the college and university level, as the flood of essay collections prepared for such courses attests.) That the essay is not more widely used for this purpose in secondary schools is perhaps part of a larger — and stranger — phenomenon found in high school English textbooks: that the anthologies make so little provision for relating the teaching of writing to the teaching of literature. It is also worth remarking that the common complaint — that of all major literary genres the essay is the most inadequately taught — finds considerable justification in the fact that so few essays are to be found in the available textbooks.

Clearly, the essay, because it is a short, versatile, and highly useful literary form, is well adapted for inclusion in anthologies at all four grade levels and for all tracks. The possibility of its use as an aid to composition, as a source of ideas, as an exercise in logical and critical thinking, as a means of becoming acquainted with authors, and as an aesthetic achievement strongly recommends it. As a significant part of man's cultural and intellectual heritage it cannot be neglected.

Because the essay is so generally neglected, we include as a footnote the names of some important essayists, which note may serve as a checklist for editors, and suggest that they include in their anthologies one or more essays by several of them.

The list represents every century beginning with the sixteenth (when Montaigne's *Essais* appeared), a half-dozen nations, and a great variety of subjects and styles. The earlier writers named have a permanent place in our culture, and of the rest most are among the best that England and America has produced in the past two centuries. Of the essays by the very recent writers in the list it is possible to say only that their quality suggests that they also may become permanent additions to our literature.[4]

To be sure, some of the authors on the list do appear in the anthologies, but with an infrequency that is notable. Of these ninety-six authors, who together are responsible for a significant part of the essay's contribution to our culture, only thirty-eight are included in one or more of the anthologies, and twenty-six of the thirty-eight authors are represented by a single essay. Seventeen

---

[4] Any list will necessarily be subjective and arbitrary. The ninety-six authors listed here were chosen because each has written one or more essays suitable for high school use, each is recognized by (some or many) critics as a master of the genre, and each has something to say in essay form that is intrinsically important. We do not imply that only these essayists should be read in high school or that all of the best essayists are here named. The list represents rather a reasonable range of choices in a four-year English program.

Henry Adams, Joseph Addison, Matthew Arnold, Harry M. Ayres, Francis Bacon, Walter Bagehot, Max Beerbohm, Hilaire Belloc, A. C. Benson, Gamaliel Bradford, Heywood Broun, Sir Thomas Browne, William Brownell, John Burroughs, Thomas Carlyle, Lord Chesterfield, G. K. Chesterton, Winston Churchill, Joseph Conrad, Abraham Cowley, St. John de Crevecoeur, Samuel Crothers, Thomas De Quincey, John Dryden, John Earle, Jonathan Edwards, Ralph Waldo Emerson, John Erskine, Henry Fielding, Benjamin Franklin, Thomas Fuller, Katherine Gerould, Wolcott Gibbs, Oliver Goldsmith, Louise Guiney, Alexander Hamilton, William Hazlitt, Oliver Wendell Holmes, Sidney Hook, William Dean Howells, David Hume, Leigh Hunt, Thomas Huxley, Aldous Huxley, Edward Hyde, Washington Irving, Henry James, Thomas Jefferson, Samuel Johnson, Ben Jonson, Charles Lamb, D. H. Lawrence, Stephen Leacock, Abraham Lincoln, J. R. Lowell, E. V. Lucas, Thomas Macaulay, Cotton Mather, H. L. Mencken, Alice Meynell, A. A. Milne, Michel de Montaigne, Christopher Morley, Lewis Mumford, John Henry Newman, George Orwell, William Osler, Sir Thomas Overbury, Thomas Paine, Walter Pater, S. J. Perelman, Bliss Perry, Edgar Allan Poe, Agnes Repplier, John Ruskin, Bertrand Russell, Sainte-Beuve, George Santayana, Arthur Schopenhauer, G. B. Shaw, Stuart P. Sherman, Logan P. Smith, Richard Steele, Leslie Stephen, R. L. Stevenson, Jonathan Swift, Arthur Symonds, H. D. Thoreau, H. H. Tomlinson, Mark Twain, Henry Van Dyke, Rebecca West, A. N. Whitehead, Edmund Wilson, Woodrow Wilson, Virginia Woolf.

anthologies have no essays by any of these authors, and ten others devote less than 1 per cent of their space to them.

The most frequently anthologized essayist is Stephen Leacock, a humorist, whose essays appear in fourteen of the volumes. The only other writers whose essays appear in ten or more of the volumes are Emerson (13), Thoreau (11), and Lamb (10). It should also be noted that many of the essays, including some of those most frequently anthologized, are excerpted. Finally, as an indication of the lack of attention given to the essay, we note that all the essays in all the volumes examined constitute only one-thirtieth of all works anthologized and that the pages devoted to them constitute only one-thirty-fifth of the total. In view of the essay's values, both pedagogic and aesthetic, this would appear to be undue neglect.

OTHER TYPES OF PROSE NONFICTION

When we turn from the essay to other types of prose nonfiction, we discover a situation startlingly different. Here we find plenty instead of paucity. The selections included under this heading are very miscellaneous, and include the following: biographical sketches, excerpts from biographies and autobiographies, descriptive sketches, excerpts from accounts of true adventures, excerpts from scientific books (including quasi-scientific and popularized scientific books), newspaper and magazine articles, extracts from journals and diaries, letters and excerpts from letters, orations, addresses, and sermons (and excerpts therefrom), excerpts from political documents, and such curios as extracts from reference works.

That those works are better lumped together as "Miscellaneous Nonfiction" (hereafter abbreviated MNF) than classed in a number of more exact categories is suggested by several characteristics that most of them share and by the criteria implicit in their selection. First of all, most of them are excerpted (and often abridged or adapted) and therefore are something less than what their authors wrote. Secondly, only a relatively small number have literary quality or give any promise of permanence. Third, the units in which many of them are placed suggest that they have been chosen for sociological or historical rather than literary reasons. Fourth, their emphasis upon such currently popular topics as the space age, electronics, travel, and communication suggests the belief that certain topics *must* be covered and that almost any selection that treats these topics is eligible for inclusion. Finally, with certain notable exceptions, most of the nonfiction included gives greater attention to information, "real-life" adventure, and social behavior than to ideas and the exercise of thinking logically and critically. At least for these five reasons, then, it seems appropriate to discuss all nonfictional prose forms, except the essay, under the heading "Miscellaneous Nonfiction."

The highest incidence of MNF as shown in Table XII is to be found in volumes designed for the ninth and tenth grades, and it will be noted that all of the books devoting approximately half their pages to MNF (ABC-9, Gn-9, Gn-10, MH-9, Scb-9) are for the first two years. The lowest incidence of MNF is found in twelfth-grade volumes. Since most of the MNF included in the anthologies is nonliterary in character, it finds its most congenial setting in ninth- and tenth-grade volumes, which are the ones that take their responsibility to literature as such least seriously. Twelfth-grade volumes, on the other hand, are, in many of the series, single-mindedly devoted to English (or World) literature and thus find much less space to print the kinds of nonliterary writing of which so much of the MNF consists. The eleventh-grade volumes in most of the series present a rather strange assortment of the literary and the nonliterary; attempting both to present a survey of American literature and to give extended representation to contemporary prose writing on subjects of current interest, they fall between two stools. Hence, the attention given to MNF is, in several of the series, hardly less in eleventh-grade volumes than in those for the two earlier years.

It is significant also that series prepared for students of lesser ability, for example HB2 and HltD, maintain a fairly constant proportion of MNF regardless of grade level, a situation in keeping with a prominent attitude in educational circles, namely, that first-rate literature is not within the grasp of second-rate students. It is here, perhaps more than anywhere else in the anthologies, that certain discriminations among students are most strongly felt. If we cared to speculate, we would say that the differentiation of the material itself, not just on grounds of difficulty and quantity, but on those of quality and essence, probably performs a real disservice to both individual students and the national interest: not only are many students deprived of their last formal opportunity to improve their taste and literary judgment, but also they are allowed to ignore important elements in their own cultural heritage and are to that extent less adequate contributors to the national community.

Table XIV summarizes various statistical conclusions about the MNF contents of the anthologies.

For the convenience of persons charged with selecting or recommending textbooks for adoption, Table XV is also included. It lists in order for each grade the single volumes that contain the largest and smallest numbers of MNF selections.

In general there is, as would be expected, a close correspondence between the ranking of volumes according to number of MNF selections and the ranking of those according to the number of pages devoted to MNF. It will be seen in Table XV that six of the sixteen volumes ranking highest in the number of MNF selections are books prepared for the second track, but that no second-track books appear among the lowest ranking.

Several comments on the information supplied by Tables XII to XV are in order. It should be noted, for example, that the figures for the eleventh and twelfth grades do not necessarily have the same significance as do those for the ninth and tenth grades. The MNF selections found in ninth- and tenth-grade volumes run heavily to articles from popular magazines and excerpts from rather ephemeral books of various kinds. On the other hand those in eleventh- and twelfth-grade volumes, while comprising some of the same kinds, frequently include also works of permanent literary worth: for example, "The Gettysburg Address," passages from the English Bible, and excerpts from the works of such writers as Thomas Macaulay, Samuel Johnson, Washington Irving, and Mark Twain. Also, some examples of the MNF, particularly in the eleventh-grade volumes, have been included, presumably for historical rather than literary reasons: for instance, excerpts from the writings of John Smith, William Byrd, and Sarah Knight. A safe rule of thumb for the interpretation of the cited tables is, therefore, that the higher the percentage of MNF selections or of pages devoted to them in ninth- and tenth-grade volumes, the less literary their general character, whereas a high percentage for eleventh- and twelfth-grade books may partly reflect the presence also of "standard" and literary works of nonfiction included for purposes of representing periods and varieties of English and American literature.

The volumes with a high percentage of nonliterary MNF are those that are dated soon after their first appearance and must be frequently revised if they are not to seem antiquated. (Paradoxically, it is the volume containing a high percentage of genuinely literary selections, no matter how ancient they may be, that does not become out-of-date.) As an illustration of this process of obsolescence at work, we may note the changes made in the "Non-fiction" section when the Harcourt, Brace series of anthologies was most recently revised. In 1952 HBM-10 appeared, having seventeen items in this section. In 1958 the Olympic edition appeared, having twenty-four items in the same section. Of the seventeen

MNF selections that had appeared in the Mercury edition no fewer than fifteen were discarded, an indisputably high rate of mortality for selections considered important enough to include only six years earlier. It would perhaps be an exaggeration to say that every deletion and every addition had been dictated by the intention of making the book seem "up-to-date." Nevertheless, that this was the intention in some of the changes is suggested by the substitution in the Olympic edition of an excerpt, "Victory on Everest," for that which had appeared in the Mercury edition, "Summit of the World: The Fight for Everest," by the same author, presumably not because one piece was literarily superior to the other, but because between 1952 and 1958 two intrepid mountain climbers in distant Asia had succeeded in conquering Mount Everest. Such newsworthiness seems totally irrelevant as a means of determining the content of an anthology of literature for use in high school English classes.[5] If timeliness or newsworthiness is indeed to be considered a principal criterion in the selection of MNF texts, then it would seem to follow that when deeper caves are explored, when larger sharks are caught, when man learns to fly faster, farther, or higher, when new chemical elements or comets or ocean depths or medical cures or fossils are discovered (the anthologies deal with all these matters), then new editions of the anthologies must be prepared.

It is difficult to approve of the present heavy emphasis that is placed by many of the anthologies upon MNF, for (1) the emphasis is gained at the expense of literature; (2) it often results in, or at least accompanies, a kind of organization that is fundamentally inappropriate for an English textbook; and (3) it tends to

---

[5] The frantic efforts to be up-to-date can also result in embarrassment for both makers and users of an anthology. HBO-11, for example, devoted a prominent and heavily illustrated page to a television quiz-show "personality" who, soon after the book's appearance, was accused of participating in a "rigged" program!

misrepresent man's cultural interests and achievements. These three effects are discussed in the following paragraphs.[6]

That the emphasis given to MNF is gained at the expense of literature is not difficult to document. A comparison of the percentages for MNF shown in Table XII with the corresponding tables for the other genres (see Tables I, IV, XIII, XVII, and XX of Appendix A) will at once indicate the disproportionate attention given to MNF. In all ninth-, tenth-, and eleventh-grade volumes taken together, MNF is given more space than any other genre except the short story. Only in twelfth-grade volumes is it outranked by poetry and drama. When one realizes that poetry, drama, and essay are the vehicles of some of the most important thoughts that mankind has entertained, he will also realize that the heavy emphasis upon MNF can only be gained by sacrificing some of man's noblest utterances.

In some instances the handling of MNF selections is indeed fantastic; for example, devoting as much as one-fifth of a volume to a lengthy abridgement of an undistinguished work like *Kon-Tiki* (RM-10), as was noted earlier, is difficult to defend on any ground; at best it is an interesting documentary narrative that has already had its day. The emphasis upon works of this kind raises again the serious question about the anthologists' criteria of selection: Are such pieces included because they are considered to be intrinsically important or because they are entertaining and "teachable" (which seems to mean capable of being readily understood without teaching)? In any case, the result is that more

---

[6] Our criticism of the emphasis placed upon MNF in the anthologies is not intended to imply that such pieces, especially when unabridged and unadapted, have no place in the English curriculum. Biographies, for example, might well be used for supplementary reading, and, if they are of the quality of, let us say, *The Education of Henry Adams*, even for in-class attention. The point is rather that the typical MNF selection is difficult if not impossible to justify for inclusion in an anthology because it adds to the bulk and the cost but not to the literary quality of the volume.

significant literature (which of course does not mean more solemn or more difficult literature) is crowded out and that the anthologies take on a decidedly nonliterary character in which there may be very little writing of real distinction. To place anything less than the usable best between the expensive covers of today's typical anthology would seem to be both bad economics and bad pedagogy.

This downgrading of the anthology from a collection of literary pieces to a kind of junior *Reader's Digest* is particularly noticeable in first-track volumes for the ninth- and tenth-grades and in second-track and developmental volumes for all grades. In such books, it is customary to find many MNF pieces, usually excerpts, that are written not by persons who have made writing a serious and principal activity in their lives but by persons whose careers are of another kind (athletes, explorers, inventors, etc.) and whose writing is, if not actually "ghosted" by someone else, only incidental to their main interests, rather casual, and very seldom distinguished. There is rarely a single MNF selection in such volumes that is a whit better than what the student could read in the next popular magazine that comes to his hand.

An important question to ask of the anthologists is this: Why should there be such a concentrated and expensive effort to make the merely average seem good and the ephemeral seem permanent? An equally important question follows: Why tamper so dangerously with the developing taste of young minds by effectively blurring, in the anthology at least, the difference between the distinguished and the mediocre? We have earlier stated that for the student in the second track, whose formal education will presumably end with his high school graduation, such books are particularly unfair, for they cause him to remain unacquainted with a large and important part of his heritage. They are also unfair to the ninth- or tenth-grade student in the first track, for they prepare him inadequately for the greater and more complex literature in the eleventh- and twelfth-grade anthologies, which he will nevertheless be expected to read.[7] One of the commonest criticisms classroom teachers make of the anthologies is that, whatever temporary "interest" they may have, they are unchallenging and ultimately unrewarding. It is significant that teachers who make this criticism generally mention the MNF selections and excerpts as the principal cause of this condition.

A second result of the overemphasis on MNF is to be seen in the organization imposed on many of the volumes, although admittedly it is sometimes difficult to distinguish here between cause and effect. The commonest kind of organization is the topical (sometimes erroneously called thematic) which is found in approximately half the anthologies examined.[8] The topical units are likely to be either frankly sociological ("Family Life" HM-9, "Sharing Group Feeling" RM-10, "The Social Swing" Hlt-10), or just as frankly scientific ("Scientific Horizons" ABC-10, "The Air Age" Gn-10, "Spotlight on Science" Hth-9).

Because literary works are neither sociological case studies nor scientific tracts, the anthologists who design units like those just named are impelled either to force literary pieces into such units or to find nonliterary pieces to fill them out. An examination of the textbooks, particularly those for the first two high school years, reveals that both practices — generally in combination, but with somewhat greater emphasis upon the inclusion of MNF than on the forcible interjection of literature — are commonly followed. When the resulting anthology becomes decidedly nonliterary in character, it probably happens for one of two reasons. The editors may have begun with a predetermined organization based upon

---

[7] This charge can be made, even more emphatically, against a large number of the textbooks used in the upper elementary and junior high school years, which, because of their literary poverty, generally informational purpose, and sociological orientation, have no right to be regarded as English textbooks at all.

[8] The organization of the anthologies is discussed at length in Chapter 7.

sociological rather than humanistic premises and then proceeded to find selections to fill out the organization. Or they may have begun with the selection of pieces suited to some utilitarian theory of education and then proceeded to devise a framework to contain them. In any case, the final results are evident: volumes that are more accurately described as socially therapeutic than as personally and humanely educative. Such books have little that is distinctively "English" about them; they could, with more appropriateness, be used for a course in "social studies." The anthology that emphasizes MNF has no clearly defined subject matter — except perhaps some amorphous generality like "The World Around Us" or an unteachable abstraction like "Growing Up." [9]

---

[9] The no-nonsense attitude of some other disciplines may be represented by the following passage from a statement drafted by a committee on high school mathematics:

> We therefore took it as a principle that the new school mathematics program must treat just the fundamental concepts and disciplines of mathematics, and just those essential procedures of the subject which most vividly convey the spirit and values of mathematics; and further that the organization and treatment of these matters must reflect the basic unity of mathematics. . . . The best response to our society's continuing need for mathematics is to keep the purposes of the new school mathematics program strictly within mathematics and to give applications of mathematics a clear pedagogical relation subordinate to these purposes.

"Report of the Committee on High School Mathematics Courses," *California Schools* (Sept., 1960), pp. 386-87.
The twelve members of the committee represented the Universities of California, Chicago, and Michigan, Yale, Columbia, Stanford, Illinois Institute of Technology, and Sacramento State College. The nearest to this noble posture that the discipline of English has come is still called merely "A Hypothesis to Test," drawn up by the Conference on Basic Issues in the Teaching of English, which reads in part:

> . . . literature should be read and studied as literature, not as documentary evidence for the social sciences. . . . Of all the "mandated" courses now in the U.S. school system English . . . is the only one which still holds the individual in focus as a human being to be developed, not as a potential "man-power resource." . . . English can re-

Fortunately, several of the anthologies, as can be seen in Tables XII and XV, maintain a preponderance of literary pieces (which, of course, may vary in quality) by keeping their MNF content down to 10 per cent or 15 per cent of the total. But those that place a much greater emphasis upon MNF are obviously in the majority. It is not surprising that some teachers who are using anthologies of this kind give more attention to the topics of the units than to the selections that are placed within them. The most charitable comment to be made on this practice is that, although it substitutes for the study of texts a free-ranging self-expression that is neither supported nor disciplined by literature, the diversion is not as serious as it might be simply because the units' contents thereby neglected are themselves not of commanding importance. This practice is, of course, far removed from the single-minded study of an essay or a poem as a wise and artistic utterance on a matter of profound human importance — which is at least one way of defining the essential nature of literary study.

Mentioned above as a third result of the overemphasis upon MNF is the possible misrepresentation of man's cultural achievement that it may bring about. When as much as one-fourth of the pages in the volumes (the average for all anthologies is 24.4 per cent) is devoted to MNF, the student is likely to draw a false conclusion, which can be either quantitative (that a large part of man's writings worth preserving has been nonfiction) or qualitative (that man has customarily set down his more important thoughts in nonfiction). That both these assumptions are false is at once apparent to anyone at home in literature. When man has wished to give expression to his most urgent thoughts, he has in-

---

main genuinely humanistic only by concerning itself clearly and boldly with the great literary tradition.

"An Articulated English Program," reprinted in *Issues, Problems, and Approaches in the Teaching of English*, G. W. Stone, Jr., ed. (Holt, Rinehart and Winston, 1961), pp. 237-39.

evitably turned to poetry, the drama, and in recent times the novel as the suitable media, for he is then free of the limitations imposed by superficial "reality." The reader also gains, for he not only is free of the same limitations but also can be present, while reading, in the dynamic and immediate cosmos through which the author represents his thought. For these literary forms the MNF selection most characteristic of the high school anthology can only be a bland and posthumous substitute — an ephemeral piece that recounts after the fact an experience that comes only at second hand to the reader. The reader then is one who, for all his attempts to "identify," is not a participant in the experience of the author as author; at best he is a listener to the words with which the writer recounts his experience. To participate in the creative act of the author, even to only a small degree, is potentially the more humane — that is, the literary — experience.[10]

Several conclusions are pertinent. The substitution in the anthologies of factual and informational writings for literature is unfortunate: for the student because his imagination is insufficiently challenged; for the community because its emerging citizens are incompletely educated; for the English teacher because his special talents are not put to full use; and for the discipline of English because its unique contribution is not fully exploited. The emphasis upon MNF at the expense of the essay is particularly unfortunate. The typical MNF selection is, first of all, an excerpt and therefore incomplete: furthermore, it has a narrative rather than logical structure. Yet, the ability to organize one's thoughts logically and coherently was perhaps never more needed than it is now. It may perhaps be symptomatic of a general weakness in our culture that the well-wrought essay should virtually disappear from high school textbooks. Related to this change also is the

---

[10] This distinction is admirably discussed in Francis Fergusson, *The Human Image in Dramatic Literature* (New York: Doubleday and Company, 1957), pp. xi-xii.

decline of the written assignment among the "activities" recommended in the anthologies: students not only read few essays; their anthologies ask them to write few essays.

We see this increase in the nonliterary content of the anthologies and the concurrent neglect of the essay (together with the expository and ideational kind of prose that it exemplifies) as the marks of a real and growing danger — nothing less than the further submergence of the humanities in the social studies and the disappearance of the individual into the faceless crowd.[11] The anthologies with a high percentage of MNF are helping to create in the students' minds the image of a prosy and pedestrian world in which man's soaring spirit is in danger of being mired.[12] Instead of encouraging this view, the anthologists should be as firm and as bold as were the members of the Committee on High School Mathematics Courses (see again footnote 9); indeed, their statement, with the substitution of "literature" for "mathematics," is as good a brief as can be found for the guidance of future anthologists.

---

[11] Dean Emerson Shuck supplies helpful documentation on this point. He quotes from the doctoral dissertation of Dorothy E. Moulton, "The Teaching of Literature in the Senior High School . . ." that professional journals have regarded literature "as instrumental to the realization of social objectives in mass education," and that even the leaders of NCTE "have been swept along by the tide." (We personally believe that the NCTE leadership is now acting to stem "the tide.") His own conclusion is much like ours: "The implications of this dominance of social scientism have extended far beyond the mere replacement or distortion of materials of the humanities in the classroom. For one thing, it has promoted the tendency in American life toward conformity and mediocrity, since the methods of social science force acceptance of the average as the ideal." Directly applicable to the overemphasis on MNF to which we have pointed is his further statement that "social scientism" has "robbed its victims of exercise in adequate control of the major ways in which human beings do most of their effective personal thinking: metaphor, lyric, story, and innuendo." Emerson Shuck, "Do the 'Humanities' Speak to Man?" *College English* 22 (May, 1961), p. 563.

[12] The pedestrianism just remarked has its literal application. The prevailing metaphor in titles of anthologies and titles of units is drawn from the pedestrian world of "trails," "roads," "highways," and "journeys" on which youth "explores" and has "adventures."

RECOMMENDATIONS

1. We recommend that editors make a particular effort to see that the essay is adequately represented in their anthologies. By adequate representation we mean the inclusion of a considerable number and variety of essays, formal and familiar, light and profound, "classical" and contemporary, on topics that are important to man simply because he is human, by authors whose wisdom guided their pen.

2. We recommend the deletion from the anthologies of all pieces of MNF that cannot be justified on artistic grounds. By these we mean articles and sketches that merely convey information, excerpts from documentary narratives — no matter how adventurous and timely — that provide no basis for generalization, and excerpts from books on technical or highly specialized subjects unless they are also humane.

3. We recommend that timeliness and the whirligig of fashion be abandoned as criteria by which to determine the anthologies' contents. We do not believe that the English textbook should or can compete with the newspaper and the magazine.

4. We recommend that all the prose nonfiction that is included be chosen on the assumption that it will be not merely assigned but taught by the teacher and not merely read but studied by the students. It must therefore be worthy of teaching and study.

5. Finally, we recommend that the number of excerpts and abridgements of MNF be drastically reduced. This reduction can be accomplished in two ways: the selections from works of permanent stature should be expanded to their original form or a substantial portion thereof, and excerpted and abridged works of only passing importance should be omitted.[13]

---

[13] If carried out, this recommendation would make a more revolutionary change in the nature and appearance of the anthologies than perhaps any other recommendation that we have made. But however revolutionary, it is in line with the proposals of almost every group of teachers and every in-

4. THE DRAMA

AS WITH several other literary genres, the problems to be considered with the drama are those of quantity, quality, and text. The three are not entirely separate, for questions about the sufficiency of the genre's representation in the anthologies cannot be answered without attention to the quality of the pieces chosen to represent it, and quality is often affected by the treatment which the texts of the chosen plays receive.

The quantity may be represented in several ways. The following table lists all dramas, including excerpts and abridgements thereof, that are included in the anthologies examined.

Table XVI of Appendix A indicates that 144 different plays are printed in the anthologies and that these plays make a total of 229 appearances. Exactly 25 per cent of these are excerpts and abridgements. The representation of various subclasses of the drama is shown in the following summary:

KINDS OF DRAMA REPRESENTED IN THE ANTHOLOGIES

Original Plays

Radio Plays	31
Television Plays	15
Movie Scripts	1
Musical Comedies	3

dividual teacher who have spoken out on the subject. As a small sample of these we mention the following publications: *Preparation in English for College-bound Students* (the Commission on English of the College Entrance Examination Board, 1960); *Joint Statement on Freshman English in College and High School Preparation* (the Departments of English of Ball State Teachers College, Indiana State Teachers College, Indiana University, and Purdue University, 1960); "College Support for the High School English Teacher: The California Experiment," in *College English* (November, 1959); *Report of the San Francisco Curriculum Survey Committee* (1960). The wishes of individual teachers are represented in Appendix F.

Stage Plays (nonmusical)　　70
Total　　120
Dramatizations of novels, short stories, etc.　　23
Pastiche (poetry)　　1
Total　　24

Various conclusions can be drawn from the above summary. It will be seen that fewer than half the plays printed are of the kind traditionally regarded as most suitable for classroom study, that is, the nonmusical stage drama. Because fifteen of the twenty-three dramatizations were designed for radio or television performance, the total number of plays, both original and adapted, prepared for those media amounts to 43 per cent of the total. What is most impressive about the conclusions to be drawn from both Table XVI and the summary is perhaps the great variety of plays that are introduced into the anthologies. The variety is underscored when we note a lack of agreement among editors in choice of plays, as indicated in the following summary:

FREQUENCY WITH WHICH PLAYS ARE SELECTED BY EDITORS

	Number of Plays
Once	108
Twice	19
Three times	6
Four times	5
Five times	3
Six times	1
Eleven times	1
Twelve times	1

Finally, as a measure of the amount of attention given to drama in the anthologies, Table XVII of Appendix A indicates the percentage of selections that are plays and the percentage of pages devoted to plays in each of the volumes and in each series.

Several significant observations can be made on the information contained in these tables. That, except in a few instances where tradition remains strong (chiefly *Julius Caesar* and *Macbeth*), the search has been for variety at least as much as for quality is suggested by the fact that only on seventeen plays (11 per cent of the total) has there been enough agreement to result in their inclusion in as many as three anthologies, and that 75 per cent of all plays appear in a single anthology. Many choices seem to have been determined by quite irrelevant criteria: introduction to television and radio, teen-age mores, the celebration of holidays, and — most frequently — "entertainment," rather than literary quality and permanence. Shakespeare is given the greatest amount of space — twenty-seven appearances of five plays, including excerpts, abridgements, and adaptations — but in all the anthologies examined this greatest of all writers in the English language nevertheless is given only 4.1 per cent of their total space — only *one-sixth the attention given to miscellaneous and largely nonliterary prose*. It should also be remembered that in forty-five volumes (62.5 per cent of the total) Shakespeare's plays are not represented at all.

Other important dramatists fare no better. O'Neill, America's leading dramatist, is represented by three one-act plays, not characteristic of his best work, for a total of ten appearances, and Shaw, England's foremost modern playwright, is represented by five plays (three of them short excerpts) appearing once each. Ibsen, perhaps the most influential dramatist in the Western world during the past two hundred years, is represented only once, as is Molière, France's greatest writer of comedies. Classical drama is completely absent. All drama written in the English language between Shakespeare's day and about 1900 is represented by two plays, Goldsmith's *She Stoops to Conquer* and Sheridan's *The Rivals*, each appearing in a single volume, the latter only as a brief excerpt. Since the Western spirit has expressed itself perhaps more vigorously in drama than in any other literary genre, these omissions are notable, especially when one observes that scores of mediocre and ephemeral pieces, perhaps topically "adapted" to the anthologists' various purposes but lacking in distinction, nevertheless are admitted.

It is of course not absolutely necessary that anthologies include dramatic works, for many suitable ones can be obtained in well-edited and inexpensive supplementary volumes; however, most anthologists have assumed the responsibility for representing this genre. With space at a premium, it would seem only reasonable that, if dramatic works are to be included, only the greatest should be admitted. Although a case could be made for certain other playwrights, this means first of all the adequate and accurate representation of Shakespeare.[1] There are at least eleven of his plays that are suitable for use in high school: *A Midsummer Night's Dream, The Merchant of Venice, As You Like It, Twelfth Night, Henry IV* (Part I), *Henry V, Romeo and Juliet, Julius Caesar, Macbeth, Hamlet,* and *King Lear.* These provide sufficient choice among comedies, histories, and tragedies, among early and late plays, among topics and themes of several kinds, and among easier and more complex works. The arbitrary restriction of the eleventh-grade volumes to American literature, among other undesirable effects, seems to prohibit the inclusion of a Shakespearean play.

The large proportion (43 per cent) of radio and television plays included in the anthologies calls for comment. Although there is no reason why such plays cannot be of as much literary merit as those written for the stage, it is apparent that many of them have been chosen primarily for the purpose of developing what the anthologists call the "appreciation" of television and radio. Taste is of course a desirable characteristic to foster, but

---

[1] No series contains four of Shakespeare's plays, and only two (Ldw and McM) contain three.

the best way to foster it, as Matthew Arnold pointed out a century ago, is to become intimately acquainted with "the best that has been thought and said." By this measure a large number of the plays included simply will not pass muster. It should also be said that teaching the appreciation of television is not the responsibility of the English teacher. His concern is teaching the reading and appreciation of literature, and the fact that literature may sometimes appear on the television screen, except that his students can then see what they *have read,* is of little intrinsic importance.[2]

Another criterion that influences the content of the anthologies is timeliness. Literature is always timely, because it speaks to every understanding reader on matters that are then (and thereafter) of great importance to him as a member of the human race. (Literature is also timeless, for it has spoken to past generations and will speak to future generations with equal pertinence.) This, however, is not the timeliness that sometimes serves the anthologists. They frequently seem to be looking for the "hit," the sensa-

---

[2] What students see on television may, of course, hardly resemble what they have read, so great is the influence that the medium exerts. It is therefore especially important that editors of anthologies be aware of the influence of the mass media upon the process of adapting literature for broadcasting. The recent report, *Television and the Teaching of English,* prepared by the Committee on the Study of Television of the National Council of Teachers of English under the chairmanship of Neil Postman, includes several relevant conclusions drawn from a comparison of Hemingway's short story "The Killers," and A. E. Hotchner's television adaptation of it. Among these are the following: (1) television programming makes inflexible demands on the time to be used in developing plot, characters, etc.; (2) "Hemingway's story is essentially one of ideas; Hotchner's version stresses action"; (3) the changed ending in Hotchner's version, "perhaps a concession to an audience accustomed to 'happy endings,'" makes a basic alteration in the story; (4) because of the huge and heterogeneous audience for the television play, the adapter felt compelled to give "social discretion priority over artistic integrity"; (5) in casting a television play the desirability of having celebrities in the leading roles, whether or not they are well suited for them cannot be ignored. The NCTE committee concludes that "the dramatic art of television is presided over by Hermes, god of commerce" (New York: Appleton-Century-Crofts, Inc., 1961), pp. 96-99.

tion, the item that makes news. A case in point, which will represent the rest, is *The King and I*, included in HBO-10. The four-page introduction makes it clear at once that this musical comedy is thought of not as literature — the only relevant criterion — but mainly as a notable event in theatrical history. It was a notable event, however, because the tunes were enchanting, the actors were excellent, the sets were impressive, the costumes were colorful, the choreography was skilfully managed, the plot was an easily accepted cliché. As entertainment on the stage *The King and I* clearly is superior; as history, however, it is faulty; as a piece of writing it is ephemeral.

How then can the inclusion of such works be justified? We believe there is no justification; and, if to include them means to omit other pieces of undoubted literary nature, their inclusion is not only unjustifiable but harmful. At best their inclusion means giving an artificial permanence to the impermanent; at worst it means omitting or abridging more deserving drama, especially that of Shakespeare.

Several additional matters of interest are suggested by the figures in Table XVII. Most of the volumes containing a relatively high percentage of dramatic selections and a relatively low percentage of pages devoted to the drama include several one-act, television, or radio plays, in some instances excerpts from longer works, but seldom a full-length drama. SF-9, for example, contains among its 125 selections 5 plays: namely, a one-act stage play, two radio plays, an excerpt from *A Midsummer Night's Dream*, and a short dramatization of a Greek myth, which average less than nine pages in length. Other volumes which include only short dramatic pieces are Hth-9 (a one-act play, two radio plays, and two television plays), Sgr-11 (two one-act plays, a television play, and an excerpt), Irq-9 (a one-act play, a motion-picture script, a radio play, and a television play), and all of the PH series (13 short pieces of various kinds). Altogether, 26 of the volumes contain only short — and usually slight — dramatic works. On the other hand 37, or about half of them, contain plays that are fifty or more pages in length, in 25 instances a Shakespearean drama. In general, these are the volumes shown in Table XVII as devoting 13 per cent or more of their pages to drama. Among books designed for use with first-track and heterogeneous classes, only one, Lipp-10, contains no drama of any kind.

An interesting observation based upon Table XVII is that the incidence of drama in the volumes for grades ten and twelve is about twice as great as that in those for grades nine and eleven. This curious situation results largely from the practice followed by most series of including *Julius Caesar* in the tenth-grade and *Macbeth* in the twelfth-grade volumes, but no Shakespeare in the other two. In only one series (Ldw) is *Julius Caesar* included where we believe it belongs — in the ninth-grade volume. Because it is probably the simplest and most straightforward of Shakespeare's works, it might well be regarded as a "freshman" play; however, in eleven of the series it is placed in the sophomore year — what appears to us an obvious instance of downgrading the literary curriculum. How thorough this downgrading has been is suggested by the plays admitted into ninth-grade volumes in lieu of a Shakespearean play — among them, Fletcher's *Sorry, Wrong Number*, McCarty's *Three's a Crowd*, Mosel's *Jinxed*, Niggli's *This Bull Ate Nutmeg*, Vullmer's *It's Your Business*, and Wishengrad's *Juliet in Pigtails*. These are hardly adequate substitutes for a Shakespeare play!

Because eleventh-grade anthologies are commonly devoted to American literature, Shakespeare is rigorously excluded from them also. One may well wonder whether the nationality of the author is the most relevant criterion of selection, especially when one looks at some of the replacements: for example, Van Druten's *I Remember Mama*, Kelly's *Finders-Keepers*, Cohan's *Pigeons and People*, Medcraft's *The First Dress-Suit*, Keppler's dramatization of *Sixteen,* and Seiler's *How to Propose.* Even the best of the substitutes in the eleventh-grade books, Wilder's *Our Town* and Sherwood's *Abe Lincoln in Illinois,* are clearly no match for the Shakespearean play thus displaced.

From the titles of many of the plays just named one may well surmise further that this is not just downgrading through the use of "easier" plays but downgrading of a special kind — the choice of pieces that exploit immediate adolescent interests. As we have said earlier, this would seem to be an unsound, if not dangerous tendency, for we must assume that the purpose of studying literature in high school is surely to help the students move toward their full adult capacity. This tendency no doubt also plays a part in the editors' great reliance upon radio and television plays, which account for almost one-half of the total. Although a play is of course not necessarily inferior because it was written for broadcasting — witness, for example, the plays of MacLeish, Benét, and Miller, which find a place in a few of the anthologies — nevertheless it is well established that most dramatic programs issuing through the mass media are deliberately held at a relatively low intellectual level.[3] In any event, the plays printed in the anthologies, excluding the plays of Shakespeare and a few others, and including many of the one-act plays and almost all the radio and television scripts, are no better entertainment than one can see on television or at the movie theater virtually any night in the week. However, plays should be chosen not for entertainment but for study and of a kind that, with the teacher's assistance in reading and comprehending, they will challenge the student's mind, stimulate him to thoughtful insights into the human condition, lead him beyond his present interests and hori-

---

[3] We are aware that any comment we could make will be less severe than that of Mr. Newton Minow, former chairman of the Federal Communications Commission, who called television a "vast wasteland."

zons, and acquaint him with significant elements in his literary heritage.

In spite of the number of plays included in the anthologies it seems clear that, except for the essay, the drama is the most inadequately represented of the principal literary genres. Although the quantity is sufficient in most volumes, the quality often leaves a great deal to be desired. Yet decisions on which dramatic works to include might be thought to be among the easiest that editors are compelled to make. First of all, there are the plays of Shakespeare, among which are not only the world's greatest but also those ideally suited for study in English classes. There are also, among others, the great plays of Aeschylus, Sophocles, and Euripides, now available in satisfactory translations. From periods later than the Golden Age of Greece, the plays of Marlowe, Jonson, Molière, Sheridan, Goldsmith, Rostand, Ibsen, Shaw, O'Neill, and the Abbey Theatre playwrights — to name a few — might be considered for inclusion, or in some instances given more adequate representation.

As with the novel, drama poses a special problem because many of the best plays for study are long. From the number of one-act plays and radio dramas in the anthologies, one might, in fact, conclude that length has been an important criterion in the choice of plays. Yet the editors have shown their willingness to devote many pages to single plays, even when they are not literary masterpieces. As examples we may note the following: *Years Ago* (Hlt-9), *The Winslow Boy* (Sgr-12); (Hlt-10), *Point of No Return* (Hlt-11), *I Remember Mama* (ABC-11). Most of the plays included are, however, much shorter than these, and many are very slight.

Such plays are difficult to defend as works to be given serious study in the classroom, for they will occupy more of the teacher's and the students' time than the results are likely to justify. Furthermore, most plays of this kind are ephemeral and, like *The King and I*, are more notable for their success at the box office than as literary works. Choosing for an anthology the plays that are successful in the contemporary theater is the equivalent of choosing novels from the list of best sellers. To print such pieces in expensive volumes to be used as textbooks in the classroom would, then, appear to be wasteful of both money and the students' learning time.

The study of dramatic literature in the classroom may provide the only chance that many young people will have to become acquainted with a large, important, and beneficial part of their heritage. This heritage is scarcely different for the high school student today from what it was for his father or his grandfather, and certainly not different in any significant way from what it was five or six years ago. We would repeat that writings that are genuinely literary never are really out-of-date, for they can strike readers of successive generations with impact and convey the sense of unique and personal communication; we are assuming, of course, that the teacher, out of his greater knowledge and wider acquaintance with literature, will be at hand to help — that is, to teach, not merely to assign and test. However, from the choice of many of the plays included in the anthologies one might indeed conclude that the goal has been to find pieces that appeal to immediately conscious interests and personally "felt" needs, that offer the least intellectual challenge for the developing but still immature reader, that, in short, need neither to be taught nor to be studied.[4] To be sure, there are several notable exceptions, including the frequently anthologized *Julius Caesar*

---

[4] "The books that really need interpretation will work best in the classroom," concludes the Literature Committee of the School and College Conference. The *Report* of this important committee, which was first published in 1940, has been virtually ignored until its recent reprinting in *Issues, Problems, and Approaches in the Teaching of English*, edited by G. W. Stone, Jr., pp. 41-65.

and *Macbeth;* yet, on the whole, less than justice is done to the drama in the anthologies.

The third problem mentioned earlier is the textual one: the extent to which the printed plays accurately represent what their authors wrote. We have already noted that 25 per cent of the plays included in the anthologies are either excerpts or abridgements. Because it is Shakespeare's texts that are most frequently tampered with, in the following pages we have considered in detail what happens to these plays when they are printed in the anthologies. Table XVI indicates that twenty-seven volumes do include a Shakespearean play. However, only three contain the full text; two of these contain only short excerpts, thirteen slightly abridged versions, and nine heavily abridged versions. Each of these versions is considered below. In addition, one anthology (HM-9) contains a twelve-page prose retelling of *Romeo and Juliet,* which has not been included in the preceding tables since it does not have dramatic form. Because the summary is of some length, is fitted out with beautiful illustrations, and is the subject of several questions in the accompanying teacher's manual, it is evident that teachers and students are meant to regard it as one of the major pieces in this volume. Yet, it is literature only at some remove — literature that has passed through the mind of an intermediary. Because it does not provide the essential qualities of the original — matter to interpret, opportunity for the imagination to work, and a challenge to the creative mind — it is an inadequate substitute, even though as summary it is remarkably skilful. It condenses, and to some extent thereby distorts the narrative, and omits all but a dozen lines of some of the most enchanting poetry that Shakespeare ever wrote. In short, it borrows from the play what Shakespeare himself borrowed from others, and omits almost all of what is peculiarly Shakespeare's own. Since it cannot be classified as drama — even as adapted, excerpted, or abridged drama — it is not considered again in this chapter.

The two volumes that contain only short excerpts are SF-9 (eight pages of *A Midsummer Night's Dream*) and SCB-9 (nine pages of *The Taming of the Shrew*). The former is not only an excerpt but an abridged excerpt that makes nine silent deletions totaling 63 lines, is equipped with numerous stage directions that range from the cute and supererogatory to the nonsensical and restrictive, concludes with "Curtain" but with no indication that there are 68 more lines before the play ends, and is renamed *A Midsummer Night s Play*, so that the last trace of the all-important dream frame is also removed. The excerpt in Scb-9, consisting of parts of two scenes from *The Taming of the Shrew*, treats the text somewhat more respectfully.

The volumes that include more than mere excerpts of Shakespearean drama vary in the manner of their editorial treatment. Four plays (*Julius Caesar, Macbeth, A Midsummer Night's Dream*, and *As You Like It*) are printed at length, although the last two only in a single volume each. The most frequently anthologized play, *Julius Caesar*, is most drastically abridged in Irq-10, which reduces the play to 45 per cent of its length. As it would be impossible for the teacher to believe that what remains is Shakespeare's play, and as the editors have candidly described what they have done (omitted "superfluous" Elizabethan language, reference to Shakespeare's time, and some minor characters, shortened some speeches and reassigned others), they at least cannot be charged with deception.[5] Eleven other volumes also include *Julius Caesar*, treating its text in various ways.

The most heavily abridged versions (excluding the anomalous

---

[5] The editorial treatment is described on pp. 202-203 of the anthology. Perhaps this severe editing is partly compensated for by the editors' remark that "A reading of [the beautiful and famous poetic passages] will show that Shakespeare does not need to be modernized. He *is* modern."

Irq-10 redaction) are thus, in order, HB49-10, HBL-10, HBM-10 and HBO-10, McM-10, and SF-10. That the versions in these six volumes misrepresent the play is apparent not only from the extent (in some volumes about one-fifth of the text) but also from the nature of the deletions. Among these deletions are passages that contain the following: (1) the description of the portents and prodigies on the eve of Caesar's assassination, which contributes to the tone of the play, signals the importance of the deed about to happen, and provides the reader with such memorable pictures as the slave with the flaming hand, the lioness whelping in the street, and the yawning graves giving up their dead (Act I, scene iii and Act II, scene ii); (2) much of the conversation between Brutus and Portia (II,i), the portrayal of her anxiety when Brutus leaves for the Capitol (II,iv), and some of the references to her death (IV,iii), which add important touches to the portraits of both Portia and Brutus as well as a note of gentleness and charm to the play; (3) except in McM-10, the entire scene in which the mob sets upon Cinna the poet merely because he has the same name as one of the conspirators — certainly one of the most effective and concise comments ever written on the dangers of ochlocracy (III,iii); (4) the efforts of another poet to reconcile the differences between Brutus and Cassius (IV,iii); (5) the confrontation of the two armies on the plains of Philippi, the futile parley between the opposing leaders, and the hint of conflict between Antony and Octavius (V,i); (6) one entire battle scene (V,iv); and (7) in the HB volumes, the closing lines of the play. At least as regrettable is the omission of much imagery and metaphorical language which give the play added dimension and depth. The mutilation of the play in these volumes is aggravated by the absence of editorial indications of the position, length, or content of the omitted parts. Thus, the danger of deception, however innocent, is ever present, as is suggested by comments on these volumes made by some teachers, who were apparently unaware that the full text was not included.

It is sometimes argued in defense of the anthologies' various abridgements of Shakespearean drama, on the grounds that there is no such thing as a single, "complete" text of a play, that a specially prepared abridgement is the "best" text for, say, the tenth grade, and that editors should therefore be allowed a relatively free hand in the preparation of a "teachable" tenth-grade version. We see no merit at all in this argument. It is true that, within narrow limits and for some of the plays, a choice of basic text is possible; but for *Macbeth* and *Julius Caesar,* the plays most commonly read in high school, there is no choice, for the ultimate copy text of each must be that in the First Folio of 1623. For most of Shakespeare's plays, including these two, we would insist, there *is* an "accepted" complete text, varying from edition to edition only slightly according to the editors' judgments on the infrequent occasions where emendation is permissible.

The view that anything less than the full text can be the "best" version for a particular high school grade is, we believe, equally invalid. Shakespeare, the master dramaturgist, supplied his own introductions to characters and events, disclosed and reinforced their motivation, devised and ordered scenes, revealed settings and moods — all with an eye to their total effect. Because of the artistic unity of his greatest plays, one can almost never delete lines with impunity, for they all contribute to the possibilities of interpretation. It is, in fact, these very possibilities of interpretation that make a Shakespearean play not only a masterpiece of human achievement but an ideally suited object for study in the classroom. While disciplining the reader, it yet provides the opportunity for unique communication with him. An interpretation may be wrong, but *several* interpretations can be "right." [6] As

---

[6] This point, which is an important part of the justification for teaching all literature, was clearly made by Professor Kittredge: "As with our fellow-

the text is abridged, the possibilities of interpretation are diminished in number and subtlety, and the channel of unique communication is choked up. Thus, there cannot be a "best" text for the tenth-grader or for anyone else except the full text, and a "teachable" text can only be one that *requires* — and profits from — teaching by an informed and perceptive instructor.

The anthologists emend as well as abridge Shakespearean texts, and even some of those who print every line substitute words here and there. The following examples in the text of *Julius Caesar*, a small number chosen from numerous instances, will illustrate the practice:

Shakespeare:	Therefore, good Brutus, be prepar'd to hear; And since you know you cannot see yourself. . . . (Act I, scene ii, lines 66-67)
McM-10:	Good Brutus, since you cannot see yourself. . . .
Shakespeare:	Good morrow, Caesar. (II,ii,109)
McM-10:	Good morning, Caesar.
Shakespeare:	That plays thee music? (IV,iii,269)
HB49, HBM, HBO, HBL:	That plays the music?
Shakespeare:	Good reasons must, of force, give place to better. (IV,iii,203)
ABC-10:	Good reasons must, of course, give place to better.
Shakespeare:	The heart of Brutus earns to think upon! (II,ii,129)
Gn-10, ABC-10:	The heart of Brutus yearns to think upon!

---

creatures in real life, so is it with our fellow-creatures in Shakspere. There neither is nor can be any exclusive or orthodox interpretation. Each of us must read the riddle of motive and personality for himself. There will be as many Hamlets or Macbeths or Othellos as there are readers or spectators. For the impressions are not made, or meant to be made, on one uniformly registering and mechanically accurate instrument, but on an infinite variety of capriciously sensitive and unaccountable individualities — on *us*, in short. . . . These principles, however, give no license to capricious propaganda. For there is one corrective and restraining proviso. Somewhere there exists, and must be discoverable, the solid fact — and that fact is Shakspere's Hamlet or Macbeth or Othello." *Shakspere* (Harvard University Press, 1916), pp. 12-13.

Shakespeare: Thy life hath had some smatch of honour in it.
                (V,v,46).
ABC-10:   Thy life hath had some snatch of honour in it.

One might be inclined to dismiss such alterations as trivial. Indeed, we selected several of the above examples because upon first thought they may seem trivial. A second thought will suggest, however, that basic principles are involved. All of the above lines in the original wording make sense, in several instances uniquely good sense in context; and there is an unwritten law among Shakespeare's editors that passages are not to be emended when they make sense as they stand, even when they present difficulties of interpretation. None of the above lines is difficult to comprehend; in fact, several of the anthologists found it necessary only to include brief glosses for such words as *earn* and *smatch*, in order to clarify the meaning of the lines. By retaining the original wording they have retained the flavor of Shakespeare's vocabulary and the original phonetic (including the metrical) values of the lines,[7] and since exact synonyms are virtually nonexistent in English, they have run no risk of altering the meaning. Others, however, emended as they pleased.

Apparently, the reason for the numerous changes was to make the text easier for the student to read. This view confronts us with a nice problem. Is it the editors' responsibility to make texts easy for students? And, if so, may they make them easy by altering the syntax, by concealing the evidence of change in the English language, and by sacrificing or at least imperiling the tonal and the ideational values of the original? Or is it instead the teachers' responsibility to make texts easy and attractive for students — in-

---

[7] Also to be regretted is the practice of substituting, for example, *you, the other, more, does, it is, are, has, suffices, your, speak, pray you,* and *loved,* for *thou* (or *thee*), *th'other, moe, doth, 'tis, art, hath, sufficeth, thy* (or *thine*), *speaks't, prithee,* and *lov'd,* as do several of the anthologies — some rather inconsistently, for these alterations affect the tone and sometimes the meter.

deed, by explaining syntactical and historical problems of language and by helping the students to discover for themselves the tonal and ideational values in the text? We believe that the proper division of labor here is self-evident: editors should provide suitable and accurate texts, and teachers should teach (not just assign) them. This conclusion keeps in clear perspective the two roles: the integrity of editors and publishers, and the central, constructive, creative, and respect-worthy function of the informed teacher.

In this discussion of editing drama in the anthologies should be noted the practice of inserting stage directions (in addition to the author's) and explanatory or narrative headnotes for the acts and scenes. Here again it is in the treatment of Shakespeare's plays that — in some of the anthologies — the practice is most objectionable. Adding the direction "She kneels" when the text reads "Let me, upon my knee, prevail in this" (*Julius Caesar*, Act II, scene ii, line 54), as do HBM-10, HBO-10, HBL-10, and SF-10, is perhaps merely supererogation. Printing "Clever Decius!" in the margin opposite the passage in which that character succeeds in persuading Caesar to ignore Calpurnia's fears and go to the Capitol (II,ii,97), as does McM-10, is perhaps merely affectation. Both of these insertions, however, deprive the reader of the opportunity to do his own thinking and visualizing, as do the numerous parenthetical modifiers inserted in the SF-10 text of *Julius Caesar;* for example, "with relief," "dejectedly," "very much disturbed," and "his good humor returning." Furthermore, these directions insist upon one interpretation and leave little room for the reader to develop his own analytical powers. In fact, the text of this play as treated in SF-10, McM-10, HBL-10, HB49-10, HBM-10, and HBO-10 is more like that in a promptbook, prepared for a particular performance, than like one printed for reading and study.

The editorial insertions can be, however, not only unnecessary or restrictive but nonsensical and even wrong. In HB49-10 and HBM-10, for example, the headnote to the last scene in the play includes this remark: "The most important detail in this scene is mentioned in the first line: a large rock on which Brutus and his friends sit down to take counsel." As the most important "detail" in this scene is the death of the protagonist, this bit of nonsense is understandably omitted from the revision of the text for HBO-10. The following will illustrate the editorial insertions that are simply wrong: in McM-10 appear these words: "He (Brutus) goes into the pulpit and looks about calmly. Cassius stands a little back of him" (III,ii). Because Shakespeare has Cassius go into another street to speak, where some of the crowd follow him, he cannot of course be in the pulpit while Brutus explains his reasons for killing Caesar. Since the editors have omitted the passage in which the citizens plan to compare impressions of the two speakers orating in different streets, they have one character left with nothing to do, and so, lacking the dramaturgic skill of Shakespeare in getting unneeded characters off the stage, they insist categorically on giving him stage room without any textual justification. We believe that these various kinds of editorial treatment do less than justice to both literature and student, because they misrepresent or misinterpret the former, and are distracting, irritating, misleading, or condescending for the latter.

Two of Shakespeare's plays, *A Midsummer Night's Dream* and *As You Like It*, except for the short excerpt already mentioned, appear in a single volume each. The former, printed in McM-9, is severely cut for class presentation. In Act I, for example, there are 36 separate deletions, totaling 70.5 lines, as well as nine emendations (most of them transitions made necessary by the deletions), and two invented lines. There are also numerous added stage directions, some of them quite elaborate, including several that have no textual justification. It could be argued that, because the text as printed in this anthology is designed for dramatization in class, the extensive directions and abridgements are justified. It should also be recognized, however, that to insist upon particular stage business, gestures, and the manner of reading the lines is to limit the possibilities of interpretation for young readers who are probably encountering their first Shakespearean play. Indeed, a very useful kind of activity for the students is to determine for themselves how particular lines should be rendered and what stage business should take place to produce the appropriate effect, for doing so will increase their understanding of the play. The elaborate stage directions, therefore, not only are restrictive of meaning but also remove some of the play's "teachability." The text of *As You Like It*, found only in Ldw-10, is much more respectfully treated. Except for a few passages alluding to cuckoldry (for example, 13 lines omitted from Act III, scene iii, and 21 lines from Act IV, scene i) and married love (for example, 4 lines omitted from Act V, scene ii), the text is given in full, free of emendation and of unwarranted elaboration of stage directions.

Macbeth, after *Julius Caesar* the play most often anthologized, is also handled with editorial respect by most of the anthologies. Although no volume contains the complete text, about the only passage deleted in varying degrees comes in the Porter's speech (II,iii), a sexual reference that all editors have excised. All but Gn-12 in the text of *Macbeth* as well as of the other plays, make a practice of substituting *-ed* for *-'d* endings, and *the* for *th'*, in some instances to the detriment of the meter. In our view the text in RM-12 is not sufficiently glossed and that in HBM-12 and HBO-12 is too heavily glossed to be of the greatest pedagogical value. We also believe that the text in McM-12 is supplied with too many and too elaborate stage directions. This is not, however, the greatest fault in the McM-12 text, which, unlike the others, is heavily abridged. It omits nine characters and ten entire scenes (including two in which the witches appear, three of the battle at Dunsinane, and the scene showing the murder of Banquo), inserts lines from the missing scenes at other places in the text, invents a few lines, omits almost three hundred lines from the scenes that are kept, and makes many small but unnecessary emendations. Shakespeare's dramaturgy is thus roughly treated, and his skilful development and motivation of character, his evocation of mood, and some of his most exciting scenes are either excised or mutilated.

The treatment of *Macbeth* in McM-12, of *A Midsummer Night's Dream* in McM-9, and of *Julius Caesar* in HB49-10, HBL-10, HBM-10, HBO-10, Irq-10, McM-10, and SF-10 we can find no way of condoning. The history of Shakespearean editing for 250 years is the record of scholarly attempts to establish an accurate and complete text of the plays, a text as close to what Shakespeare wrote as can be reasonably determined on the basis of the best and most relevant evidence. The editors of the anthologies just named would reverse this process by unnecessary and inartistic (however well-intentioned) editing. Teachers and students alike have the right to assume that their anthologies present accurate texts, a right that the teachers themselves are asserting in increasing numbers.

As we remarked earlier, the anthologies need not bear the responsibility for the drama, as it is possible to supplement them with either separate or collected editions of plays. There are now available several paperback series of the principal plays of Shakespeare, a few series of the dramas of other playwrights, and a number of collections of representative plays. A list of these can be found in the aforementioned Bowker publication (*Paperbound Books in Print*). Many of these bear the marks of authoritative scholarship and in general are textually dependable. They are not usually equipped with study aids and teacher's guides, but many contain brief biographies of the author, descriptions of the stage, and glossaries. Besides the paperback editions there are those especially edited for high school use. These are usually bound in hard covers, one play to the volume, although there is a growing tendency to publish two or more plays together so that comparative study and wider representation are possible.

1. We recommend that certainly the first and probably the second play chosen for reading in each of the four years be one of Shakespeare's. We make this recommendation because we believe that certain of the plays by Shakespeare are the most suitable that can be found for study in the high school classroom. The terminal student is entitled to the experience, and the college-preparatory student needs it as part of a progressively challenging program of reading.

2. We recommend that, if plays in addition to those of Shakespeare are used, they be chosen solely for their artistic merit and not for their topicality or their current popularity.

3. We believe that excerpts of plays should be avoided.

4. We make no recommendation about the inclusion of plays in anthologies. As we remarked earlier, good texts of suitable plays are widely available outside the anthologies. Space permitting, they could also be included in them. Nor, because we believe that an important function of the anthology is to provide a dependable literary guide for the teacher, can we recommend that some plays — for example, one-act and other short pieces — be included, and that others — for example, Shakespearean dramas — be omitted on the assumption that they will be read in separate editions. Such a solution is undesirable for it cannot be assumed that anthologies will invariably be supplemented by such separate editions. Therefore, to omit the greatest plays and to include minor ones would cause the anthologies seriously to misrepresent the drama.

5. We recommend that, whether the plays are printed in the

anthologies or in supplementary editions, their texts be treated
with respect. They should be accurately represented, and should
be accompanied by only that editorial equipment that is necessary to their comprehension. Overglossing the text is as much to
be avoided as underglossing, and glossing that arbitrarily restricts
interpretation is worse than either. Headnotes and other editorial
additions should not so fully recount what happens in the play
that the students' interest is dulled and the teacher's opportunity
to probe their understanding of it is vitiated. Editors should assume, and have the right to assume, that there will be maximum
teaching of the texts and maximum cooperation between teacher
and students in understanding and appreciating them.

5. POETRY

THE LITERARY HEART of an anthology is its poetry content. Novels
and plays can be read outside the anthology perhaps better than
within it. Essays are too few to influence the nature of the typical
volume. Many of the short stories, as we have seen, are con-
sciously juvenile or are written to formulae that are commercially
profitable rather than artistic. Much of the prose nonfiction is distinctly subliterary in quality. It is, therefore, chiefly the poetry
upon which the literary tone, the merit, and the usefulness of an
anthology must depend. Although separate collections of poetry
are available, most of the dependable ones have limitations
rather different from those that define the high school course in
literature. The most important function, then, that the anthology
can serve is that of providing students with a body of first-rate
poetry and of organizing it into a program which allows the instructor to teach it with greatest effectiveness.

QUANTITY

The anthologies examined contain a large number of poems, as can be seen from Table XIX of Appendix A. Table XIX indicates, for example, that the twenty ninth-grade anthologies examined contain 890 entries classifiable as poetry; that, because about one-fourth of these (220) appear in more than one freshman anthology, the total number of individual poems assigned to the ninth-grade is 670; and that these poems are the creations of 315 different poets.

Several conclusions can be drawn from the table. A comparison of the number of poets with the number of poems reveals that in the ninth- and tenth-grade volumes poets are represented on the average by no more than two or three poems each, whereas the average in the eleventh- and twelfth-grade volumes is about four poems per poet. This difference, although small, is the result of the somewhat greater concentration on prominent poets in the upper two grades and the very common practice of including only a single poem of a poet in the earlier grades. The larger number of poems included for the eleventh- and twelfth-grades also points to a conclusion that is in harmony with the comment made elsewhere in this report — that in most series the two later volumes are markedly more literary in character than are the two earlier ones. The right-hand column in the table shows that the average eleventh-grade volume contains more than twice as many poems as the average ninth- or tenth-grade volume, and the twelfth-grade volume about three times as many. This would seem to be a decidedly uneven distribution of attention to poetry. Finally, the table suggests a question that we find difficult to answer affirmatively: Are there 677 poets and 2516 poems (these figures include only a very few outside the Anglo-American tradition) that deserve a place in high school anthologies? We should note here also that many poems appear only once in the seventy-two volumes examined. The total number of poems making a single appearance, 2043, is more than 80 per cent of all poems included. This, too, suggests to us a startling lack of agreement among the editors on what characterizes a poem that is both artistic and suitable for classroom study. Can high school students, or even university students, be expected to form good reading habits and develop their literary taste when they are confronted with such wholesale eclecticism? A wiser course would seem to be that recommended in a report made by the San Francisco Curriculum Survey Committee: "we would change the reading of miscellaneous selections from a multitude of writers to complete works by a relatively few major writers." [1]

The attention given to poetry by the anthologies cannot, however, be measured solely in terms of numbers. The length of the poems included is also a factor, for it directly affects the amount of space given to poetry in a volume. Relatively few long poems are included, and many of those are abridged. The principal ones are listed in Table XX.

These nineteen long or moderately long poems make a total of ninety-five appearances in the anthologies examined, fifty-seven, or more than half of them, in abridged form. Most of the poems included are, however, much shorter, the more typical poems being from twelve to thirty-six lines long. Many are shorter still, including limericks, humorous two-line epitaphs gleaned from tombstones, the kind of four-line light verse beloved by some of the popular magazines, single stanzas from long poems (for example, nine lines of Spenser's *Faërie Queene*), and other small curios. The space given to poetry in the anthologies is thus much smaller than the number of poems might lead one to believe. Table XXI indicates both the proportion of poetry and the rela-

---

[1] *Report of the San Francisco Curriculum Survey Committee,* prepared for the Board of Education, San Francisco Unified School District (1960), p. 30.

tive amount of space devoted to poetry in each of the volumes and in each series.

Thus, the first-track series range in attention given to poetry from RM, which devotes more than a third (37.4 per cent) of its space to poetry, down to Hlt, which gives poetry only about one-seventh (15.2 per cent) of its total pages. Second-track anthologies give poetry still less attention, and "developmental" series, represented in the table by HltD, give it almost no space. A comparison of Table XXI with similar ones for other genres shows that the space given to poetry is less than that given to the short story in 55 of the volumes examined, less than that given to miscellaneous nonfiction in 46 volumes, and less than that given to the drama or the novel in 15 volumes. Only in 13 of the 72 volumes — most of them for the twelfth-grade — is more attention given to poetry than to *any* other genre although two volumes (HB49-12 and RM-12) devote more space to poetry than to *all* other genres.

QUANTITY

Although the anthologies must provide teacher and students with a sufficient quantity of poetry for study, it is of course the quality of the poetry included that determines the relative merit of the various series and volumes. The most obvious characteristic of the anthologies is the marked difference in literary quality between volumes prepared for the two earlier years and those prepared for the eleventh- and twelfth-grades. Because of this difference we shall consider together the anthologies for the first two years before discussing those for the later years. Since literary quality does not easily lend itself to precise measurement, we have used various means in attempting to represent it here. We have, for example, compared the poetry content of the ninth- and tenth-grade anthologies with that of various collections of poetry. Some of the latter were chosen because they are standard works; others were chosen because they present a wide range of poetry of various kinds and of various periods including the most recent. We did not expect a close correspondence between the poetry in the high school anthologies and that in the collections, but we did think that a fairly large number of individual poems would appear in both places. We discovered, however, that a few of the anthologies do not contain a single poem found in the standard collections, and that several contained only a very few such poems. Even when allowance is made for the different purposes of the two kinds of books, the disparity between them seems unduly great. One is forced to conclude that many of the anthologies for the ninth and tenth grades do not properly serve one of the most important functions of literary textbooks — the transmission of the literary heritage.

As a further means of evaluating the poetic content we have calculated for each volume the percentage of poems written by standard poets[2] and, separately, the percentage of poems substantial enough, in our opinion, to require teaching or to invoke thoughtful and critical comments by the students. This procedure recommended itself as justifiable not only because it takes into account the poetry generally regarded as a well-established part of the literary heritage, but also because it recognizes the artistic and pedagogical values of other, including contemporary, poetry

---

[2] The term "standard poets" is used here to designate writers, whether traditional or contemporary, whose literary reputations are commonly regarded as established. Those in ninth-grade volumes that can be classified as standard poets are the following: Auden, Benét, Browning, Bryant, Blake, Burns, Byron, Coffin, Coleridge, De la Mare, Dickinson, Eliot, Emerson, Frost, Goldsmith, Hardy, Heine, Holmes, Housman, Homer, Keats, Kipling, Lanier, Lindsay, Longfellow, Amy Lowell, J. R. Lowell, Masefield, Martial, McGinley, Millay, MacLeish, Masters, Poe, Robinson, C. Rossetti, Scott, Stevenson, Sandburg, Shakespeare, Teasdale, Tennyson, Whitman, Whittier, Wordsworth, Wylie, Yeats. For the tenth grade the list is about the same with some additions: Arnold, E. Browning, Gray, Goethe, Lovelace, Shelley, Suckling. Several authors on both lists are very meagerly represented, sometimes by a single poem appearing in only one anthology.

that may also be able to stimulate its high school readers toward becoming adult participants on the human scene. Finally, because of their potentially great influence upon the quality of poetry, we took into account the frequency and the extent of abridgement of poems.

Using these criteria, we have ranked in Table XXII the ninth- and tenth-grade anthologies according to the quality of the poetry they contain. Admittedly, subtle distinctions are difficult to make and more difficult to defend, and among some of the volumes we can see no appreciable difference. There were, however, clearly marked intervals in the ranking, which we have shown in Table XXII by assigning each volume to one of three groups. The volumes in the first group seem to us clearly better in their poetry content than those in the second group, and those in the second group clearly superior to those in the third group. The figures which accompany each volume in the table are not assumed to have any intrinsic validity; they represent only relative judgments. In general, the volumes listed in Group I are those that have a respectable number of substantial poems, including several by great writers, and that abridge with relative infrequency. We have noted also that by their tone and editorial treatment they do not go so far as some of the others in making literature one of the "social studies."

If the anthologies are judged by external standards, all of them will be found to be deficient in one way or another. Some force poems into topical units (for example, Tennyson's "Break, Break, Break" is put into a section called "The Social Swing" by Hlt-10). Some choose poems for nonliterary reasons (for example, Ldw-9 and Ldw-10, which make a fetish of "oral interpretation," and ABC-9 and ABC-10, which use as one of their two criteria of selection the development of "reading power," which apparently sometimes means no more than reading speed). Some include a *disproportionate* number of esoteric pieces (for example, Irq-10), of juvenile poems (RM-10), of very short pieces (Hlt-10), or of mid-twentieth century poems (Gn-9, SF2-9, Lipp-10). Many accompany the poems with questions that are literarily irrelevant, that demand recall rather than thought, or that seem condescending. Some tend to overwhelm the poem by the illustrations or the typography (for example, HBO-9, HBO-10, SF-9, SF-10, SF2-9, PH-9, PH-10). Partly because of these matters, but mostly because of the lack of adequate representation of first-rate poetry, we believe that a good anthology for the ninth- and tenth-grades has not yet appeared in this mid-century period. How far the literary anthology has strayed from its purpose is indicated by SF2-9, which contains as its *only* poet of any stature Edna St. Vincent Millay, who is represented by twelve lines of something less than her best verse.

Almost all the volumes for the eleventh and twelfth grades are markedly different in this respect, for they contain a rather large number of poems by prominent authors.[3] Tables XXIII and XXIV may provide sufficient information about their poetry content to make possible comparative judgments.

The bottom line in each of these tables indicates the percentage of all the poetry in each volume that was written by the poets listed. It also indicates of course how much was written by poets of lesser stature: for example, 22 per cent of that in Sgr-12, 58 per cent of that in HB2-12, and 66 per cent of that in RM-11. Some allowance must be made for ABC-12, HB2-12, Hlt-12, Lipp-12, and PH-12, all of which show a low percentage of poetry by the thirty-five poets named in Table XXIV; these volumes, which deliberately include "World" as well as English literature, contain a considerable number of poems outside the Anglo-American

---

[3] The authors listed in Tables XXIII, and XXIV of Appendix A are the most important of those actually appearing in the anthologies; we do not intend to imply here that these authors should or should not be included or that they should be given greater or lesser attention. The purpose of these tables is entirely descriptive.

heritage and hence are not included here among the major "twelfth-grade poets." Nevertheless, the poetry content of these five volumes is among the least adequate and their superficial "coverage" of numerous countries adds little to their worth.

As long as the anthologies prepared for the eleventh and twelfth grades have as their defining purpose the representation of, respectively, American and English literature, they seem to us obliged to include a sufficient number of poems by major American and English poets. That several of the anthologies are inadequate in this respect is obvious from the data in the tables. Other characteristics of the anthologies are also suggested by the tables. Since most of the volumes make a point of representing "modern" literature, an emphasis that in most instances becomes an overemphasis, their attention to such contemporary poets as Auden, Eliot, Thomas, and Spender seems very meager. The relative neglect of such older poets as Blake, Donne, and Hopkins suggests an unawareness by the editors of the developments in literary criticism during the past two or three decades or the conviction that these poets are too "difficult" for high school students.

Finally, there is the question whether world literature should be included. The neglect by several anthologies of numerous major authors in the Anglo-American tradition, caused by their emphasis upon the literature of the Western hemisphere (eleventh grade) or of the world (twelfth grade), is open to criticism on several counts. (1) It is at least questionable whether a high school student inadequately read in the poetry of his own culture is prepared to undertake the study of another. (2) With lyric poetry particularly, the problem of finding poems in suitable translations is a serious one; and students who are likely to be both monolingual and relatively inexperienced with the tools of critical analysis are doubly handicapped. (Paradoxically, the anthologies that give considerable attention to hemispheric or world literature are also those that seem most clearly to be aimed at "average" students.) (3) That single short poems by authors from Ecuador, Guatemala, Chile, and other South American countries adequately "cover" Latin American poetry, or that single short poems by authors from Turkey, Persia, Japan, and Greece adequately "cover" world poetry are assumptions whose validity we seriously doubt. (4) It should also be noted that the Cooperative English Program, jointly sponsored by the National Council of Teachers of English, the Modern Language Association, the College English Association, and the American Studies Association, has questioned whether world literature is properly considered a part of high school "English." [4]

There is, however, a more serious charge that can be brought against these anthologies — their miscellaneous nature, already noted as characteristic of ninth- and tenth-grade volumes. If the function of the literature program during the last two high school years is to give students the experience of literature through its serious and approximately adult study, then even the 27 "most important" authors of the eleventh grade and the 34 of the twelfth grade may be too many. But there are still more poets represented. In the anthologies for each of the two years, about two-thirds (65 per cent) of the poems included are by these authors. The rest of the poems (one out of every three) were written by no fewer than, for the eleventh-grade volumes, 203, and for the twelfth-grade volumes, 209 different authors. In addition most of the volumes contain many anonymous poems, whose authors are necessarily omitted from these totals. If the purpose of the last two years of the English program is to teach literary history, these numbers can perhaps be justified. We believe, however, that this is not the purpose intended, nor do we believe that it

---

[4] See *The Basic Issues in the Teaching of English, Basic Issue* No. 1: "What is 'English'?" This report has been recently published in *Issues, Problems, and Approaches in the Teaching of English,* edited by G. W. Stone, Jr. (Holt, Rinehart and Winston, 1961), pp. 1-22.

should be the purpose. The goal toward which most of the editors say they are reaching would be more readily attained if there were greater concentration on fewer poems, chosen not just because they were written by well-known or presently popular poets or by poets who conveniently fill gaps in the chronological or topical organization, but because they are the best poems that the best poets have written.

Before turning from the poets represented in the anthologies to the poems themselves, we may note which poets are the most frequently anthologized in each of the four years. Tables XXV through XXIX list all poets whose poetry makes ten or more appearances in the anthologies examined.

The smaller number of poets included in Tables XXV and XXVI directly reflects the narrow range of agreement among the editors on authors appropriate for the ninth and tenth grades. On the other hand, the nationalistic boundaries placed on most anthologies for the eleventh and twelfth grades make closer agreement almost inevitable. More striking perhaps are (1) the relative neglect of many major poets, and (2) the considerable attention given to lesser ones. Again, the eclecticism is a notable feature, as the great and the lesser poets stand side by side, often equally represented as if they are all equally important. These tables suggest, indeed, that the criteria that have led to the selection of poetry may be as miscellaneous as the poems themselves.

The above comments are further substantiated, particularly for the ninth grade, as we turn to the individual *poems* most frequently anthologized. Those which appear five or more times in anthologies for the ninth and tenth grades and ten or more times in those for the eleventh and twelfth grades are as follows:

Ninth Grade: Coleridge, "The Rime of the Ancient Mariner," Homer, The *Odyssey* (excerpts only, three of them in prose); Nathan, "Dunkirk"; Service, "The Cremation of Sam McGee" and the anonymous "Whoopee Ti Yi Yo"; Benét, "Nancy Hanks"; De la Mare, "Silver"; Henley, "Invictus"; Magee, "High Flight";

Tenth Grade: Teasdale, "Stars"; Tennyson, "Gareth and Lynette"; (including 4 abridgements).

Eleventh Grade: Bryant, "To a Waterfowl"; Sandburg, "Chicago"; Bryant, "Thanatopsis"; Frost, "Mending Wall"; Masters, "Lucinda Matlock"; Timrod, "Magnolia Cemetery Ode"; Dickinson, "I Never Saw a Moor"; Emerson, "Concord Hymn"; Longfellow, "The Building of the Ship" (excerpts only); Poe, "The Raven"; and the anonymous Negro spiritual "Go Down, Moses."

Twelfth-Grade: Browning, "My Last Duchess"; Gray, "Elegy Written in a Country Churchyard"; Herrick, "To the Virgins"; Keats, "On First Looking into Chapman's Homer"; *Beowulf* (excerpts only, three of them in prose); Chaucer, "Prologue" to *The Canterbury Tales* (excerpts and abridgements only); Coleridge, "Kubla Khan"; Shelley, "Ode to the West Wind"; Arnold, "Dover Beach"; Burns, "A Man's a Man for A' That"; Brooke, "The Soldier"; Browning, "Home Thoughts from Abroad"; Johnson, "To Celia"; Milton, "On His Blindness"; Shelley, 'To a Skylark"; Shakespeare, Sonnets 29 and 116; Tennyson, "Flower in the Crannied Wall," "Ring Out, Wild Bells," and "Ulysses."

Again we note the lack of agreement on poems to include in volumes for the ninth and tenth grades. Other poems among those frequently anthologized, some of which may appear to be rather strange choices, include F. P. Adams, "The Rich Man" and "Those Two Boys"; Max Eastman, "At the Aquarium"; Kipling, "Gunga Din"; the anonymous "Oh, Bury Me Not on the Lone Prairie"; Ogden Nash, "Look What You Did, Christopher"; Eugene Field, "Little Boy Blue"; and Riley, "When the Frost is on the Punkin." The obvious whimsy and the slightness of such poems as these would seem to make them better suited for elementary or junior high school readers. Indeed, judging by many of the poems chosen by the editors, one is likely to conclude that, except in a few of the eleventh- and several of the twelfth-grade volumes, poetry is thought of not as something to be taught by the teacher but matter to be read by the student unaided. There are, of course, many challenging and rewarding poems included in the anthologies, even in some of those that are the least literary. Nevertheless one may well wonder what, if anything, the student has been reading before he arrives in the ninth grade if he has not earlier, when his age made them more appropriate, received the pleasure and the profit to be derived from the humor of Service, the heroics of Kipling, the grotesqueries of Poe, the sentimentality of the cowboy ballads, and the memorable lines from those longtime national favorites by Bryant, Longfellow, Whittier, and Holmes.

GRADE PLACEMENT

The objection may be raised by some editors and even by some teachers that students are not ready for poetry of certain kinds or on certain subjects at an earlier age. This objection is perhaps implicit in such currently fashionable pedagogical devices as "reading ladders" and "developmental reading programs." Our examination of the anthologies suggests, however, that the editors themselves have no very clear principles to apply that would lead them to assign, with some degree of assurance, particular poems to particular years. This uncertainty, it may be remembered, was noted also in the discussion of the short story and, more briefly, of the drama. It is most easily seen in the assignment of poems. The following summary indicates the number of poems that have been assigned by the different editors to different grades.

POEMS ASSIGNED TO MORE THAN ONE GRADE

Grade	Number of Poems
9, 10	65
9, 11	68
9, 12	39
10, 11	46
10, 12	66
11, 12	12
9, 10, 11	55
9, 10, 12	28
9, 11, 12	5
10, 11, 12	3
9, 10, 11, 12	6
Total	393

This total would no doubt be greater if the nationalistic boundaries of the volumes for the eleventh and twelfth grades in most series had not prevented greater overlap.

Out of the total number of poems (2516) in the anthologies examined, 393 may seem to be a reasonably small fraction. It should also be remembered, however, that 2043 poems appear only once in the 72 anthologies. In other words, in 2043 instances the question of disagreement among anthologists on the proper grade placement of poems *could not arise*. That for 393 of the poems appearing in more than one anthology there should be disagreement about placement thus takes on considerable significance. It suggests, at least, that what the editors speak of as progression in the anthologies through the four grade levels is more nearly a fantasy than a reality.

It points also to the powerful effect that the method of organizing the anthologies exerts upon the selection of the contents. For example, one editor may include a poem to fit into a topical unit in the tenth-grade volume; another may use the same poem to fill a chronological gap in the twelfth-grade volume. That the nature of the poem itself may make it more suitable for the tenth grade than for the twelfth, that the poem may be too juvenile for either grade, or that its value may be so slight that it does not deserve inclusion in any volume — these are considerations that apparently are overruled by the demands of the organization. Ironically, at the same time it may be that a poem's topic is only incidental to its essential statement or that its chronological position does not provide the best context within which it can be taught and studied by teacher and students. To illustrate: Housman's "When I Was One-and-Twenty" is found in a tenth-grade anthology in a unit called "The Wooing World" (ABC-10), in one twelfth-grade anthology in a unit called "Breaking the Ties" (RM-12), and in another under the heading "Five Late Victorians" (Gn-12). Several questions suggest themselves. If the poem is easy enough for tenth-graders (as one team of editors assumes), why isn't a more complex poem used in its stead two years later? Is the poem really about "The Wooing World," or is it rather a comment on the natural recalcitrance of youth? Is this topic — or the poetic treatment of it — uniquely late-Victorian? What does it have to do with the "breaking of ties" during the pre-World War I period? These questions suggest not only that the criteria of selection may be dubious but also that the placement of selections and their organization within volumes may actually make the reading and experiencing of literature more difficult than they need be, for both teacher and student. More important still, the placement may actually detract from the poem's intrinsic values.

As Table XX indicates, quite a number of poems are found in volumes as far apart as ninth and eleventh, ninth and twelfth, or tenth and twelfth grades. Among them are, for example, "The Cremation of Sam McGee," (in six ninth-grade volumes and PH-12), "The Yarn of the Nancy Bell" (PH-9, Sgr-9, and RM-12), and "When the Frost is on the Punkin" (SF-9 and seven eleventh-grade volumes). Such poems as these would seem to be appropriate for the ninth grade, if not earlier. Field's "Little Boy Blue" appears only in books for the eleventh grade (Gn-11, Glb-11, HB49-11, HBM-11, HBO-11), as do some of the poems of Longfellow, Holmes, Whittier, and Poe which seem better suited to younger readers. It may also surprise parents to learn that their teen-agers may have to wait until the eleventh or twelfth grade to make the acquaintance of "The Highwayman," "Lochinvar," "Abou Ben Adhem," "Danny Deever," "Robin Hood and Little John," "The Charge of the Light Brigade," and numerous other pieces that they themselves were reading at an earlier age. In summary, it appears to us that most of the series have been downgraded, so that much simple poetry now appears at the most advanced levels. At the same time, however, we hasten to add that much challenging poetry of high quality has been retained by several of the anthologies.

Before ending this discussion of the distribution of poetry by grade levels, we note, perhaps only as a matter of interest, the titles of the six (of the 2516 poems) that various editors have assigned to all four high school grades (see Table XXIX). These are as follows: Coffin's "Secret Heart"; Frost's "Mending Wall" and "Two Tramps in Mud Time"; Markham's "The Man with the Hoe"; Millay's "Travel"; and Robinson's "Richard Cory." Because of the arbitrary restriction of the eleventh-grade volume in each series to American literature (two volumes, Ldw-11 and McM-11, also include a few Latin American poems), and because several twelfth-grade volumes (ABC-12, HB2-12, Hlt-12, Ldw-12, Lipp-12, PH-12) include some world — and thus American — literature, it is almost impossible for other than American poems to be on this "elite" list. One may well add that it would not have been impossible to choose somewhat more substantial poems as having such widespread appeal and range of usefulness.

EXCERPTS AND ABRIDGEMENTS

Abridgement and excerpting have been previously discussed in other connections, but the editorial treatment of the texts of poems is probably of greater importance to the users of anthologies than is the editing of texts in any other genre. The nature of poetry, especially its economy and precision of language and its structural and metaphorical unity, make scrupulous textual treatment mandatory.

There is, nevertheless, one kind of abridging that is necessary, at least in anthologies as they are presently conceived. Obviously, the whole of Milton's *Paradise Lost* or Spenser's *Faërie Queene,* if included in an anthology, would leave little room for anything else. For the editing of long poems such as these, two principal criteria should be operative: the poem to be editorially shortened should be of such overriding importance that its omission is unthinkable, and the part printed should be a natural division of the poem. Unfortunately, this kind of editing is the least prevalent. Among the few examples are the complete sections of Tennyson's *Idylls of the King* in HB49-10, Ldw-10, McM-10, RM-12. On the other hand, the longest excerpt from *Paradise Lost* comprises, not an entire section, but fragments of two sections of the poem.

The most harmless kind of editing we have found is the excerpting of brief passages from long poems: for example, 36 lines of Dante's *Divine Comedy* (Hlt-12), 28 lines of Longfellow's *Evangeline* (HBO-11), 26 lines of Pope's *Essay on Criticism* (SF-12), 37 lines of Vergil's *Aeneid* (Hlt-12), 55 lines of Arnold's *Sohrab and Rustum* (RM-12), 28 lines of Whittier's *Snow-Bound* (Scb-9). These excerpts are so minute in comparison with their sources and so obviously fragmentary that no reader is likely to be misled by them. We agree with those teachers who say that the most appropriate comment on such excerpts is that they are merely useless.

Of the abridgements that we classify as unjustifiable because the integrity of the poem is vitiated or because the reader may be deceived, some are silent, with no indication to teacher or student that the text is incomplete, and some are identified. When there is identification, the reader may be informed that the selection is an abridgement in a number of ways: it may be so designated in the table of contents, the index, or the acknowledgments of copyright; it may be identified on the page — by title, headnote, or footnote; that it is an abridgement may be surmised from the presence of ellipsis points in the text (which, however, in some volumes are not consistently present and may even have another meaning) or incidentally learned from the study questions that follow the text. Often, only persistent search turns up the editors' indication that the poem is incompletely printed. Commonly, the length, the content, and the location of the deleted part or parts are not indicated; therefore, even when abridgement is announced, the reader has no means of constructing an image of the entire poem. Occasionally an edited poem is also retitled, so that the reader may be further misled. Examples of each of these practices follow.

Unhappily, the number of silent or unacknowledged excerpts and abridgements of poems is large, nor are they confined to only a few of the anthologies now in use. In ABC-12 appears Dyer's "My Mind to Me a Kingdom Is" from which have been omitted, without indication, the third, sixth, and seventh stanzas of the original — almost 40 per cent of the poem. In ABC-9 appear twelve lines of Longfellow's "A Psalm of Life," unidentified as a fragment (it is only one-third of the poem), which is retitled "Footprints on the Sands." "Thoughts of Youth" in Ldw-9 is one stanza of the ten-stanza "My Lost Youth" by Longfellow, unacknowledged as an excerpt. Scb-9 prints as a poem entitled "Pio-

neers! O Pioneers!" a twelve-line excerpt from Whitman's poem of
that title, made up of the third, sixth, and seventh of the original
twenty-six stanzas, without indicating that the poem is incomplete and that the stanzas are not consecutive. SF-9 prints the
first seven lines of Whitman's two hundred twenty-four-line "Song
of the Open Road," silently excerpted and retitled. Sgr-11 prints
a fourteen-line passage from the middle of Emerson's "Ode In-
scribed to W. H. Channing," a ninety-seven-line poem, and refers
to it as if it were complete. The last stanza of Poe's "Ulalume,"
about one-tenth of the poem, is omitted without remark by
ABC-11, HB49-11, HBM-11, and McM-11. One stanza of Hood's
"The Song of the Shirt" is silently omitted in ABC-12, HB49-12,
HBM-12, HBO-12, HB2-9, and RM-12. One-fourth of Byron's
"When We Two Parted" is missing from the text printed in ABC-
12, and from the same volume 38 per cent of Goldsmith's "The Deserted Village" and 63 per cent of Rossetti's "The Blessed Damozel"
disappear without a trace. In Sgr-12 the opening twenty-four lines
of Milton's "L'Allegro" are omitted without indication. Although
there are many other instances of silent editing of poetic texts,
those listed in this paragraph may suggest both their frequency
and their variety. Some of them (for example, "Ulalume" and
"The Song of the Shirt") also hint that editors may have borrowed from each other, errors included.

The acknowledged excerpts and abridgements are, as might be
surmised, more numerous. The following summary will serve to
illustrate, by means of a few examples, the scope of the editing
and the editors' methods of indicating abridgement.

This list, which is intended merely to be representative, could
be greatly extended. As the summary indicates, the excerpting or
abridging may be drastic or relatively mild, and the incomplete-
ness may be plainly indicated on the page or only casually mentioned. Ellipsis points are helpful to show the location of the
omitted passage, but this device alone seems inadequate when

ABRIDGEMENTS AND EXCERPTS OF REPRESENTATIVE
POEMS IN THE ANTHOLOGIES

Author and Title	Original Length (lines)	Edited Length (lines)	Anthology	Editorial Means of Indicating Abridgement
Burns, "Lines to John Lapraik"	132	30	Ldw-12	Title and Table of Contents
Coleridge, "Dejection: An Ode"	139	20	RM-12	Study Questions
Lowell, "Vision of Sir Launfal"	347	173	Ldw-11	Study Questions
Lowell, "Vision of Sir Launfal"	347	36	HBO-10	Title
Milton, "L'Allegro"	152	128	HBM-12	Headnote
Milton, "Il Penseroso"	176	156	Sgr-12	Ellipsis points
Whittier, "The Eternal Goodness"	88	64	HBO-11	Headnote and Ellipsis points
Wordsworth, "Intimations" Ode	204	100	SF-12	Headnote, Title, and Ellipsis points

the usual three spaced periods are intended to stand, without
other indication, for half or more of a poem. We believe that
poems should be presented in such a way that there is no chance
of misconception about their length and their stanzaic organization. Some means should therefore be used to inform the student
that the poem is incomplete, preferably on the page containing
the opening lines; but it is hardly enough to state in a headnote
that "a few stanzas" have been omitted if they constitute a large
part of the poem.[5]

---

[5] We found one odd indication of abridgement: RM-12 suggests by the
title, "From the Deserted Village," that only a part of the poem is included
— but all 430 lines of it are present!

Besides the silent and acknowledged abridgements there are those which fall somewhere between. Two examples will illustrate the practice. Byron's "The Isles of Greece," a ninety-six-line song from *Don Juan,* is included in Sgr-12 in abridged form. The part printed comprises stanzas 1, 3-6, 11, and 16. The omission of the second stanza and the hiatus after the sixth are indicated by ellipsis points; the omission of stanzas 12 through 15 is not indicated, nor is the reader provided any means of knowing that more than half the poem is missing. Another example of this inconsistent practice is the treatment of Bryant's "The Antiquity of Freedom" in PH-11, which deletes 40 per cent of the poem. The entire first stanza and the closing lines of the poem are omitted without indication. A ten-line passage is omitted from the middle, but three spaced periods may perhaps be intended as ellipsis points; however, earlier in the poem there are three similar spaced periods where there is no omission. Without access to an accurate version, both teacher and reader are completely at the mercy of the anthologists in such instances as these. Led by some of the evidence to believe that the editing has been scrupulous, they are the more readily misled when editorial accuracy is inconsistently maintained.

Deception is, of course, only one of the dangers inherent in editing poetic texts. Even when omissions and alterations are meticulously identified, there is still the equally grave possibility that abridgement may result in emasculation or distortion. No one can doubt that Ben Jonson's "To the Memory of My Beloved Master William Shakespeare" has been emasculated in HBM-12 and HBO-12 when he searches in vain for some of the poem's most notable passages: "thou hadst small Latin and less Greek," "Marlowe's mighty line," "Yet must I not give Nature all; thy art,/ My gentle Shakespeare, must enjoy a part," and especially "He was not of an age, but for all time!" [6]

---

[6] The last of the passages cited, although omitted from the text, is quoted

One additional example will serve to illustrate how poems may be vitiated by abridgement. Burns's famous poem, "The Cotter's Saturday Night," is included in four twelfth-grade anthologies. In HB49-12 and SF-12 it is complete, but in HBM-12 and HBO-12 it is reduced by more than one-fourth its length. In the two latter volumes 54 lines are omitted after the stanza that ends with the line, "And, 'Let us worship God!' he says with solemn air." The omitted lines show the family at worship. In other words, the generalization is retained, but its concrete particularization is removed. We shall not be so audacious as to attempt here a full definition of poetry. We note, however, that most of the definitions we have seen stress, as essential qualities of poetry, concreteness and particularity. We can only conclude then that "The Cotter's Saturday Night," as printed in HBM-12 and HBO-12, has to some extent been "unpoemed." The ineptness of this abridgement will be further evident when it is noted that the first line after the deletion reads, "From scenes like these old Scotia's grandeur springs. . . ." Unfortunately for the reader, some of these "scenes" have vanished.

Judged by their manner of treating poetry, the anthologies give the impression of lacking confidence in literature as such. Refusing to take literature seriously *for its own sake*, they treat it as a social document, or fail to apply valid literary criteria in its presentation and interpretation, or show indifference to its integrity as art. It is not surprising then to find in the anthologies drastically — and silently — edited texts of poems that distort the orig-

---

incidentally in an inserted editorial note in HBO-12. It is worth noting, possibly as an indication of a trend toward progressively more extensive abridgement as anthologies are revised, that the poem as printed in HB49-12 contains the passages omitted in HBM-12 and HBO-12. It may be that revisions of series by other publishers would show the same trend; however, because earlier editions of other anthologies are no longer in sufficiently general use, we have not included them in our survey and, therefore, have not been able to make the same kind of detailed comparison as was possible with the Harcourt, Brace series.

inals and deprive them of their unique spirit and appeal. The unsuspecting student is the helpless victim.

In addition to the distortion of a poem by abridgement, its text may be inaccurately represented through careless editing or reliance upon an invalid copy text. The following versions of Blake's "The Tiger" will illustrate.

Blake's text	Text appearing in Gn-12
Tiger! Tiger! burning bright	Tiger, Tiger, burning bright
In the forests of the night,	In the *forest* of the night,
What immortal hand or eye	What immortal hand or eye
Could frame thy fearful symmetry?	*Framed* thy fearful symmetry?
In what distant deeps or skies	(5) In what distant deeps or skies
Burnt the fire of thine eyes?	*Burned that* fire *within* thine eyes?
On what wings dare he aspire?	On what wings *dared* he aspire?
What the hand dare seize the fire?	What the hand *dared* seize the fire?
And what shoulder, and what art	And what shoulder, and what art,
Could twist the sinews of thy heart?	(10) Could twist the sinews of thy heart?
And when thy heart began to beat	*When* thy heart began to beat,
What dread hand forged thy dread feet? *	What dread hand *formed* thy dread feet?
What the hammer? What the chain?	What the hammer, what the chain,
In what furnace was thy brain?	*Knit thy strength and forged* thy brain?
What the anvil? What dread grasp	(15) What the anvil? What dread grasp
Dare its deadly terrors clasp?	*Dared thy* deadly terrors clasp?
When the stars threw down their spears,	When the stars threw down their spears,
And watered heaven with their tears,	And watered heaven with their tears,
Did he smile his work to see?	Did he smile his work to see?
Did he who made the Lamb make thee?	(20) Did he who made the lamb make thee?

---

* Blake's line in the engraved version was "What dread hand and what dread feet"; the line as given above is presumably the poet's own later emendation. Both versions of the line are therefore regarded as having authorial validity, and reputable modern editors have chosen between them.

Tiger! Tiger! burning bright   (stanza missing)
In the forests of the night,
What immortal hand or eye
Dare frame thy fearful symmetry?

Besides the omission of the final stanza and changes in punctuation and capitalization, there are, in Gn-12, no fewer than twelve
corruptions of the wording itself (indicated above by italics).

In addition to Gn-12, seven other anthologies (ABC-12, HB49-
12, HBM-12, HBO-12, McM-12, SF-12, Sgr-12) include Blake's
"The Tiger." Of these Sgr-12 contains the Blake text as given
above, and ABC-12, McM-12, and SF-12 use the alternate line 12
from the engraved version but otherwise print this text.

We cannot insist too much that high school anthologies incor-
porate the results of sound literary scholarship, meticulous textual
editing, and informed literary criticism. We believe that literature is a serious discipline that deserves to be taken seriously; and
by "serious" we mean neither solemn nor dull. Literature — well
chosen, well edited, and well taught — is exciting rather than solemn, and it is the trivial that proves to be dull. It is apparent from
the 2516 different poems that a very large number of them were
chosen, not by the only sure criterion — the literary importance,
but for secondary reasons — because they are "easy," because they
have topical interest, because they lend themselves to "group activities," because they can be made to evoke social awareness,
because they represent "coverage" of certain periods or places,
or perhaps merely because anthologists have a personal predilection for them. When such secondary or irrelevant criteria of selection are combined with misleading or inaccurate editing, literature is placed in double jeopardy. Students who are being
introduced to literature can hardly be expected to regard with
dignity and respect compilations of readings that do not reflect
the central elements and values of that discipline. Moreover, the
teacher's task is, in the long run, thereby made more difficult, for,

as teachers themselves are the first to know — particularly now when they must compete with the prestigious sciences — he whose subject does not evoke respect *as a serious and important body of matter for study* finds it difficult to maintain for himself the degree of respect that makes the successful teaching of it possible.

RECOMMENDATIONS

1. We recommend that the poetry included in the anthologies for all four grade levels be chosen for its high literary merit, and that this criterion be met before topicality, historical or typological representativeness, timeliness, and the demands of the organization are taken into account. Only if selection precedes arrangement can quality be assured.

2. We recommend that, without necessarily reducing the quantity of poetry, a much smaller number of poets be represented per volume than is now the case with most anthologies.

3. We recommend that, before they admit the esoteric and the unusual, anthologists make certain that they have represented, as fully as possible, the poetry central to the Anglo-American literary heritage.

4. We recommend that poems which tell an uncomplicated story, appeal to young emotions, or are expressed in fairly unsophisticated language be used in the ninth and tenth years and not reserved for the eleventh and twelfth grades because of the nationality of their authors, and that in general the poetry content of the anthologies make progressively greater demands upon students as they proceed through a volume and through a series.

5. We recommend that at least one-third of an anthology's pages be devoted to poetry.

6. We recommend that, if long poems are excerpted, the fact be clearly indicated and that the excerpts chosen be representative and, whenever possible, consist of natural divisions of the entire works. We see no value at all in minute excerpts.

7. We recommend that poems never be abridged, simplified, adapted, or otherwise altered. If a poem can be included only by altering its text, then another poem of equal merit that can be printed in complete form should be substituted for it.

CHAPTER 3

Organization and Coverage

THE ORGANIZATION of the anthologies is hardly less significant than content for reaching an evaluation of them. Although a volume containing a high proportion of inferior and nonliterary selections cannot be metamorphosed into a superior and literary anthology by its organization, one whose contents are generally acceptable in themselves can be seriously vitiated by inappropriate arrangement. And an arrangement that stresses values more pertinent for science, social studies, or general knowledge than for literature can move a textbook outside the proper area of English studies entirely. The method of organization is, therefore, an important consideration for those responsible for selecting anthologies for their schools. It is even more important for the teacher, whose conduct of classes in literature is likely to be influenced by the editors' arrangement of the contents. Because of the importance of the anthologies' organization to both those who adopt and those who use them, we have made a detailed analysis of the arrangements found in all the anthologies we have examined. As many of the results of our analysis as possible are presented in tabular form. The analysis and accompanying description are followed by our interpretation of the findings and by recommendations for improvement.

As we noted earlier in discussing the literary quality of the selections, here also the most remarkable feature of the anthologies as a group is the difference between the ninth- and tenth-grade volumes on the one hand and the eleventh- and twelfth-grade volumes on the other. The favorite method of organization in the books for the two earlier years may best be designated as the topical,[1] whereas the books for the later years employ a variety of methods among which the chronological is the most frequently used.

All the books have divisions of some kind, and forty of them also have subdivisions. Either the main divisions or the subdivisions may be regarded as "units," although the term itself is used in somewhat less than a third of the volumes, this practice being commoner among the ninth- and tenth-grade books than in those for the later grades.[2] All the divisions in a volume may be of the same kind, but in about half the books they are drawn from two or more different categories. Volumes in which a single system does not predominate we have designated as having a "mixed" arrangement. In addition to the "mixed" arrangement, the arrangements adopted are the two previously mentioned (topical and chronological), the geographical, and the typological. The dominant system of organization in each of the anthologies we have examined, in both main divisions and subdivisions, can be described by one of these five terms, as is shown in the following summary.

---

[1] We have designated as topical all sections or "units" that are made up of selections chosen because they treat a common topic (for example, "The Animal World," "Growing Up," "Conquests of Science"). Some editors call such units "thematic" — in our opinion a misuse of the term. We have discussed at length the difference between topical and thematic units in our book, *Dialogues on the Teaching of Literature* (New York: Bookman Associates, 1960), pp. 184-198.

[2] We have noted the tendency, particularly in the better anthologies, to abandon the term "unit," even though the concept continues to be employed.

DOMINANT SYSTEMS OF ORGANIZATION IN THE ANTHOLOGIES

System	Ninth Grade Divisions		Tenth Grade Divisions		Eleventh Grade Divisions		Twelfth Grade Divisions		Totals Divisions	
	Main	Sub	Main	Sub	Main	Sub	Main	Sub	Main	Sub
Topical	15	4	10	5	5	2	4	1	34	12
Typological	3	0	7	1	0	4	2	5	12	10
Chronological	0	0	0	0	10	3	9	4	19	7
Geographical	0	0	0	0	0	0	2	0	2	0
Mixed	3	7	0	1	2	3	0	0	5	11
	21	11	17	7	17	12	17	10	72	40

The numbers in the above summary represent individual volumes. Thus, thirty-four or almost half of the volumes are arranged topically, all but nine of them being books for the ninth and tenth grades. Tenth-grade volumes also make frequent use of typological arrangement. Chronological arrangement, the commonest system in the eleventh and twelfth grades, is not used at all in ninth- and tenth-grade books. Geographical arrangement is the least used, and then only in the twelfth grade. The variety of systems is greatest in twelfth-grade volumes, followed in order by those for the eleventh, tenth, and ninth grades. Of the forty volumes that subdivide their main sections, over one-fourth (11) draw upon two or more systems, with no single order predominating, and are thus classified as having "mixed" systems of secondary organization.

When we turn from the dominant systems of organization to the individual units or other divisions of the anthologies, we must add four kinds to the five already mentioned. One of these, the thematic, appears occasionally but with nothing like the frequency that editors regularly suggest in their prefaces or tables of content. By "thematic unit" we mean one made up of selections whose essential statements comment upon a human quality or trait (for example, courage, love, vanity). Thus, in HBO-9 we classify the fourth subdivision, "Loyalties," as thematic, but one appearing later in the book, "Man's Conquest of the Air," which the editors call thematic, we prefer to classify as topical. Another kind of division has as its only unifying element the expression of or the appeal to a certain mood. Most examples of this kind are units made up of humorous pieces, often limericks and other light verse (for example, units titled "Just for Fun," "The Funny Side," "High Jinks"). A third kind combines two criteria and is designated as the "combination" unit in the tables. Examples of this kind are "Lyrics of Labor" (typological-topical), "Poems of Love and Friendship" (typological-thematic), "American Songs" (geographical-typological). Finally, there are a few units that are so miscellaneous or so general as to make their classification quite meaningless (for example, "The Pleasures of Reading," "Words Are Wealth," "All True," "Words of Widsom," and "Treasures of Our Heritage"). The unifying element in such units as these is at best casual; they seem to have as their chief reason for being a catch-all function, providing a place for pieces that editors wished to include but found no other way of fitting into their organization. We have also included as "miscellaneous" such a unit as "Television as Literature."

One curious practice to be noted in ninth- and tenth-grade volumes is that although most units contain several selections — the range in the typical volume is from four to twelve pieces — some books include a "unit" made up of a single (usually long) work. In most instances this "unit" is typological, consisting of a novel or a play, and most frequently called simply "The Novel" or "The Drama." We have found, however, a few instances of the one-item "unit" which the editors have attempted to fit into a topical organization (for example, the unit entitled "One Boy's Life" in SF-9, which consists solely of an abridged and partly adapted long excerpt from Dickens's *David Copperfield*).

Tables XXX through XXXIII of Appendix A indicate some of the more important details of organization.

For the convenience of the reader, the above data are summarized in Table XXXIV, in which the figures have been converted to percentages.

Several comments are suggested by these tables. Evidently, consistency of organization is not highly regarded by the editors, for in almost half the volumes their main divisions are drawn from two or more different categories, and no volume has subdivisions that all belong to the same order. The only series that maintain a consistent organization within the main divisions of each of their four volumes are HltD, PH, and Sgr, and of these only HltD uses the same kind of organization (the topical) throughout all of its four volumes. Consistency of organization seems to be more highly regarded in the volumes for the two later years and is most notably lacking in the volumes for the ninth grade. It may be argued that inconsistent arrangement is based upon illogicality and is therefore bad; however, we find no particular virtue here in consistency as such unless the elements maintained in a consistent order are themselves relevant to purpose and unless these elements are thereby enhanced. In the anthologies these elements are the units, and there is no positive correlation between quality of units and consistency of organization. We have observed, in fact, that appropriate units often occur in volumes with a highly inconsistent organization and that among the volumes maintaining the greatest consistency in their arrangement are several of the qualitatively poorest anthologies we have found.

We have noted also the lack of flexibility in many of the anthologies, particularly those arranged topically or chronologically. If a teacher finds himself compelled to use a particular volume and does not wish to proceed through its units *seriatim*, he may find the labor necessitated by reorganization to be hardly less than that originally expended by the editors in devising the arrangement that he now rejects. About the only help that editors provide is an index (or second table of contents) arranged by literary types. The index will expedite the teacher's reorganization of the anthology, but of course it will not supply literary pieces more appropriate for typological units than those originally chosen by the editors *for their topicality or chronological position.* Characteristically, a book arranged by topic has no subdivisions and thus no internal organization that might be of help if the teacher should wish to use it otherwise than in its existing order. In books of this kind, indexes are especially necessary. In chronologically and typologically arranged volumes, subdivisions, which are often present, can help to reorganize the contents in lieu of a special index, which is usually absent. In none of the volumes, however, have we found much real flexibility, in spite of indexes and internal subdivision, chiefly because the anthologies show the results of imposing an order upon the material. We believe that in the compiling of literary anthologies *selection must precede and be largely independent of organization,* and that these two editorial steps should not be confused. Otherwise there is no safeguard for literature *as literature;* for if organization plays a prior and dominant role in the editing, unworthy pieces may be admitted and literary pieces will be included to serve other — and almost inevitably lesser — ends.[3]

There are other general comments on the organization of the anthologies that cannot be easily represented in tabular form. Some of the volumes contain still smaller subdivisions than those indicated in the tables, most notably HB49-11, HBM-11, HBO-11, McM-11, and Sgr-12. Several of these are too short to be consid-

---

[3] We have discussed this matter at some length in *Dialogues on the Teaching of Literature,* especially pp. 171-175, 202-203. The reader may also recall the warning of Matthew Arnold on what he calls the fallacy of the historical estimate and the fallacy of the personal estimate. These are discussed in his essay, "The Study of Poetry," which he wrote as *his* introduction to an anthology. Perhaps it should be required reading for all anthologists!

ered as units, but they are helpful for further marshaling of the contents. Most volumes for the eleventh and twelfth grades have, besides their chronological, typological, or topical organization, a further and overriding limitation — the geographical or nationalistic, since it is customary to reserve the eleventh year for American and the twelfth year for English literature. The exceptions are as follows: ABC-12 (English and World literature), HB-12a (World literature), HB2-12 (modern literature from any source), Hlt-12 (English and World literature), HltD-11 and HltD-12 (nonliterary readings), Ldw-11 (literature of the Western hemisphere), Ldw-12 (English and Continental literature), Lipp-12 (no geographical limitation, but mostly English and American literature), PH-12 (World literature), Sgr-12a (World literature). The volumes for the ninth and tenth grades, with the possible exception of Lipp-10, have no geographical boundaries, although they run heavily to American writings.

GEOGRAPHICAL AND CHRONOLOGICAL ORGANIZATION

The last exception just named suggests a further comment. *All Around the Land,* as Lipp-10 is titled, *uses* literature (some of it rather slight) for a nonliterary purpose, as is indicated by the titles of its six units: "Introducing a Continent," "Going Abroad at Home," "In the Country," "In Town," "At Work," and "In the Old West." This kind of organization is, we believe, more appropriate for a textbook to be used in history or geography than in an English class. We have classified most of the units in Lipp-10 as topical, since their contents were obviously chosen because they deal with a common topic — aspects of American life. They might also have been classed as geographical, because they all deal with a particular nation, but we have preferred, in such ambiguous situations as this, to follow, as nearly as possible, literary (which here means biographical) criteria in classifying the units in the anthologies. That is, American literature is written by American authors, but it is not necessarily *about* America and Americans, and so also for English, Canadian, Latin American, and Continental literatures — a statement that seems self-evident. Two additional volumes will serve to illustrate. PH-12 has six divisions: "United States of America," "Canada and Mexico," "Latin America," "Europe," "Africa," and "Asia," and, although the book is titled *Literature of the World Around Us,* because of some of the divisions it might better have been titled "Literature *about* the World Around Us." Several of the selections, although about the various continents, are not by natives of those regions and thus cannot represent the literature *of* Africa, *of* Asia, and so forth. Similarly, Sgr-12a, titled *Prose and Poetry of the World,* includes several selections apparently because they are about regional topics, not because they represent regional literatures; for example, pieces by *American* authors *about* Spain, Singapore, Russia, Mexico, and Denmark. Whatever the merit of such pieces, the point we would make here is that, if they are presented as literature *of* rather than *about* various parts of the world, they appear in false guise, that the students are not thereby becoming acquainted with those literatures (the apparent purpose of such volumes), and that, to the extent that the units are composed of works by non-native writers writing *about* foreign lands, which have been chosen and arranged for this reason, they have a more legitimate place in textbooks for the social studies than in those intended for English classes.

A somewhat similar situation is found in several of the chronologically arranged volumes. Five volumes (ABC-11, RM-11, Sgr-11, ABC-12, and SF-12) include within chronological units modern pieces about earlier periods (which sometimes bulk larger than the selections from earlier literature which they accompany): for example, ABC-11 includes part of a play by Sidney Kingsley (1943) in the unit "The Years of the Revolution"; RM-11 includes Benét's short story, "A Tooth for Paul Revere"

(1938), in the unit "The Birth of a Nation"; Sgr-11 includes Ogden Nash's humorous poem, "Look What You Did, Christopher!" (1933), in the unit "Foothold in the Wilderness" — alongside excerpts from Captain John Smith's *True Relation* and *The Bay Psalm Book;* ABC-12 includes Thurber's "The Macbeth Murder Mystery" (1937) in the unit "The Elizabethan Age"; SF-12 includes an adapted excerpt from Marchette Chute's *The Innocent Wayfaring* (1943) in the unit "Chaucer's England." One would not of course object to such pieces as student readings, especially as supplementary readings; but one must object to the substitution of secondary for primary material and to the usurping of the valuable page space that the former is given. Why not give this space to additional pieces actually written during America's Colonial and Revolutionary periods and in Chaucer's and Shakespeare's England?

Our objections to this practice of transforming, at least in part, either geographical or chronological divisions into topical units are not, however, directed only at the space they preempt. "The Past Through the Eyes of the Present," as the ABC volumes characterize such secondary material, is precisely that — the past *edited* and *interpreted*. The literature has filtered through another mind before it reaches the student, and his opportunity to confront the past at first hand, to read about it in the words of men and women who were there, is thereby lessened; and as it is lessened so is the educative potential of literature, for the reader becomes less free to weigh the evidence, assess the authors' meaning, experience the impact of their words, and draw his own conclusions — in short to think, critically and creatively. A term now commonly used to characterize such practices as this is "spoon-feeding," which, one would think, should no longer be necessary for high school juniors and seniors.

The chronological and geographical methods of arrangement are also subject to other abuses. An evident purpose of most

eleventh- and twelfth-grade volumes is to provide a sense of literary history and national literatures. If this is also the teacher's
purpose, he will not wish to use any of those that do not convey
this sense: HBL-11, Hlt-11, HltD-11, Lipp-11, PH-11, HB2-12,
HltD-12, Lipp-12, PH-12, Sgr-12a. He would also be well advised
to avoid several others: McM-11, which has an arrangement that
is best described as freakish; SF-11, a highly eclectic and not very
satisfactory experiment in combining historical and modern
pieces; McM-12, a volume that has an account of English literary history in which poems and short excerpts are interspersed;
Rm-11, a confusingly organized book in which chronology competes with other orders; and those (ABC-11, Ldw-11, HB2-11,
HBM-11, HBO-11, Sgr-11, and SF-12) that have an excessive
proportion of recent literature. Several volumes follow the practice
of introducing modern literature first (often arranged typologically) and then going back to the beginning for a chronological
representation of literature that comes up to about 1900. These
two sections, usually titled by some such rubric as "America (or
England) Today" and "America's (or England's) Past," are, in
several anthologies, of about equal length, as can be seen from
the figures in Table XXXII. Volumes that adopt this reversed system are the following: ABC-11, ABC-12, HB49-11, HBM-11,
HBO-11, and, in a modified form, RM-11 and SF-11. We were
interested to learn that some teachers believe that the first section
in such volumes is, as one teacher expressed it, "a complete waste
of space." We ourselves see nothing objectionable, and indeed
something beneficial, in preceding the earlier literature with a
selection of modern pieces — if certain precautions are taken:
the sections of modern literature should be kept within appropriate bounds (probably not more than about 20 per cent of the
total contents), and they should be made up of selections that
have real literary merit. Unfortunately, these two precautions are
not always present in the volumes so arranged.

It also goes without saying that chronologically arranged volumes should reflect chronology with accuracy. That anthologies differ in this respect can be seen in the summary below. For purposes of comparison, nine selections from the literature of colonial America are represented in the summary. These, in the chronological order of their composition, are as follows: (1) Smith, *True Relation* (1608); (2) *The Mayflower Compact* (1620); (3) Bradford, *History of the Plimmoth Plantation* (1630-1646); (4) *Bay Psalm Book* (1640); (5) *New England Primer* (*ca.* 1690); (6) Knight, *Journal* (1704); (7) Sewall, *Diary* (the passage chosen was written in 1720); (8) Byrd, *The History of the Dividing Line* (1729); (9) Edwards, *Sinners in the Hands of an Angry God* (1741). Although some of the anthologies also include other selections to represent early America, these appear with sufficient frequency to supply a satisfactory basis for comparison. In the following summary the numbers refer to the correspondingly numbered selections above, and the order of the numbers in each column represents the order of appearance of the selections in the volume named. Some allowance must be made for special elaborations of the arrangements (for example, the internal subdivision in HBO-11); even so, however, it appears that chronology is followed rather loosely in some of the anthologies.

CHRONOLOGICAL VARIATIONS IN CERTAIN
ELEVENTH-GRADE ANTHOLOGIES

ABC-11	Glb-11	HB49-11	HBM-11	HBO-11	Ldw-11	MCM-11	Rm-11	Sgr-11
1	1	4	4	1	1	2	1	1
8	3	5	5	8	8	8	3	4
2	8	9	9	6	6	3	5	5
3	5	6	6	3	7	4	6	9
4	6	8	8	4	4	9	8	
5	7			5		5		
7			9					
6								

Having criticized the abuses of chronological and geographical units, we must now say that we consider neither, even when properly used, the ideal kind for the organization of literature in high school courses. Theoretically, one can make a case for both, for a work of literature has its origin in a particular time and a particular place, and it may bear the characteristic marks of that time and place upon it. Practically, however, as the anthologies themselves indicate, chronological and geographical arrangements tend to pervert the study of literature, for the teacher is likely to find himself conducting a class in geography or literary history rather than literature. The evidence is abundant in the anthologies: scores of pages given over to historical introductions, sometimes more than are devoted to the selections; study questions and especially review questions at the ends of units that stress information about time and place rather than thought about literature; maps, charts, tables of dates, illustrations, and suggestions for "activities" that emphasize historical and geographical *facts*. Many unit titles carry this same emphasis: for example, "Moving Westward," "War Between the States," "Time of Peril," "From Ocean to Ocean," "Building the Towns and Cities." Indeed, some of the volumes themselves as earlier noted also bear titles which shift the emphasis away from literature. This misplaced or faulty emphasis in editorial apparatus and titles we believe symptomatic of an unfortunate development — the submersion of English in the social studies.

There is further objection to chronological and geographical arrangement. We have noticed that some of the anthologies so organized include inferior pieces or find it necessary to abridge long works in the interests of the arrangement itself. If the whole span of literary history is to be represented, then selections must be found for all periods, even though such representation may mean leaving out other, superior and complete pieces that happen to have been written in periods that overwhelm editors with their richness. Editors are then likely to indulge the fallacy of the historical estimate, of which Matthew Arnold wrote. Or, to fill out their geographical arrangement, they may have to search out writings by, for example, Central American or Near Eastern authors (and adequate translations of them), which may prove to be inferior to much American or English literature necessarily omitted because of the demands of the organization.

We conclude that, at most, the organization should actively aid students and teacher to become involved with the best literature as directly and as quickly as possible, without excessive "background" material and editorial apparatus; and that, at least, it should not cause the denial to students of first-rate literature. Unfortunately, several of the anthologies arranged chronologically or geographically fail on both counts.

Here perhaps is the best place also to register a protest against one of the commonest practices in the anthologies, to which we have several times alluded, namely the reserving of the eleventh- and twelfth-grade volumes for, respectively, American and English literature. It is understandable why most editors and many teachers think that there must be provision in the high school literature courses for the treatment of these two national literatures as distinctive bodies of material deserving of chronological study within their geographical contexts. Our objection is not, however, to this purpose but rather to the effect that the practice has upon literary study in the entire four years of high school. In essence, this effect is one of downgrading the anthologies. Reserving much of the best American and English literature for the last two years because it is needed to fill out such chronological units as "The Romantic Revolt," "The Elizabethan Age," and "The Flowering of New England" results in the impoverishment of the anthologies for the ninth and tenth grades, which are consequently filled with many pieces that are "timely," "entertaining," "appealing to adolescent interests," but of dubious literary merit.

Another result of this practice is that much simple literature, more suitable by its intellectual and emotional appeal for freshmen and sophomores than for juniors and seniors, turns up in the eleventh and twelfth grades simply because it happens to have been written by historically important American or English authors. All of these pieces would probably be more congenial to freshmen, who could read them simply as poems and stories that appeal to youthful emotions and comment upon appropriate human concerns.

Still another result of the traditional anthology structure is that certain authors, no matter how important, cannot be included in the books for certain grades because of the accident of their nationality. The principal example is Shakespeare. We were pleased to discover that many teachers require the reading of a Shakespearean play or two in the junior year; but to do so they must go outside their anthology for a text. The eleventh-grade anthologies are forced by their organization to settle for plays of lesser quality because Shakespeare was not an American and because dramatic genius has not been a particular forte of earlier American authors.

Finally, as a result of the present system national literatures are distributed by years, which affects the eleventh-grade volumes particularly and is, we believe, of doubtful merit. It is exemplified in volumes with such titles as *Adventures for Americans, America Today,* and *To Be an American.* The editors were no doubt motivated by laudably patriotic considerations, as is suggested not only by the titles and the internal organization but also by frequent editorial comment; yet an examination of such books shows that they have probably done a disservice to the cause they espouse. It is a sad fact that the volumes making the most obvious show of patriotism in their organization are among the poorest in quality of the eleventh-grade anthologies. By including a high proportion of selections that are clearly inferior and short-lived, they have not presented American literature at its best and thus have removed, or at least diminished, one reason for the young reader to be proud of his national heritage.

This kind of anthology probably reflects also a fallacious theory of the purpose of formal education, resulting from the confusion of ultimate with proximate goals. Reaching proximate goals — for example, equipping students with knowledge, with critical and analytical ability, with responsible habits of mind — is within the school's capacity. The actual attainment of ultimate goals — for example, producing good citizens — is probably beyond its grasp, although it can help to supply reasons why it is desirable to be a good citizen. This is perhaps only a variation on an old adage: although you can lead a horse to water, you cannot make him drink — but you can make him thirsty.

If "excellence in education" [4] is accepted as a reasonable goal — as well it might be — then we would define "excellence" for the English class as consisting of the best literature, respectfully presented, thoughtfully taught, and carefully studied — a proximate goal that is within the reach of both anthology editors and classroom teachers, and one that has value in pointing to ultimate goals, including that of good citizenship.

Two examples will sufficiently illustrate the confusion of goals. *America Today* (PH-11) contains eight units: "America Is Strength," "America Is Ideals," "America Is Neighborliness," "America Is Faith," "America Is Beauty," "America Is Laughter," "America Is Enthusiasm," and "America Is Promises." This colorfully elaborate arrangement (which, the editors go to the trouble of saying, avoids "chauvinism") is implemented as follows: more than one-third of the space is devoted to short stories, most of them slight pieces reprinted from popular magazines and Sunday supplements; more than one-fourth of the space is devoted to miscellaneous nonfiction, almost all of it nonliterary; although a

---

[4] *Report of the San Francisco Curriculum Survey Committee,* p. 7.

few of America's best-known poets are represented, only one-eighth of the pages are allowed both for their poems and for those of the minor poets included; American drama is represented by four lesser plays, three of them short and two of them written for radio and television; 83.5 per cent of all the selections were written since 1900, many of them by contemporary authors, and of the remaining 16.5 per cent representing three centuries of American literature only one piece antedates 1800; in spite of the editors' assertion that each selection included was "written to be complete in itself," more than ten per cent of the pieces are condensed, abridged (in two instances silently), excerpted, or, in one instance, expurgated (silently). This, we think, does not reflect a culture in which a thoughtful American can take much pride. Two comments suggest themselves: the grand promise of the organization is not fulfilled by the meager contents; and the unit titles themselves suggest that America is a *fait accompli* rather than a "land of opportunity," where what is congenial is not so much vigorous endeavor as an attitude of relaxed complacency.

The second example, for which we go outside the organization of the anthologies, is closely related to the second comment made just above. We refer to the covers of the books, which, as we have already remarked, are in some instances quite gaudy. Several of these bear colored illustrations, often of Americans at play. One might well ask what is the relevance of these recreational activities for the study of literature. Our criticism, however, touches a still more important issue, as can be seen when we compare these covers with those on some of the twelfth-grade volumes of English literature: the sovereign riding in the royal coach (ABC-12), the guards at Buckingham Palace (Gn-12), the Houses of Parliament (HBM-12), the queen on her throne (HBO-12). The difference, of course, is in the symbolism. Whereas Americans are shown as leading a carefree country-club existence, the English

are represented by traditional symbols of their national greatness.[5] This contrast is striking to say the least.

Since anthologies for the eleventh and twelfth grades have
long been reserved for American and English literatures, the solution of this problem will not be easy, for tradition dies hard, and
there are, as we have said, telling arguments for the discrete treatment of national literatures, particularly of one's own native
literature. Yet the opposing arguments are perhaps even more
compelling. A possible compromise would be to assign literary
selections to the four volumes regardless of the nationality of
their authors, making certain only that everything admitted is
first-rate and that simpler pieces are put in the earlier years and
the more complex ones in the later years. Then, for students who,
it is thought, should acquire some knowledge of American and
English literary history,[6] a small supplementary volume could be

---

[5] It is only fair to add that many of the anthologies avoid this exhibi-
tionism on their covers. America is also represented by a desert scene (HBM-
11), an eagle (HBO-11), a cattle roundup (HB2-11), a farmer looking at
his fields (Hlt-11). We find nothing objectionable in these except perhaps
the added expense.

The Harcourt, Brace Laureate edition, published since this section was
written, has eliminated entirely the illustrated covers for all volumes for
grades nine through twelve. While to other eyes this practice may seem to
be an example of retrogression in cover design, we prefer to regard it hopefully as an admirable re-emphasis of the fact that the inside, not the outside,
of a book is what really counts. We would rejoice even more if we could
believe that Harcourt, Brace's example forecasts the beginning of a trend.

[6] These would presumably be college-preparatory students. It is necessary
to add, however, that few, if any, colleges require of their entrants anything
like a systematic knowledge of literary history. The following statement, endorsed by sixty college and university departments of English in California,
perhaps represents the prevailing view (Quoted from "College Support for
the High School English Teacher: The California Experiment," *College English*, November, 1959, reprinted as NCTE Publication R-23):

> The departments sponsoring this statement are convinced that the study
> of selected masterpieces, contemporary and classical, rather than the
> extended review of English and American literary history, affords the
> best training and develops the best reading habits.

A similar view was recently expressed more or less officially. In an editorial prepared, one which tells its story briefly and without reliance on the clichés that are the stock in trade of many eleventh- and twelfth-grade anthologies. This compromise would not only free the anthologies for literature and the absolutely essential editorial apparatus; it would also bring together to their mutual advantage the history of American literature and the history of the literature in which it has its roots. This sense of relationship,[7] together with the sense of proportion that is likely to accompany it, is generally absent in the traditional anthologies. Although American literature has a history of only three and a half centuries, whereas there are about thirteen centuries of English literature, and although America has yet to produce writers of the stature of Shakespeare, Chaucer, and Milton, the anthologies do not reflect these obvious facts, and in several instances the eleventh-grade volume is the bulkiest in the entire series.

That as much genuine literature of America and England as is now contained in the series could be included if the proposed change were made is, we believe, beyond doubt. We suspect, indeed, that the amount would be greater, not less. The space for

---

in *The English Journal* (December, 1961, p. 638), an NCTE organ, appeared the following statement:

> . . . curriculum patterns in literature need serious attention. . . . For example, why are so many schools sticking to a chronological survey of American and British literature in the eleventh and twelfth grades? Though the pattern was handed down from the colleges, most of them, ironically, have now abandoned it in elementary courses. . . . Are we teaching literature or are we teaching anthologies?

[7] Edward Tyrrel Channing's Phi Beta Kappa oration of 1818, "Literary Independence," the manuscript of which was only recently discovered in the Library of Congress by Professor Richard Beale Davis, has this wholesome and still timely advice for editors and English teachers (first printed in *The Key Reporter,* Vol. XXVI, No. 3, Spring, 1961):

> Let no American ever measure his patriotism by the zeal with which he disclaims all dependence on English minds — he might as well cut himself off from the purest, warmest sympathies; snap the costliest bonds of affection; separate himself from man to prove his solitary independence.

it would be available if the present huge bulk of nonliterary material were abandoned. A look at the present situation is provided by the following summary, which indicates the distribution of the contents of all the anthologies according to nationality of author.

DISTRIBUTION OF CONTENTS ACCORDING TO NATIONALITY OF AUTHOR
(in percentages)

Grade	American	English	Foreign (in translation)	Classical (Greek and Roman)
Ninth	75.6	15.6	7.9	0.9
Tenth	71.4	18.0	8.6	2.0
Eleventh	98.4	0.4	1.2	0.0
Twelfth	9.4	68.8	19.6	2.2
All volumes	59.6	29.2	10.0	1.2

The high concentration of American literature in eleventh-grade volumes and of English literature in twelfth-grade volumes (the latter somewhat reduced because some series now devote their final volumes to World literature) is the natural consequence of the chronological and geographical organization in the last two years. It might seem that American literature receives a heavy emphasis also in the first two years; however, much of the material represented by the above percentages for those years is, as we have shown, nonliterary in character. We saw earlier that the selections classed as "miscellaneous nonfiction" constitute a large percentage of the contents in ninth- and tenth-grade volumes. Almost all of this material is by American authors and hence is included in the high percentages for those years in the above summary. Also included in these figures are the many slight poems, stories, and plays previously noted, which are best characterized not as nonliterary but as second-rate. Thus, in spite of the percentages, the *literature* of America does not fare as well as it should. Much of what has been said about American literature also applies to English literature.

Indeed, the whole matter of "coverage," as it is customarily called by the editors, is in need of re-examination. The "coverage" of American and English *literature,* as we have seen, is inadequate. Furthermore, if we assume that it is part of the English teacher's responsibility to teach literature in translation — as most teachers apparently believe — then, in spite of the editors' assertions in their prefaces (especially to ninth- and tenth-grade volumes) that they have adequately represented both native and foreign literature, it is evident from the above summary that anthologists have provided relatively little opportunity for the teacher to discharge that responsibility. Their assertion that they have adequately represented both contemporary and older literature is also controverted by the facts, as is shown in the following distribution.

DISTRIBUTION OF CONTENTS ACCORDING TO DATE
(in percentages)

Grade	Pre-Twentieth Century	Twentieth Century
Ninth	24.6	75.4
Tenth	26.6	73.4
Eleventh	47.2	52.8
Twelfth	65.0	35.0
All volumes	44.7	55.3

That three-quarters of the contents of ninth- and tenth-grade volumes have been chosen from the writings of the past sixty years and only one-quarter from all the earlier centuries would hardly lead one to conclude that "all literature is adequately represented." Even in eleventh-grade volumes, which are heavily oriented toward the historical approach, all literature written before 1900 gets less than half the space. The facts of coverage according to date are actually more one-sided than the figures in the above table suggest, for the bulk of pre-twentieth century literature appearing in the anthologies is from the nineteenth century. Thus, all literature written before 1800 is very meagerly represented except in a few of the volumes for the eleventh and twelfth grades.

The concentration in the last two years of such older literature as is included and its virtual absence in the two earlier years seem to us also to have several bad effects, some of which are comparable to those already pointed out as deriving from the concentration of American and English literature in the junior and senior years. In addition, an acquaintance with "Our Cultural Heritage" (another purpose mentioned by several of the editors) remains little more than a promise when the anthologies for half the high school course in literature almost completely ignore all literature old enough to have become part of anyone's heritage. As the acquaintance with this heritage diminishes, to the same extent is weakened an important common bond among men and an important aid to their self-improvement. As Sir Richard Livingstone once remarked, "To know one's age, and nothing else, is useless. We must be able to criticize and judge it. . . . Otherwise we risk being captives of our own day and slaves to its attendant delusions." A superintendent of schools has recently stated the case in even bleaker terms: "Once our western civilization has lost direct contact with the classics in the arts and in literature, no one will have to destroy it for it will have already been destroyed. . . . There exists the real danger that young moderns of the 'rock 'n roll age' will destroy civilization by simply losing contact with that portion of the past which has proven its greatness." [8]

That the anthologies now de-emphasize literature written before 1900 is a self-evident fact.[9] That much great and usable lit-

---

[8] William H. Fisher, Superintendent of Schools, Las Vegas, New Mexico, as quoted in *The CBE Bulletin*, May, 1961, p. 10.

[9] Without intending to single out the Harcourt, Brace series as any worse than others in this respect, we cite them to indicate what seems to be a

erature of various countries and earlier periods is entirely omitted is also a self-evident fact. That the anthologies nevertheless find the space for large quantities of writing that is mediocre, trivial, or dated is, we believe, yet another self-evident fact. In our opinion, the reasons for these facts are: (1) the adoption of faulty criteria by which to select the materials to anthologize, and (2) the restrictive and enervating effect of many of the schemes of arrangement by which the anthologies are organized. Because these two reasons are interrelated, we include here in our observations on organization and coverage some comments on criteria of selection also. These matters can best be discussed in terms of the most-used of all arrangements — the topical.

TOPICAL ARRANGEMENT

Chronological and topical organizations differ strikingly in a very important practical respect: it is virtually impossible to produce a chronologically arranged anthology that does not contain a considerable body of literature; it is not only possible but all too probable that a topically arranged volume will contain little or no literature. In the former, literary texts may be overwhelmed by the machinery of history, but the teacher can detach them from the impedimenta; if the section of modern writings is unduly large, it may contain much chaff along with the grain, but

---

trend in the increasing de-emphasis of earlier literature. The trend can be seen in the following figures:

Edition	Twentieth-Century Selections (per cent)	Pre-Twentieth-Century Selections (per cent)
HBM-9 (1952)	71	29
HBO-9 (1958)	78	22
HBM-10 (1952)	70	30
HBO-10 (1958)	76	24

It should be added that 11 ninth-grade and 8 tenth-grade volumes in other series give even greater attention to twentieth-century writings than do HBO-9 and HBO-10.

for the sections devoted to earlier periods, time will have taken care of the winnowing; if the chronological context does not provide the best setting in which to teach the poem or story or play, the teacher can, albeit with some difficulty, provide another. The important point is that literature is made available and students can see it on the page.

Topical organization, on the other hand, is by its very nature — at least as that nature is revealed in a large number of the anthologies — uncongenial to literature. Typically, the editors speak expansively in their prefaces of "aims," "goals," and "objectives," which may include such noble purposes as introducing students to an "abundance of good literature" and "expanding students' horizons." One may well wonder, however, especially after looking at the tables of contents, whether these statements of purpose are more than some ritualistic formula required of anthologists. The editors are on more familiar ground when they speak of "developing reading skill" and "appealing to students' interests," the two purposes most frequently cited. We have mentioned earlier that there is a misconception of "English" implicit in the former, for every teacher is a teacher of reading, but a *high school English teacher* is primarily a teacher of *the reading of literature*. It is in implementing the latter, however, that the topical organization plays its influential — and usually detrimental — part. "Appealing to students' interests" is by most of the anthologists taken to mean "appealing to students' *present* interests," particularly as these have been determined by educational "research" (that is, by questionnaires on which students register their "likes" and "dislikes"). At the same time the ability of real literature to *create* interest and the capacities of teachers to stimulate their students to *find* interests and to *become* interested in what may not have appealed to them earlier are vastly underrated. In short, the topically arranged anthology shows little confidence in either literature or teachers.

As might be expected, the topical units appearing most frequently in the anthologies are those dealing directly with adolescence and its problems: the family, getting along with others, growing up, dating and romance, sports, vocations. A large number also deal with science and natural history: the space age, transportation and communication, the atom, the sea, animals. In other words, topical units are more likely to be drawn from the social sciences and the natural sciences than from the oldest and most relevant discipline — the humanities. It is for this reason, perhaps more than for any other, that many anthologies have lost their character as "English" books and put literature in a subordinate position.

The emphasis reflected by topics dealing with the natural and social sciences is, in our opinion, faulty. It is faulty first of all because it is based upon an improper view of the function of literature — what may be called the bibliotherapeutic view. That literature can have a powerful influence upon mankind has been believed by a long line of men who have thought deeply on the subject — among many others, Plato, Quintilian, Xenophon, Horace, Vergil, Sidney, Spenser, Pope, Addison, Johnson, Wordsworth, Shelley, De Quincey, and Arnold. But literature cannot be prescribed; it is not a remedial specific like a doctor's prescription. Its potency derives from both its rational and its irrational components, including an indefinable one called "art," and the accurate diagnosis of social and psychological ills for treatment by bibliotherapy is merely a presumption. In other words, virtue — whether social or personal — is not inculcated by teaching it *directly*, and literature, when it succeeds in influencing mankind, does so through its persuasive eloquence.[10] Neither does literature

---

[10] This point was recently made by a sociologist, Harvard Professor George Caspar, during a symposium sponsored by the American Council of Learned Societies on the subject, "The Relationship Between the Humanities and the Social Sciences" (ACLS *Newsletter*, March, 1961, p. 5):

deal primarily with man as a social animal but with particular men as unique and many-faceted beings. Even a poem like Whittier's *Snow-Bound* is not so much about a family and its "togetherness" as it is about the unique characteristics of its individual members and especially about the reminiscing narrator. In short, literature does not treat sociological topics specifically. These are properly the concerns of textbooks in sociology, anthropology, vocational guidance, and home economics rather than those of literary anthologies, for a work of literature is not a social tract.

Topical units drawn from the natural sciences are removed even farther from the province of literature. Except perhaps for the subgenre called science fiction, literature is not *about* science. When the writer draws upon science, he may do so in one of several ways. His characters may be scientists, as in the novels of C. P. Snow, but they are first of all human beings who must solve their particular problems. He may find in science a source of metaphoric language (for example, John Donne's famous compasses), or he may anthropomorphize the scientific object (for example, Emily Dickinson's railway train), or he may show its effect upon human beings (for example, Thomas Hood's sweatshop). But one would hardly put "A Valediction: Forbidding Mourning," "I Like to See It Lap the Miles," and "The Song of the Shirt" into topical units titled, respectively, "Scientific Inven-

---

. . . between the social sciences and certain of the humanities a clear line can indeed be drawn. That is the line between the sciences on the one side and the arts on the other. . . . Literature is certainly trying to tell the truth about man, but it is rather obviously not trying to do it by methods characteristically scientific. Nor is it just trying to tell the truth. What literature can do is to . . . persuade us . . . of what man is capable of, ought to be capable of, and ought not to be capable of. Just because it is art and not science, literature can persuade us . . . what the values themselves ought to be. And for this reason great literature is precious. . . . All it can do is offer us a choice and be eloquent. But in its eloquence it has all the advantages over a science.

tions," "Transportation," and "Manufacture." That the anthologist do not often make such ridiculous assignments of literature suggests that it does not lend itself to organization under scientific topics. In short, literature does not treat scientific topics specifically. These are properly the concerns of textbooks in aeronautics, zoology, oceanography, engineering, physics, chemistry, and astronomy rather than of literary anthologies, for a work of literature is not a scientific treatise.

There is an additional reason why, in our opinion, anthologists are misled when they attempt to capitalize on the prestige of the natural sciences. Science thrives upon discovery and change, and what is believed today may be disproved tomorrow. A scientific "truth," as the scientists themselves say, is merely the explanation that will account for all presently known and conjectured properties or manifestations of matter (or non-matter!) under study. Nothing could be more remote from literature, which attempts to arrive at permanent truths that have their origin, not in the world of nature, but in the heart and spirit of man. Furthermore, organization of the anthologies by scientific topics actually may perform a disservice to science itself. These topical units make demands that are best met by factual and informative prose written on a technologically simple level, so that it is within the grasp of most high school students. The technological complexities must, of course, be supplied by classes and textbooks in the sciences. But in addition to technological knowledge, probably the most important faculty of the future scientist, which is also the one that literature can help to develop, is imagination. We firmly believe that, not the pieces that largely make up the topical units involving sociology or science, but great and challenging literature — for example, the plays of Shakespeare, the poetry of Chaucer, Donne, Milton, Blake, and Keats, the novels of Fielding, Austen, Dickens, Dostoevski, Hawthorne, and Melville — are the best whetstones of the imagination that textbooks for English classes can supply.

Not only is the theory that lies behind the topical organization of many of the anthologies faulty; the practical results of its application may be defective. These results are chiefly of three kinds: the literature that is included may be forced into topical units that misapply or misinterpret its meaning; almost all literature written before the present is likely to be omitted; literature may be displaced by nonliterary material. The following examples will serve to illustrate the first of these. Tennyson's "Break, Break, Break" and Psalm 107, among other selections, are placed by ABC-10 under the heading "the Briny World," a designation that ignores the human qualities stressed in the two poems: grief, fear, piety, the sense of inadequacy. In Hlt-10, Shakespeare's "O Mistress Mine" appears in a unit titled "The Social Swing," an assignment that both slights the intrinsic nature of the song and ignores its context in *Twelfth Night,* where Sir Andrew, when given a choice, specifically requests Feste to sing of love, for, as he says, "I care not for good life." The classification of Dickens's "A Christmas Carol" in Ldw-9 as a story of "Home Life" leaves little room for either its chief character or its central meaning. One of the strangest selections in the unit, "America Is Neighborliness," in PH-11 is Shirley Jackson's short story, "The Lottery," whose characters must surely be among the most unneighborly neighbors to be found in literature! It may be evident from even these few examples that editors are inclined to organize literature into topical units by its accidents rather than by its substance.

The second result named above, that topical organization discourages the inclusion of older literature, is readily documented, as can be seen from Tables XXXII and XXXIII of Appendix A. This table lists all anthologies in which three-fourths or more of the selections are from the twentieth century.

The correlation between topical organization and proportion of recent literature is obviously very high. Even the few exceptions are more apparent than real. The geographical organization of PH-12 is at times ambiguous, as we have already noted, and might almost as well be classified as topical. In the mixed orders indicated for ABC-9 and HBO-9 there are more topical units than any other kind. Although the main divisions in HB2-12, Sgr-10, and HBO-10 are typological, the subdivisions — which provide the actual teaching units — are predominantly topical. In contrast, the volumes arranged chiefly or entirely by literary genres average about 63 per cent twentieth-century selections (the range is from 51 per cent for Irq-10 to 70 per cent for HB9-10), and those organized chronologically average about 35 per cent twentieth-century selections (the range is from 14 per cent for RM-12 to 51 per cent for HBM-11).

To illustrate the third result is difficult only because the evidence is so copious. Unit after unit in the anthologies, whether social or scientific, contains nothing at all by those whom we have called standard authors and very little else that can be called literature. Units like "Let's Explore Careers!" "Seeing Your Parents' Side," "Stepping Out," "Exploring with the Scientist," and "Our Electronic World," to name only some of the more obvious examples, are in themselves incompatible with literature. Not literary writers but social and natural scientists are the ones directly concerned with these topics. To be sure, we have heard of a professor of education who interpreted *Hamlet* for a group of prospective English teachers as a lesson in "Growing Up," and some teachers apparently have tried to make *Romeo and Juliet* serve as a source book on family problems.[11] However, we would like to

---

[11] Cf. G. W. Stone, Jr., "Cooperative English Program Notes," PMLA, LXXVI (May, 1961), viii:

Our hope is that throughout the school system those professing to teach English will think constantly of the unique contribution which English

think that such teachers are few, and we feel rather confident that in these plays Shakespeare was not writing about either adolescent psychology or "Family Living." Unfortunately, however, many of the anthologies encourage just such perversions of literature. But since even the most social- or scientific-minded anthologist soon realizes that the opportunities for this kind of interpretation of literature are not endless, he resorts to one of two expedients. He creates a topical unit whose title is so broad as to admit almost anything; for example, "The World of People" (ABC-10), "Facing Problems" (HBM-9), "The Art of Living" (HBO-10), "By Their Deeds" (Hlt-12), "People Are Important" (HM-9), "People and Problems" (SF2-9). (One might well ask whether literature could possibly be about anything else!) Or, he fills out his units with magazine articles and excerpts from books that are directly concerned with sociological and scientific matters.

It must be acknowledged that not all topical units in the anthologies are entirely deficient in literature, and that there are some which do include several significant literary pieces. On the other hand, there are many that contain no literature at all. Judging by the results, we must conclude that topical organization is, of all presently used arrangements, the least appropriate for high school anthologies of literature. Nor are its mistreatment and neglect of literature *as literature* its only shortcomings; even for the intended social values it seems inadequate. So far as the organization is concerned, the topical order is the anthologies' counter-

---

as English (not as a handmaid of the social science) can make to the minds and imaginations of students. The aesthetic impact of *Romeo and Juliet* as a play will differ for different persons and for different ages, but students might well be introduced to it as a play — with all the tensions that are built up and released, with all the impact which the language has for character revelation, plot movement, and aesthetic charge. To view it as the basis for exploration of family problems, father and daughter relationships, mother love, teen-age romance, and nursing seems to us to be utterly removed from the purpose of the art of drama.

part of the advice held out by some educators — "speak to youth in its own language" — which is a corollary of the well-worn command, "reach the student where he is." However, the incongruity of the speaker and his language when he affects the style of his hearer is likely to invoke merely the latter's ridicule. Or, as the teen-ager might express it (or might have expressed it — the terms are out-of-date almost at once), the adult's attempt not to be a "square" is in itself "square." [12] Adolescents expect adults to speak like adults, not like adolescents, if for no other reason than their resentment at outsiders invading their premises. The editor who tailors literature to fit adolescent problems is doing something not greatly different and thus runs the same risk of ridicule — of himself and of literature. Also, such tailoring of literature is largely ineffectual, for it smacks of preachment. Youth can surely see through the pretense of passing off social instruction as "enjoyment" or "appreciation" or "adventure." Finally, it is self-defeating. The derivation of "education" indicates that it means "leading out," but the constant parading of adolescents in front of themselves seems merely narcissistic. A proper role of education, including that part of it represented by the anthologies, is to help the student profit from adolescence as he grows through it and to make sure that he leaves it behind when he outgrows it. St. Paul's famous remark puts the case succinctly: "When I was a child, I spoke like a child, I thought like a child, I reasoned like a child; when I became a man, I gave up childish ways." (1 Cor. 13:11.) Topical organization, because it tends to be incongruous, ineffectual, nonhumanistic, and self-defeating, is, then, inappropriate for an anthology of literature — even if its contents are intended for the lesser purpose of *socializing* its readers.

---

[12] This matter is admirably treated by Edwin H. Sauer in *English in the Secondary School* (New York: Holt, Rinehart and Winston, 1961), p. 102ff.

TYPOLOGICAL ARRANGEMENT

The organization of units according to genres or types is, along with the chronological and the topical, one of the most frequently used methods. It is perhaps the best for determining the order of *printing* (not necessarily of *teaching*) literary texts. It can almost automatically exclude nonliterary material if the genres chosen for representation are limited to prose fiction, the essay, the poem, and the drama. It demands relatively little editorial machinery, and what is included can be made directly relevant to literature and literary purposes. Since most genres have a long history, the inclusion of earlier literature is encouraged. It can be used to embrace the literature of one nation or of many. Because most literary figures likely to be studied in high school have written their best work in a single genre, it allows for some internal organization by author. Of all the ways of organizing anthologies it is probably the least subject to arbitrary manipulation, for the form of several of the genres is self-evident. Perhaps its greatest advantage is its flexibility, which enables the teacher to reorganize the contents — for example, thematically — without either doing an injustice to the literature or foregoing the particular virtues that the editors have built into their volume.

Abuses of the typological order are of course possible, but they are relatively few. The abuse that is most damaging — as it is also in an anthology organized in any other way — is the one already mentioned: the inclusion of inferior pieces and the expansion of sections devoted primarily to nonliterary types. It is significant that volumes having a high percentage of nonliterature are usually those containing one or more typological units made up of miscellaneous nonfiction. As we have seen, as much as half the contents of some volumes belong in this category, and the average for all volumes is almost 25 per cent. The literary character of anthologies arranged typologically could be enhanced simply by the deletion of such units, an improvement that could be made more easily in them than in anthologies organized in other ways. Teachers who believe in the primacy of literature in English classes find it relatively easy to ignore these units or to use them only as "free" reading. The best solution, we believe, is to restrict the anthologies to the genres that are most likely to be represented by unequivocally literary selections (poem, essay, short story, and — if length is not an obstacle — drama and novel) and to leave to the discretion of the teacher the assignment or encouragement of *supplementary* reading in nonfiction (preferably entire works instead of the excerpts and condensations upon which the anthologies depend), guided by the knowledge of individual students that is available to teachers but not to anthologists.

The second abuse of typological organization is of fundamental importance to the organization itself, which it tends to destroy. This is the mistyping of the selections included. Generic distinctions are highly useful in literary study and indispensable to critical facility. For the students' sake, it also seems especially important in this scientific age to be exact wherever exactness is possible. To misclassify descriptive sketches, journalistic articles, factual narratives, and excerpts from biographies as "essays," and excerpts from novels or books of nonfiction as "short stories" is to deprive these terms of their usefulness, to confuse the students by blurring distinctions, and to mislead them into believing that all literary discriminations are hopelessly arbitrary and subjective. Probably the most curious instance of such misclassification which we have found appears in ABC-11; an excerpt from Thomas Wolfe's long prose work, *You Can't Go Home Again,* is printed to appear as a poem and classified in the table of contents as an essay, so that *three* genres are confused. The commonest kind of mistyping is, however, the naming of almost anything a "story."

The third abuse to which anthologies arranged by genre are

subject is the inclusion of editorial machinery that does not keep in steady focus the chief purposes of literary study. The unduly elaborate treatments of minor critical matters are of this kind, and the *excessive* attention to the scanning of poetry, which tends to make of literary pieces joyless corpses for dissection. (Incidentally, the kind of scanning described in the anthologies is quite mechanical and shows no awareness of recent developments in phonology.) Of this kind also is the introduction to a typological unit that discusses the history of a genre but says little about its characteristics and gives the student no advice on how to gain some mastery over the form.

These abuses of the typologically arranged anthology are easily enough avoided. Unlike those which are found in a volume arranged chronologically, geographically, or topically, they do not permeate the whole book. Although the anthologist who adopts this organization is as much committed to it as is he who adopts one of the other arrangements, he is unlikely to subordinate literature to its history or place of origin and, most important, as long as he stays with the clearly literary genres, he is less likely to include nonliterary pieces. In short, it is possible, indeed quite easy, to keep peripheral matters in a secondary position and the literature itself central.

ORGANIZATION BY RELATIVE DIFFICULTY

There is one other order that should be mentioned. It is not self-evident, for unlike those already discussed, it is not indicated by unit titles and may exist alongside any of the others. This is the order of difficulty — that is, the arrangement of selections so that the simpler pieces precede those that are more complex and the student is steadily challenged to develop his skill as a reader. This order is important within a single volume, but it is more important within an entire series. It is of practical concern to both teacher and students, although it is of course not unique to the study of literature. It is the basis upon which "reading ladders" and "developmental reading" programs are built, and depends in some degree upon quantitative measurement (for example, word-frequency and length of sentences), although some elements required for its application (for example, degrees of intellectual and emotional complexity) are not subject to precise quantification. It is the one order that nearly all the anthologists mention in their prefaces, usually with emphasis. It is also the order that we have found to be least consistently maintained in the anthologies, especially when all the volumes in a series are considered together.

Some volumes for the ninth and tenth grades begin with the short story, probably the easiest genre for the inexperienced reader, and end with a novel (perhaps troublesome chiefly because of its length) or a play, which is likely to be difficult for most students because it demands a particular kind of intellectual reconstruction. Volumes of this nature (for example, HBM-9, Irq-9, Ldw-9, McM-9, SF-9) show some degree of progression in complexity. A larger number (for example, ABC-9, Gn-9, HB2-9, Hth-9, HM-9, Lipp-9, PH-9, Sgr-9) show little or no progression, the pieces coming near the end of the volumes being approximately of the same degree of difficulty as are those at the beginning. In volumes of the latter group, a real sequential program of reading, one that proceeds from the easier to the more demanding, has apparently been thwarted by the presence of another kind of arrangement, the ubiquitous topical organization.

When entire series instead of single volumes are considered, the lack of progression is at least equally evident. The amount of space given to the short story, for example, remains relatively constant through the four grade levels, and the stories selected for eleventh- and twelfth-grade anthologies, like those in the volumes for the two earlier years, are chiefly of the easily read commercial-formula variety. The drama furnishes another kind of evidence. Although one of the most demanding of literary types, the attention given to it year by year fluctuates in a curious way: Ninth grade, 9 per cent; Tenth grade, 16 per cent; Eleventh grade, 9 per cent; Twelfth grade, 19 per cent. These figures suggest that, not the degree of complexity and difficulty but other factors — especially the topical arrangement of ninth- and tenth-grade volumes and the geographical limitations placed on those for the two later years — have determined the contents and have thereby in varying degrees vitiated the progressional character of the series. The table indicating that 393 poems have been assigned to various levels by the different editors lends further support to this conclusion. We have also noted earlier in this chapter that simple and even slight poetry is frequently included for the later years. As additional evidence we include the following summary showing the distribution of selected short stories in the anthologies according to grade levels.

DISTRIBUTION OF SELECTED SHORT STORIES

Short Stories	Assigned Grade Levels	
The Outcasts of Poker Flat	ABC-9	Gn-11
The Devil and Daniel Webster	Gn-9	ABC-11
The Open Window	Hlt-9	SF-12
The Tell-Tale Heart	SF-9	Hlt-11
Sixteen	Lipp-9	HBM-11
The Silver Mine	HBM-9	Lipp-12
To Build a Fire	Gn-9	Sgr-11
The Split Cherry Tree	Sgr-9	Gn-11
Bill	SF2-9	ABC-11
The Jumping Frog	ABC-9	SF-11
The Snob	HB2-9	Hlt-12
All Yankees Are Liars	Hlt-9	HBO-12

The evidence of such contradictory conclusions reached by the editors as is indicated in each of the pairs in the summary suggests either that progressive difficulty is often inoperative as a criterion for the arrangement of selections or that editorial judgments in this respect cannot be trusted. Neither can it be concluded that one series is consistently "easier" than another, maintaining a sequential program but beginning somewhat lower on the scale of difficulty, for one team of editors that selected the stories in each of the pairs found one story easier and one more difficult than did their counterparts for the other series. In the last two pairs, the contradiction in judgment is even more remarkable since both first- and second-track series are involved. From the evidence noted, which merely represents the variety and quantity that could readily be adduced, it is apparent that the series of anthologies do not supply by themselves a sequential program of readings, and that the well prepared and widely read teacher is still needed to pick and choose among their multifarious contents.

The remaining ways in which anthologies are organized require less comment, among other reasons because they are less widely used. The arrangement of pieces by their moods cannot go far in organizing volumes since its potentialities are severely restricted, and in any case it seems wasteful. This order would be helpful if, for example, one's purpose were to identify the sources of the comic or to characterize national humor, but such purposes are more sociological than literary and pose philosophical problems that most high school students are not yet ready to attempt. At the same time, this kind of arrangement blocks a useful avenue to literary study. By associating pieces that have some *other* element in common — for example, their thematic statement — but *differ* in mood, the teacher has at hand a supply of related selections with which to reach students of different temperaments and motivations while illustrating the variety of approaches that writers use in their literary treatments of similar matters. Thus, to associate Ogden Nash's "Kindly Unhitch That

Star, Buddy" (which appears in three anthologies) with plays, stories, and poems that deal with human ambitions in a variety of ways would provide teacher and students with a greater number of significant and literarily relevant points of comparison to discuss and write about than would its inclusion in a unit on humor.

Of the several organizational plans we have discussed, the thematic organization, although little used in the anthologies, is potentially the best of all arrangements, for it exploits the very stuff of literature in the construction of the framework. Thus, it brings literary pieces together, with a minimum of editorial machinery standing in the way, for whatever benefits can be derived from their close association. However, it is, as we have shown, subject to abuse — perhaps more so than is any other. It can readily encourage the teaching of the themes instead of the literature. In the hands of an ill prepared and poorly read teacher, it can lead to critical license and the violent perversion of literary pieces. If it is mechanically followed in the classroom — especially if the theme of each unit is announced in advance — it can be deadly and is likely to make literary study little more than a routine exercise in deduction. It therefore requires a teacher of superior ability and well-developed critical powers. Of editors it also makes huge demands: a widely ranging, detailed, and intimate acquaintance with literature and the ability to detect its subtlest discriminations and nuances. Furthermore, since thematic interpretation depends so fully upon particular contexts and even upon the temperament of the interpreter (note that after 360 years there is still room for perceptive readers to argue about the meaning of *Hamlet*), it is highly unlikely that a generally acceptable anthology arranged entirely by themes could be produced. For the teacher who can profitably teach literature in a thematic arrangement for the potentially great benefits that it can contribute, perhaps the best that editors can provide is an anthology with enough flexibility, in whatever arrangement it uses, to allow such a teacher to reorganize the contents thematically according to his own best lights.

RECOMMENDATIONS

1. We recommend that topical organization and topical units be abandoned by the anthologies. We have found no topical unit that is entirely acceptable and many that are wholly unacceptable. The temptation to include pieces because they "fit" rather than because they are literary appears to be too great to resist. As a consequence, the study of literature, although a long-respected discipline, has lost curricular status.

2. We recommend that the contents of anthologies for all four years be arranged according to their literary genres. Although we are not convinced that this method of organizing the contents necessarily provides the best possible order for teaching them, it is the arrangement least likely to do them an injustice and is a sufficiently flexible plan to allow the individual teacher to design his own program.

3. We recommend that the traditional assignment of American and English literatures to the eleventh- and twelfth-grade volumes be discarded as unduly restrictive, and that instead the best of American and English literature be more evenly distributed over the four years.

4. We recommend that comprehensive experiments be conducted with the thematic method of organizing literary programs.[13]

5. We recommend that editorial apparatus having as its main purpose the support of the arrangement itself be made as unobtrusive as possible.

---

[13] In *Dialogues on the Teaching of Literature* we strongly recommend the thematic arrangement of literature and attempt to show in some detail how it might be worked out.

CHAPTER 4

Editorial Apparatus

No ONE can leaf through the anthologies without being aware of the amount of space devoted to the editorial apparatus within the volumes. In quantity this space extends from the generous to the overwhelming. The apparatus itself, we believe, ranges in importance from the trivial and irrelevant to the most essential, and in quality from the erroneous to the most scholarly. The facts are shown in Table XXXV of Appendix A, where only the volumes in series are included, although for comparison we have made similar counts for a sampling of anthologies not in the three- and four-volume series. To represent these we have chosen SF2-9, HM-9, and Irq-9, the corresponding figures for which are introduced whenever relevant. Except for two columns (15 and 17) which list percentages, Table XXXV presents the total number of pages devoted to each kind of apparatus in each volume and in each series. In order to discover exactly how much space is devoted to the apparatus and how much to the selections, we have counted fractional as well as whole pages. Therefore, a volume shown in the table as having seven pages of pictures may have seven full-page plates, a larger number of illustrations that are less than full-page size, or a combination of full-page and fractional page illustrations, but in any case occupying an amount of space equal to seven full pages in that particular volume. Because of the collage-like appearance of many of the volumes, a meaningful count of pages devoted to the editorial machinery could be obtained only in this way.

The tables of contents range in size and format from the brief and unadorned (Gn, Hlt, Ldw, Lipp, McM, RM) to the very elaborate (ABC, PH). The tables of contents in ABC are, in effect, doubled, for the pages containing titles and pagination are followed by another set of pages containing pictures and captions that refer to the various divisions of the volumes. Other preliminaries in the anthologies (column 2) include prefaces (usually brief), acknowledgments, and introductions. Most notable among the introductions are the "Color Sections" in HBM, the heavily illustrated articles by present-day writers in HBO, and the pages in PH-10 containing color photographs of high school students which accompany several poems written by them.

Under the heading "Body" in Table XXXV are two columns of figures pertaining to the organization[1] of the books ("Unit Introductions" and "Unit Follow-ups") and two similarly labeled columns pertaining to the individual selections. Unit introductions (column 3) are relatively brief in topically arranged volumes, usually containing from a paragraph to three pages of editorial prose about the topic and a drawing or photograph, often in color. These volumes vary greatly in the elaborateness of their unit introductions. The typologically arranged volumes have somewhat longer unit introductions, which ordinarily contain an account of the history of the genre, occasionally make suggestions for reading the selections (for example, HBM and HBO), and sometimes reproduce portraits of the principal writers in the genre. Longest of all are the introductions to the units in chronologically arranged volumes. These are made up of "background material"

---

[1] Tables XXX to XXXIII of Appendix A, identifying the kinds of organization in the various anthologies may be helpful to the reader of this paragraph.

about the politics, the social conditions, the principal events, and the literary history of the periods, and commonly are lavishly illustrated (among other, Gn-11, HBM-12, HBO-10, RM-12, SF-11, Sgr-12). These introductions often contain maps, charts, and tables of dates, as well as photographs and drawings representing the times.

In most volumes the "Unit Follow-ups" or "postviews" (column 4) are shorter than are the introductions to units. The chief elements to be found here are review questions for the entire unit, a list of "activities," and a bibliography of suggested additional readings. Bibliographies are present in most of the volumes. Two series, Gn and Lipp, have no review questions or activities, although the latter has a series of "Unit Tests" in an appendix.

The introductory matter to individual selections (column 5) may consist of a headnote on the topic or circumstances of the selection, a biographical sketch of the author, a portrait of the author, an identification of the source if the selection is an excerpt, or some combination of these. A few volumes (for example, Hlt-9, RM-10, SF-10, and the entire Lipp series) give very little space to such headnotes, but others, particularly the books for the eleventh and twelfth grades, give the introductory material a generous amount of space (for example, Gn-12, Ldw-11, Ldw-12, RM-11, and the entire HBM and HBO series).

The material following individual selections (column 6) consists chiefly of study or review questions, suggestions for activities, and vocabulary drills. Less frequently, lists of titles for supplementary reading are included. These are in addition to the similar elements following the units. The series giving the most space to these matters are Hlt, Sgr, ABC, and Gn. Some questions are of the kinds that can be used to promote discussion; however, many others merely test the student's ability to recall what has been read. Of this latter kind the most notable are those in the ABC series, almost all of which are "objective" (matching title and author, multiple choice, etc.). The ABC volumes regularly include "Reading Scoreboards" also, by which the student can determine his reading rate. The average number of suggested activities per volume, whether following units or selections, is 635. The number of questions is even greater.

In column 7 of Table XXXV the figures represent the number of pages given to pictures (photographs, line drawings, engravings, reproductions of paintings, etc.) that are actually inserted in the selections themselves, and that are intended to illustrate. These pictures are in addition to those found in various other parts of the anthologies and accounted for in the figures in columns 1, 2, 3, 5, 8, 13, and occasionally elsewhere. The most lavishly illustrated volumes are those in the SF, HBO, and HB2 series; however, because of the numerous pictures in the introductions, special color sections, and tables of contents, the volumes in the PH, HBM, ABC, Gn, and RM series also give the immediate impression of being heavily illustrated. Pictures illustrating the texts are generally scenes from the stories, plays, poems, and prose nonfiction, and represent the editors' or the artists' conception of characters, incidents, and settings. In several instances the illustrations are photographic — scenes from stage performances, motion pictures, or television programs. In every case the possibility exists that the illustration will influence the reader's understanding, interpretation, or appreciation of the selection that it accompanies. The pictures found elsewhere in the anthologies (and not represented in column 7) are unlikely to have this effect. They are included rather to provide background material, to motivate the student to read, and sometimes (we suspect) merely to add to the colorfulness of the book.

Some of the most recent books use color very heavily, and there has been much experimenting with the effects of colored backgrounds for the letterpress, of bleeding and overprinting and of other typographical techniques. In a few instances apparently there has been an attempt to use colors that correspond with the mood of the selection (for example, in HBO-12 the first witches' scene in Macbeth has white letterpress on a black background). In general, however, one is chiefly impressed by other qualities — the ingenuity of the designers and the lavishness of their product.

The figures in column 8 in Table XXXV represent a variety of items included in some of the anthologies. Among them are jokes and cartoons, discussions of the novel which are not accompanied by selections, a history of the English language, and suggestions for speaking, choral reading, and related matters.

All the volumes contain indexes arranged by author or title or both (column 9), and many have indexes arranged by literary type as well. It should be noted also that the volumes arranged typologically have no need of such an index and that certain other volumes (for example, PH-10 and all those in the Sgr series) have a second table of contents (and therefore are included in column 1), which classifies the selections by literary genre. No anthology contains an index of first lines.

The practice of glossing difficult and unfamiliar words (column 10) varies widely. The SF series includes a glossarial appendix that in both appearance and size resembles a miniature dictionary. The ABC, HB49, HBM, HBO, HB2, Hlt, and Sgr series also append rather extensive glossaries. Most of those that contain no such appendix (Ldw, Lipp, McM, PH) — as well as several that have an appended glossary — use footnotes to explain unfamiliar terms, although in Lipp and PH the glossing is very light. In the Gn series the glossary lists only proper names and critical terms, while footnotes take care of the explication of the text. The glossaries in the HB49, HBM, HBO, and HB2 series have numerous entries which refer the user to one of the vocabulary sections that follow the selections; these series also use footnotes for glossing difficult words and proper names. The glossarial appendix in RM-11 and RM-12 is limited to literary terms. The entries in all the glossaries except those in the RM and Gn series are brief, usually consisting of synonyms or short definitions. Many of the literary terms in RM and Gn are given a paragraph of explanation. In all the glossaries the meanings given are confined to those pertaining to the uses that the words have in the respective volumes. One example will illustrate the practice. In Hlt-11 *creased* is defined only as "grazed (with a bullet)," even though in the commonly used dictionaries at least two or three additional meanings are given for *crease* as a verb. The alternative meanings, often including the primary and commoner meanings, are ignored if they do not apply to the words as used in the anthology. Of the volumes not included in these series, the following are representative: SF2-9, like the SF series, contains a miniature dictionary; the glossary in HM-9 follows the majority practice and resembles those in the ABC, HB, and Hlt series; Irq-9 contains no glossary.

Only eleven volumes in five of the series (ABC, HB49, HBM, Ldw, Sgr) contain an appendix of biographical sketches (column 11). In each instance the sketch is short, usually a paragraph of 100 to 250 words, and limited to the prominent facts of the author's life. Most of the volumes without a biographical appendix include sketches of the authors' lives in the headnotes to selections or in a box inserted in the text (counted in column 5). The biographical appendix apparently is thought to be best suited to volumes that are topically arranged. Only two series contain items that can be listed as "General Review" (column 12). Each volume in the ABC series has a two-page section called "Time for Inventory," consisting of very general questions under such headings as "Comprehension," "Rate of Reading," "Using Source Material," and "Reading and Visualizing." ABC-12 also contains a section titled "Analyzing Your Reading," made up of passages to be read and marginal questions to be answered. All volumes in the Lipp series include an appendix of "Unit Tests" provided in an "A" and a "B" form.

Miscellaneous items included in appendices (column 13) are as follows: chronological tables of dates and historical events; all volumes in the ABC series have maps and charts showing the books' "coverage" of times and places; there are descriptions of the literary genres in RM-10, Sgr-12, and several volumes in the various HB series; there are articles on America in the Modern World in the eleventh-grade volumes of the HB49, HBM, and HBO series; McM-11 and McM-12 contain quite lengthy accounts of literary history in which poems and prose excerpts are interspersed; the SF volumes have brief notes "To the Teacher."

The total number of pages devoted to editorial apparatus (column 14) ranges, in ninth-grade volumes, from a low of 116 (McM) to exactly twice that number (HBO); in the tenth grade from 148 (PH) to 265 (HBO); in the eleventh from 157 (McM) to more than twice that number (HBO); in the twelfth from 151 (McM) to almost three times as many (Gn); and for the series from a low of 578 (McM) to a high of 1281 (HBO).

In percentage of pages devoted to the apparatus, the individual volumes range from a low of 20 per cent (McM-9) to a high of 50 per cent (Gn-12). The volumes not in the above series and chosen as representative show the following proportions: SF2-9, 46 per cent; HM-9, 38 per cent; Irq-9, 27 per cent.

The figures in column 16 of Table XXXV represent the actual number of pages, including fractional pages, that are devoted solely to the texts of poems, short stories, novels, plays, essays, and miscellaneous nonfiction offered as readings for the students. It will be seen that on the average there is one page of editorial apparatus for every two pages of text. Finally, column 18 indicates the total number of pages in each volume and in each series.

The editorial apparatus is, however, not confined to the books which the students see; a great deal more of it is included in the separately published volumes — called, variously, manuals, handbooks, and guidebooks — that are prepared solely for the teacher's use. These contain a wide variety of matter: additional questions and activities, suggestions that teachers may follow in leading class discussions, aids for the teacher in analyzing and evaluating selections, additional vocabulary exercises, answers to the questions in the anthologies, bibliographies, lists of phonograph records, films, and other audio-visual aids, suggestions for guiding the students' responses, suggestions for reading improvement, objective tests on the selections and units, suggested assignments, suggested "snap quizzes," lists of famous passages, "clues for appreciation," suggested "listening experiences," and much additional "background material." This editorial matter is, of course, supplementary to that in the anthologies themselves.

EVALUATION

To evaluate the editorial apparatus in the anthologies we have sought those criteria which are most conducive to the effective teaching and study of literature, most appropriate to the purpose of literature, and most trustworthy in guiding our examination of the vast amount of data. These criteria we have concluded to be the following:

1. *Quantity.* Is there enough (or too much) editorial apparatus? Does it inhibit the teacher from performing in his area of knowledge and competence? Does its bulk tend to overwhelm the literary selections or compete unfairly with them for the available space? Does its quantity invite a lack of discrimination in its application? Is any of it merely waste?

2. *Relevance.* Does the apparatus contribute to the comprehension, analysis, and evaluation of literature? Does it recognize the essential nature of literature as a moral-aesthetic product of the

human mind and spirit or does it make literature a servant of the social studies and the natural sciences? Does it encourage mere busyness or does it stimulate the mind and evoke the imagination?

3. *Tone.* Is the editorial prose appropriate to both literature and students? Is it patronizing, extravagant, precious, dull, pedantic, commonplace, merely clever, sentimental? Is its tone either dogmatic or unduly permissive? Does it have some stylistic quality in its own right? Are the illustrations and editorial comments in harmony with the spirit of the selections and the nature of literature?

4. *Helpfulness.* Does the apparatus give sufficient guidance to the student so that he can perform the tasks required? Does it do much of the student's work for him? Are the demands it makes possible of fulfillment? Does it encourage the misinterpretation of literature? Does it restrict the imagination of the student? Does it challenge him to steadily increasing exertion?

5. *Accuracy.* Are the facts correct? Is the scholarship adequate? Are the questions and suggestions for activities based upon sound critical principles? Do the interpretations and analyses have contextual probability?

We have attempted to apply these criteria to the various elements in the editorial apparatus.

Quantity

At the outset we recognize that some kinds of editorial apparatus are probably indispensable: tables of contents, indexes, either glossaries or explanatory footnotes (although some volumes manage to omit both by including only selections with no difficult words), and acknowledgments. Others may be desirable: introductions to units, lists of questions, some biographical information, and bibliographies of supplementary readings. However, several of these are more appropriate for the manual, where they can be thoughtfully considered by the teacher and selected by him for use with a particular group of students. This latter practice has at least two advantages: it allows the teacher greater freedom of deliberate choice, and it runs no risk of confusing students by confronting them with a mass of editorial matter in which the trivial and the important, the relevant and the irrelevant, the challenging and the patronizing may stand side by side in indiscriminate array. Teachers report that nothing puts students off quite so much as a plethora of editorial equipment; for they are led by it to conclude, understandably, that what is regarded as important are the facts that the introductions contain, the answering of the numerous questions, and the busyness required by the activities, rather than the fullest possible comprehension of the text which they surround. And when the text itself is slight, the student may be as frustrated as the man in the fable who, after removing layer after layer, found nothing at the center of the onion. But whether the full editorial apparatus is incorporated in the anthology or whether some of it is reserved for the manual, it is clearly excessive. An anthology devoting 34 per cent of its space to machinery (the average for all the series) very often has much expensive and unusable bulk, while in many instances, as we have demonstrated in preceding chapters of this report, it may include relatively few selections of enduring quality to which this machinery is applied. The extreme example is SF2-9, a glossy volume of 608 pages which devotes 46 per cent of its space to machinery but contains no selections by authors who are truly great and only a handful by authors of any significance whatsoever. For such, Shakespeare's title makes the most appropriate comment, "Much ado about nothing."

That the editorial machinery is excessive is also suggested by the anthologists' various practices themselves. If, for example, we take the smallest number of pages devoted to each of the items listed in Table XXXV, we see that for ninth- and tenth-grade volumes the space required for the machinery would amount to about 12.5 per cent and in those for the upper years to about 19 per cent, or about 16 per cent for all volumes. Although these figures must be regarded only as rough approximations, that — while modest, they still manage to come to so much — is at least suggestive. Our own conclusion, which we attempt to document in the following pages — as well as that of many teachers who have written to us — is that a large amount of the space given to editorial machinery is simply wasted. We shall go even further. Much of the machinery is harmful as well as wasteful, for it misdirects the student, misrepresents the literature, or acts as a barrier between the two. When the machinery bulks large, it also diminishes the space that is available for the selections.

As examples of waste — a few out of the many that could be cited — the following are notable. All the color sections can hardly be used by teacher or students. Students give them a passing glance, and teachers who regret the omission of selections begrudge the space that they occupy. The introductory essays that replace them in the HBO series (82 pages) are little better. Although charmingly written (by Jesse Stuart, Jessamyn West, Clifton Fadiman, and J. B. Priestley) and luxuriously illustrated, they do hardly more than delay the texts of the selections. Their counterparts in the ABC and PH series are of similar negligible value. The thesis of several of these introductory pieces is that writers find their inspiration everywhere — a not very profound conclusion that, in any case, it might be better to allow students to arrive at inductively.

It will be noted that the HBO series devotes almost three times as much space to this introductory and largely pictorial material as does the HBM series. The examples in the following summary, though drawn from the volumes of only one publisher, will further illustrate this trend to expand the editorial machinery as anthologies are revised, even if to do so requires cutting back the selections.

SHOWING THE EXPANSION OF EDITORIAL APPARATUS
AS ANTHOLOGIES ARE REVISED
(Number of pages)

Selection	HB49	HBM	HBO
Julius Caesar	62	73	82
Macbeth	59	63	70
The Valiant	17	18	21
Silas Marner	122	134	124
Prologue to The Canterbury Tales	13	15	17½

In each instance the expansion is apparently caused by the increase in number or size of the illustrations, in the number of questions and activities following the selection, or in the amount of introductory matter. Although fewer pages are used for *Silas Marner* in HBO-9 than in HBM-9, the text is also shorter, since the latest revision contains a more heavily abridged version of the novel. The lines included from Chaucer's *Prologue* are progressively lessened; although all three editions have 508 lines in a Modern English translation, HB49-12 contains 169 lines in the original Middle English, HBM-12 contains 82 lines, and HBO-12 has 64 lines. Thus, more space is required to present less text, as the editorial apparatus, in this instance in the form of illustrations, continues to expand.

The excessiveness of the machinery may be illustrated in still another way. The text of a short piece, particularly a poem, may be so obscured by the apparatus that it is almost overlooked. For example, in RM-11 a twelve-line excerpt from Masters's *Spoon River Anthology* is preceded by a half-page of introductory matter and followed by another half-page of comments and questions. In Sgr-11, two-thirds of a page is required to contain a four-line poem by Dorothy Parker and the accompanying apparatus. In the volumes of the HBO series and in HM-9, short poems by Sandburg, Frost, Dickinson, Stevenson, Kilmer, and others are almost eclipsed by the brightly colored illustrations. In such instances the poem may become secondary, as if it were a caption for the picture. The pictures, particularly in the HBO series, are often things of beauty and great technical skill; unfortunately, these very qualities tend to make the poems seem even less important to the immature and perhaps reluctant reader. In HBO-12, five pages are devoted to T. S. Eliot, of which one and a half pages are occupied by illustrations and one page by a biographical sketch and other machinery, so that the poems themselves are given only about half the total space. In HBM-12, twenty-seven lines excerpted from *The Faërie Queene* are surrounded by almost two pages of apparatus; in fact, the student is not allowed to read Spenser but instead is offered three isolated stanzas (from one of the longest poems in the English language!) as examples illustrating the editorial comments.

Not only single works but the entire contents of a unit may be overwhelmed by the machinery of the editors; for example, in ABC-12, of the 54 pages given to "The Age of Victoria" almost half (25.5) are devoted to introductory matter, questions, comments, objective tests, a bibliography, "Reading Scoreboards," a chart, and sundry other items (the proportion might have been even greater if this series used pictures to illustrate the texts). In varying degrees excessive apparatus is present in the eleventh- and twelfth-grade volumes of most series. In these anthologies, most of which are chronologically arranged, the extensive editorial equipment places undue emphasis upon the framework, and the selections tend to become mere samples. Even if the purpose of the English course in these grades were the acquisition of a knowledge of literary history, the teacher is virtually compelled by the apparatus to proceed deductively and the students are prevented from the more significant and memorable experience of beginning with the texts and, from them, drawing the evidence that makes for documented conclusions. If, however, the purpose of the English course is to give the students a direct and intimate acquaintance with the literature itself — as we believe it to be — much of the machinery serves only as a barrier. The temptation to include vast quantities of "background material" and to devise a multitude of activities and questions appears to have been almost irresistible, especially in the upper grades, but in some series and single volumes for the ninth- and tenth-grades also. We are therefore pleased to be able to commend those volumes in which the apparatus is kept closer to the essential minimum — Irq-10, in which the machinery is unobtrusive; RM-12, for the restraint shown in its questions and activities; MGH-9 which, as one teacher remarked, has "mercifully little" machinery; and the ABC series for its minimal use of pictures.

On the other hand, anthologies may omit necessary apparatus; the volumes in the Lipp series, for example, provide so little information about the selections that they are left in a vacuum and the student is not provided help in establishing them in context.

Excessive editorial apparatus also results in a lack of discrimination. Several series have numerous questions, as many as ten or fifteen, following even a short and mediocre selection. The common result is that some of the questions are distinctly inferior, clearly irrelevant, and unhelpful. Questions that deepen or sharpen the students' acquaintance with the text stand alongside others that encourage random discussions of broad and vaguely defined topics. The solemnity with which both kinds are presented is likely to obscure, for many students, the fact that they are not all equally important or pertinent.

Several of the series supply an abundance of questions and activities following selections or units, notably Hlt, ABC, Sgr, SF, HBM, and HBO. In ABC-12, for example, Barrie's play, *The Old*

Lady Shows Her Medals, is followed by seven questions on plot and meaning, a request for five character sketches, some lines to be practiced orally, six passages of dialect to be read, fifteen words to be pronounced, nine phrases to be enunciated clearly, fifteen words to be looked up in the dictionary, directions for a discussion of the scenery, costumes, and staging of the play, and six suggestions of additional activities ranging from the reading of other plays, to clipping newspaper reviews, to acting out a scene with puppets, to looking up the biography of Barrie, to the presentation of a play before the class. The teacher is unlikely to undertake it all but will select as he sees fit; however, he is given no help in selection, for there is no indication that some of these matters are more important than others. The good teacher who has time for class preparation will select wisely; the teacher whose own literary education is weak or who is subjected to the common harassments of high school teaching will be inclined to take the easy way out: "The first row will prepare exercise one, the second row exercise two, etc.," or "Choose one of the suggested activities and be prepared to tell the class how you would carry it out," or "Write out the answers to the first ten questions." The results are all too obvious: meaningless homework for the students, uneven benefits that depend upon mere chance, the teacher's loss of some degree of control over his subject, and ultimately, the students' loss of respect for the subject.

There is a striking difference between anthologies prepared for high schools and those intended for colleges in respect to their use of editorial machinery. Our analysis of college anthologies has been limited to a few books, but those we have examined keep the editorial apparatus below 20 per cent, chiefly by avoiding organization by units and therefore all the unit machinery, by including few or no illustrations, and often by leaving all the questions and activities to the teacher's own devising. This seems to us an eminently sane practice. It is also one that assumes an expert knowledge of literature by the teacher; but this assumption also should be an entirely reasonable one. After all, literature is his principal subject matter. Indeed, there should be — and can be — a close similarity between the teaching of literature in college and high school, since the instructors on both levels are presumably striving toward the same goal, namely, helping their students to a sensitive acquaintance with literature, and are presumably concerned, equally, in asserting the integrity and the dignity of their subject. Hence, the difference in amount of machinery in the two kinds of books is probably both unnecessary and undesirable. It is difficult to believe that anthologies at least for seventeen-year-old high school upperclassmen should be so completely unlike those for eighteen-year-old college freshmen. One decisive change that would encourage better articulation between high school and college (a widely advertised desideratum) is the jettisoning of most of the editorial apparatus so that both teacher and student can concentrate on the important matter, the texts themselves.

Relevance

The excessive use of editorial machinery would not be so objectionable if all of it were relevant. Irrelevance is found principally in two places — in the questions and in the activities suggested. Questions that follow units and selections should, we are convinced, lead the student back to the texts rather than into vaguely defined areas of "experience" and should place comprehension ahead of application, particularly when the application depends upon relationships that at best are tenuous and tangential. The activities may be irrelevant in several ways. They may ask for mere "busywork" that is a perversion of the "learning by doing" doctrine. Several anthologies place much emphasis upon group activity that may have only a slight connection with what has just been read: forming a "fan club" (SF-10), forming an "adventure club" (SF-9), "group speaking" (HB2-9), "group writing" (HBO-9, HBM-10, HBO-12, Ldw-9). The group activity may be complicated as well as irrelevant. The following from Ldw-10 will illustrate: "Make a scrapbook of stories from . . . magazines. A committee may be appointed to pass judgment on the stories brought in, and another committee may classify the stories under such headings as sports stories, detective stories, local color stories, or on some other basis of grouping. Perhaps a third committee can find illustrations or make decorative headings." Students are directed to sources of mediocre stories; nothing is said about reading them; the topical kind of classification suggested requires little more than skimming; nothing is said about the merit of the stories or the need for valid criteria in selecting them. Group activity can also lead to a perversion of the democratic process. Hlt-12, for example, asks students to make a chart of battles mentioned in the nine works of a unit they have just completed and to list for each the time, the hero, the enemy, and the outcome "when you have arrived at answers *on which you can agree* . . ." (emphasis added). In short, one determines history by majority vote! [2]

Some activities suggested are very slight; for example, cartoon contests (HltD-9), "scrambled" stories (SF-9), identification of settings (Scb-9). Other activities suggested make demands that are both irrelevant and impossible: "research" on San Francisco's Chinatown (HBL-11); "a study of the woman suffrage movement, the development of modern scientific psychol-

---

[2] Group activities are particularly irrelevant in English classes. A useful corrective is to be found in Channing's Phi Beta Kappa oration of 1818 that was cited earlier on p. 148: "Look through the history of Literature, and you will find that single minds, living and working apart, forming independent estimates of things, taking upon themselves the responsibility of their thoughts, and 'pursuing glory at their own peril,' — that these have been the only efficient minds, the only minds that have made important accessions to knowledge. — Would you alarm them with the reproach of singularity or of impudent pretensions?"

ogy, or the effects of modern wars" (Hlt-12). In such instances as these, the student is asked to begin his "research" outside the literature he has read and often to stay outside it. The questions and activities, by concentrating on factual matters, may be more closely related to the organization of the book than to the texts it contains. Or they may show other kinds of disproportionate emphasis; for example, on reading rate (the ABC series) or "speech activities" (the Ldw series). In these instances the selections are often little more than springboards from which the editors leap into something other than literary study.

The irrelevance that is most harmful, however, is that produced when literature is made to serve other ends, particularly those of the social studies and the natural sciences. The following suggested activities and questions will illustrate this common practice.

A panel discussion on the following topics: "Proper dress for the teen-age girl," "Proper dress for the teen-age boy," "Planning a teen-age dance and party," "How to be popular." (HB2-9)

A class vote on the most popular television programs. (ABC-11)

A list of popular magazines that are to be rated as "Good," "Average," and "Poor." (HBM-10; in HB49-10 the third rating was "Trash," but in keeping with the general tone of the revision the descriptive word was softened.)

A rating scale for the parents in the stories read ("Parents often judge you in one way or another. This is your chance to turn the tables"). (Hlt-9)

A question that asks merely for physical information: "What statistics show the greater depth and steepness of Hell's Canyon?" (Lipp-10)

How far this kind of activity can be pressed is shown by the following example. SF2-9 directs the students to make a chart "showing what you have learned about the habits of wild animals." A printed sample illustrates the form it is to take: horizontal rows labeled "wolves," "beavers," "otters," "diamondbacks," "bees," and vertical columns headed "food," "shelter," "communication," "methods of sensing danger," "methods of caring for the young." Where the rows and columns intersect, the students are to write in such answers as "dams," "rattles," "nectar." One might ask whether it is necessary for the students to read these selections in order to know the answers; he would certainly wish to ask whether this exercise is not more relevant for a biology than for an English class.

Although one must admire the ingenuity rather than the relevance of activities like these, he will also find that several anthologies succeed in staying rather consistently with matters that are more appropriate. Among these we make special mention of Scb-9, Sgr-10, SF-11, Ldw-10, RP-9. We also commend the Lipp series for the form of its questions, even though they are not always relevant for a literary anthology; this series deserves special mention for giving the questions a context of discussion and comment which helps to indicate to the student their significance. At the opposite pole are, among others, HM-9, Hth-9, Hlt-10, HB2-11, SF2-9, in which a large proportion of the questions and activities make literature subservient to the social and natural sciences. Lying somewhere between these extremes are most of the volumes in the HBM and HBO series. These contain many activities and questions that are pertinent to literature and that can aid the students in comprehension and appreciation; but alongside them are many others that are irrelevant and distracting.

Two activities that can be relevant to the purposes of English and are valuable in their own right we find greatly understressed. One of these is the memorization of poetry. There are very few instances where this is even suggested. In the Ldw series students are occasionally asked to "add one of the poems . . . to your memory collection," but this practice is notable in the anthologies chiefly for its infrequency. Yet there is probably no better way for the reader to make literature intimately his own.

The other neglected activity is writing. Although we have counted more than 35,000 "activities" that are suggested in the anthologies, we have also found that only 3.2 per cent of them specifically ask the student to write. The single volume having the highest percentage of writing activities is Irq-9 (10.8 per cent), and the series having the highest percentage is RM (7.8 per cent). Other single volumes ranking relatively high are Glb-11 (8.7 per cent), Irq-10 (8.5 per cent), and RP-9 (6.3 per cent). The series include Ldw (5.2 per cent), HBM (3.9 per cent), Hlt (3.9 per cent), and HBO (3.7 per cent). At the lower end of the scale are PH (0.2 per cent), Gn (0.7 per cent), SF (1.0 per cent) among the series, and among single volumes Scb-9 (0.5 per cent) and HM-9 (1.6 per cent). We believe that even the highest percentages are much too low, for writing — or rather composition—is as much a part of the English teacher's responsibility as is literature. Furthermore, since literature can provide ideal subject matter for writing assignments, this neglect is particularly unfortunate. The possibility of achieving the greatly desired "articulation" of the several facets of English studies is not exploited, and instead we find a physical and almost unbridgeable gap between reading and writing that is dramatically represented by the existence of two completely different sets of books for English classes, a problem we will discuss at greater length in the second part of this volume. In the one book the student is told to write but is given little help with subject matter that he can control and the teacher can evaluate; in the other he is provided with a large store of subject matter but is rarely told to write about it. Furthermore, this separation is maintained in spite of the numerous curricular developments throughout the nation that show with what remarkable success composition and literature have been integrated to their mutual advantage in individual classrooms and districts.

Even when writing is included among the activities suggested, it is often inadequately treated. We find seven principal weaknesses in the treatment of writing in the anthologies: (1) the students are asked merely to restate in their own words what they have read, so that their own critical powers are not called into play; (2) they are asked to write on a topic that has no important relationship to what they have read; (3) they are encouraged to write badly; (4) they are asked to report on "research" that is likely to result in a patchwork of secondhand extracts from reference books and perhaps in plagiarism; (5) they are given topics so vast that no one but an already skilful writer could deal with them adequately; (6) greater emphasis is placed upon "creative writing" than upon exposition; (7) greater emphasis is placed upon writing by the group than by the individual. The following assignments taken from the anthologies will illustrate these various shortcomings.

(1) Summarize the story line in six or seven statements. Use the two below and add others. . . . [HBM-9]
    Write a one-page version of Jeremy's story, using at least seven of the words or phrases in the list. [Hth-9]

(2) . . . have you some vivid memories of a favorite picnic or some favorite meal? Write an account of it, using vividly observed details to help your audience share your special experience. [Lipp-10]

(3) From one of the selections in this part choose what seems to you to be the most important and newsworthy event. Then write a news story as though the event just occurred. Write your story in standard newspaper style. . . . Organize the facts in the order of their decreasing importance so that the story can be cut at almost any point. You can also have some fun writing a headline for your story. [Hlt-12]

(4) Prepare a report on Indian symbol writing. [Glb-11]
    Present to the class a special report on one of the following topics or on some related topic of your own choosing. . . . Costumes of the Period, The Crusades, The Black Death, etc. [SF-12]

(5) Could you add some new verses of your own [to Anderson's "Hi-

Yo, Hi-Yo, Discernible Today"] and vary the choruses to fit them?
[HBO-10]
Write a sequel to . . . [in nearly every anthology].
(6) As an experiment in group writing, you might compose a first
line of your own [to a limerick]. Let everyone in class carry it on
from there. The results will be unpredictable! [HBO-9]

The inadequacies of several of these types of assignment are
readily apparent. Restatement of what the student has read, although relevant, develops neither the ability to organize discrete
materials nor facility in critical thinking. Writing on a personal
experience, as well as neglecting the relationship between reading and writing, puts the teacher in an unfavorable position for
giving maximum guidance to the inexperienced writer. "Playing
up angles" and arranging paragraphs in the order of diminishing
importance result in writing of a kind that places ease of rapid
reading above orderly treatment of subject and sensationalism
above integrity. The usual "research" topic must be pursued in
libraries that were not intended to provide adequate facilities for
genuine research and is likely to result in no more progress in
composition than is represented by the greater ability to write
footnotes. Many of the "surveys" and "reports on research" demand
investigation in breadth and depth that are not yet within the
grasp of the young student; he may thereby be persuaded to over-
simplify and to draw conclusions from insufficient evidence. Although the writing of verse and original stories may provide some
variety in written assignments, the kind of writing that can give
the best training in composition for all students, whatever their
vocational aims, is that which requires the logical organization
of ideas — that is, exposition; also, unwarranted praise of a
student's "creative writings" frequently leads to frustration and
disappointment when they are later subjected to impartial criticism. And writing the first line of a limerick that is then completed by others reduces writing to a parlor game.

Group writing seems to us a particularly questionable kind of activity. If it is to result in real composition and if it is to be a genuinely cooperative enterprise, each member of the group will need to possess at least the following qualifications: the ability to cooperate in organizing the activity so that all members actually contribute; a knowledge of the subject; an awareness of the knowledge of the subject possessed by each of the other members of the group; some knowledge of the psychology of group process; a means of arbitration on points of grammar, logic, and rhetoric that will prevent the compromises on these matters from representing only the lowest common denominator of the participants' knowledge and facility; a motivation that leads each member of the group to resist the uncritical acceptance of the ideas advanced by the most vocal member.

We suspect that several of these qualities must be deliberately cultivated if they are to appear even among experienced writers. In the meantime, individual students should be encouraged to write by, from, and for themselves.

Composition is at best a difficult undertaking, for it requires the skilful management of words and sentences — the subtlest and most sophisticated tools that man possesses. The inexperienced writer therefore needs much assistance in learning to control them and clear directions for their application to an assigned topic. Yet, the editors often provide little help. They may even misdirect the student, as this example will illustrate. In Sgr-11 the student is asked to write a report on one of several topics. Among them is the following: *"Philip Freneau and His Poems.* Read 'The Wild Honey Suckle' and 'The Indian Burying-Ground' and summarize the thought of each. What part did Freneau play in the war?" If the student actually follows this advice, he is almost certain to fail as a writer; for he is told to head in at least two directions at once, to draw conclusions from minimal evidence, to trace relationships that go beyond the scope of the topic; he is not provided with or encouraged to discover for himself an idea or thesis that will control his essay. An assignment could hardly be more ineptly formulated than this one.

After examining the thousands of activities and questions provided by the editors, we conclude that their most remarkable qualities are ingenuity, variety, and abundance rather than relevance to the readings. Their purpose seems rather to give the student something to keep him busy than to stimulate his mental growth. The thorough revision which they undergo as new editions are prepared suggests also that they have been determined by expediency, first guesses, reckless experiment, inattention to the psychology of knowledge, and sensitivity to the competitive market. In short, what they lack is a clear sense of purpose, a guiding principle that is relevant to the literature which they accompany.

We suggest, therefore, that no activity or question be admitted into the anthologies unless it satisfies the following criteria: (1) it should encourage the student to involve himself with matters that are not uniquely personal and private; (2) it should provide clearly defined boundaries within which success *can* be achieved; (3) it should be related to the central concerns of the literature that suggests it; (4) it should extend the reader's comprehension of what he has read by inducing him to assess what he has derived from his reading, to formulate his thoughts thereon, and to give them appropriate expression.

We are convinced that topics can meet all four of these requirements and still provide sufficient range to obtain variety and to allow for individual differences among both students and literary selections. We are also convinced that if literature is not the only subject matter that can be exploited for the teaching of composition, it still remains the best, and therefore, to slight written exercises in the anthologies or to separate literature from composition by isolating the two in separate series of textbooks is to perform a grave disservice to English as a curricular subject in the schools.

Tone

The tone established by the editorial apparatus is of serious importance in determining the value of an anthology, but it is much more difficult to evaluate than either the quantity or the relevance of the machinery. Even an anthology containing many first-rate selections may be cheapened by the inclusion of such "gimmicks" as jokes and cartoons, particularly when they are unrelated to the selections and have no justification except the amusement they provide (for example, ABC-9 and Sgr-11). We would also classify as a trick the inclusion of a group of stories and poems by high school students (as in PH-10); to print such pieces in an expensive and physically durable volume designed for a captive audience is to give an air of commonness to what is really uncommon — namely, literature of distinction. Illustrations may also establish the tone; their contribution and effect are discussed at the end of this chapter.

The editorial machinery sometimes seems intended primarily to "sell" literature (a phrase that, unfortunately, is sometimes used by both editors and teachers), and consequently the methods of the huckster are introduced into the anthologies. Prefaces describe the contents as "fresh," "crisp," "brief," "exciting," "appealing," "attractive." When an anthology is revised, attention is called to the number of selections that are "new," that favorite word of television commercials (HBM-10 uses "new" ten times in its preface). Selections are said to be "timely," "up-to-date," "in keeping with the spirit of modern youth," or the current prestige of other disciplines (for example, "a planned correlation between literature and science") is exploited. The song of the hawker, which may also be heard wherever the editors' prose appears (for example, in HM-9 and in some volumes of the HBM,

HB2, and PH series), seems to us inappropriate for an anthology of literature. Literature is not to be made "attractive" to students, but students are to be attracted to literature. The latter role is properly the function of the informed and enthusiastic teacher; the anthology's primary role is to make the literature available.

The tone may also be detrimental when the editors continually emphasize a special predilection. The most notable example is found in the ABC series. Most of the selections are accompanied by the admonition to students to note down the time when they begin and finish the reading, the number of words in the selections is given, and "Reading Scoreboards" are provided so that each student can compute his own reading rate. The reader can hardly fail to conclude that literature exists primarily for the development of speed in reading. It is not surprising to find in the preface to ABC-12 that the editors regard speed, along with "comprehension" and "vocabulary enrichment" as "of equal and primary importance." Sir Francis Bacon's remark seems to us more appropriate for literature: "Read . . . to weigh and consider."

The tone that is most pervasive in the anthologies, however, is one that reflects the editors' attitude to the students. This tone is frequently one of permissiveness. Suggested activities following the selections are often introduced with the words, "You may wish to [find, write on, discuss]" (HM-9, SF-10, HBO-10, HBM-9, Irq-10, ABC-11, and many others). There are several variations on this rubric: "It may be fun to . . ." (SF-9), "If you would like to do some writing . . ." (ABC-12), "It would be an interesting project to appoint a committee to . . ." (Hth-9). This permissiveness may sometimes upset the teacher's plans; for example, the teacher may not want the students to consult the text for the answer to a question, but the editors overrule him: "You may use your text for help" (SF-10). In fact, in the midst of all this permissiveness the teacher must often feel helpless, a functionary without a function. But there are amusing moments also. When the students are asked, "Would you like to write a love poem in the style of the Cavaliers?" the chorus of No's must be deafening (and, of course, "No" is a proper answer to the question). Teachers have a right to expect that publishers choose their editors because of their special knowledge and competence; however, the permissive attitude that pervades the anthologies goes far to undermine the teachers' confidence in the editors. In ABC-12, for example, *Macbeth* is followed by this statement (among others) under the heading "Further Adventuring": "If you would like to do some writing, try one of these suggestions or another of your own choosing: (a) a character sketch of Macbeth or of Lady Macbeth, (b) a letter Lady Macbeth might have written in answer to her husband's, (c) the doctor's report on Lady Macbeth's illness, (d) a pastoral poem." Not only does the wording make the whole exercise permissive, but also there is inadequate direction for those who "would like to do some writing." We believe that students, teachers, and the state of English in the curriculum would all benefit if editors proceeded on the assumption that literature is a serious discipline and that the principal business of students is to master it.

The editorial prose in the anthologies often has other characteristics as well. The tone may be simply chatty: "You are going to be interested in Jim and Stella and Betty and their folks. They're a good family to know" (HB49-9). This kind of prose, found, for example, in ABC-9, Hlt-10, HBM-10, HM-9, SF-9, HBO-10, HB2-10, HBM-11, Lipp-10, becomes effusive and coy. It conveys nothing so much as the impression that the editors prize above all comradery with their readers. Activities following selections are thus headed "Let's be off!" (HBM-11), "Over to you" (HBO-10), "Talking it over" (SF2-9), "It's your life" (Irq-9). The heading is sometimes ingeniously worded to call attention to the relationship between questions and the selections they follow: "No Tears,

Please," following Carew's "Disdain Returned," "No Swinish Words," following Andersen's "The Swineherd," "Exchanging Ideas — Not Hearts" following Sidney's "My True Love Hath My Heart" (ABC-12). In Lipp-10 the introduction, after announcing that "There are scores of ways to look at the continent on which we live" (a geography textbook?), calls its six sections "excursions" (they are clearly intended for summer tourists rather than serious travelers!), and ends, "Are you ready for the take-off? All abo-oard!" When the account of ancient Rome that prefaces *Julius Caesar* in HBM-10 was revised for HBO-10, the objective manner of treatment was replaced by a personalized "you-were-there" style. Examples could be added almost indefinitely. This affected breeziness has led teachers to remark of the editorial prose that "It often seems written for kiddies, for it is oversimplified and chatty, the apparatus geared for spoonfeeding." The cloying nature of such prose is likely to insult the good student, to leave the poor one unmoved, to put the readings in an unfavorable position, and to puzzle the teacher (is he to instruct his charges or to treat them with fond indulgence?).

The combination of permissiveness, casualness, and juvenility may result in the misdirection of both teacher and students. Students are encouraged to believe that all opinions, no matter how offhand and undocumented, are of intrinsic and equal importance. When the editors ask, "Do you agree or disagree with Shakespeare that love should be an 'ever-fixed mark,' regardless of what happens?" (Hlt-12) or "Do you agree with Pope that pride is the greatest cause conspiring to blind one's judgment?" (Ldw-12) they force the student to deal with ideas extracted from their context. Such questions may be important, but what is more important at this point in the student's education and relevant to the subject matter of English is that he know precisely what Shakespeare and Pope have said, how and why they said it, and what it contributes to the totality of their poems. The student will have a whole lifetime to think about love and pride, either in the abstract or in terms of his personal life, but he has only the present moment to discover — and perhaps to benefit from — what keen observers of the human scene have had to say about love and pride.

The juvenile approach to literature may have another unpleasant result also, which can be illustrated by the following passage from a unit introduction in Hlt-9: "You want to know what other teen-age boys and girls are saying and doing. And you probably find it reassuring to learn that many young people face the same difficulties that perplex you. Willie Baxter, Huck Finn, and Jasmine Griffith are teenagers like you." This insistence that the youthful heroes and heroines are "teenagers like you" is possibly the natural extension of the attitude found in most elementary readers today, which portray the various Dicks and Janes going through their daily, and not very exciting, routines. Although, to be sure, there is something of every boy in Willie and Huck and something of every girl in Jasmine, young readers are attracted to these stories not because their characters are "teenagers like you" but because they lead lives of their own, confront and solve — or fail to solve — their own particular problems in surroundings and situations that are somehow different from the reader's. This would seem to be the meaning of the "vicarious experience" of literature. But that experience is vitiated by the steady insistence on the kind of teen-age empathy that is encouraged by the editors' chatty and patronizing prose.

We also suggested earlier that editorial prose should have some stylistic quality. It is altogether possible that such prose, as well as the selections themselves, will influence students. It is particularly necessary, therefore, that editors assume responsibility for their own language. That they have not always done so is indicated by the following representative sentences (ironically, the grammatical and rhetorical flaws in these sentences are some-

times treated at length in the grammar and composition series is-
sued by the same publishers).

How does the author get his ideas across? (PH-10)
He has written for radio, the movies, short stories, magazine serials,
    and a novel. . . . (HB2-11)
Although the sestet discusses a different topic than the octave . . .
    (Sgr-12)
. . . of course *Julius Caesar* is in poetical form, even though the lines
    are not rhymed. This is because they are written in blank verse,
    which is unrhymed and not divided into any set stanzas. (HBM-
    10)

Slang, chatty colloquialisms, unparallel construction, awkward
splits, and circular logic are hardly appropriate to editorial prose.
There is so much editorial prose in the anthologies that is con-
sciously juvenile, inappropriate, or inadequate that we are
pleased to cite those that are largely or wholly free of it: SF-11,
SF-12, HBO-12, HB-12a, MGH-9, Irq-10.

Helpfulness

In general, we have found that the editorial machinery supplies too much rather than not enough help to the students. Some
editors, for example, provide subheadings, headnotes, and summaries that do much of the student's work for him. In Gn-12 the
comments that precede each scene of *Macbeth* furnish many of
the answers to the questions that follow the text. In HBM-11
Washington's "Farewell Address" is fitted out with subheads like
a newspaper article. In SF-12 an analytical outline precedes a
section of *In Memoriam*. In HBO-12 subheads are inserted in
"L'Allegro" and "Il Penseroso." Numerous additional examples
could be cited. We find three principal objections to such practices: (1) Much of the work that the student should do is already
done by the editors. (2) The teacher's control of his subject is
lessened. (3) The editors provide a single interpretation — their

own. This interpretation may be oversimplified or even eccentric; but even if it is unobjectionable on other grounds it discourages students from taking the initiative, from arguing for their own interpretation, and thus from exercising their own powers of analysis and imagination.

The glosses that are provided, whether in footnotes or in an appendix, are also inclined to be excessive. We see little reason for glossing common words in their primary meanings. The extent of one's vocabulary has been found to be a reliable index of knowledge and intelligence; it is revealing to discover that the anthologies have such a low opinion of their users in these respects. At the same time, however, they often hamper the development of vocabulary by discouraging the habit of consulting the dictionary. Words that are defined in dictionaries that are available to high school students should not be glossed in the anthologies. Instead, the glosses should be limited to foreign words, archaisms, neologisms, and other words that are not included in the commonly used dictionaries.

At the same time that anthologies provide too much help in defining common words, they sometimes provide too little help by omitting the metaphorical or connotative values of words. The following example will illustrate. In *Julius Caesar*, when Antony first sees the body of his slain friend and leader, he says to the conspirators:

> I know not, gentlemen, what you intend,
> Who else must be let blood, who else is rank. . . .

The word *rank*, the major editors of Shakespeare and historical lexicographers agree, here means "overgrown," "ripe," "ready to be cut down (as weeds)." The passage thus carries a figurative overtone suggesting that Caesar was indeed a noxious growth, and the reader has the pleasure of recognizing both the literal and the metaphorical meaning of the lines. But only one of the twelve anthologies that include *Julius Caesar,* SF-10, glosses this passage in a way to suggest the fullness of its meaning: "who else, like overtall weeds, must be cut down." HB49-10, HBL-10, Ldw-9, McM-10, RM-10, and Sgr-10 do not provide any explanation of the line; Irq-10 omits the passage entirely; Gn-10 glosses *rank* as "too powerful," ABC-10 as "too full of blood; too powerful," and HBM-10 and HBO-10 as "next to be killed." Since a sizable portion of the fun in reading Shakespeare derives from recognizing the metaphorical language as supporting or commenting upon the literal meaning of the lines, and since most of the anthologies give no assistance in capturing this fun, it is little wonder that students are not excited by the text — *as they could be.* Furthermore, when the editors insist on a single contextual meaning like "next to be killed," they may mislead the reader into believing that it is the lexical meaning of the word.

Some anthologies give the impression that the words glossed have been chosen at random: Hlt-9 glosses Shakespeare's *habit* but not his *pleasance* or Coffin's *tierces;* Hlt-12 glosses three words in a poem of Surrey but not a half-dozen others that are also archaic; Gn-9 chooses to gloss from O. Henry's "The Ransom of Red Chief" such words as *brake, lackadaisical, contiguous,* and *renegade,* but not *fraudulent, yeomanry, sylvan, somnolent, acceded, proclivities,* and a dozen others that would seem to be equally difficult. Perhaps none of these words should be glossed, but in any case the inconsistency is inexplicable.

Glosses have only one purpose: to aid the student in reading a particular text. They should neither fail to give this help nor hinder the attainment of a larger purpose — the formation of the habit of thoughtful reading. In the light of this conclusion we believe that glosses should satisfy the following requirements: (1) they should encourage rather than discourage the development of good habits in the use of dictionaries; (2) they should not make unnecessary the discrimination among several possible meanings of a word; (3) they should not distort meaning by defining words either out of context or only in the literal context; (4) they should make readers aware of additional, especially metaphoric and extended, meanings of words; (5) they should omit no essential information that is not readily available to students.

Another piece of editorial apparatus included to help the student is the biographical sketch, either prefixed to the selection or contained in an appendix. These sketches are usually helpful for giving the student a frame of reference, although many of them are short and are restricted to factual details. We have noted, however, that what may be a crucial bit of information, the date of the selection, is sometimes missing. Also, the details chosen for inclusion are not always the most helpful; as a teacher remarked, he found it more important that his students know what else the author has written than that his father was a ropemaker. The principal charge to be brought against the anthologies in their treatment of biography is, however, their inconsistency. Hlt-9, for example, identifies the authors of the longer selections but not those of many short poems that are included, even though the authors of the latter may be equally important. On the other hand, some anthologies, for example, ABC-9 and SF-10, include biographical sketches of such well-known authors as Shakespeare, George Eliot, Mark Twain, and Sir Walter Scott, but not those of many lesser-known contemporary writers. It may be that the latter are relatively unimportant; yet it is evident that the student has other convenient sources of information to which he can turn for the biographies of well-known authors but probably none beyond the anthology itself for minor and recent writers. Here, as with the glossaries, there seems to be a lack of controlling principle. It should be added, however, that most volumes for the eleventh and twelfth grades are both consistent and generous in providing the necessary biographical data.

Among the helpful elements in the anthologies are the bibliographies of suggested additional reading. Some of these are carefully related to the units which they follow: for example, RP-9, SF-10, HBO-11, Sgr-12. These bibliographies list works which not only are relevant to the units but also are of some intrinsic and often permanent value. On the other hand, the bibliographies in some volumes, for example, Hth-9 and HM-9, run heavily to teen-tales and other ephemera. A few volumes, for example, ABC-12, emphasize secondary rather than primary readings in their lists of suggestions. A curious practice is occasionally found and can be represented from HB49-9: this anthology includes in its section on drama six short and relatively easy plays but lists, among others suggested for supplementary reading *As You Like It* and *A Midsummer Night's Dream.* Thus, the easier — and in this instance, slighter — plays are made available for teaching and study; the more difficult and enduring plays suggested are presumably left for the students to struggle through on their own.

The questions included to direct the students' reading of the selections are generally helpful, at least for the more superficial purposes of following the story line and noting the factual details. Many of the questions in the Ldw series, for example, which are classified by a rather elaborate set of symbols, are designed to recall details, but few are concerned with finding the central idea or discerning the author's organization. Other volumes that provide similar questions are those in the ABC and HB2 series, RM-10, and Hth-9. Many of these are helpful, although they often encourage merely rote learning of fact and identification rather than challenging the imaginative and analytical faculties. But questions are sometimes more ambitious, even when there is little help provided for answering them. For example, ABC-12 asks, "How would you describe the literature of the early nineteenth century?" By this time, if all the contents of the chapter have been assigned, the students will have read seven pages of highly capsulized information supplied by the editors, 830 lines of poetry, one piece of contemporary prose, and an excerpt from a modern biography. A description of early nineteenth-century literature based upon this relatively small amount of evidence would almost certainly be inadequately documented and probably oversimplified as well. The situation becomes more confused when crucial or difficult terms like "romantic," "realistic," "sentimental," and "Renaissance" are undefined (as in HBO-10, Ldw-12, and Hlt-12).

Among miscellaneous helps in the anthologies at least three deserve special commendation. SF-9 and SF-10 contain helpful transitional passages and useful discussions of "The Author's Craft." HBM-9 includes several unit introductions that give real assistance to the student; for example, the section on reading poetry. The discussion and comment into which the study questions are introduced in the Lipp series furnish a more helpful context and a better perspective than most anthologies provide. Among miscellaneous helps that we find particularly objectionable are the overblown, chatty, and supererogatory headnotes to selections and stage directions in plays.

In assessing the helpfulness of the anthologies, we arrive at two apparently contradictory conclusions: they provide either too much or too little assistance. Too much help is given on matters that should be left largely to the teacher and his students. These are chiefly matters of finding the meaning, defining common words, and interpreting texts. On the other hand, too little help is given in the phrasing of topics for writing assignments, in the glossing of connotative meanings, and in the explanation of puzzling texts. These are matters on which most students and many teachers require much help. We believe that it is possible for editors to find the golden mean between too much and too little help, but they will do so only when all editorial apparatus is first measured by two standards — the essential nature of literature and the primary function of anthologies.

Accuracy

In previous chapters we have pointed out several kinds of errors that occur in the anthologies. These are errors in the editing of texts, examples of which will be found in the chapters on the novel, the short story, the drama, and poetry. There are also errors in organization; for example, placing Malory before Chaucer in a chronologically arranged volume, or, as already cited, classifying an excerpt from a novel as a short story. Additional examples of these kinds will be found in the chapter on organization and coverage. Here we are chiefly concerned with the accuracy of the editorial apparatus itself.

On the whole, the anthologies are relatively free of factual error. They are less satisfactory in their critical judgments, many of which tend to be oversimplified and categorical or to be based upon unidentified and even dubious principles of literary criticism. In the following paragraphs we have attempted to represent the kinds of inaccuracies in the anthologies, both of fact and of judgment, by means of typical examples.

A few of the factual errors occur in connection with the illustrations. For example, on a page of pictures in RM-12 appears the caption, "England in the thirteenth century became a tight little island with towers of stone soaring heavenward. . . ." The picture appearing beside the words "towers of stone" is of Westminster Abbey, whose towers were not built until about 1739. But more often the errors are found in the comments on the selections. HBO-11 describes the sonnet without distinguishing between its principal forms, and attributes to the kind it describes, the Italian, a feature that is a characteristic of the English sonnet. In Sgr-12 the comment is made of "Chevy Chase" that the letters v and u "sometimes get mixed up," whereas they were simply alternative forms of the same letter. In Ldw-12, Wordsworth's "It Is a Beauteous Evening" is said to be addressed to the poet's sister instead of to his natural daughter Caroline. HBO-10 calls "What Is So Rare As a Day in June" the author's title as if Lowell himself had separately titled this excerpt from *The Vision of Sir Launfal*. HBM-10 calls *Henry V* one of Shakespeare's "earlier histories," although, except for the partly Shakespearean *Henry VIII*, it was the last history play he wrote. From these examples one may conclude — rightly — that most of the factual errors are relatively minor. As we have said, they are also relatively few.

Another kind of imprecision in the anthologies arises from the categorical or oversimplified statement. From Irq-9 we learn that "Homer teaches no lessons in his epics," although countless readers, from Xenophon onward, have thought that he does. HB2-11 calls Parkman "America's greatest historian," without qualification and without giving a reason why he is said (by the editors) to be the greatest. In spite of our lack of knowledge about Shakespeare's early life, HBM-10 states categorically that "For years he had acted in his own plays, and it was indeed acting that had first drawn him to London. . . ." HBO-12 properly identifies Auburn in Goldsmith's *Deserted Village* with Lissoy in Ireland but does not mention that the poet also had in mind the English villages affected by the Industrial Revolution (see line 57: "A time there was, ere England's griefs began"). Irq-10 comments that "The all-knowing-author approach . . . certainly makes for greater unity in the [short] story," although Henry James and his numerous followers have pretty thoroughly discredited this view. Nor is it always true that "the novel covers a longer period of time [than the short story]," as Sgr-9 states without qualification. Irq-10 also assumes that interest in the short story must be achieved by either "surprise or suspense," thus leaving out of account the "slice-of-life" stories, those in which character is more important than plot, and those that please by satisfying the expectation established in the beginning. Ldw-12 declares without qualification that "there is in the poetry [of the eighteenth century] no sincere expression of everyday life, everyday joys, and everyday troubles." As a final example of the categorical statement we mention this particularly inept comment made in ABC-12: "In *Hamlet* there are several villains but none more despicable than an old man named Polonius."

In a rather large number of instances the critical implications of the editorial apparatus are misleading or ambiguous, as the following examples indicate. Gn-11 places Irving, Hawthorne, Poe, and Bryant in a chapter called "The Rise of a National Literature," and Harte, Twain, Parkman, and Lincoln — as well as the usual New England and Southern authors — in a chapter called "The Age of Romanticism," thereby failing to indicate that some of the writers in the first group may also be "romantic" and that some of those in the second may not be. HB2-12 offers an oversimple definition of comedy: "A play in which the leading characters successfully overcome obstacles." Many tragedies — even one as stark as *King Lear* — fit this definition. HBM-12 omits the opening passages in "L'Allegro" and "Il Penseroso," and then justifies the deletion with the comment that "these passages are difficult and contribute little if anything to our enjoyment of the musical, clear lines." The presumption of the editors in tuning up the "organ voice of England" is remarkable. Ldw-12 takes a somewhat similar view of Pope's heroic couplets, finding little in them but "monotony" and ignoring the internal flexibility, the witty antithesis, and the skilful balance that perceptive readers, including modern critics, have pointed out. McM-11 asks the reader of Poe's "Ulalume" to "observe that if you repeat Ulalume a few times you will feel a melancholy sadness. By repeating lines Poe makes the reader catch his breath in a sort of quick sob." This is perhaps pneumotometric criticism? RM-10 dispatches "realism" and "romanticism" in short sentences: "Fiction that deals with life as it is commonly lived day by day is known as realistic fiction. Fiction that deals with fanciful characters in fanciful situations and consequently with strange happenings is known as romantic fiction." We suspect that these definitions misrepresent a large body of distinguished fiction, which cannot be so conveniently labeled. HBO-12 remarks of Swift's *Gulliver's Travels,* "In short, the land of the horses is an ideal state," a comment that no alert reader of the Fourth Book (it is only summarized in this volume) would make, for it rests ultimately on the false assumption that Gulliver is Swift. Even when the clichés are not erroneous, they may still be misleading. HBM-9, for example, so oversimplifies historical time in the following passage that the reader can hardly fail to be confused by the rapid transitions from the fifteenth to the eighteenth to the twentieth century: "After the printing press was invented, books and magazines became common and a great audience of readers was created. To satisfy the needs of this new audience, writers turned the old tales into a new form — prose narratives or fiction. Thus novels and short stories came to be the most popular reading fare of modern times." As a final example of editorial apparatus that may mislead the students we cite the organization of HBO-9. A group of short stories and a group of poems are followed by a group of nonfictional pieces. The third group appears under the heading "Adventures in Reality." But what is "reality": Orville Wright's flying the first airplane, but not Keats' urn-inspired meditations on the transitory and permanent aspects of being? It is likely that the greater reality is in fiction, not fact. Until anthologists make this distinction, they will be performing a disservice to both literature and students.

The editorial apparatus has only one purpose: to assist teachers to teach and students to comprehend the literary content. It should therefore help to make the difficult comprehensible, not more difficult. It should not distort by misinformation or misdirection. It should not lead students to believe that what is complex is really simple, but rather it should help them to understand the complexity. And not least, it should make use of the results of literary scholarship and criticism. Since high school students are likely to be defenseless against inaccuracy in scholarship and naïveté in literary criticism, it is the responsibility of editors of high school textbooks, even more than of editors of textbooks for experienced readers, to be meticulous in their scholarship and informed in their criticism. We cannot believe that the editors of most of the anthologies have taken either responsibility with sufficient seriousness. The prevalence of the historical cliché and the retention of critical theories that have long since been exposed as fallacious suggest above all that much editorial content of anthologies, even in the most recent of those we have examined, is obsolete.

Because illustrations occupy so much space in the anthologies and because the trend is apparently toward even more pictures, we call particular attention to them in the following paragraphs. That they are excessive is only hinted at by the figures in Table XXXV, column 7. These figures, as was earlier noted, account only for the pictures that are inserted in the texts in order to illustrate them. Actually, all illustrations in a volume are likely to occupy much more space; for example, HBO-12 has 48 pages of pictures inserted in the selections, but it has 63 additional pages of pictures in the unit introductions and other parts of the book. Altogether these occupy 13.5 per cent of the total pages. This is the equivalent of devoting about every seventh page throughout the book solely to pictures; furthermore, pictures are given space equaling 25 per cent of that given to all the poems, stories, essays, plays, and nonfiction in the entire volume. HBO-12 is one of the most heavily illustrated anthologies that we have examined, but others, including volumes in the HBM, HB2, SF, RM, and Gn series, as well as HM-9 and SF2-9, are not far behind.

A recent innovation in some anthologies is the "picture story" or "picture article." These occupy from four to eight pages, are made up almost entirely of pictures, and contain almost nothing for the student to read. They may be on any subject: a day in the life of a teen-ager, training to be a track star, the Ozzie Nelson family of television fame, working with a summer theater company, etc. The anthologies that include these are in general the most juvenile in tone — SF2-9, HM-9, and the HB2 series. Special mention should be made of a picture story in SF2-9, "Out of Control," which consists of five pages of photographs from the television show of the same title, followed by the script. The student is asked to "read" the photographs, and in the text itself much emphasis is placed upon the technicalities of television photography. One might object to the transplantation of television violence into the classroom for a captive audience (brass knuckles, for example, play a part in "Out of Control"), but even more basic is the objection — not just to this item but to all "picture stories" — on the grounds of relevance. While public protest that "Johnny can't read" becomes louder, pictures are introduced into the textbooks in place of words!

Irrelevance of illustrations shows up in other ways also. The Lipp series, for example, prints at regular intervals of about ten or twelve pages full-page photographs which have little or nothing to do with the selection into which they are inserted. Although technically excellent (they are said to be prize-winning photographs), their general irrelevance and the regularity with which they appear give an artificial tone to the volumes. In some anthologies (the PH series and HM-9, for example), many illustrations are more appropriate for the social studies and the natural sciences than for literature.

The illustrations may be judged by their tone as well as by their quantity and relevance. The splashy colors used in SF2-9 and the jumbled appearance of many pages in the HBO series, for example, seem more appropriate for an old-time circus poster than for a volume of literature. We believe that the principal effect is to cheapen the contents — as, ironically, the books are made more expensive. Students can hardly be expected to take it seriously if the tone established by their textbooks suggests that it is as nonfunctional and decorative as the pictures and other parts of the editorial apparatus make it seem.

Our principal objection to the illustrations in many of the anthologies is, however, that they unduly restrict the imagination of the reader. The most satisfying picture of a character or a setting — and the only one that is personally valid — is the mental image that the reader himself creates. Indeed, the illustrations tend to vitiate two of the doctrines most vigorously promulgated by professional education. By forcing the readers to accept the pictorial representation of characters and settings printed on the page, the anthologies ignore Individual Differences and lessen the opportunity for Creative Thinking. One of the chief values of literature in the classroom derives from the student's confronting the text itself and, by close application to it, arriving at an interpretation that is both contextually probable and personally satisfying. This is too great a value to be compromised by editorial or pictorial intrusion. We believe that the best pictorial illustrations of texts are those that are least intrusive and call the least attention to themselves. We therefore prefer black-and-white to colored illustrations, simple line drawings to fully sketched portraits, and any kind of drawings to photographs. The more the illustrations insist upon detailed representation, the more they are likely to restrict the imagination. Most restrictive of all are photographs from stage, motion picture, and television performances, which not only insist upon particular and limited interpretation but also identify fictional characters with well-known actors.

Because of the vast bulk of editorial machinery in the anthologies — more than thirteen thousand pages of it in the series alone

— we have had to be content with examples, but enough of them have been provided perhaps to show that there is much room for improvement. We see three ways in which they can be improved in respect to editorial apparatus. (1) An appropriate and consistent principle should determine what machinery is admitted and what is rejected. At present the anthologies give the impression that anything can be included — perhaps in the belief that someone somewhere may be able to use it — no matter how incongruous or irrelevant it may be. The result is the miscellaneousness that we have described in this chapter. (2) Because up to half the machinery is required merely to establish the organization of an anthology and to keep the student aware of it, much of the apparatus could be eliminated by simplifying the organization. (3) Whatever the principle decided upon and whatever the organization used, a drastic reduction in the amount of machinery should be made. More space for literary texts would thereby be available within the same covers. But there is another reason, perhaps equally important, why it should be reduced. Authors, at least the good ones, say what they have to say (with whatever complexity is required), introduce the reader to it in the proper circumstances, reveal what is necessary in their own good time, and stop when there is no more to say — all within the twenty lines of the poem, the five acts of the play, or the five hundred pages of the novel. In short, the author is his own best commentator, and therefore much of the editorial apparatus is simply unnecessary. What should take its place is the assistance of the informed teacher in disclosing potential meanings and the concentration of the students on the texts themselves. This distribution of responsibility would go far toward maintaining literature in its proper place in the curriculum, for students would then be studying literature (and not its periphery), teachers would be teaching it (from the texts rather than from the editorial apparatus), and editors would make it available. Beyond the texts, the anthologies might provide only the essential context and a critical vocabulary that would enable students to talk and write about the selections with some degree of precision. Since the texts themselves would then dominate the anthologies, they and not the machinery would set the tone; much of the irrelevance and misdirection, the clichés and the oversimplifications would disappear. Perhaps then we would not have to "continue forever appearing on the author's doorstep," [3] but could enter his house. And not least, the joys that generations of readers have found in literature might become possible in the classroom.

---

[3] Vincent E. Miller in a review of new reprints of well-known novels, *College English*, 22 (May, 1961), p. 600; this review makes several telling points in short space.

PART II

The Grammar
and Composition Series

CHAPTER 1

Grammar and Composition Series

Scope of the Report

Although many additional books of various kinds (workbooks, handbooks, vocabulary booklets, spellers, etc.) were included in the total number of publications inspected in the course of this study, the following report is based primarily on detailed examination of fourteen sets of textbooks here designated under the general title "Grammar and Composition Series." With two exceptions[1] these sets include four volumes each and are intended to be used in grades nine through twelve. The oldest series included in the study (HB *Living Language*) carries the copyright date 1953. It is probable that other, older editions are still in use in some school districts; however, information obtained by canvassing publishers, state departments of education, and a large number of representative districts throughout the United States leads us to believe that the sets examined in this study include all that are in extensive use at the present time. The following

---

[1] Scott, Foresman, *Guide to Modern English,* includes grades eleven, twelve, in a single volume. McGraw-Hill, *Your Language,* twelfth-grade volume was not available in time for this study.

series, listed alphabetically by publishers, are the subjects of this report:

Allyn and Bacon: *Effective English* (Meade, Haugh, Sonke) 1961.
American Book Company: *Our English Language* (Bailey, Walker, McPherson, Reed) 1957.
Ginn: *English Skills* (Hook, Guild, Stevens) 1959.
Ginn: *Better English* (Herzberg, Guild, Hook, Stevens) 1955.
Harcourt, Brace: *English Grammar and Composition* (9-Warriner, Whitten, Griffith; 10-Warriner, Griffith; 11-Warriner, Mersand, Griffith; CC-Warriner, Griffith) 1958.
Harcourt, Brace: *Living Language* (9, 10, 11-Blumenthal, Frank, Zahner; 12-Frank, Zahner, Schendler) 1953.
Heath: *English in Action* (Tressler, Christ; 11-Tressler, Christ, Terino; 12-Tressler, Christ, Starkey) Seventh Edition, 1960.
Lippincott: *English for Today* (Gray, Hach) 1955.
Macmillan: 9-*Our English Language* (Pollock, Sheridan, Williams) 1961; 10-*Essentials of Modern English* (Pollock, Sheridan, Williams, Anker) 1961; 11-*Language Arts and Skills* (Pollock, Sheridan, Roody, Williams, Adams) 1961; 12-*The Art of Communicating* (Pollock, Sheridan, Hunter, Doll) 1961.
McGraw-Hill: *Your Language* (9-LaBrant, Painter, Anderson, Baldridge; 10-LaBrant, Painter, Jameson; 11-LaBrant, Leary, Bird, Painter) 1956, 1959, 1960.
Row, Peterson: *The New Building Better English* (9, 10-John, Yates, De Laney; 11-John, Yates; 12-De Boer) 1961.[2]
Scott, Foresman: *Guide to Modern English* (9, 10-Corbin, Blough, Vander Beek; Upper Years-Corbin, Perrin) 1960.
Scribner's: *English at Work* (Bryant, Howe, Jenkins, Munn) 1956.
Singer: *Enjoying English* (Wolfe, Beyer, *et al.*) 1960.

Content of the Series

Classified in general terms, the contents of the several series are summarized in Table I of Appendix B.

The quantitative analysis represented by Table I requires some explanatory comments. First, although the table represents the

---

[2] The 1960 edition, also examined, differs in no significant detail; hence no reference is made to it in the tables or comments which follow.

proportions, in terms of number of pages, allotted to the three large classifications of Grammar; Usage, and Mechanics; Composition; and "Other," it in no sense reflects the *organization* of the books analyzed. No volume in any of the series is divided as such into such clearcut sections as Grammar, Usage, and Mechanics; Composition; and "Other," as might seem to be implied by the table — nor, indeed, does the tabular presentation in any sense imply that in our view any volume should be so arranged. The various patterns of organization used in the several series are described hereafter.

Second, some explanation of the three main headings used in the table is here necessary. Under the heading "Grammar, Usage, Mechanics" are counted all the pages that have to do with parts of speech and parts of sentence, phrases and clauses, sentence classifications, principles of sentence construction, and closely related matters; levels of usage, including occasional extensive lists or indices (as, for example, the 243-page index in Scott, Foresmen — Upper Years); and punctuation, capitalization. In all of these texts, pages counted include those given to explanation, example, and exercise. Under the heading "Composition" are counted all pages having to do with written composition involving units larger than sentences (pages having to do with the writing of isolated sentences — for order, variety, etc. — are included in the count of Grammar, Usage, and Mechanics). Forms included under this heading are paragraphs, "themes" or essays, reports or research papers, both personal and business letters, and "imaginative" forms when these are treated primarily as parts of the students' active writing program. Pages are counted that present writing instructions and assignments, lists of writing topics, selection and limitation of topics, models or illustrative pieces of writing, outlining, directions for revision and proofreading. Under the heading "Other" are counted pages given to a miscellany of topics and activities in such a wide range as to make identification and enumeration impractical in this place. Included, at the one extreme, are topics intimately related to composition, such as spelling and word study, and, at the other, topics the relevance of which is less certainly established, such as telephoning, answering doorbells, and dating. The extent and diversity of contents here identified as "Other" will be discussed in the appropriate section of this report.

Finally, the authors of this report wish to acknowledge the fact that the page counts represented in Table I, Appendix B, are only as precise as page-by-page examination of the books, conducted over a limited period of time, could make them. Our aim in this analysis was to render an entirely objective classification of the contents, such that anyone else undertaking the same analysis would arrive at approximately the same figures. However, the nature of the contents, in which many treatments of topics and activities overlap or shade into others, and the organization, particularly of certain sets of books in which determined efforts at integration or fusion are made, have combined to make our aim of absolute objectivity an ideal rather than an actual achievement. For example, chapters in some books begin with several pages of rather general "motivation," involving, perhaps, the devising of imaginary situations which then provide occasion for a variety of activities — writing, conversation, panel discussion, and, in connection with these writing and speaking activities, exercises in grammar, spelling, vocabulary. On the next page is the outline of a single chapter from one of the volumes.[3]

Merely to distribute the contents of such a chapter — and the series contain many such — among the three columns of Table I, Appendix B, is a task that involves fine distinctions and, undoubtedly, many arbitrary decisions. In these cases our aim was, at the least, to make our decisions consistent from volume to volume and from series to series. Fortunately for the objectivity of the in-

---

[3] Scribner's, *English at Work*, 9, Chap. 4, pp. 86-114.

A GAME TO BE REMEMBERED

Writing Your Ideas:
  Thinking together
  Focusing attention
  Planning your theme
  Opening sentences
  Further helps
  Improving your writing
  Responsibility sheet 4

Speaking Your Ideas:
  Listening to the ideas of others
  General procedure
  Practice in listening

Aids to Communication:
  Getting the verb right
  Mastery test A
  Mastery test B
  How to study spelling
  Spelling lesson 1

itial analysis represented by Table I, not all of the series are so organized as to make classification of content particularly difficult, and some are so organized as to make it a simple matter of chapter-by-chapter calculation. This statement, however, is not meant to imply any necessary correlation between the relative ease with which contents can be classified by page-count and the merit of the series, for it is conceivable that one series in which integration of content makes classification and precise counting of pages peculiarly difficult is superior to another in which clear division of topics makes classification a mechanical matter.

Series Organization: Emphasis and Proportion

The foremost fact of series organization is made apparent by Table I, namely, that each of the broad categories of Grammar, Usage, and Mechanics; Composition; and "Other" is given approximately equal attention, in terms of space, at each grade level throughout any particular series. Thus, for a typical example, Ginn, *English Skills*, gives 172, 175, 139, and 191 pages, respectively, to grades nine, ten, eleven, and twelve for Grammar, Usage, and Mechanics; 82, 93, 76, and 103 pages for Composition; and 194, 200, 249, and 174 pages for "Other." This count suggests a somewhat lighter emphasis on Grammar and Composition in the eleventh grade, with a correspondingly heavier emphasis on "Other," and a heavier emphasis on Grammar in the twelfth grade, with lighter emphasis on the "Other." Only a few of the series show a truly pronounced emphasis or de-emphasis on any one of the three categories in any one year. Singer, *Enjoying English*, shows wide variation in the space given to Composition, with 34 and 53 pages in the ninth and tenth grades against 116 and 99 in the eleventh and twelfth grades. McGraw-Hill, *Your Language*, shows a sharp drop in attention to Composition, from 113 pages in the tenth grade to 45 in the eleventh, and a corresponding rise in "Other," from 234 in the tenth to 336 in the eleventh. Certain series appear to emphasize Composition in the tenth and twelfth grades, for example, American Book, *Our English Language*, and Scribner's, *English at Work;* but others, notably Lippincott, *English for Today;* Macmillan, *Language Arts and Skills;* and Singer, *Enjoying English*, give most space to Composition in the eleventh grade.

Though other, comparable variations are made apparent by Table I, the fact remains that the most conspicuous feature of the fourteen textbook series as they are represented in that table is the remarkable evenness of the page counts grade by grade in each of the three columns. This fact inevitably raises a basic question that will be pursued hereafter in the detailed sections of this report. Since Grammar, Composition, and "Other" receive approximately equal attention quantitatively at each grade level over a four-year span, what provisions are made for *progression* from year to year? Obviously, if the same topics were treated in the same manner and to the same depth in successive volumes of a series, there would be no true progression, but only *repetition*. This aspect of the total problem of organization, the extent to which the authors of the several series manage to achieve actual progression rather than mere repetition while treating the same general topics in each of the four years, is a principal matter for later detailed analysis.

Organization within Volumes

Along broad lines, the mechanical facts of organization within volumes of the fourteen series are expressed in the final three columns of Table I, Appendix B. Organizational details will, of course, be a concern of each detailed section in this report. Here it is appropriate only to supply brief explanatory comment.

Table I shows that six over-all organizational plans are used in volumes of the series:

Activities followed by Handbook	(A&H)
Handbook followed by Activities	(H&A)
Activities, Handbook, Activities	(AHA)
Integrated A&H	(Int)
Alternating A&H	(Alt)
Unclassified	(Unc)

Of these plans, the most frequently used is the first. Six of the series use the A&H plan in all four volumes; one more (the Macmillan series) uses it in grades ten, eleven, and twelve, but uses H&A in grade nine; one more (the Row, Peterson series) uses it in grades nine, ten, and eleven, but uses H&A in grade twelve; and, finally, another (the Scott, Foresman series) uses it in grades nine and ten, but falls into the Unclassified category in the volume designed for the upper years. Thus the A&H arrangement is used in a total of 32 of the 54 volumes examined.

In the typical A&H arrangement, the volume is divided into two parts. In the first of these are included all writing, speaking, listening, reading, thinking, and other activities, with accompanying motivation, instruction, assignments, lists of theme topics, models, etc. In the second are included instruction and exercises in grammar, usage, mechanics, spelling. Often the two-part division is definitely marked as, for example, in the Heath series, where the first group of eighteen chapters is headed *Language Activities* and the second group of seventeen chapters is headed *Handbook;* and in the Allyn and Bacon series, where the first eleven chapters are headed *Using the Language Arts* and the latter eleven are headed *Learning about Language.* Some of the series, however, notably the two Ginn series and the Harcourt, Brace *Living Language,* show no such formal division by the use of separate headings, as in the typical cases above, but the division is nevertheless clearly marked by the nature of the chapter headings; thus, for example, Ginn's *Better English,* 9, shifts after Chapter 18 ("Movies, Radio and Television Programs, and Recordings") from an Activities to a Handbook content, Chapter 19 being titled "Writing Good Sentences" and treating subjects, predicates, objects, modifiers, and sentence classifications. Finally, typical A&H volumes tend to be divided very evenly, about half the total number of pages going to activities and half to the handbook. One notable exception to the half-and-half rule of the typical A&H arrangements is Lippincott's *English for Today,* in which grade nine is divided 426-161; grade ten, 464-85; grade eleven, 442-111; and grade twelve, 474-91.

The H&A organization is used in only one complete series of four volumes (Harcourt, Brace, *English Grammar and Composition*), in the first volume of Macmillan, *Our English Heritage,* and in the fourth volume of Row, Peterson, *Building Better English.* Certain organizational features of the Harcourt, Brace series may be appropriately summarized at this point. The volumes of this series are not divided in the usual two-part way: one part Handbook, the other Activities. Rather, the volumes for grades nine and ten have six parts each, with Parts I and II given to grammar and usage, and with Part VI in grade nine and Part V in grade ten given to mechanics — capitalization, punctuation, etc. The volumes for grades eleven and twelve have eight parts

each, with Parts I and II given to grammar and usage, and
with Part VII in grade eleven and Part VIII in grade twelve
given to mechanics. In addition, these volumes for the upper
years include handbook-style treatments of sentence structure
in Part V, eleven, and in Parts III and IV, twelve. But, indeed, it
should be mentioned here that the Harcourt, Brace series is unique
among all the series in following a typical handbook treatment of
topics, with respect to both organization and content. Thus, in all
the volumes of the series, not only typical handbook topics such
as parts of speech, parts of sentence, and punctuation, but also
topics under the general heading of composition — paragraphs,
research paper, letters — and the variety of topics under what is
called "Other" in Table I are treated in handbook style. This basic
difference between the Harcourt, Brace *English Grammar and
Composition* and all of the other series will be noted in connection with each of the detailed sections of this report.

Of the remaining two volumes in which the H&A arrangement
appears, the Row, Peterson twelfth-grade volume and the Macmillan ninth-grade volume, the former is the clearer example.
The first 170 pages of this volume fall under the formal heading
Handbook of Language Mechanics and treat the usual materials
of grammar, usage, and mechanics, while the remaining 181
pages fall under the heading *Using Language to Communicate*
and take up the usual forms of writing and a variety of "Other"
topics. The Macmillan ninth-grade volume, on the other hand,
does not fall at all definitely into the H&A category and might
justifiably be placed in the Unclassified group. This volume begins with two chapters on vocabulary and study habits. It moves
next to six chapters treating, respectively, simple sentences,
nouns and pronouns, verbs and verbals, agreement of subject and
verb, modifiers, and compound and complex sentences. Thereafter it takes up a variety of activities involving writing, speaking,
listening, and concludes with a treatment of mechanics. Thus

the only claim of this volume to the H&A classification is its early six-chapter concentration on usual handbook matters.

A similar problem of classification occurs with Singer's *Enjoying English,* the only series identified in Table I as AHA — Activities-Handbook-Activities. The volumes of this series follow a common arrangement consisting of five parts: Part I, Experiences in Speaking, Listening, and Writing; Part II, Thought and Language Problems (or comparable wording); Part III, Language Skills and Correct Usage (or comparable wording); Part IV, Grammar Aids to Mature Expression (or comparable wording); Part V, Forms and References for Everyday Use (or comparable wording). In this arrangement, Parts I and II involve a great variety of activities; Parts III and IV present the usual handbook materials; and Part V presents letter writing, club meetings, applications and interviews, library exercises, etc. The basis for classifying the volumes of this series as AHA is the presence, at the approximate middle of each volume, of 200 to 250 pages of typical handbook material, separating the activities with which the volume begins and ends. Contradicting this classification is the author's own statement in the preface to each volume that each book of the series provides an "integrated program of self-expression, attack on common errors of usage, analysis of language meanings, and mastery of grammatical principles." Supporting this claim is the fact that an attempt at "integration" is indeed made, for example, in the "Experience Units" of Part I where, along with a variety of writing, speaking, and listening activities, attention is called to spelling, sentence building, recognizing sentences, keeping sentences apart, using sentence patterns, using exact verbs, etc.

The only series listed in Table I as Integrated is Scribner's *English at Work* which makes a thoroughgoing attempt at such an arrangement. The following unit is from the Scribner's grade nine volume:

CHAPTER 3: A PET OF ONE'S OWN

Writing Your Ideas:
  Thinking together
  Opening sentences
  Planning your theme
  Better communication
  Beginning sentences for
    themes
  Further helps on this
    assignment
  Responsibility sheet 3

Aids to Communication:
  End punctuation
  Run-together construction
  Use of comma with *and* or *but*
  Commas in a series
  Comma after *yes* and *no*
  Mastery test A
  Mastery test B
  Spelling demons

Speaking Your Ideas:
  Animals and their characteristics
  An oral English program
  Planning your talk
  Conducting the program
  Judging the recitation

It will be observed that this unit begins with preparation for and instruction in writing, moves on to speaking, and ends by concentration on punctuation. Each of fourteen units in the volume follows the same general pattern, with varied emphasis each time under "Aids to Communication." Thus Chapter 4, "A Game To Be Remembered," begins with writing and speaking and emphasizes the verb; Chapter 5, "Manners," continues the verb emphasis; Chapter 8, "Finding a Pen Pal," involves letter writing and emphasizes capitalization; Chapter 11, "Fun Out-of-Doors," takes up the simple sentence; Chapter 12, "Shopping Problems," deals with the compound sentence, and so on. Thus, in the course of the fourteen units many aspects of grammar and mechanics are treated by instruction, exercise, and mastery test; spelling, it should be mentioned, is a feature of each unit.

Finally, although the volume ends with a section identified as a "Handbook of Grammar and Usage," this section runs to only 50 pages, in contrast to the usual handbook in other series which is typically around 200 pages; moreover, this handbook differs from others by being in fact a *continuation*, in the form of additional exercises and tests, of the specific grammatical and mechanical treatments begun in the fourteen writing and speaking units. Thus, for example, Chapter 13, "Wishful Thinking," has emphasized complex sentences; at the end of the unit appears the note, "Additional work on complex sentences begins on page 501," and on page 501, in the handbook, further exercises are preceded by the note, "Continued drill from Chapter 13, pages 320-333." This is the pattern followed in all volumes of the series. The handbook section in this series is thus uniquely composed of additional study geared to writing and speaking units.

Only one other distinct plan of organization found in the series remains to be mentioned here — the Alternating plan, which appears in the American Book Company's *Our English Language*. The basic device of this organization can be illustrated simply by noting chapter headings from the grade nine volume: 1. "Leisure-time Fun"; 2. "Simple Sentences"; 3. "Time for Letters"; 4. "Compound Sentences"; 5. "Practice in Paragraphs"; 6. "Complex and Compound-complex Sentences." The volume contains twenty-nine chapters in this alternating pattern, a chapter involving an activity of writing, speaking, or listening, followed by a chapter treating some grammatical or mechanical topic; finally, Chapter 30, "Year-round Helps," of about 80 pages, reviews the materials of the preceding chapters. This style of organization falls about halfway between the typical Activities-Handbook plan and the Integrated organization.

Remaining to be mentioned in this introductory portion are those volumes (McGraw-Hill, *Your Language*, grades nine, ten, and eleven; and Scott, Foresman, *Guide to Modern English*, Upper Years) which follow no recognizable pattern of organization and have therefore been identified in Table I as "Unclassified." The problem may best be indicated by a summary recital of chapter titles from Part I of the McGraw grade nine volume: 1. "The Term Begins"; 2. "Words"; 3. "Choosing Leaders and Talking to Each Other"; 4. "Writing"; 5. "Taking Care of Details"; 6. "Listening"; 7. "The Report"; 8. "Letters"; 9. "Out-of-class Affairs"; 10. "The Big Book, the Dictionary"; 11. "Languages of the World"; 12. "Everyone Daydreams"; 13. "Telling the Time"; 14. "Words on the Air: Listening"; 15. "Usage"; 16. "Words: More Than Meets the Eye"; 17. "Using Words in Different Ways"; 18. "Plays"; 19. "On Guard!" Part II follows the five sections: 1. "Speaking"; 2. "Spelling, Punctuation, and Capitalization"; 3. "Grammar"; 4. "Usage and Selection of Words"; 5. "Preparing Papers and Writing Letters." Because of the two-part division, with the presentation of Mechanics, Grammar, and Usage in the second part, the volume would seem superficially to fall into the Activities-Handbook classification. However, the arrangement fails to fit that classification in three basic ways: first, many elements usually placed in typical handbook sections, notably verb forms and usage, are included in Part I; second, some activities usually included in the activities section, notably speaking, preparing papers, and writing letters, are here repeated in Part II after being treated in chapters of Part I; and finally, the typical handbook materials of mechanics, grammar, and usage, while they are here included in Part II, are not given recognizable handbook treatment.

The fourth and final book that falls into the Unclassified category, Scott, Foresman's upper years volume, consists of two parts. Part I begins with a chapter on levels of usage. It then moves to four chapters on the steps in writing — getting ready, planning, writing, and revising. Next it presents five chapters dealing with "words" — meaning, use, using dictionary, how words work, and word forms; two chapters on avoiding sentence errors and writing good sentences; two more chapters on writing — the research paper and "special types," including business and personal letters, school examinations, questionnaires, and reports; two chapters on speech activities; a chapter called "Taking Tests"; and a final chapter on punctuation. Thus Part I includes, in an order not readily classifiable, elements of the typical two-part Activities-Handbook textbook. Part II is an alphabetically arranged index, consisting of 203 pages in which are combined some of the features of a dictionary, a grammar and usage handbook, a book of rhetoric, and a general reference book. Inclusion of this index, occupying two-fifths of the total space, makes this volume unique among the textbooks examined.

CHAPTER 2

Grammar, Usage, Mechanics

ANALYSIS AND DESCRIPTION

THAT THE related subjects of Grammar, Usage, and Mechanics together claim a high proportion of the total pages contained in each volume of all series examined is made apparent by Table I of Appendix B. For the sake of convenience, the relevant figures from that table are repeated in Table II. As may there be seen, six of the series give nearly one-half of their space to Grammar, Usage, and Mechanics; seven give approximately one-third; and one gives less than one-fifth. The highest number of pages is given by HB[1]* (1162); the lowest by Lippincott (410). The highest percentage is given by Scott, Foresman, *Guide to Modern English* (49 per cent); the lowest by Lippincott (18 per cent).

It will be noted further that in all series approximately equal numbers of pages are given to Grammar, Usage, and Mechanics at each grade level, and thus approximately the same *proportion* is given to Grammar, Usage, and Mechanics in each volume that is given in the total series. The highest number of pages given in any one volume occurs in HB [1], grade twelve (351); the lowest in Lippincott, grade twelve (90). The HB [1] represents a

*HB[1] — Harcourt, Brace, *English Grammar and Composition.*

gradually rising emphasis in each year after grade nine; the Lippincott number represents only a slight drop from previous years. The most remarkably even number of pages given in successive years is shown by Macmillan, whose individually titled volumes number respectively 225, 220, 220, and 231, with a spread of only 11 pages from least to most. The widest spread is represented by Scott, Foresman, *Guide to Modern English,* with 206 pages in grade nine and 317 in the final volume — a difference of 111 pages; it is to be noted, however, that this final volume is intended for use in both grades eleven and twelve.

In summary, it is evident that at least *quantitatively* each series gives approximately the same attention to the combined subjects Grammar, Usage, and Mechanics at each grade level.

This fact at once raises a fundamental question that must serve as a focal point throughout the remainder of this section: if the volumes of series do not differ significantly from each other *quantitatively* in their attention to Grammar, Usage, and Mechanics, are there other ways in which they do differ significantly in the treatment of these subjects? Do they, for example, differ in the grammatical topics treated? Are parts of speech treated in one volume and not in others? Or are the eight parts of speech distributed among the several volumes, with nouns and verbs treated in one, adjectives and adverbs in another, pronouns and prepositions in another, conjunctions and interjections in another? Are simple, compound, complex, and compound-complex sentences allotted one to each volume? Are phrases divided between the first two volumes, clauses between the second pair? Are certain complements taken up in early volumes and others reserved for later? Are structural errors, such as dangling modifiers, faulty parallelism, faulty subordination, fragmentary or run-together sentences divided among the volumes? Are problems of case, number, agreement, tense similarly distributed? Are rules of punctuation apportioned equitably among the four volumes?

Or if there are no significant differences in the grammatical-mechanical topics treated from volume to volume, is differentiation based on other principles, such as manner and depth of treatment? Does, for example, the expository style of the textbooks become more complex in successive volumes? Are new concepts added from year to year that deepen students' understanding of parts of speech, problems of usage, and the conventions of punctuation and capitalization?

It is obviously not feasible, in a limited space, to answer all of the questions — of which those above are only examples that point to the basic problem — with respect to the grammatical-mechanical topics treated in each of the fifty-four volumes examined. It is therefore necessary to limit the presentation of detail to a few selected topics with the expectation that textbook treatment of these will be understood as representative of all such topics. To this end, we have selected topics certain to be treated in all series, important enough to serve as examples, and at the same time sufficiently restricted to permit detailed analysis. These topics are Parts of Speech, Agreement of Subject and Verb, Punctuation and Capitalization, and Subject and Predicate — Sentence Recognition. Table III of Appendix B presents the number of pages assigned to these topics in each volume and the total for each series.

Parts of Speech

Two observations are to be made with reference to that portion of Table III that pertains to Parts of Speech: (1) there is an extremely wide range in attention given to the parts of speech according to the series totals; (2) fairly uniform attention is given to the parts of speech in each volume of each series.

In the main, the very wide discrepancies evident in series totals for parts of speech are reflections of basically contrasting methods of organization employed by the textbook authors. For the most part, those books that show relatively low page totals include a distinct treatment of the parts of speech as parts of speech, separate from treatment of their usage as parts of the sentence. This treatment is sometimes, as in HB [1], contained in a single chapter headed "The Parts of Speech." Included in such a chapter are definitions, illustrations, and exercises involving identification of nouns as nouns, pronouns as pronouns, without reference to use as subject, object, etc. In contrast, books that show a high page total are likely to be those in which the main organization of the handbook, (or equivalent) portion of the volume is based on individual chapters for each part of speech, treated in all aspects of form and function. Examples of this kind of organization are to be found in both of the Ginn series and the American Book Company's *Our English Language,* among others.

The method of the latter, a representative volume, will serve to exemplify this kind of organization. In the ninth-grade volume, six chapters are given to the parts of speech, as follows: (1) "Ideas about Nouns"; (2) "Speaking of Pronouns"; (3) "Using Verbs"; (4) "Adjectives and Adverbs"; (5) "The Practical Preposition"; (6) "Conjunctions and Interjections." The treatment of the parts of speech handled in this fashion may be demonstrated by noting the contents of the chapter on nouns: "What Is a Noun?" "Taking Inventory," "Using Exact Nouns," "Singular and Plural Nouns," "Writing Possessives," "Common and Proper Nouns," "Case of Nouns," "Nominative Case," "Objective Case," "Two Punctuation Problems," "Word Study," "Time for Review," "Have you Accomplished the Purposes?"

In contrast to this method is that, for example, of Row, Peterson, *Building Better English.* Here, in the ninth-grade volume, appears a single chapter of 16 pages titled "Recognizing Parts of Speech." About two pages are given each part of speech as part of speech; thus nouns are defined, classified as proper, common, concrete, abstract, collective, and compound; the various classes are illustrated; and four written or oral exercises present problems in identifying and classifying nouns. The same pattern is followed with pronouns and the other parts of speech. Following the single chapter given to the eight parts of speech, seven of the remaining nine chapters in the handbook section treat the uses of particular parts of speech in building sentences, thus: "Using Nouns to Build Sentences," "Using Pronouns to Build Sentences," etc.

In summary, two contrasting ways of presenting the parts of speech are used in the textbooks: (1) a separate chapter, or section, discussing *all* parts of speech as part of speech, with subsequent chapters in the handbook treating parts of the sentence (subject, predicate, complement) and phrases and clauses, involving the parts of speech as they are relevant in discussion of these latter topics (of this organization HB [1], any volume, provides the clearest example); (2) a separate chapter for *each* part of speech, or for small groups of parts of speech, using these as focal centers for discussion of sentence parts (of this organization the clearest example is furnished by Allyn and Bacon, *Effective English,* grade twelve).

It is not our purpose at this point to comment on the relative effectiveness, or efficiency, of the two basic plans. Each has its advantages and its disadvantages; repetition is inevitable by either method, and each method results in a number of "leftovers" — such as verbals, phrases and clauses, compound and complex sentences, agreement — which have to be discussed outside the main frame. Variations upon, and even drastic departures from, these principal organizations are evident among the series examined, most notably in those that attempt "integration" of the usual handbook materials with all other materials of writing, speaking, and listening. The effort at "integration" results in distributing pieces of information about parts of speech as parts of speech and as elements of sentence among all, or nearly all, chapters in the volume. Of this practice the best example is furnished by Scribner's *English at Work*, any volume. In the volume for grade ten, Adjectives and Adverbs are thus given one page in Chapter 3, "Your Public and You"; Verb Information is given a page in Chapter 4, "Building a Paragraph"; Detecting Trouble in Verbs has ten pages in Chapter 9, "Drivers, Good and Bad"; Adjectives and Adverbs have eleven pages in Chapter 11, "How the Mind Works"; Pronouns have five pages in Chapter 14, "Listening," etc. As may be noted in Table III, this kind of series shows a relatively low total amount of space given to parts of speech; on that point, however, the following paragraph makes a comment.

The count of pages given to parts of speech, as shown in Table III, is probably less precise than the count for any other item in the several tables. For volumes having a chapter devoted to the parts of speech as parts of speech, counting is a mechanical task, and the result can be precise. For volumes which attempt discussion of individual parts of speech in all their aspects of form and function, the task of separating out just those pages which treat the part of speech as part of speech is impossible of exact performance; hence the count for such volumes, in Table III, represents the total discussion of the parts of speech, not just that portion which considers them as parts of speech, and in these cases the totals run much higher than for those volumes in which parts of speech are treated distinctly as parts of speech.

More important, however, than the question of the total amount of attention accorded parts of speech in a given series is the question of differentiation in the treatment from volume to volume. Generally speaking (allowing for rare exceptions in the treatment of interjections), each part of speech is given attention in each volume of each series.

Further, *not only are all parts of speech treated in each volume of each series, but also they are treated in essentially the same manner and to approximately the same depth in each.* That is to say, parts of speech are defined, exemplified, discussed in their various uses as sentence parts, and made the subjects of written or oral exercises in each volume of each series. It is manifestly impossible, in limited space, to show in detail the repetitive treatments of all parts of speech in all volumes of the series examined; accordingly, it will be necessary here to proceed by limited example.

Since its treatment in the textbooks, as well as analysis here of its treatment, involves the least complexity and difficulty, we begin with the interjection as it is represented in a few of the series, taken at random:

Allyn and Bacon, *Effective English:* In Volume 1, page 215, the interjection is defined as "a word that shows strong or sudden feeling. It often precedes an exclamatory sentence" and is illustrated by "Oh." In Volume 2, page 231, it is defined as "a word which stands alone to express strong or sudden feeling. It often precedes a sentence that explains the feeling expressed" and is illustrated by sentences containing "Oh!" "My goodness!" and "My!"; it is also represented in a diagraming demonstration, page 256. In Volume 3, page 215, it is defined as "a word which is used to express emotion or strong feeling. Interjections are sounds or cries which express fear, anger, surprise, or sorrow — often emotionally toned slang words," is illustrated by twelve expressions, and mentioned as an item in punctuation, page 375. In Volume 4, pages 374-75, it is described as derived from Latin *interjectio,* defined as "a remark that is inserted," having characteristics as follows: expresses feeling or emotion, has no grammatical relation to rest of sentence, is followed by exclamation point or question mark when used alone, or by a comma when used

to begin a sentence; is illustrated by "Oh?" "Well!" and "Why!";
and is made the subject for a library problem, involving the location and identification of interjections.

A second typical treatment of the interjection is represented
by American Book Company, *Our English Language*. In Volumes
1, 2, 3, and 4, the interjection is defined, illustrated, diagramed,
and used as the subject of a ten-sentence exercise involving punctuation and capitalization.

What has been briefly summarized concerning the treatment of
the interjection in the two series above holds true for virtually
all of the series examined. Exceptions include the Scribner's
series, *English at Work*, and the Harcourt, Brace *Living Language*, which omit discussion of the interjection entirely, and
the Scott, Foresman *Guide to Better English* and the Macmillan
series (individual titles), both of which omit the interjection in
the first volume but treat it in the remaining volumes.

The treatment of the parts of speech may be illustrated further
by detailed analysis of the textbooks' handling of a considerably
more substantial part than the interjection — the noun. Since it is
not feasible to describe in detail the treatment of the noun in
every volume, we present in Table IV a quantitative summary in
terms of pages given to the noun in each volume of each series,
and describe a single typical treatment in detail.

It is necessary first to distinguish in Table IV between those
totals marked (*) and all of the others. The considerable difference between the high totals of the former and the relatively
low totals of the latter is a reflection of basically different methods
of organization described earlier. In the former, virtually all
matters pertaining to nouns, or in which nouns figure, are brought
together in one chapter, as in American Book Company's chapter
"Ideas About Nouns" in the volume for grade nine: Taking Inventory, Using Exact Nouns, What Is a Noun? Singular and Plural
Nouns, Collective Nouns, Writing Possessives, Common and

Proper Nouns, Case of Nouns, Nominative Case, Objective Case, Two Punctuation Problems, Word Study, Time for Review, Have You Accomplished the Purpose? In addition, the summary section of this volume, "Year-round Helps," featuring additional exercises on all points covered in the body of the volume, includes numerous items pertaining to nouns.

The latter form of organization, reflected in much lower page counts for nouns, may be exemplified by reference to Ginn, *English Skills,* grade nine. In this arrangement, and included in the count of pages, are first the chapter, "What's in a Name? Nouns," in which are treated Common, Proper, and Collective Nouns, and a small section under the title "Spell by Rules," in which are treated Plurals, Contractions, and Possessives of Nouns. Series counts included in Table IV that are not marked (*) represent approximately these same aspects of the total treatment of nouns, and do not represent pages given to nouns as subjects, objects, appositives, etc., as the counts for the series marked (*) do.

Actually, even the higher counts hardly do more than approximate the full attention, both direct and oblique, that is given to nouns; they do not, for example, include pages given to noun clauses, to the various phrases in noun uses, or to noun problems that arise in connection with capitalization and agreement. Perhaps the most accurate and complete count of actual attention paid to nouns is that shown in Table IV for Row, Peterson, *Building Better English.* Here the treatment of nouns falls under two chapter headings: Chapter 19, "Recognizing the Parts of Speech," in which nouns are defined, classified, illustrated, and made the basis of four written and oral exercises; and Chapter 21, "Using Nouns to Build Sentences," which treats nouns in their various uses and forms and in relation to the major problems that arise in sentence building. The only noun matters regularly treated in the textbooks but not included under either of these two chapter headings (which are the basis of the count shown in Table IV) are capitalization, formation of plurals and possessives, and noun clauses — all of which are treated elsewhere in the volume.

Despite the imperfections in Table IV that result from the use of contrasting organizations in the treatment of nouns, such quantitative representation shows the two main facts with sufficient clarity: *that all the textbooks give considerable attention to nouns, and that approximately the same attention is spread with notable uniformity among all volumes of each series.*

While Table IV thus adequately represents the amount of space given to nouns in the volumes of each series, it does not touch the more fundamental question of differentiation among volumes on any basis other than the quantitative. It is obviously not feasible here to compare the details of what is *said about and done with* nouns from volume to volume of each series, and from series to series. It will be necessary, therefore, to let detailed analysis of treatment by one reasonably typical textbook series stand for all, with additional comments to mark unusual variations that appear in certain other series. For this purpose, the fairest choice is undoubtedly Ginn, *English Skills,* which devotes a comparatively modest number of pages to nouns, treats all of the noun matters that are regularly treated in the majority of textbooks, and discusses them in a manner that is as nearly "standard" as any. An account of this typical treatment follows.

In the volume for grade nine the main discussion of the noun as a part of speech is presented in Chapter 18, "What's in a Name? Nouns." Here nouns are first characterized as names. A preliminary exercise asks students to identify the names included in nine brief sentences. Common nouns are next distinguished from proper nouns in an exercise of ten sentences. Collective nouns are then represented in an exercise of six sentences that include words like "class," "committee," and "family." Four definitions follow: of the *noun,* as name of a person, place, or thing . . . the name of a quality or idea, which cannot be seen; of a *common* noun, as a name which may be applied to any one of a class of persons, places, or things; of a *proper* noun, as the name of a particular person, place, or thing; and of a *collective* noun, as the name of a group or class and not of a single person or thing. Next are presented three rules: a proper noun begins with a capital letter; a collective noun used to name members of a group as a unit takes a singular verb and a singular word referring to it; a collective noun used to name the members of a group as separate individuals takes a plural verb and a plural word referring to it. Finally, exercise sentences ask students to identify nouns, to distinguish common from proper nouns, and to choose the appropriate verb or pronoun to accompany collective nouns used as subjects; two testing exercises on common, proper, and collective nouns complete the treatment of nouns in this chapter.

Typical additional attention is given the noun in later chapters of this volume, notably Chapter 24, "Punctuation and Capitalization," under the heading Capital Letters, and Chapter 25, "Spell by Rules," under the heading Plurals, Contractions, and Possessives of Nouns.

In the volume for grade ten the main discussion of the noun as part of speech is again presented in Chapter 18, "What Everyone Should Know about Nouns." Here nouns are first characterized as names, and a preliminary exercise of three sentences asks students to identify the nouns. Next, with the same sentences as exercise material, distinction is made between common and proper nouns. Next, collective nouns are introduced through an exercise of three sentences, using the words "band" and "team." Four definitions follow: of the noun, as the name of a person, place, thing, or an idea; of the common noun, as a name applied to any one of a class of persons, places, things, or ideas; of the proper noun, as the name of a particular person, place, thing, or idea; and of the collective noun, as the name of a group or class and not of a single person, place, or thing.

Next are presented three rules: a proper noun begins with a capital letter; a collective noun used to name members of a group acting as a unit takes a singular verb and a singular pronoun or adjective; a collective noun used to name members of a group acting as separate individuals takes a plural verb and a plural pronoun or adjective. Next are presented three exercises asking students to recognize and distinguish common and proper nouns and to use verbs correctly with collective nouns. Finally, concrete and abstract nouns are introduced, exemplified, used as the basis of exercise, and defined as follows: a noun which names a person or thing is called a concrete noun; a noun which names an idea is called an abstract noun. The chapter concludes with testing exercises on collective, concrete, and abstract nouns.

Additional attention is given nouns in a chapter on punctuation and capitalization and to plurals, contractions, and possessives of nouns in a chapter on spelling.

In the volume for grade eleven the main discussion of the noun is again presented in Chapter 18, "Nouns and Pronouns." In a preliminary exercise based on five sentences, common, proper, collective, concrete, and abstract nouns are distinguished. Next comes a list of definitions as follows: of a noun, as name of a person, place, thing, or idea; of a common noun, as a name that may be applied to any one of a class of persons, places, things, or ideas; of a proper noun, as the name of a particular person, place, or thing; of a concrete noun, as name of a thing that is evident to one of the five senses; of an abstract noun, as name of an idea that is not evident to the five senses; of a collective noun, as name of a group or class and not of a single person, place, or thing. Rules follow: a proper noun begins with a capital letter; a collective noun that names the members of a group as a unit takes a singular verb, pronoun, or possessive adjective; a collective noun that names the members of a group as individuals takes a plural verb, pronoun, or possessive adjective. Finally, practice and testing exercises ask the student to distinguish between concrete and abstract nouns, distinguish between singular and plural uses of collective nouns, and use abstract and collective nouns accurately.

Additional attention is given nouns in a later chapter on punctuation and capitalization and to plurals, contractions, and possessives of nouns in a chapter on spelling.

In the volume for grade twelve the main discussion of the noun is presented in Chapter 12, "Learning More about Nouns and Pronouns." Nouns are first described as names of persons, places, things, or ideas and are divided into two chief classes, common and proper, with exercise questions on these classes. Next concrete and abstract nouns are exemplified and made the subjects of exercise questions. Collective nouns are next given similar treatment, with exemplification and exercise questions. There follows a set of definitions: of a noun, as name of a person, place, thing, or idea; of a common noun as name applied to any one of a class of persons, places, things, or ideas; of a proper noun, as name of a particular person, place, thing, or idea; of a concrete noun, as name of a thing that can be perceived by one or more of the five senses; of an abstract noun, as the name of an idea that cannot be perceived by the five senses; and of a collective noun, as name of a group or class of people or things and not the name of a single person or thing. Next come two rules: when a collective noun represents the group or class as acting as a unit, the verb should be singular; and when a collective noun represents the members of a group or class as acting as separate individuals, a plural verb should be used. There follow two exercises of ten and eleven sentences respectively, the first involving identification of kinds of nouns, common, proper, abstract, concrete, and collective, the second involving agreement of verbs with collective nouns. There is finally a testing exercise of eleven sentences involving distinction of common and proper nouns and recognition of singularity or plurality of collective nouns.

Additional attention is given nouns in a chapter on punctuation and capitalization and to possessives of nouns in a chapter on spelling.

The preceding summary of the treatment of nouns and noun matters through grades nine, ten, eleven, and twelve may stand as representative of the treatment of parts of speech in general through these grades in the Ginn series, *English Skills*. With allowance for variation in organization of materials, it may stand also as representative of the treatment accorded parts of speech in other series examined. The primary fact made apparent by this analysis is this: *that each part of speech is given essentially the same treatment in any volume of any particular series that it is given in all other volumes of that series.*

Agreement of Subject and Verb

The treatment of the agreement of subject and verb as reported here can justifiably stand as representative of the treatment accorded matters of usage generally. Agreement is a topic treated by all textbooks in the several series examined, and, as shown by the relevant column in Table III, is presented with a high degree of regularity from volume to volume and from series to series. Although any other major problems of usage — as those involving case and reference of pronouns, comparison and placement of modifiers, principal parts of verbs — may appear to have equal claim to be selected as the example for analysis, the matter of subject-verb agreement has the advantage of being at once highly important and relatively concentrated with respect to the place it occupies in any given series. Whereas other usage problems are touched on here and there at widely dispersed points in some of the textbooks, depending on the type of general organization employed by the authors, treatment of subject-verb agreement is likely to be confined to one or two chapters or sections of chapters, and hence it lends itself more readily to accurate comparison of volume with volume and series with series.

Table III shows that space given to subject-verb agreement in the several series ranges from a top of 63 pages (HB [1]) to lows of 14 pages in each of the Ginn series and 12 pages in the McGraw-Hill series (which, however, is represented by only three volumes in this report). The more typical treatments use from twenty-five to forty pages. It is accurate to say that in the main the textbooks cover a common body of matter in the form of explanation, exemplification, and drill; it would therefore be difficult to select any one series that might appropriately be termed "eccentric" in its coverage of this topic. Of all the series, the one that appears to be most representative in the handling of subject-verb agreement is Heath, *English in Action,* which, as is shown by Table III, gives 43 pages to subject-verb agreement, distributed evenly by grade, 13, 10, 10, 10; among the several series, these numbers are neither very high nor very low.

In the volume for grade nine, agreement is treated in Chapter 24, "Making Verbs Agree with Their Subjects." First is stated the basic rule: A verb agrees with its subject in number (singular or plural). It is pointed out that a verb ending in *s* is ordinarily singular, and that the procedure for making verb agree with subject is as follows: Ask yourself first; What is the subject? Second: Is it singular or plural? Then choose the correct verb form. Next follow a number of practice exercises: (1) Using *doesn't* and *don't* correctly (8 sentences); (2) Agreement with *you* (5 sentences); (3) Using correct verbs in inverted sentences (20 sentences); (4) Making verbs agree with their subject (50 sentences); (5) Agreement with compound subject (16 sentences); (6) Making verbs agree with their subjects (50 sentences); (7) Rapid drill on agreement of subject and verb (24 subject-verb combinations); (8) Noting verb errors (jotting down errors heard); (9) Mastery test on agreement of subject and verbs (20 sentences); (10) Mastery test on agreement of subject and verb (20 sentences). Special problems illustrated in connection with these exercises include the following: (1) phrase after subject; (2) subject with *and;* (3) compound subject, but one idea; (4) *or, nor;* (5) collective noun; (6) *the number of, a number of;* (7) *each, every,* and similar words. Typical instructions for the practice exercises include: "Say each sentence aloud until it sounds right to you." Total number of sentences for exercises and mastery tests: 213.

In the volume for grade ten, agreement is treated in Chapter 24, "Making Verbs Agree with Their Subjects." There is first a diagnostic test on agreement of verb and subject (20 sentences). Next is stated the basic rule: A verb agrees with its subject in number. It is pointed out that a verb ending in *s* is usually singular, and that the verb *to be* is irregular. The special problems of *doesn't* and *don't, you,* and the inverted sentence are treated as in the volume for grade nine. Next follow a number of practice exercises: (1) Making verbs agree with their subjects (10 sentences); (2) Using verbs and subjects correctly (12 subject-verb combinations to be used in sentences); (3) Making verbs agree with their subjects (20 sentences); (4) Studying agreement of verb and subject (10 sentences); (5) Solving all agreement problems (25 sentences); (6) Rapid drill on agreement (8 problems of subject-verb combinations); (9) Mastery test on agreement of verb and subject (20 sentences). Special problems illustrated in connection with these exercises include the following: (1) phrase after subject; (2) sentences with predicate noun; (3) positive and negative; (4) *and;* (5) *or, nor;* (6) *each, every,* and similar words; (7) collective nouns; (8) singular nouns ending with *s;* (9) *who, which, that.* Total number of sentences for exercises and mastery tests: 125.

In the volume for grade eleven, agreement is treated in Chapter 28, "Using Correct, Vivid Verbs." First is presented a diagnostic test on agreement of verb and subject (20 sentences). Next is stated the basic rule: A verb agrees with its subject in number. It is pointed out that a verb ending in *s* is singular, whereas a noun ending in *s* is plural. The special problems of *doesn't* and *don't, you,* and the inverted sentence are treated as in volumes for grades nine and ten. Practice exercises follow: (1) Choosing correct verbs (14 sentences); (2) Agreement of verb and subject (24 problems of subject-verb combinations); (3) Using correct verbs (16 sentences); (4) Mastery test on agreement of verb and subject (20 sentences). Special problems illustrated in connection with these exercises include the following: (1) sentence with predicate noun or pronoun; (2) positive and negative; (3) modifiers (prepositional phrase) after the subject; (4) *who, which, that;* relative clause following *one of;* (5) *and;* (6) *or, nor;* (7) nouns plural in form but singular in idea; (8) *each, every;* (9) collective noun. Total number of sentences in exercises and tests: 94.

In the volume for grade twelve, agreement is treated in Chapter 23, "Finding the Right Verb." First is presented a diagnostic test on agreement of verb and subject (20 sentences). Next is presented the basic rule: A verb agrees with its subject in number and person. It is pointed out that a verb ending in *s* is singular, whereas a noun ending in *s* is plural. The special problems of *you,* the inverted sentence, and *doesn't* and *don't* are treated as in the volumes for grades nine, ten, and eleven. Next follow a number of practice exercises: (1) Choosing correct verbs (16 sentences); (2) Agreement of verb and subject (30 problems of subject-verb combinations); (3) Using verbs correctly (16 sentences); (4) Mastery test on agreement of subject and verb (20 sentences). Special problems illustrated in connection with these exercises include the following: (1) positive and negative; (2)

sentence with predicate noun; (3) *who, which, that;* relative clause following *one of;* (4) *and;* (5) *or, nor;* (6) plural in form but singular in idea; (7) *each, every;* (8) collective nouns. Total number of sentences in exercises and tests: 100.

Total number of sentences used for exercises and tests in the four volumes of the series: 532.

The foregoing account of subject-verb agreement as that topic is treated in the Heath series is offered as the fairest choice to stand as representative. As shown in Table III, several series give greater attention to agreement, others less. In general, the special problems or "trouble spots" given special attention in the Heath series are the same that receive special attention in other series. The only considerable difference between the treatment of subject-verb agreement in the Heath series and that in certain other series, notably those that use an "integrated" or "alternating" type of general organization, is that in the Heath series the topic is characteristically restricted to a single chapter, or section of a chapter, in each volume, whereas in the others the treatment is dispersed, often widely.

The primary fact made apparent by our study of agreement is this: *that the topic of agreement of subject and verb is given essentially the same treatment in any volume of any particular series that it is given in the other volumes of that series.*

Punctuation and Capitalization

As may be seen in Table III, the mechanics of punctuation and capitalization receive a very considerable amount of attention in each volume of each series. In general, this topic receives, volume for volume, greater attention than the parts of speech; indeed, it receives greater attention than any other topic covered in the typical handbook section of any series. Table III shows an extreme series range, from the highest totals of 270 and 213 pages, respectively, for Harcourt, Brace, *English Grammar and Compo-*

sition and Scribner's *English at Work,* to the lowest figures of 41 and 65 pages, respectively, for American Book Company's *Our English Language* and Lippincott's *English for Today.* It is to be remarked that the two series showing the highest totals also represent extreme opposites in general organization — the Harcourt, Brace series representing the clearest example of the straightforward handbook type of organization and the Scribner's series representing the clearest example of the "integrated" textbook; what these two contrasting types of organization mean for the treatment of punctuation and capitalization is that in the former instance treatment is confined to one primary section of the text and in the latter it is distributed throughout the text.

Because of the very large space given by most series to the complex of matters under punctuation and capitalization, it is not feasible in limited space to present a detailed account of the treatment given to the entire topic. The purpose will best be served by limiting detailed analysis to a single area, namely, the relatively specific, but highly important, matter of comma punctuation. To introduce this analysis a comparative table will be useful at this point.

As may be seen in Table V of Appendix B, there is considerable range in the space given to comma punctuation, from the high of the two Harcourt, Brace series, 81 and 77 pages, to the low of American Book Company's *Our English Language,* 15, and Lippincott's *English for Today,* 22 pages, a reflection in part of the contrasting types of organization represented by the two pairs of series. It will be observed that nine of the fourteen series shown in the table concentrate the treatment of comma punctuation in a single chapter (shown as "ch" in the table) or to a single section of a chapter; all rules, explanations, examples, and exercises on comma punctuation are in these texts confined to the one chapter, which is typically placed in the handbook section, often under a more comprehensive heading such as "Mechanics." Frequently in these same texts additional passing attention is paid to special uses of the comma in connection with writing assignments, such as business and personal letters. Students are often admonished to be careful with punctuation in proofreading their written work. These references are made only in passing, however, and because they usually amount to no more than a sentence on each occasion they have not been included in the count of pages. The contrasting type of organization finds rules and exercises distributed or dispersed (marked "d" in Table V) throughout the volume, without the use of any substantial handbook chapter or section devoted to punctuation. Actually, only one series, that of the American Book Company, is marked "d" in Table V. Four others, however, are marked "ch&d" to indicate use of both a relatively substantial handbook section and a distribution of attention to punctuation throughout the volume.

In order to represent the textbooks' treatment of comma punctuation adequately in this report, it is necessary to take for analysis a typical example of each major kind of organization — that is to say, of the "ch" and the "ch&d" classifications shown in Table V. Avoiding the high and low extremes in page counts, we present a detailed account of the Macmillan series to exemplify the "ch" treatment, and of the Singer series to exemplify the "ch&d" treatment. To complete the account, it will be necessary to comment additionally on the single example of the "d" treatment found in the American Book Company series.

In the volume for grade nine of the Macmillan series, the treatment of punctuation is presented in the final section called "The Mechanics of Writing." Comma punctuation occupies ten of the thirty pages there given to punctuation in general. An initial general comment precedes the stating and illustration of individual rules: "A comma signals a slight pause. Guard against overusing it. Like medicine, it should be used only according to directions." There follow rules in this order: (1) "Use commas to separate words, phrases, and clauses in a series." (2) "Use a comma to separate an introductory word, phrase, or clause from the rest of the sentence." (3) "Place a comma before the conjunction that joins two main clauses in a compound sentence." (4) "Use commas to set off a non-restrictive clause from the rest of the sentence." (5) "Use commas to set off a non-restrictive participial phrase from the rest of the sentence." (6) "Use commas to set off non-restrictive words or phrases in apposition." (7) "Use commas to enclose words used in direct address." (8) "Use commas to set off words and phrases of slight importance which interrupt sentences." (9) "Use a comma between the name of a city or town and the name of its state or country. If you write a complete address as part of a sentence, use a comma between items." (10) "Use a comma after the salutation of a friendly letter and after the complimentary close of a friendly letter and of a business letter." (11) "Use a comma or commas to set off or enclose the words in dialogue which tell who the speaker is." (12) "Use commas to set off contrasting expressions introduced by the word *not*." (13) "Use commas to set off words and phrases transposed from their normal order in a sentence." (14) "Use a comma when words are omitted from parallel word groups." (15) "Use a comma to set off a participle separated from the word it modifies." (16) "When no specific rule applies, but there is danger of misreading, use a comma."

It should be explained that although these sixteen rules are given in the order here reproduced they are separated from one another by explanatory comments, examples, notations of exception, and, in certain instances, special "do not" instructions — for example, with Rule 1, "Do not use a comma between the last adjective in a series and the noun which the series modifies," and, with Rule 4, "Do not use commas to set off a restrictive clause from the rest of the sentence." In addition to rules and the various explanatory devices, the section includes punctuation exercises totaling 85 sentences, including a general review exercise. The exercises are preceded by the instruction to "explain the comma usage in each case."

In the volume for grade ten, the treatment of punctuation is presented as section eleven of the Handbook, where comma punctuation occupies 10 of the 11 pages given to "End Marks and Commas." Rules are stated in the following order: (1) "Introductory words such as *yes, no, well, why,* and *oh* are followed by a comma." (2) "A participial phrase at the beginning of a sentence is followed by a comma." (3) "A long adverbial clause at the beginning of a sentence is followed by a comma." (4) "A succession of prepositional phrases at the beginning of a sentence is set off by commas." (5) "Words and phrases moved to the beginning of a sentence from their normal position are set off by a comma." (6) "An appositive is set off from the rest of the sentence by commas." (7) "Words of direct address are set off by commas." (8) "Parenthetical expressions are set off by commas." (9) "In dates and addresses of more than one part, set off every part after the first from the rest of the sentence." (10) "Non-restrictive clauses are set off by commas from the rest of the sentence." (11) "Non-restrictive participial phrases are set off from the rest of the sentence by commas." (12) "Place a comma before the conjunction that joins two main clauses in a compound sentence." (13) "Commas are used to separate the parts of a series." (14) "Commas are placed between the coordinate adjectives that modify the same noun." (15) "Use a comma to separate words or phrases that might be mistakenly joined in reading." (16) "Use a comma when words are omitted from parallel word groups."

As in the volume for grade nine, these rules are separated from one another by explanatory comments, examples, special "do not" instructions, etc. Also included are five punctuation exercises totaling 85 sentences.

It will be observed that although the order of rules is changed and the wording of some rules is altered, with some regrouping of items, the sixteen rules in each volume actually cover the same sentence elements and situations. Further, although the sentences employed in exercises in the two volumes differ in content, the same punctuation practices are tested in both.

Since, in the Macmillan series, the treatment of comma punctuation in the volumes for grades eleven and twelve is identical to that in the volume for grade ten, it will not be necessary here to repeat the details. The order and wording of the rules are identical in the three volumes, as are also the examples and explanatory comments, in every detail. The same number of exercises, five, covering the same problems, is included in each of the three volumes. Sentences included in these exercises differ, however, for each volume, and there is some difference in the number of sentences included in each exercise, as follows:

Exercise 1: 15 sentences in grades ten and eleven; 14 in grade twelve.
Exercise 2: 20 in grades ten and twelve; 18 in grade eleven.
Exercise 3: 20 in grade ten; 18 in grades eleven and twelve.
Exercise 4: 20 in grade ten; 18 in grades eleven and twelve.
Exercise 5: 10 in each of the grades.

Although sentences included in the exercises differ from volume to volume, the patterns are frequently similar, as will be observed in the following examples:

Exercise 1
grade 10: Why no one had told us about the fire.
grade 11: Why every picture in my roll of film was spoiled!
grade 12: Why there are many amateurs who do excellent repair work.

Exercise 2
grade 10: Please mail the package to me at 14 East Seventeenth Street New York 11 New York.
grade 11: Send your contributions to Mr. Frank Quinn 1851 West 107th Street Chicago 43 Illinois.

Exercise 3

grade 10:   Dr. Powers who lives next door is a famous brain sur-
geon.

grade 11:   Mr. Moss who teaches industrial arts has just bought
a station wagon.

grade 12:   Her sister Joan who lived near us in Tulsa is now eighteen years old.

Exercise 4

grade 10:   Harry's rude thoughtless reply bothered us all day.

grade 11:   It was one of those warm muggy days in early September.

grade 12:   The line of weary hungry students moved slowly into
the cafeteria.

Exercise 5

grade 10:   Below the men were working quietly.

grade 11:   Inside the fire was burning brightly.

grade 12:   Inside the gaiety continued for many hours.

Although the Macmillan series is here used to represent typical
"ch" treatments of comma punctuation, it should be pointed out
that the series is not precisely representative in its use of *identical* materials (except exercise sentences) in grades ten, eleven,
and twelve. In the volumes of any other series, though coverage
of comma rules, together with explanatory exemplification, is essentially the same at each level, yet order and wording of rules
are varied from year to year, different examples are prepared,
and explanatory wording is altered, so that superficially the treatment of comma punctuation may appear markedly different at
each grade level. It should also be pointed out here that the foregoing description of Macmillan's identical repetition of comma
treatment throughout three grade levels is not intended as an ad-
verse comment. Rather, this case of undisguised repetition is here
pointed to as effectively dramatizing a primary fact about handbook materials and their treatment in successive volumes of any
series. The critical comments which conclude this section on

Grammar, Usage, and Mechanics will be found to center on this fact.

To represent the "ch&d" treatment of comma punctuation, the Singer series, *Enjoying English,* will be described in sufficient detail to make apparent the differences between the two major approaches. The right of this series to be used as the example is based first of all on the page count, which is average in comparison with others. The Row, Peterson series might have equal claim with the Singer series to be used as the example and is omitted mainly because it has figured earlier in this report as the example for parts of speech.

The essential difference between the "ch" treatment and the "ch&d" treatment is that whereas the former confines its discussion of comma punctuation to one chapter or section, with occasional passing reference to commas elsewhere, the latter takes up comma usage fairly regularly in connection with discussion of kinds of sentences and of sentence elements: for example, at the time the compound sentence is introduced, attention is drawn to the use of the comma; similarly, when adverb and adjective clauses are introduced, the conventional comma usage is defined and may be the basis of an exercise. Besides this passing treatment, the "ch&d" texts include a summary chapter or section on comma punctuation, which may or may not be as full as that included in the "ch" texts.

Thus, *in the Singer volume for grade nine,* the first reference to comma usage occurs in connection with the use of quotations, when the use of the comma is illustrated in connection with such examples as, "My brother said, 'Really, I'm sorry.'" The next reference is made in connection with compound sentences, when the rule is stated that a comma is placed before the conjunction that joins the independent clauses; at this point also comma punctuation serves as the basis for two written exercises. Commas are next mentioned in connection with appositives, and the rule is stated that appositives and their modifiers are usually set off by commas; commas again figure in an exercise here. Commas are next mentioned, and rules given, in connection with adverb and adjective clauses; there is an exercise requiring students to distinguish between restrictive and non-restrictive adjective clauses. Similarly, elsewhere in this volume, commas are briefly treated in connection with the salutation and closing of letters, in addresses, and with dates.

Comment is relevant here that in this volume the practice of directing attention to comma punctuation at the time of introducing sentence elements is not followed through with perfect consistency; thus, whereas adequate attention is drawn in connection with the introduction of adjective and adverb clauses, no reference is made to commas in connection with, for example, the introduction of participial phrases. Other, comparable occasions for mention of relevant comma rules are also passed by.

The concentrated treatment of comma punctuation occurs in this volume in the chapter "Making Sense with Punctuation." Initially are presented comments on the importance of comma punctuation, demonstration of the relation of punctuation to meaning, and a general punctuation exercise. Next follow the statement and exemplification of rules. While these rules differ in no notable particular from those reported in the analysis of the Macmillan series, there is a difference in the organization. In the Macmillan series rules were simply listed, without grouping; here they are grouped under headings "A" and "B," as follows: under "A" are included words like *yes, no, well,* dates, addresses, omission of words, salutations and closings, and nouns in direct address; under "B" are included elements in a series, independent clauses with conjunction, direct quotations, adverb clauses, parenthetical elements, introductory transitional and participial phrases, non-restrictive clauses, and appositives; in addition, near the end of the chapter, allowance is made for commas to prevent misreading. Accompanying the statement of rules, explanations, examples, and notation of special problems are some thirteen exercises of three major kinds: given sentences to punctuate; punctuation of paragraphs from dictation; and original writing of sentences and paragraphs to illustrate the comma rules. The total number of sentences used for exercise is lower than that for the corresponding Macmillan volume, but the greater variety of other exercises brings this aspect of the comma treatment to approximate quality with that volume.

In the volume for grade ten, commas are mentioned in connection with the discussions of compound sentences, quotations, letters, adjective and adverb clauses, and appositives; these occasions coincide with those noted in the volume for grade ten.

The concentrated treatment of comma punctuation in this volume is presented in the chapter "Clearer Meaning Through Punctuation," with comma punctuation occupying six of the twenty-one pages. The eight rules of the ninth-grade volume are here expanded to thirteen and are listed rather than divided into two main groups. These thirteen rules cover the identical situations described in the preceding volume, and are listed in the following order: words, phrases, or clauses in a series; independent clauses with coordinating conjunction; direct quotation; introductory phrases and clauses (participial phrase, adverb clause); parenthetical words and phrases; non-essential (non-restrictive) clauses; nouns in apposition, with their modifiers; *yes, no,* etc.; items of a date; items in an address; informal salutations and complimentary close; nouns in direct address; omission of words. In addition to explanatory comments, notation of exceptions, and examples, the section includes thirteen exercises, including individual sentences, paragraphs, a letter, dictation, and some original writing; some exercises involve the semicolon as well as the comma.

In the volume for grade eleven, commas are mentioned in connection with the discussions of complex sentences (adverb and adjective clauses), compound sentences, interjections, introductory phrase (participial, nominative absolute), letters, and quotations. The concentrated treatment is presented in the chapter "Punctuating for the Reader's Convenience," in which comma punctuation takes up five of the twenty pages. In this section comma rules are divided into two groups, "Six Old Friends in Comma Usage" and "Eight Comma Rules for Major Sentence Constructions." Rules in the first group include *yes, no, oh,* etc.; items of a date; items in an address; omission of words; salutations and closes; nouns in direct address. Rules in the second group include words, phrases, and clauses in a series; independent clauses with coordinating conjunction; direct quotation; introductory adverb clause; introductory phrases (participial, infinitive phrase of purpose, prepositional phrase with a gerund, prepositional phrase to prevent misreading, plainly transitional phrases; non-restrictive (parenthetical) words and phrases; non-restrictive (parenthetical) adjective clauses; nouns in apposition and their modifiers. Besides special comments and examples as noted for preceding volumes, the treatment includes six exercises of the kinds noted before, and again involves semicolons in certain exercises.

It will be noted that the rules in this volume cover the same items as are covered in previous volumes, the only notable expansion being the fuller treatment of kinds of introductory phrases that are conventionally set off.

In the volume for grade twelve, commas are mentioned in connection with discussions of complex sentences, compound sentences, interjections, introductory phrases, including nominative absolute, and quotations. The concentrated treatment is presented in the chapter "Sensible Punctuation," in which comma usage takes up seven of the twenty-two pages. In this treatment the rules again total fourteen, in the following order: words, phrases, and clauses in a series; independent clauses with coordinating conjunction; direct quotations; introductory adverb clause; introductory phrases (participial, long prepositional, transitional); non-restrictive (parenthetical) words and phrases; non-restrictive (non-essential) clauses; nouns in apposition and their modifiers; *yes, no, oh,* etc.; items of a date; items in an address; omission of words; salutations and closes; nouns in direct address. Besides special comments and examples, the section includes seven exercises, including three that involve semicolons.

The two textbook series described in the foregoing pages may stand as representative of the treatment given to comma punctuation by a majority of the textbooks examined. It will be observed that the rules covered are common to all, though no exact number of rules is common to all. A lower-than-average number signifies that two or more rules have been grouped under a single heading; a higher-than-average number signifies that items sometimes grouped together are treated separately. It will be further noted that although the precise wording of rules differs from series to series, and, indeed, often from volume to volume, it is in fact the same body of rules that emerges in each instance. Also to be noted is the fact that in these volumes the terminology of punctuation rules is the terminology of sentence grammar: rules are expressed in terms of adjective and adverbial clauses, appositives, participial phrases, etc. The main facts made apparent by this analysis are these: that there is considerable uniformity among the various series in both the matter and the manner of treating comma punctuation, and, more significantly, *that comma punctuation is given essentially the same treatment in any volume of any particular series that it is given in all other volumes of that series.*

Brief characterization now needs to be made of two series in which treatment of comma punctuation varies from that of the majority. The first of these is that marked "d" in Table V. The American Book Company gives no chapter as such to the subject, but handles commas in two ways: (1) reference to comma usage, including statement of a rule, examples, and exercises, in connection with discussion of parts of speech and elements of the sentence; (2) a list of comma rules, without amplification, in a general chapter, "Capitalization and Punctuation." While superficially this treatment appears to resemble that marked "ch&d" in Table V, significant differences become apparent on analysis. In the "ch&d" volumes, the principal treatment of commas is contained in the chapter or section devoted to comma punctuation, in which rules are stated, general explanation and point of view toward punctuation given, illustrations of rules provided, and exercises included in substantial quantity; in these volumes, attention to relevant comma problems in connection with discussion of particular sentence elements is relatively slight and not necessarily included in every case. In the American Book Company's series, on the other hand, the concentrated presentation of comma rules is atypically confined to approximately one page in each volume, and is in the nature of a formal recapitulation of rules defined, illustrated, and used as the basis of exercises throughout the book. Thus, for example, the standard rule that non-restrictive adjective clauses are set off with commas is stated and illustrated at the time adjective clauses are introduced for discussion; the rule that independent clauses joined by a coordinating conjunction take a comma is stated and illustrated at the time compound sentences are discussed, etc. After this generally systematic attention to the relevant comma problem in discussion of particular parts of speech, sentence elements, and kinds of sentences as they are presented, the eventual listing of comma rules is a formality.

The remaining series that is in part atypical so far as comma treatment is concerned is McGraw-Hill's *Your Language*. The series follows the normal "ch" arrangement, and in this respect conforms with majority practice; it conforms also in that its eleven stated rules (grade nine) do in fact include all the items regularly mentioned in other sets of comma rules. The treatment, however, differs from that in other textbooks in these respects: (1) the section on comma punctuation is presented in each volume before such sentence elements as adverb and adjective clauses, participial phrases, and appositives, which are terms regularly used in comma rules, have been introduced to students; (2) the result of this placement is that certain key rules are necessarily stated less precisely than in other series; (3) the resulting general effect is one of considerably less firmness of direction in the use of comma punctuation than appears in other series. A few examples will suffice to illustrate these characteristics. In the volume for grade nine the second rule is stated as follows: "We use commas to set off *long* introductory phrases or dependent clauses, when the comma aids in reading." In other series, the particular kinds of introductory phrases and clauses (e.g., participial phrases, adverb clauses) are regularly specified so that the rule will not be mistakenly applied to introductory noun clauses or infinitive phrases as subjects, etc. Further, the above statement of this rule is atypical in its addition of the qualifying clause, "when the comma aids in reading," a clause which lends a quality of imprecision that is not found in any statement of the rule contained in other textbooks. The "standard" statement approximates that used in Harcourt, Brace, *English Grammar and Composition:* "Use a comma after an introductory adverb clause, an introductory participial phrase, or a succession of introductory prepositional phrases." A second illustration of atypical treatment of comma punctuation in the McGraw-Hill series will be noted in the statement of the third rule in the volume for grade nine: "We use commas to set off phrases and clauses that may be omitted without affecting the main clause. (You may be interested in knowing that such a clause or phrase is called *non-restrictive.*)" The statement is atypical in its unselective grouping of "phrases and clauses" and in the imprecision of its wording in "without affecting the main clause." More typically, two rules are made of this one, the first defining the punctuation of non-restrictive adjective clauses, the second identifying parenthetical expressions, or interrupters; as typically stated, these rules preclude the likelihood of students using them to justify setting off virtually all modifying phrases in sentences and thus stripping all sentences down to the essential elements of subject and predicate; the punctuation "The box, of apples, was on the table" and "A man, with a limp, walked down the road" would seem to be not only allowed but required by the wording "that may be omitted without affecting the main clause." A third illustration of atypical treatment of comma punctuation in series will be noted in the statement of the fourth rule in the volume for grade nine: "Participial phrases are often set off by commas. Examination will show you the pattern of the participial phrase." This rule is atypical in three respects: first, the situations identified by examples used to illustrate the rule — "Entering the room, we saw many familiar faces" and "The stranger, noticing us at last, arose and extended his hand" — have already been covered by the second and third rules, respectively; second, the wording "often set off by commas" is not marked by the firmness of direction that characterizes the statement of rules in other series; third, in other textbooks the form and function of the participial phrase have normally been defined prior to the statement of the rule, so that students presumably know in advance to what element the rule has reference and what it is that they are to punctuate without need of the addition, "Examination will show you the pattern of the participial phrase." The examples of atypical treatment taken from the volume for grade nine are here selected as representative of the treatment of comma punctuation throughout the series; and, indeed, they may stand as representative of the treatment given all other matters of grammar, usage, and mechanics in this series.

Recognition of the Sentence

A final topic which is of basic importance and yet of sufficiently restricted character that its treatment can be made the subject of detailed analysis here is that which centers upon identification of the sentence as a unit with essential parts. The relevant figures are presented in Table VI of Appendix B.

It should be stated at once that although the page counts shown in Table VI are intended to represent only that space which is given to instruction and practice in the recognition of sentences, the diverse interpretations of the topic as it is treated by the authors of different series have made it impossible to ensure that the count recorded for one series represents exactly the same thing as that recorded for another. For typical treatments, the count includes all space given to definition of the sentence, explanatory comments, examples of basic sentence patterns, discussion of subject and predicate, exercises designed to practice or test "sentence sense," and coverage of additional matters immediately relevant to the problem of distinguishing the sentence, as sentence, from all other units. Diversity of treatment has resulted from varying interpretations of which matters *are* necessary to, or relevant to, this problem. Thus, to illustrate, for the ninth-grade volume of the Allyn and Bacon *Effective English* series the unusually high count of 22 pages is reported on the evidence of the authors' own titling of a twenty-two-page chapter as "Recognizing Sentences." In fact, this chapter includes materials relevant to verbs, nouns, pronouns, compounded elements, and sentence classifications that, in other textbooks, are not directly associated with the immediate problem of sentence recognition or building "sentence sense." The full count is nevertheless recorded in Table VI on the grounds that to do otherwise — that is, to identify and count only those pages which in our view are precisely relevant to the problem — would be to misrepresent the intent of the authors.

as indicated by their chapter heading. Many comparable difficulties have arisen with other textbook series: some authors, for example, have included attention to "comma faults," "run-on" or "run-together" sentences, and "fragments" in their treatments of sentence recognition, while others have not; some have included pages of diagraming, etc., which partly but not wholly concern sentence recognition. With these allowances made for diversity, the page counts shown in Table VI may stand as fairly representing the space given to the problem of sentence recognition. Among half a dozen series, either of the Ginn series, the Harcourt, Brace *English Grammar and Composition,* the Heath series, or the Macmillan series are notably representative of the treatment given to sentence recognition. Since others of this group have been used to exemplify treatment of other grammatical matters, the Harcourt, Brace *English Grammar and Composition* is chosen for the purpose. Certain comparisons of special matters and certain comments on atypical treatments will follow this volume-by-volume summary.

In the volume for grade nine, matters pertinent to sentence recognition are contained in Chapter 2, "The Parts of a Sentence." The treatment begins with distinction made between conversational and formally written sentences. The sentence is next defined as follows: "A sentence is a group of words containing a verb and its subject and expressing a completed thought." Contrast of completed thought with fragment is next made and serves as a basis of an exercise of twenty items. Subjects and predicates, simple and compound, are next defined, distinguished, and illustrated and made the basis of exercises, as are also compound subjects and verbs. Additionally, attention is given to the subject in an unusual position and to the understood subject, as "you" in an imperative sentence.

In the volume for grade ten, matters pertinent to sentence recognition are contained in Chapter 2, "The Sentence: Subject and

Predicate, Single-Word Modifiers." The chapter begins with a definition of the sentence as follows: "A sentence is a group of words containing a verb and its subject and expressing a completed thought." There follows brief discussion, with illustration, of the use of incomplete expression in conversation to stand for complete thought, and contrast is made of that usage with standard practice in writing. Next the subject and predicate are introduced, defined, exemplified, and made the basis of an exercise of ten sentences. Simple and complete subjects, simple and complete predicates are next distinguished and used as the basis of three exercises. There follows discussion of the subject in an unusual position, of the understood subject, and of compound subjects and verbs. Finally, additional attention is given to the meaning of "completed thought," and the immediate treatment ends with two exercises which require distinguishing between complete sentences and fragments and further require completion of the given items that are fragmentary. After this point the discussion turns to sentence classification and to various complements; this latter discussion, being clearly separated from the preceding, is not included in the page count.

In the volume for grade eleven, matters pertinent to sentence recognition are contained in Chapter 2, "The Parts of a Sentence." First a diagnostic test is given requiring identification of subject, verb, and complement. Next a definition of the sentence is given as follows: "A sentence is a group of words expressing a completed thought." This definition is accompanied by examples contrasting sentences and fragments. Next follow treatments of the sentence classified according to purpose, simple and compound subjects and verbs, and the problem of finding the subject when it is out of the normal word order. The section ends with a treatment of complements; although this part begins by relating complements to the problem of recognizing sentences, the discussion of complements is not included in the count in Table VI.

In the volume for grade twelve, matters pertinent to sentence recognition are contained in Chapter 2, "The Parts of a Sentence." First is given a diagnostic test requiring identification of subject, verb, and complement. Next a definition of the sentence is given as follows: "A sentence is a group of words expressing a completed thought." This definition is accompanied by examples contrasting sentences and fragments. Next follow treatments of the sentence classified according to purpose, simple and compound subjects and verbs, and the problem of finding the subject when it is out of the normal word order. The section ends with a treatment of complements; although this part begins by relating complements to the problem of recognizing sentences, the discussion of complements is not included in the count in Table VI.

While it is not included in the page count, additional attention is given to the problem of sentence recognition in all volumes of the series, as follows: grade nine, Chapter 4, "Writing Complete Sentences," instruction and exercises on fragments and run-on sentences, 13 pages; grade ten, Chapter 4, "Writing Complete Sentences," instruction and exercises on fragments and run-on sentences, 13 pages; grade eleven, Chapter 6, "Complete Sentences," instruction and exercises on fragments and run-on sentences, 14 pages; grade twelve, Chapter 4, "The Completed Sentence," instruction and exercises on fragments and run-on sentences, 10 pages.

It may be concluded that the principal volume-by-volume differences in treatment of sentence recognition in the series are the following: (1) abbreviation of the definition of the sentence in the second pair of volumes; (2) slight alteration of the order in which items are taken up; (3) decrease in number of exercises in the second pair of volumes. With allowances made for ordinary variations of wording, organization, and emphasis, the series described may stand as representative of most of the series examined. The main facts made apparent by this analysis are these: that there is considerable uniformity among the various series in both the matter and the manner of treating the problem of sentence recognition; and, more significantly, *that the topic is given essentially the same treatment in any volume of any particular series that it is given in the other volumes of that series.*

The latter observation may be further illustrated by comparing treatments of one specific item that is of central concern to all of the series, namely, the definition of a sentence. Because of the emphasis assigned to "the sentence" in all volumes of every series, it seems desirable to record here the definition given in each volume of each series. As will be seen, most series carry essentially the same definition throughout the series; major and minor variations in the handling of definition are made apparent by the following summary. For convenience in making comparisons, the several series are classified in three groups.

Group 1: In the American Book Company's *Our English Language,* grade nine, the sentence is defined as follows: "A sentence is a group of words that makes sense when it stands alone. A sentence gives a complete thought." This definition is repeated without change in each of the four volumes.

In Ginn's *English Skills* the definition is as follows: grade nine: "A sentence is a group of words expressing a complete thought. It names the subject and states or asserts something about the subject. The statement or assertion is called the predicate"; grade ten: "A sentence is a group of words expressing a complete thought. It contains a subject and a predicate"; grade eleven: "A sentence is a group of words expressing a complete thought and containing a subject and a predicate"; grade twelve: "A sentence is a group of words expressing a complete thought."

In Heath's *English in Action* the definition is as follows: grade nine: "A sentence expresses a complete thought. It contains a subject and a predicate, either expressed or understood." This definition remains the same for grades ten, eleven, and twelve.

In Macmillan's series (separate titles) the definition for grades nine, ten, eleven, and twelve is as follows: "A sentence is a group of words that expresses a complete thought by means of a subject and a predicate." [2]

In Scribner's *English at Work* for grades nine, ten, eleven, and twelve the sentence is defined as follows: "A sentence is a complete statement of a happening or a condition. The two essentials of a sentence are a subject and a verb, though one or both of these parts may be unexpressed."

In Ginn's *Better English* for all four grades the sentence is defined as follows: "A sentence is a group of words expressing a complete thought."

In the foregoing group of textbooks, including the Harcourt, Brace series earlier analyzed, *the sentence is defined in each volume of each series, and it is defined in virtually the same words each time.* Among the series that follow, greater variations will be noted.

In the textbooks comprising Group 2 (Singer's *Enjoying English*, Harcourt, Brace's *Living Language*, Allyn and Bacon's *Effective English*, Row, Peterson's *The New Building Better English*, and Scott, Foresman's *Guide to Modern English*), greater variation occurs in the definition of a sentence than among those in Group 1; nevertheless this variation is relatively slight.

Even in those volumes in which the sentence is not formally defined, the components of the sentence are nevertheless so presented that the typical image of a sentence as a group of words

---

[2] In the volumes for grades ten, eleven, and twelve is quoted this definition: "Each sentence is an independent linguistic form, not included by virtue of any grammatical construction in any larger linguistic form." (Leonard Bloomfield, *Language*.) The quotation is followed by the statement, "We shall make use of a simpler definition," which is that cited for the series.

making complete sense and containing subject and verb is definitely indicated; further, in those series which omit formal definition from one or two volumes, the definition that is included in
the remaining volumes is normally a version of the "standard"
definition employed by most series. Second, in volumes in which
a degree of reluctance to repeat the "standard" definition is evident, characteristics ascribed to the sentence (e.g., the Allyn and
Bacon grade nine) nevertheless add up to those that are usually
included in this definition; in addition, in at least one volume of
this kind of series, a "standard" definition is somewhere included.

Finally, it is significant that in the comparatively few series
which deviate considerably from usual practice in defining the
sentence — either by omitting definition or by attempting an
atypical description of the sentence — discussion of the topic of
sentence recognition characteristically runs much longer than in
other series; basic matters that in Group 1 volumes may be dis-
patched in two or three pages may in some Group 2 series take as
many as twenty pages (e.g., Allyn and Bacon grade nine, Table
VI).

Group 3: The only series that properly belongs to Group 3, as
representing the greatest deviation from typical practice in the
treatment of sentence definition and closely related matters, is
McGraw-Hill's *Your Language.* It is not feasible, in limited space,
to attempt a full account of this deviation for each of the three
volumes that have been examined. Initially, it should be pointed
out that this series, as Table VI shows, takes more space for the
topic in the three volumes examined than any one of the other
series takes for four volumes; it may be added that, even so, the
count for this series does not include all items covered by the
counts recorded for certain other series, whose authors managed
to include, for example, classification of sentences according to
both structure and purpose, together with examples and exercises,
within the section devoted to the basic matter of sentence recog-

nition. One reason for the unusual amount of space recorded for this series is *the repetition of the same details within volumes*. A second reason is the inclusion of much gratuitous information and comment presented in uneconomical form.

Most of the differences that separate this one series from all of the others in the treatment of basic sentence matters would seem to derive from a single difference, which is that of *purpose*. All of the other series, despite such variations as have been exemplified in the foregoing summaries, have in common the apparent purpose of making the idea of the sentence and its essential components as simple and clear as possible for students who will use the information in their writing; to this end, as scrutiny of the content makes evident, definition, example, explanatory comment, and exercise were definitely selected and organized. On the other hand, the McGraw-Hill series works, by a variety of means, towards the diametrically opposed purpose. First, a very considerable amount of space in this series, beginning in the ninth-grade volume, is given to conversation, in both example and exercise, with the result that the emphasis of training is upon "sentence-words" and "sentence-phrases" rather than upon "full sentences." Typical exercises in the volume for grade nine begin as follows: (1) "Look at the following conversation"; (2) "Write a conversation like that in exercise 1"; (3) "Make up four imaginary conversations of from four to six lines each"; (4) "Write a telephone conversation between two people who are making a date to meet for dinner or a movie. Both are being overheard, and they are trying to say very little. Make use of sentence-words and sentence-phrases as much as you can." Secondly, the sentence, which is defined briefly and in direct terms in typical series volumes, is here *not* defined, but the following statements are made the basis of class discussion: (1) "A sentence is a group of words that contain [sic] a subject and a verb"; (2) "A sentence is a group of words containing a subject and a verb and expressing a complete thought",

(3) "A sentence may be a word, phrase, or subject-verb combination which expresses a clear thought in a given conversation or piece of writing." Third, the volumes contain inconsistencies or half-contradictions at key points; for example, this statement occurs in the ninth-grade volume: "Whether it makes a statement, asks a question, makes a command or request, or expresses strong feeling, a full sentence usually has two main parts," and in the tenth-grade volume occurs this statement: "Every full sentence has two major parts: subject and predicate." Fourth, the volumes include expository sentences and passages, even at the most crucial points, which appear not to be aimed at clarity, the primary virtue of textbook exposition. Thus in the volume for grade nine: "Like predicates, a sentence may have both a simple subject and a complete subject." From the same volume: "Sentence-words, sentence-phrases, and full sentences may express any one of four meanings, as you may see in the examples below: make statements, ask questions, give commands or requests, express strong feelings." From the volume for grade eleven: "To form the basic framework of a sentence, the noun-structure and verb-structure that are tied together cannot be subordinated." In all its characteristic expository passages, the volume for grade eleven avoids the usual textbook virtue of clarity by making what is essentially simple appear highly complex; thus, for example, are presented instructions for finding the subject and main verb of the sentence, "In the evening she usually studies while I do the dishes":

The preposition *in* subordinates the first noun-structure *the evening;* that cannot be the subject. The word *usually,* an adverb, subordinates itself and therefore cannot be any part of the framework. And the word *while* (from List 5d) subordinates the clause that follows it. Even though the noun-structure *I* and the verb-structure *do* are tied together (both first person singular), they are subordinated and therefore cannot be the subject and main verb of the sentence. That leaves *she* and *studies,* the subject and the main verb.

In the volume for grade eleven, after two pages of prose of the kind just quoted, the subject of a sentence is thus defined:

We can now give an exact definition of the subject of a sentence. The *subject* of a sentence is either the first unsubordinated noun-structure, as in the basic framework and Variants 1 and 5; or it is the noun-structure between the two parts of an uninterrupted verb-structure, as in Variants 2 and 3. Command sentences have no subject (Variant 4).

In the same volume the question of the subject in a command sentence is thus explained:

Variant 4 has no noun-structure tied to the verb-structure.

Dance!

This is a command. It is the only type of sentence in English that does not have a subject. In fact, the signal of a command is a main verb with no ending and with no subject tied to it. Sometimes there is a noun-structure before the main verb in a command, but it is not tied to the verb:

You be careful!

In this example, *you* is the noun of address. It could only be [sic] the subject if the verb was [sic] tied to it.

A final example from the same volume will perhaps suffice to suggest the extent to which this series deviates from the normal textbook aim of clarity. The following are directions for an exercise in distinguishing adjectives from adverbs:

In order to recognize Pattern Two, you have to be able to tell an adjective (Frame 1) from an adverb (Frame 2). An adverb subordinates itself and, therefore, cannot be part of a basic sentence pattern. The modifier-structure in Pattern Two has to be unsubordinated, of course. That means that it has to be an adjective because adjectives do not subordinate themselves. The following pairs of sentences look very much alike, but in each pair one of the sentences has Pattern Two and the other has Pattern One with a subordinate structure. Which is which?

Table VII, Part A, of Appendix B, represents the analysts' comparative evaluation of the treatment given Grammar, Usage, and Mechanics in the textbook series examined; Part B represents the analysts' direct estimate of this treatment, without reference to comparative ratings.

Coverage

The heading *Coverage* necessarily refers primarily to full series rather than to individual volume treatment. As foregoing tables dealing with selected topics — Parts of Speech, Subject-Verb Agreement, Sentence Recognition, and Comma Punctuation — have suggested, nearly all series cover a central, standard body of information in a fairly uniform manner. Coverage here does not refer so much to *depth* as to *breadth* of treatment; consideration of depth has entered into the rating when, in the opinion of the analysts, certain items of basic concern were found to be passed over so lightly in a given series that these items could not properly be counted as "covered." No series fails to deal in some detail with principal matters such as parts of speech, parts of sentence, major problems of usage, capitalization, and punctuation. Outside the main common ground, however, larger differences appear. There are differences, for example, in coverage of the possible functions of the several kinds of phrases: some texts, to illustrate, omit reference to the use of prepositional phrases as nouns; some make no mention of the "nominative absolute" or "absolute phrase." Some texts fail to treat problems of grammatical parallelism within the sentence. Elliptical clauses are often left unmentioned, though these might well be treated both in connection with comma punctuation and in connection with the fault of the dangling modifier.

In arriving at the rating given in Table VII to each series under the heading (1) "Coverage," we have made numerous checks on specific items that tend to lie outside the central body of commonly treated matter. Table VIII presents the results of one such check. In this particular case, each volume of each series was examined for its treatment of the pronoun in and about the infinitive phrase — as subject or object, as predicate pronoun of the infinitive with a subject (example: They thought him to be *me*) and as predicate pronoun of the infinitive without a subject (example: He was thought to be *I*). In Table VIII "no" means that none of these uses is discussed; "s" means that subject is discussed; "o" means that object is discussed; "p" means that one condition of the predicate pronoun is discussed; "all" means that all uses of the pronoun in relation to the infinitive are made clear. It will be noted that four of the textbook series give students no explicit instruction in the uses of pronouns in relation to infinitive phrases; two instruct only in the use of the subject of the infinitive; one treats only subject and object of the infinitive; three others are incomplete in one or more ways; and four treat all aspects of the problem. It is true, of course, that no single "touchstone" is likely to be perfectly reliable, and it would be incorrect to conclude from the evidence of Table VIII that all series which fail to treat pronoun-infinitive problems fully will also be found notably deficient in their general coverage of the fairly standard body of grammatical matter. On the other hand, we have found the treatment of pronoun-infinitive problems a reliable indicator in the following way: that those series which have treated these problems fully have also covered both the "standard" body of material without significant omissions and a higher than average number of such details as lie just outside this body. Reminder should be made here that the observation just made pertains only to *coverage*, in which respect most of the series are approximately equal; the following criteria must also be considered before any final judgment is made about even that one part of a grammar and composition textbook that deals with grammatical matters. It should finally be stated that we have found no serious fault with most series in the matter of coverage as the term is here defined; as foregoing representative counts of pages make evident, the main body of grammar, usage, and mechanics is not only covered by most series, but covered four times.

General Clarity

Two points should be made at once: first, that "general clarity of presentation" is here used as a very broad but by no means merely impressionistic rubric, which takes many factors into consideration and which overlaps and in part encompasses other items used in the rating shown in Table VII, especially items three, four, and five, and to a degree also items six, eight, and nine; second, that general clarity of presentation has very evidently been, for the authors of most textbook series, a matter of primary concern. It is fair to point out at once that, as shown in Table VII, we have found it possible to give a satisfactory rating to approximately as many textbook series under the heading of Clarity as under the heading of Coverage.

With few exceptions, the series evince a serious effort to be clear in the treatment of grammar, usage, and mechanics in the following major ways: (1) use of a variety of printing and editorial devices; (2) use of a simple, direct, open style of writing; (3) inclusion of abundant examples and exercises; (4) allowance of considerable space for important topics, including space for repeated treatments of most. In principle, and in moderation, there can be no doubt of the usefulness of these means of achieving clarity.

Nevertheless, we have become convinced that *excess* in any of these means, though it may result in perfect clarification of a given item at the moment, can, ironically, stand in the way of mastery; that is to say, *the very care to achieve clarity can result in making learning more difficult or in preventing it.* Many textbooks, by aiming to make the going as easy as possible, make retention of vital points difficult. Resembling their counterparts in the literature anthologies, pages that are striking in their use of five or six different colors, that use as many different sizes and styles of type, and that feature cartoons, whether relevantly or irrelevantly, risk the possibility of distracting rather than concentrating the reader's attention. The use of a very great amount of space — say thirty pages to cover the rules of punctuation — is no guarantee that the student will assimilate what is indispensable from those thirty pages, where the presentation of vital detail is interrupted by cartoons, color pictures, and passages of pleasant chat contributed gratuitously by the author. The fact is that the conventional rules for the use of the comma can be printed and exemplified in a single page, and such a page, though less "easy going" than thirty pages, can be mastered more readily than thirty pages.

Lack of economy in presentation, thus, we find to be the principal enemy of General Clarity in the treatment of grammar, usage, and mechanics, when General Clarity is understood in terms of *mastery* and *retention* rather than in terms of the ease with which students can read through pages of low-density prose. We have found those textbooks deserve the highest rating on this item that have sought clarity through economy, with the least use of distracting features of any kind.

Organization within Volumes

Organization within the volume can affect general clarity in a number of ways. We have considered that, on the whole, the organization which presents grammatical and mechanical matters in a single, unified section of the volume tends most towards clarity. Although we understand that grammatical and mechanical matters are to be both studied and used throughout the year, and that they are always to be integrated with expression, particularly writing, we find the effort to achieve integration directly, by distributing bits and pieces of grammatical information from beginning to end of the volume, even when these bits are pulled together for summary and review at the end, quite unsatisfactory. Not integration, but fragmentation is achieved in this way. To present instruction in and practice with, say, nouns, in connection with the initial theme assignment is clearly futile, since obviously no theme can be written with nouns alone. Neither, in our opinion, is integration achieved by the practice of alternating chapters involving writing and other activities with chapters treating grammatical matters. If the efforts of some authors to "enforce" integration in these ways are to be applauded because integration is a worthy aim, it is nevertheless necessary to state that these same ways have inevitably so dissipated the presentation of grammatical matters that the general clarity (again in the sense of mastery and retention) of the treatment must be given a low rating. True integration is a desideratum that has not been achieved by any of the textbooks examined, and we consider it doubtful that any textbook will ever achieve it. We question further whether any textbook should try. We believe that integration is something which can occur only in the minds of students, that teachers have or can have a great deal to do with it, and that textbooks can be most useful not by sprinkling grammatical information over all pages of the volume but by presenting it in clear, orderly, and economical fashion so that any particular part of it can be readily found and applied. Whatever their other virtues may be, efforts to integrate heterogeneous materials by the simple act of *printing them together in chapters* are found to be ruinous with respect to organization and clarity in the treatment of grammatical matters.

The remarks above consider some effects of the volume's overall organization upon the treatment of grammatical matters. In those textbooks in which grammar, usage, and mechanics are mainly confined to a single "handbook" section, or treated in chapters set apart from composition and other activities, organization is invariably found to contribute more to clarity than in textbooks in which these matters are scattered. But noteworthy inequalities of organization are evident also among those books that *do* confine grammatical matters to a definite section, and these also are reflected in the ratings presented in Table VII (3). Perhaps no textbook writer has solved perfectly the multiple and complex problems of *order* in the presentation of basic grammatical information. Every system of beginning and continuing a particular topic appears to have certain disadvantages and to run up against special snags. Thus, for example, if the textbook writer begins with the simple sentence, introducing subject and verb, he at once encounters a degree of awkwardness in the fact that the nouns and pronouns that can serve as subjects and the verbs that can serve as predicates have not yet been introduced. On the other hand, if he begins with the parts of speech, they must be first treated in a kind of vacuum in which definition and example are alike relatively meaningless; and thereafter they must be treated again in relation to their uses as elements of sentences. Many of the textbooks examined reveal the effects of honest grappling with the countless and probably inevitable problems of just this sort. Some have succeeded better than others in avoiding awkwardnesses and serious troubles. A few have unfortunately fallen into a veritable quagmire of difficulties. When comma punctuation, for example, which is conventionally, and no doubt necessarily, discussed in terms of sentence elements, is presented *before* the necessary sentence elements have been introduced, great awkwardness results. Perhaps the combination of pronouns and complements has occasioned greater organizational difficulty than any other one matter. Complements are sometimes taken up early, along with subject and verb, under the general heading "Parts of the Sentence"; expositional problems then result because pronouns and their case forms have not yet been introduced, so that the initial treatment of complements must simply miss its main reason for being. Pronouns, in fact, with their protean forms and many involvements, have caused great organizational difficulty for all textbook writers. In the most unsatisfactory treatments of the pronoun it is necessary to use the volume's index to run down the particular information that one seeks — and the likelihood of a casual student's doing so would not seem strong. In typical volumes, not all that is needed is said about the pronoun in any one or even two chapters or sections: some information may be found under the pronoun as a part of speech, some under parts of the sentence, some under headings like "Reference," some under "Verbals," etc. It is not unusual for a textbook writer to deal with pronouns in half a dozen different places, under as many headings, and the regrettable fact is that the student must already know his grammar in order to conduct a successful search for the specific information he needs. One indication of the relative success of the writers in organizing their grammatical material is the number of places in which they have had to take up pronouns and pronoun problems, that textbook being best in this respect which manages to cover most pronoun facts and problems in a single place.

The treatment of the pronoun is perhaps, in this sense, the best single touchstone by which to judge the organization of grammatical and mechanical matters within a volume; we have found that, generally speaking, if a textbook writer has found an efficient means of bringing together all that must be said of the pronoun, its various forms, uses, and relations, that writer has also found satisfactory, or most nearly satisfactory, ways of treating other parts of speech, phrases, clauses, kinds of sentences, and the rest. On the other hand, if his basic organization has required him to spread vital pieces of pronoun information about under a variety of headings in the volume, his organization will have required him to give similar piecemeal treatment to other parts of speech and sentence elements. "Mastery," in these circumstances, we consider to be unlikely, even impossible. Relative success or failure in these respects is reflected in the ratings of Table VII (3).

Particular Explanations

For the most part, textbook writers have followed traditionally fixed patterns in presenting definitions, statements of principle, and rules, these then being followed characteristically by examples to illustrate. Further, for the most part, they have aimed at clarity, if not always at economy, in these explanations; hence, for most textbooks, we have found little cause to assign widely differing ratings on this item of judgment. Numerous samples of particular explanations have been recorded in foregoing pages, most notably in connection with definitions of the sentence, and with rules of punctuation, and the point is partially treated above also, under the heading "Coverage."

It is true, certainly, that *organization* of the grammatical section has sometimes adversely affected the force of particular explanations, even when these are in themselves clearly stated, when the explanations are presented in terms that have not as yet been made clear; an example has been cited earlier, of a presentation of comma rules in terms of sentence elements before the elements have been introduced. The most serious difficulty with particular explanations, however, has arisen in those very few textbooks whose authors have sought to introduce markedly unconventional systems of explanation, with the result that what in fact may be a relatively simple matter, and is made even childishly simple by most textbook writers, is made grotesquely complex merely by the abundance of the authors' painful and unnecessary prose. Although a negligible amount of this unfortunate kind of "explanation" occurs in a number of series, it is present in sufficient quantity to be ruinous in only one, McGraw-Hill's *Your Language.*

Two further matters need to be mentioned. Teachers who use the textbooks that we have examined have often registered complaints on two points that are relevant here: first, that textbook writers occasionally change some of their grammatical terms between volumes of a series, or use alternate terms for the same items even within a volume, with resultant confusion for students; second, that writers often put great emphasis on relatively simple matters, or on matters that do not have immediate bearing on actual problems of grammatical expression, and give inadequate attention to the most difficult and most urgent grammatical explanations. We have found justification for these criticisms in only a very few places in a very few textbooks. Although authors, as has been pointed out earlier, have often spread their information about in the textbook, under a variety of headings so that it proves difficult to find, yet for the most part they have somehow, somewhere, presented what is vital. In these respects the lone major exception is the McGraw-Hill textbook series cited above, which consistently elaborates the gratuitous and slights or obscures the essential.

Progression within Volume

Failure of satisfactory progression shows up in the form of repetition. Unquestionably, a certain amount of repetition is inevitable in any volume in which the attempt is made to cover and explain adequately the main body of information on Grammar, Usage, and Mechanics. Moreover, it is very probable that a degree of deliberate repetition is desirable, both to establish connections between the familiar and the unfamiliar and to aid retention of vital facts and principles. For the most part, we recognize in the textbooks examined a serious effort to treat necessary grammatical matters clearly, with a minimum of wasteful repetition.

The key to avoidance of such repetition is of course a satisfactory solution to the complex problems of organization. Generally speaking, wasteful repetition is best avoided in those textbooks in which all or nearly all relevant information on a given major topic — pronouns, for example — is confined to a single chapter or section; on the other hand, the greatest amount of wasteful repetition results from a scheme of organization that requires several additional treatments of the pronoun, to continue the same example, after the initial one. Problems of organization exist for which we do not pretend to have wholly satisfactory solutions; we can only report that in our view some textbook writers, more successfully than others, have found organizational means of avoiding undue repetition without omitting vital parts and without jeopardizing general clarity of presentation. On these considerations our ratings in Table VII are mainly based.

One other kind of repetition, in addition to that occasioned by inefficient organization, needs mention here. A very few of the textbooks deliberately "go over the same things twice" — or at least many of the same things — once in the "traditional" way, with standard definitions and statements of relationships, and again by means of some experimental adaptation of the "new, scientific" way. The mildest illustration of this practice may be seen in the Macmillan volumes for grades nine and twelve, in each of which some ten pages are given, respectively, to "New Ways of Looking at Language" and "The Structure of English," though elsewhere in the volume grammatical matters are covered adequately. A much more unfortunate case of this kind of repetition occurs in McGraw-Hill's *Your Language*, especially in the volume for grade eleven. In this volume grammatical matters are first treated by one system in three chapters — "Signals and Structures," "Connecting the Structures," and "What Sentences

Can Do" — with a total of eighty-six pages, and thereafter repeated, with mixed "traditional" and "structural" terminology, in a ninety-seven-page handbook section on "Grammar and Usage."

Progression within Series

We are not alone in regarding repetition, in all the series examined, as *the most serious single fault* of the treatment given to grammar, usage, and mechanics. Lack of progression from volume to volume, or simply repetition, is the common theme of criticisms sent us by hundreds of teachers in the course of our study. As an example of such tiresome repetition, on page 489 of the twelfth-grade volume, the Scribner's series offers the following admonition: "Avoid using *them* boys instead of *those* boys, *theirselves* for *themselves*, and *hisself* for *himself*. Such usage is unacceptable." That the editors should feel it necessary to give instruction at the level of literacy signified by these examples on what is in fact page 2055 of their total series does not exactly exhibit confidence in the effectiveness of the preceding 2054 pages. The Scribner's series is not unique in this respect; all the series examined imply comparable distrust of their own cumulative effectiveness.

Much evidence of the purely repetitious character of the textbooks in the treatment of grammatical matters from year to year has been supplied in foregoing pages of this report, both in the tables up to Table VI and in the discussion of representative topics such as parts of speech, punctuation, treatment of sentence recognition, and so on. What has there been presented by example only might as readily be extended to include all of the aspects of grammar, usage, and mechanics that are treated in the textbooks. If other conclusions arrived at in the present report tend sometimes to be debatable, this one is not: *the fact is that, in all the textbooks examined, essentially the same body of grammatical and mechanical matter is covered at each grade level in essen-*

tially the same ways and at essentially the same depth. Claims made in the prefaces of many series that yearly progression has been achieved must, we find, categorically be declared false so far as treatment of grammatical matters is concerned. The extent to which they are true for treatment of other aspects of the English program will be discussed hereafter.

Some textbook writers, more than others, have obviously sought ways of giving successive volumes at least the appearance of newness and addition. Chief among their methods are the following:

1. *Use of new drill and test sentences.* All of the textbooks have this feature.

2. *Use of different orders of presentation.* In none of the textbook series, however, do changes in the order of presenting grammatical matters amount to more than meaningless juggling of items. In some instances the organization of later volumes is definitely inferior, by being more confused, to that of the first one or two volumes; it may be supposed that the more confused arrangements in these cases have resulted from attempts to vary, for the sake of mere variation, an initial organization that was the textbook writer's first and best solution.

3. *Omission of certain items from some volumes.* Though for the most part all basic matters are covered in each volume of a series, occasionally some topics — such as verbals, special pronoun uses — are withheld from the first volume or even the first two volumes. More rarely, a topic treated in the first two volumes is omitted from the third or fourth volume. Occasionally certain items are omitted from some one volume of the four. But the tables showing that full treatments of subject and verb agreement, punctuation, the noun, etc. are regularly included in all volumes of a series may stand as essentially valid for the main body.

4. *Addition of certain items to later volumes.* A very few series,

most notably McGraw-Hill's *Your Language,* gain an appearance of progression in the treatment of grammatical matters by including in successive volumes an increasing amount of information, or allusions to information, on the study of the English language and language in general. Brief comment has been made on this practice in foregoing pages. Further comment in this report will be found in the section headed "Other," for in our view the varieties of linguistic information under question may be more appropriately discussed under that heading than under the heading of Grammar, Usage, and Mechanics.

We should make one fact perfectly clear at this point, namely, that we do not charge textbook writers with personal dereliction in having failed even to create a successful illusion of progression from volume to volume in their treatments of grammatical and mechanical matters. On the evidence of the textbooks themselves, we must suppose that two facts are at least as obvious to the writers who have wrestled with the problem of progression as they are to us. The facts are these:

1. All such basic matters as parts of speech, parts of sentence in their kinds and relationships, capitalization, punctuation, etc. need to be covered adequately in the volume for grade nine.

2. When these matters have been covered adequately once, *there is truly nothing to add that is at once relevant and significant;* hence the three remaining volumes must either be simply, and intolerably, repetitious or move off to other fields.

That these are indeed facts, the textbooks themselves, together with the workbooks that accompany eight of the series examined, provide the irrefutable proof. No textbooks deliberately present a wholly inadequate coverage of basic grammatical matters in the ninth grade in order to allow opportunity to extend the coverage in the tenth and thereafter in the eleventh and twelfth grades. To do so would be simply absurd. Universally, the writers recognize that parts of speech, structural elements, rules of punctuation and capitalization need to be made available to students for their use in the ninth grade. No writers present, for example, nouns and pronouns in the ninth grade, adjectives and adverbs in the tenth, verbs and conjunctions in the eleventh, prepositions and interjections in the twelfth; any writer who did so, we have no doubt, would be universally challenged. The nature of the grammar of the sentence, and the nature of the need for this grammar particularly in written expression, make such a distribution, or any variation of such a distribution, unthinkable. There is thus no alternative to the presentation in the ninth-grade volume of all grammatical information that is relevant to problems of written expression. Having once presented this information adequately, writers of four-year series textbooks have no choice thereafter but repetition.

We believe that all of the facts of Grammar, Usage, and Mechanics that are essential for written expression by native English speakers and writers can be covered in fewer than 100 pages. Against this reasonable total, for convenient contrast, may be set the following representative four-year series totals:

Allyn and Bacon	774
Harcourt, Brace (*English Grammar & Composition*)	1162
Heath	858
Macmillan	896
Scott, Foresman (3 volumes)	777
Singer	856

The lowest total given to Grammar, Usage, and Mechanics by a four-volume series is that of Lippincott: 410 pages, or by our estimate, approximately four times the space needed.

In our opinion, which is based entirely on systematic review of the contents in series reported on for this study, nothing but positive harm can result from the practice of presenting high school students with four successive treatments, in as many volumes, of the basic facts of grammar, usage, and mechanics. Further, in our view, textbook writers who have made the most earnest and ingenious efforts to achieve variation (progression being an impossibility) in these treatments have succeeded only in making matters worse rather than better. All of the evidence amassed by our study of the textbooks tends to but one conclusion: *that the needs of students will be served best by placing in the hands of ninth graders, to be used thereafter as needed through the twelfth grade, a single, brief handbook of grammar, usage, and mechanics.*

We call attention to the fact that two of the publishers whose books we have examined have already moved, if ever so slightly, in the direction we recommend. First, the Macmillan series (separate titles), though it includes the usual four volumes, uses the identical handbook section, except for drill sentences, in the volumes for the tenth, eleventh, and twelfth grades. This same section might better be used also for the ninth grade. Also we do not see that any useful purpose is served by changing the drill sentences from year to year. Second, the Scott, Foresman series, *Guide to Modern English,* is a three-volume series, the third volume being used for both the upper grades. In our opinion, the relevant parts of the handbook section of the third volume, totaling under 100 pages, should serve throughout four high school years.

We further believe that the handbook section included in the fourth volume of any one of the series examined would better serve the needs of high school students throughout the four years than do the four handbook sections presently designated for use in different years.

Better than this makeshift arrangement, however, which should be adopted only by schools that have a larger number of series volumes already on hand and relatively new, is, as we have said, the adoption of *a single four-year handbook.*

Relevance of Information and Activities

Serious though it is, the inclusion of extraneous matter is a much less troublesome problem in the sections of textbooks given over to Grammar, Usage, and Mechanics than it is in the sections treated in this report under the headings of "Composition" and "Other."

It is nevertheless a fact that certain textbook writers, more effectively than others, have indeed confined their grammatical sections to relevant and economical discussion. Others have, in varying degrees, indulged themselves in personal chat with students, devising student-life situations, ingenious motivational approaches, elaborate analogies of the "familiar" kind, etc., with the result that while the total space given to the grammatical sections is considerably expanded, the space given to precisely relevant grammatical explanation, example, and exercise is actually decreased. A peculiarly troublesome kind of extraneous matter that has found its way into a very few treatments of grammatical matters can best be identified here as "talk about" language — about language in general, about the "American" language, about the "scientists" who have made "exciting, new discoveries" in language, etc. If this "talk about" language is sometimes academically interesting, or interesting for its eccentricity, it is more often merely curious, seeming odd and out-of-place. It has the appearance of being scraps of information half-digested by the authors from summer-session linguistic courses. In any event, it does not, generally speaking, bear clearly upon the great and serious problems involved in helping students to write and speak more effectively.

Happily, a majority of the textbooks are either completely devoid of the kinds of random extraneous matters identified above or limit their remarks on these matters so sharply that the danger of obscuring vital instruction is negligible. Further, as has been stated above, in the more extreme cases, for example, in the Mc-Graw-Hill *Your Language* series, it has been possible, for purposes of this report, to separate out such indulgences from the main treatment of grammar and to count them under the heading of "Other," where in the appropriate section of this report, they are more fully examined.

For the most part, in these series in which grammatical and mechanical matters are discussed in a single, concentrated section, virtually no irrelevant matter is discernible; in others, when these matters are distributed piecemeal throughout whole volumes, there is invariably an intrusion of alien activity and information, roughly "motivational" in character.

Tone

Like the problem of extraneous matter, the problem of tone is more satisfactorily managed in the treatment of grammatical matters than in the treatment of writing and other matters. It should be pointed out that "tone" here is used in a broad sense; it includes all that pertains to the style and apparent attitude of the textbook writer in addressing his topic and the students who are to gain information and acquire skill from his treatment of the topic; it includes items as diverse as distracting pictorial illustrations, on the one hand, and bad expository prose sentences on the other. In short, it includes everything that bears on the writer's manner in addressing his task. As in the anthologies of literature, tone may be businesslike and serious; it may be pretentious, inflated; it may be condescending; it may be "chummy"; it may be cajoling, motherly. It may cater to students, or it may arrogantly present its matter. For the most part, with few notable exceptions, we have found the tone of writers most satisfactory *in those sections given to grammar, usage, and mechanics.* We have not found it uniformly satisfactory in the treatments of "Composition" and "Other." Accordingly, discussion and illustration of the important question of tone are reserved for those later sections of the report.

Sense of Purpose

We have repeatedly suggested that the treatment given to Grammar, Usage, and Mechanics in the textbooks should carry a sense of what the study of these matters is, in the most direct sense, *for*. We have gone on the assumption that the purpose of instruction in these areas is to provide students with the particular knowledges and skills that they need in solving certain basic and ever recurring grammatical and mechanical problems of expression, *primarily* written expression. If ours may seem to some a narrow view of the purposes of grammatical study, it is nevertheless the unqualified view of the present report. *We believe in grammatical study, for high school students, as means, not end.* Our basic assumption has figured to some degree in the ratings of textbooks on each of the items included in Table VII; for obviously sense of purpose must be taken into account in judging "Coverage," as it must in judging "Organization with Volume," "Relevance," etc. Our rating under the heading "Sense of Purpose" is therefore, in large measure, a general, or summary judgment.

Table VII shows considerable variation in the ratings of this item. Some textbook writers coldly "lay it all out" — parts of speech, parts of sentence, usage, punctuation, etc. — for students to "master" as a body of knowledge, with no attempt, direct or indirect, to relate the information to problems of expression. At the other extreme, some writers make valiant efforts to relate grammatical study as intimately as possible to expression. Two methods are prominent among the latter: first, use of an organization which includes treatment of one or two parts of speech, sentence parts, or rules of punctuation at a time, in chapters that involve writing, with the result that grammatical matters are distributed throughout the volume; and, second, use of drill exercises which require that the students write sentences using particular parts of speech, sentence elements, commas, etc., rather than merely identify these in given sentences. Though we acknowledge and applaud these efforts, we have pointed out and must repeat that certain practical disadvantages result from them. The first method so scatters grammatical matters about that items are hard to find and even harder to master as a whole body of usable information; further, it may well be of no real use to a student assigned to write his first theme to place in that same chapter instruction on one part of speech, say the noun, when in fact he needs to make use of all parts of speech and all sentence elements in writing his theme. To learn about nouns for the first theme, about pronouns for the second, about adjectives for the third, and so on, is not necessarily to approach either writing or mastery of a total functional body of information.

The second method, using sentence building instead of analysis based on given sentences, is unquestionably preferable to incessant drill in identifying parts in sentences written by other people, in inserting commas into other people's sentences, and so forth. But this method, too, has a fault: students are asked, in turn, to "build sentences with nouns," "build sentences with pronouns," "build sentences with verbs," "build sentences with adjectives," etc. — but the fact is that no one "builds sentences with nouns," or with any other parts of speech. We build sentences and paragraphs and essays with *ideas* and with detail in the form of fact, example, etc., in the course of which process we make use of nouns, pronouns, and all the other parts of speech. In our view, thus, the second method confronts students with a basically false conception of what writing is: we do not write to use parts of speech, but to express ideas, facts, feelings.

Virtually no textbook makes a deliberate attempt to show students, *at the time that new grammatical elements are introduced, the major direct relationships between knowledge of those particular elements and specific problems of expression.* It seems a waste, for example, to introduce participial phrases and to discuss their form and function without, at the same time, identifying the particular problems of structure and punctuation that use of participial phrases poses for the writer. No textbook has gone through the body of grammatical and mechanical matters in the way suggested, relating each item of grammatical knowledge to the specific major problems that arise with its use. All of the textbooks emphasize the "what" and the "how" of grammatical knowledge without simultaneous explanation also of the "why." If this lack alone determined the ratings of the textbooks' treatment of grammatical information, it would be necessary to record them as universally unsatisfactory.

CHAPTER 3

Rhetoric and Composition

ANALYSIS AND DESCRIPTION

TABLE IX of Appendix B presents such general facts and figures pertaining to the series' treatments of rhetoric and composition as lend themselves readily to quantitative summary. With the addition of selected matters that do not lend themselves to tabular presentation, the items of this table furnish the materials for the descriptive account that follows.

Amount of Attention

Two points are of special interest here: first, the total amount of attention given by series authors to the various aspects of instruction in rhetoric and composition; second, the actual amount of writing required or expected of students, in terms of number of writing assignments.

Computation of the total amount of space given to rhetoric and composition has proved to be a long and exacting task. In most series, as will be explained in the following section on organization, attention to rhetoric and composition is distributed widely between the covers of the volume. Instruction pertinent to rhetoric and composition is sometimes found inconspicuously placed in the midst of chapters not primarily concerned with either; on the other hand, chapters which by title might be expected to be concerned wholly with rhetoric and composition are found on examination to include pages or sections that cannot appropriately be counted with either. The complex and subtle problems of separating the germane from the nongermane for purposes of computation may be exemplified by referring to two typical ones, those having to do with motivational matter and those having to do with letter writing. First, many of the series follow rather elaborate patterns of "working up" to actual writing assignments. Often, as for example with exercises in narrowing topics and outlining, pages are definitely countable as preparation for composition; but perhaps as often the activities here loosely designated "motivational" appear to be ends in themselves rather than approaches to composition. It is in these latter cases that decisions of what to count toward composition and what not to count have been peculiarly difficult. Second, letter writing, which figures conspicuously in all the series, and in all volumes of most, has been found to involve much that concerns composition only secondarily and other matters, such as the etiquette of personal notes, invitations, acceptances, and the like, primarily. Instruction in the handling of business correspondence regularly involves space devoted to classification of the kinds and purposes of business letters and to diagrams and explanatory information on how to address envelopes, fold letters, etc. In short, much that is included in the series under "Letters" appears on examination to belong rather with "Other" than with Composition.

These are but two areas among many in which it has been necessary to decide somewhat arbitrarily between counting and not counting. Yet, in defense of our final computations, it is to be said that we have scrupulously sought to apply the same decisions to comparable cases in all the series; further, it is to be made clear that our decisions have generally been on the generous side, so that in any instances of faulty judgment it is probable that the figure given for "Total Rhetoric and Composition" is higher, not lower, than a strict count would allow.

These figures, as may be seen in Table IX, show a wide range in pages assigned to Composition, from a high of 560 pages for the Lippincott series to a low of 179 pages for the Harcourt, Brace *Living Language*. On the average, from one-sixth to one-fourth of the total space in a series relates to instruction and practice in Rhetoric and Composition. In most series, as has been made apparent earlier in Table I of Appendix B, the proportion of space given to Rhetoric and Composition is lower than that given to either Grammar or "Other." Evaluative comment on the significance of this difference is reserved for the concluding portion of this section.

Not less significant than the total amount of space given to the treatment of rhetoric and composition is the total number of writing assignments required or recommended. Column 3 of Table IX shows the count for each volume of each series, together with totals for the series. Once more, it must be stated that the count is in every case rather generous than severe. Our intent has been to include in the count every writing exercise that involves units substantially larger than individual sentences, but to omit such exercises as outlining and comparable writing activities that are preparatory in nature. Exercises in copying or rewriting given material have also been omitted. Even with these omissions, the count includes a wide diversity of writing assignments, which would hardly be allowed under a strict interpretation of the term "composition." The range extends from telegrams to research papers, and from minutes of club meetings to critiques of television programs. It should be added that several series follow a practice of making "optional" assignments — that is to say, assignments beyond those required of the entire class, to be performed by students who choose to perform them; we have included fewer such writing assignments in the count, with the result that the totals for some series are higher by as much as one-third than they would otherwise be. On the other hand, merely "alternate" assignments, allowing choice by the student of one from among several possibilities, have been counted as single assignments.

Table IX makes apparent the very considerable range among the series in number of actual writing assignments, from a high series total of 414 (ABC, *Our English Language*) to a low of 56 (Scribner's, *English at Work*). The same two series also represent the high and the low for individual volumes, the ABC volume for grade twelve making 133 writing assignments and the Scribner's volume for grade eleven making 13. The distribution of writing assignments within volumes and within series is described below.

Organization-Distribution

Column 4 of Table IX presents a three-way classification of the distribution of writing instruction and practice within volumes of each series. Before comments are made about the distribution within volumes, however, note should be taken of the distribution of emphasis on writing within series.

On the evidence of column 3, one general point is first to be made, namely, that material on writing is distributed uniformly among the volumes of most series, some series having virtually identical figures during two or three of the four years. In general, if the series total is comparatively high, the figure for any one year of the series is also comparatively high; conversely, if the total figure is low, that for any one year is also low. There is thus, among all the series, no case of a conspicuously weighted year of composition, or of a conspicuously slighted year. It will be observed, however, that of the fourteen series examined, seven give fewest writing assignments in the ninth-grade volume, and four make the fewest assignments in the tenth-grade volume. On the other hand, the highest totals are spread with remarkable evenness: three series give most writing assignments in the volume for grade nine, three in the volume for grade ten, two in the volume for grade eleven, five in the volume for grade twelve, and one gives equally high numbers to grades eleven and twelve. To the extent that the number of writing assignments is indicative, it thus appears that in the series as a whole somewhat less emphasis is given to composition in the ninth grade and somewhat more in the twelfth; a minority of series, however, reverse this general tendency. It would nevertheless be inaccurate to state that any one year of the four shows significantly greater emphasis.

Column 4 of Table IX reflects the practice of textbook writers in either distributing or concentrating writing assignments and writing instruction within individual volumes of the series. It will be observed that in eight of the fourteen series each volume has been rated "M" to signify that in these volumes material falling under the general head of composition is "moderately" distributed — that is to say, spread over a considerable number of chapters or sections, but not spread throughout the volume or even completely throughout that portion of the volume that is distinct from the handbook section. In this frequent arrangement, from one-third to one-half of the total chapters apart from the handbook include some writing instruction and at least one writing assignment. Volumes following this arrangement may sometimes devote two or three consecutive chapters primarily to subjects like "Mastering the Paragraph" and "Narrative Writing," these being followed by chapters on "Personal Problems," "Newspapers and Magazines," or "Radio, Television, and Motion Pictures," each of which may involve some special writing assignments; these, in turn, may be interspersed by chapters on speech activities, library units, vocabulary units, etc., which do not typically include formal writing assignments. Thus, in the "M" classification, as many as eight chapters may involve writing instruction and assignments, these chapters being set among, or alternating with, as many more chapters given to activities other than writing, and involving writing either incidentally or not at all. In order to characterize this type of arrangement more specifically, the relevant content of one very typical series is summarized below. The following are the principal composition chapters of the Ginn *English Skills* series.

Grade 9:   ch. 3 — personal letters; ch. 6 — writing directions; ch. 7 — account of interview; ch. 12 — paragraphs; ch. 13 — biographical book report; ch. 15 — writing verse; ch. 16 — movie review, etc.

Grade 10:   ch. 10 — paragraphs; ch. 11 — business and social letters; ch. 12 — reports; ch. 13 — experience themes; ch. 14 — reports on movies, television, radio; ch. 15 — news story, feature, editorial, etc.

Grade 11:   ch. 3 — letters; ch. 7 — paragraph development; ch. 8 — rewriting test questions, writing practice examinations; ch. 9 — book review; ch. 10 — written report; ch. 11 — various newspaper forms, evaluation of magazine; ch. 12 — write an advertisement; ch. 13 — writing about television programs, movies, etc.

Grade 12:   ch. 2 — personal and business letters; ch. 4 — book review; ch. 5 — autobiography, personal stories, short story; ch. 7 — précis; ch. 8 — persuasive editorial or article; ch. 9 — written report; ch. 10 — poetry.

As will be noted, each volume includes seven or eight chapters mainly involving writing; interspersed are chapters involving a considerable diversity of activities, exemplified as follows: "Getting Along with People," "Making Your Voice Serve You Well," "Words and Your Dictionary," "Improving Reading Skills," "Clear Thinking in Discussions," "Parliamentary Law in Club Meetings," "Courtesy in Everyday Situations," "Making Announcements and Introducing Speakers," "Arriving at Decisions Through Discussions," etc.

In contrast to the plan of spreading writing instruction and assignments over a sizable portion of the volume is that of concentrating (marked by "C" in column 4) attention to writing in a single section or small number of chapters grouped together. An example of this practice, which is represented by only two complete series, is afforded by the Harcourt, Brace *English Grammar and Composition* series. The practice of this series is summarized below.

Grade 9: Writing confined to Part III, following Part I, Grammar, and Part II, Usage, and preceding sections on Aids to Good English, Speaking and Listening, and Mechanics. Chapters in Part III include Paragraphs, Compositions, Letters, Stories, and Reports.

Grade 10: Writing confined to Part III, following Part I, Grammar, and Part II, Correct and Effective Sentences, and preceding sections on Speaking and Listening, Mechanics, and Vocabulary. Chapters in Part III include Paragraphs, Compositions, Narrative Writing, and Letter Writing.

Grade 11: Writing confined to Part VI, following sections on Grammar, Usage, Speaking and Listening, The Library, and Sentence Structure, and preceding sections on Mechanics and Examinations.

Grade 12: Writing confined to Part VI, following sections on Grammar, Correct Sentences, Clear Sentences, Smooth Sentences, and The Library, and preceding sections on Speaking and Listening and Mechanics.

Chapters on writing in Grades eleven and twelve essentially repeat the forms used in Grades nine and ten.

In yet a third kind of organization of content relating to composition (marked "W" in column 4), writing instruction and assignments are widely distributed either throughout the entire volume or throughout the volume except for the handbook section, which in these volumes tends to be slighter than average. An example of this practice, which also is represented by only two series, is afforded by Scribner's *English at Work*.

Grade 9:   Themes, paragraphs, letters, or other writing in each of the first 14 of 19 chapters.

Grade 10:   Autobiography, letters, paragraphs, reports, and other writing in each of the first 12 of 19 chapters.

Grade 11:   Paragraphs, dialogues, research papers, letters, and other writing in each of the first 14 of 19 chapters.

Grade 12:   Career theme, letters, arguments, essays, research papers, book reviews, and other writing in each of the first 14 of 20 chapters.

      In this series virtually all chapters (aside from the handbook) include some writing along with other activities in an "integrated" program.

The foregoing discussion, supplementing column 4 of Table IX, presents in the most general terms the facts on distribution of writing instruction and practice both within volumes and among volumes of a series. Another aspect of the question involves the order and placement of the various *forms* of writing both within years and over the period of four years. Discussion of this topic follows.

Forms

Quite apart from purpose (description, exposition, etc.), the *forms* of writing (in units larger than the sentence) for which instruction and assignments are given in the textbooks collectively include the following, listed here in (approximately) a descending order of emphasis:

1. "theme"
2. paragraph
3. letter (friendly, business)
4. review (movie, radio, television, magazine, book)
5. news article (story, feature, editorial, interview)
6. research paper (term paper, library report, "investigative theme")
7. drama (dialogue, radio, television script, one-act play, "socio-drama")
8. autobiography, diary

9. poetry (couplet, free verse, ballad, limerick, parody)
10. essay (article, familiar, formal)
11. précis, summary
12. story (personal narrative, incident)
13. "rewrite" (from one level of style to another, etc.)
14. adaptation (story to play, etc.)
15. paraphrase
16. announcement, bulletin board notice
17. minutes of club meeting
18. club constitution
19. telegram
20. classified advertisement

The term "theme," which heads this list, accounts for roughly one-half the total number of writing assignments in the textbook series. Themes are assigned in most textbooks of each grade level. Although an occasional series prefers to use some other designation, such as "paper" or "composition," "theme" is by far the most common term for written exercises in the textbooks. It is used, in fact, to stand for virtually every kind of written exercise, whether descriptive, expository, or narrative. It may be short — a single paragraph; or it may be several thousand words in length, as in the case of the "long investigative theme." Although textbook writers often refer to the "one-paragraph theme," the term more commonly is used to designate writing of more than one paragraph; but length is not a determining factor in what is and what is not a "theme," nor is content or purpose. "Theme" may be distinguished from "essay," in the usage of the textbooks, only as the more general may be distinguished from the specific; all "essays," formal or informal, are themes, but of course not all "themes" — which can be descriptive or narrative as well as expository — are essays. The range of topics considered appropriate for themes is literally without limit. This range is surveyed below in the section on "Sources."

Themes, as has been stated above, are ubiquitous in the textbooks, being assigned in every year and at any given point, early, middle, or late, in any year. The two principal forms that, after the "theme," receive the greatest amount of attention among the series as a whole in number of pages and number of writing assignments made are the paragraph and the letter. The single year of greatest concentration on the paragraph is the tenth, six of the series giving that year the highest number of pages; three series give the highest number of pages to the paragraph in grade nine, three in grade eleven, and only one in grade twelve — which year, for the greater number of series, shows least emphasis on the paragraph. As may be plainly seen, there is no agreement among the series on a year for greatest emphasis on instruction and practice in writing the paragraph.

Within volumes, the placement of material on the paragraph also varies from series to series. In the greater number of series, this material comes relatively early. It should also be added that the practice of most series is to concentrate discussion of the paragraph in one chapter or section of the volume, rather than to spread this material over several chapters. On the other hand, many paragraph writing assignments are made in chapters other than the special one in which the paragraph is formally discussed; thus, while typically instruction in the paragraph is confined to one section, practice in writing it is spread fairly widely. Further detail on the treatment of the paragraph will be found below under the heading "Instruction."

Columns 7, 8, and 9 of Table IX show, respectively, the number of pages assigned to letters and letter writing, the number of writing assignments for friendly letters, and the number of writing assignments for business letters. As with the paragraph, most series spread the treatment of letters rather evenly over the four years, the most even distributions being represented by both Ginn series, *English Skills* and *Better English*, by Heath, by HB[1], and by Singer. But, indeed, most series are remarkable rather for the evenness of this distribution than for their scanting of any one or two years; only ABC and HB² give significantly unequal attention to letters over four years. It will be noted that *no* series entirely omits attention to letters in any one year. It will be noted also that no one year generally shows a conspicuous emphasis, above other years, in attention to letters.

Of passing interest here is the practice of several series in presenting a substantial number of pages which discuss letters and letter writing without making direct assignments to write letters. Thus, for example, Macmillan gives four, six, and six pages, respectively, to letters in grades ten, eleven, and twelve, and makes no writing assignments in these years. McGraw-Hill gives six and seven pages to letters in grades ten and eleven without writing assignments. HB² gives a total of 36 pages to letters but makes only five writing assignments in four years, with none in grades ten and eleven. Generally speaking, and as might be expected, those series which give the greatest amount of space to letters, personal and business, also present the most complete coverage of the many types and purposes of letters.

As may be seen by comparing totals in columns 6, 8, and 9 of Table IX with totals in column 3, a very considerable part of the total writing experience of students during four years is represented by paragraph and letter writing. For example, of A & B's 145 writing assignments, 58 are paragraphs and letters; of Ginn¹, 307 and 87, of HB¹, 164 and 67. On the whole, assignments to write paragraphs and letters represent one-fourth to one-half of the total number of writing assignments. Since the form variously referred to in the textbooks as "theme," "paper," "composition," itself claims approximately half the total number of writing assignments, it is apparent that assignments in the remaining seventeen forms identified above are thinly covered.

It should be pointed out here that certain of these latter forms are assigned in chapters in which composition is not the principal aim. Thus the "review" of a motion picture, radio or television program comes typically in a chapter which discusses motion pictures, radio, and television; the "news article," in a chapter which treats newspapers and magazines; the "minutes of a club meeting," in a chapter on parliamentary procedure or formation of clubs, and so forth.

One final form recurs with sufficient frequency and takes sufficient space in the textbooks to require special attention here. This is the longer piece of expository prose based on some kind of study and variously identified as a research paper, term paper, report, source theme, investigative theme, etc. These terms are not completely interchangeable among the textbooks. The term "report," for example, may in one set refer to the typical research project which terminates in a long paper complete with footnotes and bibliography, but in another set it may represent a much briefer account of material looked up in the library and even presented orally. Column 10 of Table IX indicates the distribution of instruction and practice relating primarily to the longer research paper but also including the shorter kind of report. In this column the symbol "O" means no material in that year; the symbol "R" means report, which may be long or short, and possibly either oral or written in finished form; the symbol "Res" means inclusion of a formal research project so designated by the textbook. As will be noted, the most common grade for the unqualified "Res" designation is the twelfth, when all series but Lippincott have extensive instruction and practice. The second most common placement of the research paper is the eleventh grade, when seven of the series have material designated resarch, and five more designate a "report." The tenth grade includes only one "Res" symbol, but eight textbooks have some sort of "R." It is to be further noted that seven of the series, or exactly half of those examined, include either a report or formally designated research paper in every year. Of the remaining series, three have some form of report or research in three of the years; two have research papers in two of the years; and two have research papers in only one year.

Source Materials and Topics

Essentially, the discussion which follows attempts to answer, with as much detail as is possible in very limited space, a question that must be of first importance to student users of these textbooks, to their teachers, to an objective analyst of the books, and quite evidently to the authors of the textbooks. The question is this: "*What do the textbooks recommend that students write about?*"

In the broadest terms the answer is that students are assigned to write about *themselves and the immediate interests of their adolescent worlds:* their families, their friends, their neighbors, their streets and communities, their school, their hobbies, their personal experiences. It is appropriate here to quote directly from typical textbook series. Since there is remarkable uniformity, the following statements assembled from several series will serve to represent the points of view of all series examined.

Heath, *English in Action,* grade twelve: "Your own experiences, your reading, your observation of people, places, and things, your listening activities will give you ideas for themes.

"Your part-time job, for example, will provide you with half a dozen subjects. If you are a baby sitter, you may write on one of the following: Children I have sat with; One memorable evening; Economic advantages of baby-sitting; How I became a baby sitter. . . ."

Allyn and Bacon, *Effective English,* grade ten: "The three chief sources for your theme material are your own personal experiences, conversations with other people, and books (including encyclopedias and other reference works). Much of your writing this semester will be drawn from personal experiences: I was there; I felt it; it happened to me." (p. 27.)

Singer, *Enjoying English,* grade nine: "The authors of this book believe that any student can speak and write well when he chooses the topic closest to his heart. Perhaps this topic is money for a movie; perhaps it is a moment with a boy friend or girl friend; perhaps it is a problem with your father or mother about dating or coming home late; perhaps it concerns your daydreams of your future." (p. 2.)

Scott, Foresman, *Guide to Modern English,* grade nine: "Your classmates would enjoy reading about some of the exciting, sad, unusual, or amusing things that have happened to you or that you saw happen. For example, you might tell how you won the fishing contest at Indian Lake or about the practical joke that cost your brother the leading part in the seventh-grade pageant. As you can see, the incidents you write about need not be any more startling or spectacular than the ones you talk about. . . . Some of the people and places that have impressed you or amused you or aroused strong feeling on your part would also make good subjects for papers. . . . Perhaps the most useful sort of paper you might write is an explanation of how to make or do something or how something works. Your hobbies, clubs, and other activities provide a number of subjects for such explanations. . . . Many ideas for another sort of explanatory paper come from the countless talks you and your friends have about personal and social problems, especially those of people your own age. . . . In some papers you might aim to make your ideas about a problem seem so reasonable and convincing that readers will adopt them. For example, suppose that you take a very dim view of the week-night curfew for teen-agers in your town. . . ." (pp. 129-30.)

Row, Peterson, *Building Better English,* grade ten: "Since you write best about the things that you know, the topics for your first writing efforts should be taken from your own ideas and experiences. Your thoughts, interests, attitudes, and personal experiences will suggest many subjects which can be developed into entertaining compositions.

"Secondhand experiences, those that you secure through reading, television, motion pictures, radio, or talking with people, are other fertile sources of theme ideas." (p. 125.)

The preceding representative excerpts from textbooks adequately define the general area from which all of the books examined draw the topics that are recommended for themes of every purpose — description, narration, exposition, argumentation — and in all forms, from paragraphs to the "investigative theme."

Topics for writing are presented in two ways in the textbook series: (1) with each direct assignment to write is presented a list of suggested topics; (2) either at the end of the volume or at the ends of individual sections, or in both places, are presented extensive lists of additional topics. It is obviously not possible here, in limited space, to record all of the topics suggested by even one of the series, for if there is one feature common to all series it is the abundance of suggested topics for writing. To demonstrate the remarkable unity of the textbooks in this basic matter, it will therefore be necessary to proceed, first, by describing representative practices and listing a substantial number of topics selected from Ginn, *English Skills*, a typical series, and, second, by listing a very few representative samples from a number of the remaining series.

GINN, GRADE NINE. *First list of topics* is presented in Chapter 12, p. 171; students are to write a topic sentence for each, and later to choose one as basis of a paragraph: 1. "My Hobby." 2. "My Camp." 3. "Our Back Yard." 4. "My Worst Embarrassment." *Second list of topics,* for a theme of two or three paragraphs: 1.

"What I Learned at Camp." 2. "Why I Like My Hobby." 3. "Why Every Student Should Belong to a School Club." 4. "What 'School Spirit' Means to Me." 5. "What I Should Consider in Choosing My Vocation." 6. "Why Every Boy Should Own a Dog." *Third list* is for a "report": 1. "The Manufacture of Phonograph Records." 2. "Poisonous Snakes in the U.S." 3. "Early American Cooking." 4. "U.S. Department of Conservation." 5. "Housekeeping in the Future." 6. "What the Experts Say about Golf." 7. "A Famous Woman Athlete." *A Classified List of Theme Topics* is included at the end of this volume. This list classifies 175 topics under the following heads: Descriptions, Reminiscences, Character Sketches, Processes, Explanations, Persuasions and Arguments, Comparisons and Contrasts.

GINN, GRADE TEN: Topics for a *descriptive paragraph:* "walking down the hall of your school," "riding up to your school on your bicycle," "riding on an elevator or escalator in a department store." Topics for an *initial theme:* "a well-planned city park," "a city in the rain," "the old cemetery," "the woods at night," "night baseball," "snow on the farm." Topics for *a report:* "three-dimensional television," "artificial satellites," "foreign customs," "historical sites in New England," "unusual occupations," "how to hold a tennis racket." The *Classified List of Theme Topics* at the end of this volume includes 100 topics under the headings Home and Friends, School and Community, Life in a Democracy, One World.

GINN, GRADE ELEVEN: *Topic sentences for a paragraph:* "The student council is important in our school," "In my opinion, —— is one of the greatest recent scientific developments," "Last summer I learned a valuable lesson at camp." Topics for a *three-paragraph theme:* "breakfast — as prepared by Mother, by Sister, by Me"; "what my family thinks about my telephone friends," "my brother writes home from college — to Mother, to Dad, and to the Girl Next Door." The *Classified List of Theme Topics* at the end of this volume includes 165 topics under the headings of Description, Characterizations (Types), Characterizations (Individual), Processes, Explanation, Persuasion, Argumentation, Comparison and Contrast, Reminiscences.

GINN, GRADE TWELVE: Topics for *personal experience* story: "failing to arrive home at the promised time," "my first pay check," "on getting up in the morning." Topics for *a report:* "a famous building," "the Boston Tea Party," "an improvement in agriculture," "a famous inventor," "a well-known woman."

Allyn and Bacon, *Effective English,* grade ten: Topics for "a theme of more than one paragraph": "the chivalry of today," "the essentials for success," "the values of regular church attendance," "the importance of planning my future."

American Book Company, *Our English Language,* grade twelve: Topic sentences for paragraphs: "There are TV programs to please all kinds of persons," "Candy may be all right for you but it isn't for me," "You wonder why my brother doesn't call you for dates."

Harcourt, Brace, *English Grammar and Composition,* grade twelve: Topics for a paragraph of comparison or contrast: "Our new car and our old car," "Country life and city life," "Intramural sports and interscholastic sports," "The book version of a novel and the movie version."

Heath, *English in Action,* grade nine: "Ideas" for a story-theme: "I was cook," "I go bargain hunting," "Dad lays down the law," "The joke was on me," "Just plain scared."

Lippincott, *English for Today,* grade eleven: Topic sentences for paragraphs: "The party last night was great fun," "The ability to type is a valuable skill," "Teaching tricks to a dog is not easy," "The story of my nickname is interesting."

Macmillan, *Our English Language,* grade nine: Topics for paragraphs: "swimming on a hot day," "a science experiment," "an exciting adventure," "having my picture taken," "walking to school," "the school bus," "keeping a diary," "an unexpected tumble," "being a freshman."

McGraw-Hill, *Your Language,* grade ten: Topics for "explanations": "how to install dual exhausts," "the four-barrel carburetor," "the duties of a lifeguard or camp counselor," "T-formation football," "how to read a weather map," "aims of a boy scout or a girl scout," "hi-fi equipment," "new equipment at the dentist's," "a new farm implement."

Scott, Foresman, *Guide to Modern English,* grade nine: Topic sentences for paragraphs: "Being a baby sitter is not always an easy job," "You can tell quite a bit about people's character by the way they dress," "If I were a dog I'd hate to live in a city," "Miss ——, my history teacher, has a fine sense of humor," "I never let bad weather interfere with my plans," "Many high school students don't know how to study," "Last week I learned the importance of 'A stitch in time saves nine,'" "High school is more interesting than junior high," "Being the baby of the family is not always an advantage," "A bargain is not always a bargain."

Scribner's *English at Work,* grade twelve: Topics for themes: "the struggle to be well dressed," "what my relatives think of me," "people who find fault with me," "the mistakes of umpires," "team jealousies," "my family's interest in my dates," "obnoxious people in public places," "borrowing and borrowers."

Numerous as are the examples listed above, they represent in fact only a minute fraction of the total number of "suggested topics" supplied by the textbook writers. It may be stated categorically that no textbook series has provided an inadequate number of such suggestions; indeed, all evidence points to the conclusion that "thinking up" topics for writing claims a major part of the energy that goes into preparation of any series. One significant aspect of this fact is discussed in the Evaluative Summary that concludes this section of the report.

Instruction

With few exceptions, all of the series examined include a very considerable amount of space for instruction in the art, or skill, of composition, ranging from the details of word choice through the rhetoric of sentences to the preparation and final proofreading of long reports.

Typically, instruction in composition falls under the following heads:

1. Use of concrete and specific nouns, action verbs, figurative language.
2. Construction of rhetorically effective sentences.
3. General principles such as order, unity, coherence.
4. Selection of topic.
5. Narrowing of topics for composition.
6. Gathering of material.
7. Outlining.
8. Specific instruction for each of the various forms — the paragraph, the friendly letter, the business letter, descriptive, narrative, and expository exercises, "themes," stories, dialogues, poems, reports, etc.
9. Preparation of the final draft, and proofreading.

With widely varying degrees of emphasis, all series have something to say under each of the headings above, and with rare exceptions they give attention to all of these matters in each volume. It is further to be observed that instruction given tends in all cases to be of a standard kind, drawn from a common reservoir. Whereas certain volumes give more space to instruction in principles of composition than others, yet essentially the same elements of advice are included in all. It is manifestly possible here to select only a few of the principal subjects which receive attention and to characterize the treatments of these that appear most typical of the series as a group.

One compositional problem which receives extensive and virtually universal treatment is that of *narrowing the topic*. A typical set of directions for accomplishing this preliminary step is contained in Harcourt, Brace, *English Grammar and Composition*, grade nine, as follows:

11b.   *Limit the Subject*

Having chosen a subject for an interesting composition, ask yourself: Is the subject narrow enough for a short theme? If not, how can I limit it? For compositions of only two or three pages, you cannot handle a big subject well. In fact, you should learn to choose a *part* of a subject to write about.

Suppose, for instance, that you chose, in Exercise 1, to write on "fishing." This general subject includes all kinds of fishing, in fresh water and in salt water, as well as all ways of fishing, from cane poles to harpoons. It also includes every type of fish, from a crayfish to a whale, and every kind of bait, from earthworms to mullet. To cover the general subject "fishing" in a brief composition is impossible. If, however, you limit this subject by choosing only a part of it, you can handle the subject well in a short paper. For example, you could fully develop such limited topics as "How To Catch Bass," "Four Tips on Fresh-Water Fishing," "Using a Spinning Reel," "The Differences in Artificial Lures," or "A Tangle with a Stingaree."

There follows a series of three examples of the process of limiting subjects, of which the first will serve illustrative purposes here:

General Subject: Automobiles
Limited Topics: The Art of Washing a Car
    The Best Low-priced Car on the Market
    How to Clean a Carburetor
    Kinds of Mufflers
    Recent Improvements in Automobile Tires

The section of instruction concludes with an exercise in identification of limited and unlimited topics and with a specific writing assignment as follows:

Exercise 3.
Before continuing your study of this chapter, try your hand at writing a brief composition. Select an interesting subject that you know something about. Perhaps you will choose one of those listed in Exercise 1 or Exercise 2. Limit your subject so that you can develop your ideas well in 300 words or less. Writing this composition will help you to understand better the advice given on the following pages.

The treatment in the volume for grade ten of the same series is very similar to that in the volume for grade nine.

The treatment of "limiting a subject" outlined above from a single series corresponds very closely in all respects but one to that of all other series examined. It differs from the greater number only in being more succinct and businesslike.

The problem of "narrowing a topic" or "limiting a subject" is taken up most frequently and fully in connection with instruction for writing a report or other kind of extended paper. It is related also to that of achieving unity in, specifically, the paragraph.

With the exception, in a few series, of the report or term paper and, in yet other series, of personal and business letters, the form or unit for the writing of which the most detailed instruction is given, we have earlier indicated, is the paragraph. Columns 5 and 6 of Table IX show, in terms of total pages and number of writing assignments, the universally heavy emphasis given by textbook writers to the paragraph. In a typical series which, over all, lists 400 "suggested topics," as many as 250 of these are topics suggested for paragraphs.

In short, omitting a few series (Harcourt, Brace, *Living Language,* and the Lippincott and McGraw-Hill volumes) typical series not only give large space to the paragraph in terms of total pages, number of suggested topics, and number of actual writing assignments, but tend to concentrate their fullest and most explicit instruction in the art or skill of composition upon the paragraph unit.

In broadest terms, this instruction includes: (1) the use of *models,* sometimes merely for examples, sometimes for detailed analysis; (2) insistence on and practice in the use of *topic sentences;* (3) identification and illustration of various *methods of development* (example, analogy, etc.); and (4) consideration of possible kinds of *order.* Because the material covered, as well as the pattern of covering it, is virtually the same in a majority of texts, it will be possible to represent the practices of all fairly adequately by first presenting a detailed account of the practices of a single series that incorporates in its treatment virtually all that is contained in the other series together, and thereafter by supplementing this account by specific references to other texts. For the first purpose the single series that may most fairly stand for all is the American Book Company's *Our English Language.*

This series gives a full chapter to the paragraph in each volume, as follows: grade nine, "Practice in Paragraphs"; grade ten, "Polishing Paragraphs"; grade eleven, "Better Paragraphs"; grade twelve, "A Clinic for Paragraphs."

In the volume for grade nine, 16 pages, the materials of instruction, in order, can be summarized as follows:

1. Definition: "A paragraph is a sentence or a group of sentences developing a single topic. A paragraph is set off by indenting the first word."
2. Presentation of two imperfect paragraphs for analysis.
3. Topic sentence: "The sentence which tells the main idea of a paragraph is the *topic sentence.*"
4. Exercise in identifying the topic sentence in each of three brief paragraphs.

5. Exercise in identifying topic sentences in five paragraphs from student's history or science book.
6. Exercises in selecting and writing appropriate topic sentences.
7. Presentation of "kinds" of paragraphs — explanation, description, argumentation, and narration — involving use of topic sentences and actual writing of illustrative paragraphs.
8. Two writing exercises to practice use of conversation.
9. Presentation (with writing exercises) of ways to develop paragraphs: example, details, reasons.
10. List of transitional words and phrases with exercises in using them.
11. Review of instruction on paragraphs in the form of eight "standards for good paragraphs," as follows:

    "A good paragraph deals with only one topic."

    "A paragraph of explanation, description, or argumentation usually contains a topic sentence."

    "All the sentences help to develop the topic."

    "The sentences are arranged in a natural order."

    "Transitional words, phrases, and sentences help to make a smooth-flowing style."

    "The first sentence catches interest."

    "The last sentence makes a good conclusion."

    "The first word of each paragraph is indented."

12. Additional review including the following:

    Answering questions on the text ("What is a paragraph?" "What is a topic sentence?" etc.).

    Writing of paragraph from a given topic sentence ("Summer [winter, spring, autumn] is my favorite season") using details as method of development.

    Writing of paragraph from given topic sentence, details, and concluding sentence. The topic sentence: "Yesterday I had a spell of 'fall weather'."

    Writing an anecdote made up chiefly of conversation.

    A "paragraph game" for the whole class, using a judge, a master of ceremonies, a timekeeper, with rest of class as panel members. Gist of game is 1-minute speech by each of panel members, to be judged for (1) getting off the topic, (2) stalling for time, (3) making an error in usage. Points are added or lost on various grounds, the team winning that has most points after all class members have participated.

The volumes for grades ten, eleven, and twelve are basically similar.

Even if space permitted, no significant purpose would be served here by summarizing treatments of the paragraph in other series with so much detail as that used in this account of one sample text, inasmuch as there is such general uniformity in the treatments of all series that it is fair to say that the one example represents all with respect to the central facts. That is to say, textbook treatments of the paragraph are uniform in the following principal ways: (1) in their coverage of basic items of instruction — definition of paragraph, emphasis on topic sentence, methods of development; (2) in their use of "model" paragraphs, both good ones for analysis and inferior ones for criticism and rewriting; however, differences do exist in the qualities of paragraphs chosen for these purposes, and this fact needs brief comment. Some textbook writers make use of student examples; others (for example, writers of the series used in the foregoing analysis) use paragraphs written by themselves expressly for the purpose; and yet others use paragraphs quoted from magazines, textbooks, or other books, with typically a science or social content. These latter are normally well-organized pieces of prose, illustrative of the use of topic sentences, of well-defined order, and of definite methods of development in terms of examples, details, comparison or contrasts, etc.; (3) in their choice of suggested topics for practice in writing paragraphs. Comparison of the foregoing samples taken from a single series with the lists of representative topics, including paragraph topics, presented earlier in this section of the report will make it evident that uniformity prevails among all the series in this important respect; (4) in their repetition of virtually identical items of instruction and practice exercises from volume to volume. Although column 5 of Table IX shows that not every series presents extensive treatment of the paragraph in each volume, yet several do so, and others treat the paragraph fully in three out of four volumes. In all of these, approximately the same degree of similarity is evident in the treatments from volume to volume as is evident in the foregoing summary of the sample series.

Because such uniformity exists, it is possible to characterize the textbooks' treatment of the paragraph with reasonable fairness through the detailed account presented above of the treatment in a single representative series. At the same time, because in virtually all series the paragraph is the unit of composition (beyond individual sentences) that is most emphasized and most fully treated, it is possible to let treatment of the paragraph stand, for the most part, for treatment of composition in general. And, more particularly, the presentation of *instruction* in the principles of the paragraph may be considered to stand generally for instruction in composition.

Yet another, and very different, aspect of instruction in composition, or writing, figures largely in all of the textbook series, and so requires attention here. Unfortunately, practices vary so widely in the treatment of this aspect, which will here be designated very loosely as *rhetoric*, that the problem of adequate representation in small space is severe. In the first place, whereas treatment of such a unit of composition as the paragraph is typically confined to a single chapter or section of each volume, treatment of rhetoric, which involves items as diverse as choice of words, effective order of elements in sentences, economical expression, figurative language, etc., is typically distributed under many headings and among many chapters and sections of volumes; indeed, it often appears in the form of merely a few words of advice which are incidental to the main topic just then being treated in the textbook. For this reason, no count of pages representing quantitatively the space given to rhetoric and closely allied matters is included in a table, for it could not be accomplished with sufficient accuracy to ensure fairness in a comparative view of the several series.

That all the textbook writers have made provisions for encouraging *effectiveness* of writing, beyond mere correctness is, however, amply demonstrable. It will be useful here to record principal chapter and section headings from several series to suggest the scope and nature of these provisions:

Allyn and Bacon, *Effective English*
  "Using Expressive Words," "Writing Is Creative," "Improving Your Writing Style," "Using Figurative Language."

Ginn, *English Skills*
  "Make Your Sentences More Effective," "Variety — the Spice of Sentence Life," "Make Complex Sentences Effective," "Build Sentences Effectively."

Harcourt, Brace, *Living Language*
  "Pinning Down Word Meanings," "Shifting Word Order in the Sentence," "Effective Writing," "Metaphor Makes Meaning Vivid," "Building Effective Sentences."

Heath, *English in Action*
  "Forceful Verbs," "Building Better Sentences," "Be Specific: Call a Dog a Beagle," "Varied Sentences," "The Right Word at the Right Time," "Studying Words in Action," "Vivid Verbs," "Writing Pleasing, Forceful Sentences," "Use Vivid, Exact, Specific Words."

McGraw-Hill, *Your Language*
  "Using Words in Different Ways," "Metaphor, The Way You Put It," "Loading a Sentence to Capacity."

Singer, *Enjoying English*
  "Grammatical Keys to Forceful Sentences," "Making Colorful and Varied Sentence Patterns," "Concrete Details."

In the foregoing summary, some items represent entire chapters, some represent substantial sections of chapters, and yet others represent only brief passages. Brief as it is, the summary will perhaps suffice to show that the series cited, in each volume (although the latter fact is not specified in the summary), give attention to means and standards of effective, rather than to merely correct, choices and arrangements of words, sentence elements, and sentences.

So many are the possible points of attack on the complex problem of teaching students to write better than merely correctly that it is hardly possible here to represent with adequate detail the total effort made by even a single series; and even so, since no single series is perfectly typical, that method of representation would not adequately characterize the approaches of the textbooks in general. A reasonable solution would appear to be to reproduce in some detail the approach made by successive volumes of a single series to a principal aspect of the large problem. As will be seen in the general summary above, a few major points of attack tend to appear with especial frequency in the several series. Description of the treatment given the central one of these, in volumes that are as nearly typical as any, will serve to exemplify details of instruction and practice.

For this purpose, analysis follows of the treatment given by the Heath series, *English in Action,* to the general problem of *effective construction of sentences.* On the one hand, this series most consistently represents the serious efforts of all series to deal with this basic matter; and on the other hand, this particular matter represents, for most series, the central point of attack on the total problem of effective writing.

Grade nine. In the volume for this grade the principal treatment is contained in Chapter 34, "Building Better Sentences." Items of instruction and practice follow in this order:

1. Illustration of effective and ineffective sentences through two contrasting accounts of "an exciting meeting between a boy and a wild stallion."
2. Instruction, with examples, in using "subject-not-first" sentences. Practice (12 sentences) in revising given "subject-first" sentences.

3. Instruction, with examples, in "streamlining" sentences by cutting out deadwood, using appositives. Practice (42 sentences).

4. Practice in "streamlining" a given theme (21 short sentences) by using "subject-not-first" sentences, getting rid of useless words, and using appositives.

5. Instruction, examples, and practice in the use of direct quotation to replace indirect quotation; a brief story entitled "Dishes" to be re-written.

6. Instruction, examples, and practice in the use of complex sentences to replace compound sentences; an original story-theme to be written (first report card, first train ride, first visit to the dentist, etc.) and revised according to these instructions: ". . . place before a sentence the figure 1 if you have put something other than an adjective before the subject, 2 if there is an appositive in it, 3 if it contains a direct quotation, and 4 if the sentence s complex." As model a story-theme, "Fishing at Night," is presented.

Grade ten. In the volume for this grade the principal treatment is contained in Chapter 30, "Writing Effective Sentences," the content of which is summarized in the following order:

1. Instruction in writing concise sentences, with examples to illustrate excision of useless words; exercise (20 sentences) in *correcting* sentences containing extra words: e.g., "Thomas A. Edison he was able to produce synthetic rubber from the goldenrod."

2. Added instruction, with examples, to eliminate repetition, other deadwood; exercise (20 sentences) in cutting out deadwood.

3. Added instruction, with examples and exercises, in reducing clauses, using appositives, complex sentences, participles and gerunds.

4. Instruction in writing "clear sentences," with examples and exercises in avoiding incorrect omissions, arranging modifiers and paired conjunctions, specifying antecedents of pronouns, using direct quotations.

5. Instruction, with examples and exercises, in writing unified and varied sentences; an original theme about "an unforgettable experience," with sentences to be improved "in the ways studied." (Same instruction as in volume for grade nine.)

6. Final review of chapter; 25 sentences to be *corrected;* e.g., "Although George is not as tall as me, he can shoot baskets very good in-

deed," "A heavy bank of gray clouds laid in the valley all day long," "Dad bought two bicycles, red in color, for my brother and I."

Grade eleven. In the volume for this grade the principal treatment is contained in Chapters 30 and 31, "Writing Clear, Concise Sentences" and "Writing Pleasing, Forceful Sentences."

Chapter 30

1. Instruction in writing concise sentences, with examples to illustrate excision of useless words; exercise (16 sentences) in "cutting out deadwood." E.g., "Never try to discuss a question of which you know nothing about." Exercise in rewriting paragraph from a student's theme.

2. Instruction, with examples and exercises, in writing *clear* sentences, avoiding dangling participles, misplaced modifiers, faulty placement of pairs of conjunctions (not only . . . but), awkwardness, sentence shifts, inaccurate connectives ("Cyrano de Bergerac loved Roxanne for many years, and he never dared tell her of his feelings"), ambiguous reference of pronouns, indefinite pronouns ("In the Carlsbad Caverns they have one huge cave nearly a mile long").

3. Instruction, with examples and exercises, in writing to express *clear thinking:* avoiding inaccurate statements ("Detective Stories are my favorite activity"), mixed metaphors, illogical statements.

4. Summary: rewriting a given letter for greater clarity and conciseness.

5. Final review of "clear, correct, concise sentences," 12 sentences to rewrite; e.g., "The setting of *Avalanche Patrol* takes place in the Rockies."

Chapter 31.

1. Instruction, with examples and exercise, in writing varied sentences: short and long, subject not first, use of question, command, or exclamation, direct quotation.

2. Instruction, examples, and exercises in writing *forceful* sentences: use of appositives, compound predicates, complex sentences, participles, active voice.

3. Instruction, examples, and exercises in writing *unified* sentences: avoiding disconnected statements, rambling sentences, overlapping constructions ("Gray's is the store that sells the book that has the song that pleased the pupils that saw the Maskers' show").

4. Instruction, examples, and exercises in using parallel structure.

5. Review: 25 sentences to be improved "by using the methods shown in this chapter."

6. Final review: improving a given theme, "My Hobby."

Grade twelve. In the volume for this grade the principal treatment is contained in Chapters 26 and 28, "Making Sentences Clear and Concise" and "Building Pleasing, Forceful Sentences."

Chapter 26.

1. Instruction, examples, and exercises in writing concise sentences by eliminating wordiness, using simpler constructions, avoiding tautology, unnecessary preliminaries, and flowery language.

2. Instruction, examples, and exercises in writing clear sentences by avoiding ambiguous reference of pronouns, indefinites (it, you, they), dangling participles, infinitives, and elliptical clauses, misplaced modifiers, sentence shifts, inaccurate connectives.

3. Instruction, examples, and exercises in expressing clear thinking through choice of accurate words, use of logical statements.

4. Review: 22 sentences to be improved; examples: "On pulling the right-hand drawer it stuck slightly," "The librarian sent the books to the bindery which needed refinishing."

With allowances for varied emphases and devices for approaching the highly complex problem, it may be said that textbook series generally cover a common body of principles for effective writing style; in this area the industry and the ingenuity of the authors appear to be second only to those employed in thinking up topics for composition. There can be no question that all have taken most seriously the challenge of aiding students to write better rather than merely correctly.

EVALUATIVE SUMMARY

Part A, Table X of Appendix B represents the analysts' comparative evaluation of the treatment given rhetoric and composition in the textbook series examined; Part B represents the analysts' direct estimate of this treatment, without reference to comparative ratings.

Number and Distribution of Writing Assignments

The basic question implied by the heading above, and by the item that it represents in the evaluative table, is this: *Do the series examined provide, by means of a sufficient number of writing assignments distributed throughout the year, for a steady emphasis on practice and instruction in writing?*

With the exception of a few that are notably short (Table IX, column 3), we find that most series are adequate with respect to number of writing assignments alone, without reference to other relevant considerations. We have assumed that a sufficient writing program might be maintained on the basis of a single piece of writing (paragraph, theme, book report, or other form involving more than unrelated sentences) assigned approximately once each week throughout the year. With allowances made for some inevitable interruptions and disruptions of the program in occasional weeks, a reasonable total number of such pieces during each year would be around 30; and if approximately this number were maintained through four years, the total number of writing assignments required of each student would be around 120. All but two of the four-year series make at least this many assignments, and several far exceed it.

A related matter, however, is that of the distribution of these assignments both within given years and over the full four years. Five of the series fall short of 30 writing assignments in at least one year, though perhaps not seriously short. More serious, in our opinion, is the practice in as many as eleven of the fourteen series of confining primary emphasis on composition to a comparatively small number of chapters — in some instances to only one or two — in each volume. Although rigid confinement of writing experience to a few weeks in each year can hardly be the true intention of the authors of these series, this arrangement implies that the teacher will devote one short period, perhaps of two or three weeks, to having the class study and practice writing, with all the rest of the year given to other activities in which writing either does not figure at all or is in any event not primary. Such a practice would appear so obviously indefensible as to require no special comment here. The question of distributing writing assignments is of course intimately related to that of the overall organization of the volume. In this respect, if not in others, those volumes in which the authors have found means to include writing as a major aim in most chapters would appear to have a definite advantage. On the other hand, the practice of concentrating attention upon major principles of composition in a few chapters, while distributing actual assignments widely, would appear also quite satisfactory and even preferable. In volumes in which both instruction in principles and the bulk of writing assignments are confined to a very few chapters, it would seem essential that authors make their true intention unmistakable — if such is their intention — namely, *that the writing assignments made in these chapters should be spread over the entire year and not confined to a few weeks.* Authors of some series have neglected to make this point clear.

Emphasis — Forms and Purposes

In the heading above, "Forms" refers to paragraphs, essays, themes, research papers, letters, stories, dialogues, etc., the full catalogue of which is extensive and is only partially covered, in terms of principal forms for which assignments are made by the textbooks, in the appropriate foregoing section of this report. "Purposes" here refers to the standard classification, such as exposition, description, narration, and argument.

The assumption on which the rating given in column 2 of Table X is based is that the primary emphasis in the writing experiences of the general high school student should be upon exposition, in the forms of paragraph and essay, or "expository theme." This is not to say that we consider no other forms and purposes of writing ever to be appropriate for high school students. Undoubtedly there should be elective opportunities, ranging from occasional to frequent, for narration and description, and for imaginative forms such as poems and stories. But the core of the composition program we consider to be expository writing, in the forms of paragraph and essay.

That the paragraph form is adequately represented by most series, in both number of pages and number of actual writing assignments, is shown by columns 5 and 6 of Table IX. Five series show high totals of more than forty paragraph-writing assignments over the four years, with two series having fifty assignments or more. On the other hand, six series show totals of twenty assignments or fewer, ranging down to two series with four and three, respectively. All those in the latter group would appear to us to fall short, some slightly and others seriously. Assignment of forty paragraphs over the four years would seem a reasonable, or even modest minimum. The paragraph also would appear a valid and profitable form to be practiced in each year; hence distribution might reasonably be expected to be comparatively regular, and indeed such is the case with most of the series. Four of the series place a conspicuous emphasis on the paragraph in a single one of the years; this practice does not appear to us to be a justifiable one. On the other hand, seven series show no actual assignments in paragraph writing in one or more years; this practice appears to us to be equally indefensible.

In the matter of space given to treatment of the paragraph, most textbooks again appear to be adequate, if, indeed, not somewhat more than adequate. Two series give totals of more than 90 pages, and seven give 70 pages or more to discussion of the forms, purposes, arrangements, and methods of development of the paragraph, and to models and writing instruction. The possibilities of excessiveness in the repetition inevitably involved in such totals are considered below in the section on "Progression." Two more points with regard to space given to the paragraph are relevant here. First, two of the series give no space at all to the paragraph in the volume for the ninth grade, and three others give slight attention to it, whereas it might be supposed that full treatment of this basic form would be indispensable in that grade. Only four series give most space to the paragraph in the ninth grade. Four others give conspicuously greatest space to it in the tenth grade, whereas most others hold to a notable balance either in all four years or in three of them; only two of the series give observably greater attention to the paragraph in grades eleven and twelve. Our point of view, which is reflected in the ratings of column 2, is that postponement of adequate paragraph treatment and practice beyond the ninth grade is a serious fault.

Second, in five of the series there appears a marked disproportion in the amount of space given to discussion of the paragraph and the actual number of assignments to write paragraphs. For example, in a volume of one series 23 pages are given to discussion, with only three paragraph assignments; in another, 20 pages are given to discussion, with but one writing assignment; and in others comparable but less conspicuous discrepancies appear. It would appear reasonable, on the contrary, to expect a decreasing number of pages of discussion after the ninth grade volume, without, however, a decreasing number of assignments.

Paragraphs are of course but one, though basic, aspect of the large matter of emphasis in forms and purposes taken into consideration in arriving at the ratings of column 2. It will be observed that Table IX includes no page or assignment breakdown in terms of the four principal classifications according to purpose — exposition, description, narration, and argumentation. Though such a breakdown would be highly useful in showing comparative emphases in this respect, the fact is that examination of the textbooks proved the impossibility of achieving anything approximating accuracy in this kind of analysis. Examination of typical topics for writing in typical series reveals that the student's finished product might fall into any one of the four classifications according to purpose, or might involve equal parts of all four. Review of the foregoing section on "Source Materials and Topics" will suggest, most likely, a generally heavy emphasis on narrative in actual student compositions; yet most of the topics summarized in that section would lend themselves to other purposes if students were deliberately instructed to handle them so. We must nevertheless conclude *that the emphasis is not steadily or primarily upon expository writing in any one of the series.*

Finally, it is necessary to comment briefly on what appears to be a general failure of reasonable proportioning in volumes that present elaborate treatment and extensive practice of one specific form of writing, namely, the letter. Table IX, column 7 shows a high mark of 214 pages given to letters by one series, with total assignments of 76 business and personal letters to be written. Five series include more than 100 pages dealing with letters; one series includes 113 letter-writing assignments, and eight of the series include more than 40 such assignments. What we consider to be undue proportion given to letters is reflected in the ratings of Table X, column 2. Though it would be difficult to fix a number of pages or assignments categorically, with the assertion that any higher number would be excessive, we find it reasonable to assert that all but four of the series appear to us absurdly excessive in their treatments of letters.

Of the great variety of random forms of writing that are only partially catalogued in the foregoing discussion of Rhetoric and Composition, such as minutes of club meetings, advertisements, telegrams, announcements, bulletin board notices, it is our view that such items can form no part of a serious program of composition, and an undue proportion of them in any series has figured adversely in the rating shown in Table X, column 2.

Instruction — Principles and Techniques

The main strength of most textbooks, with regard to instruction in the principles and techniques of composition, lies in their treatment of the paragraph — and, we believe, appropriately so. With only two exceptions, namely, in those series which simply fail to give sufficient assignments in writing paragraphs to put instruction into practice, all series may be considered adequate in this respect. The major points of instruction, such as unity, coherence, and emphasis, use of topic sentence, methods of development, and problems of order, are covered with relatively uniform explanation and degree of completeness, though with one qualification that is discussed below. In the use of illustrative paragraphs, an important means of instruction in virtually all series, greater differences have been observed, and these are among the factors taken into consideration in arriving at the ratings in Table X, column 3. For the most part, exemplary paragraphs used for analysis and for demonstrating the several methods of development and kinds of order are clear examples and serve this most immediate purpose well. Nevertheless, in certain series the model paragraphs are totally lacking in distinction as models of prose and appear to have been chosen only because they deal with topics similar to those regularly assigned for student composition — sports, school activities, family, hobbies, etc. For such "models," textbook writers have chosen paragraphs from popular magazines or newspapers, have written "models" themselves, or, in other instances, have used pieces written by high school students. Although we recognize that argument can be made for the use of models that are "close to home" and to the student's own level, the fact is that the world's prose literature is packed with an infinity of paragraphs that represent true distinction, that is to say, which combine genuine literary merit with rich possibilities of illustration. We have therefore tended to favor in our rating on this point those series that most reflect their authors' search for true distinction in all pieces of writing that are used as models, and we have tended to disapprove of the use of any and all models from student writers.

A second representative aspect of instruction that has figured in our rating on this point is that of limiting subjects. Most texts devote considerable space to practice in limiting large topics to narrower ones deemed more suitable for brief papers. In their coverage of this kind of preliminary activity the textbooks are approximately equal, with the exception that about half of the series include the same degree of attention to the problem in all volumes, whereas others stress it more heavily in one or two volumes. No series, in our view, falls short of adequacy in this matter. Again, however, a qualification is necessary and is discussed below.

Further, as has been shown in the foregoing summary of the treatment accorded matters of word choice, conciseness of expression, arrangement of sentence elements for effectiveness, and similar aspects of the complex problem that may loosely be termed rhetoric, or "building better sentences," most series cover all details with sufficient thoroughness — indeed, they characteristically give relatively full treatment to all aspects of the problem in each volume. Often the most elaborate treatment given this aspect of composition is presented in connection with *descriptive* or *narrative* writing rather than *expository* writing; it is in this connection, for example, that most attention is given to figures of speech, to selection of vivid verbs and modifiers, etc. Once again, most series have been found to be quite adequate in these matters but for the qualification that is discussed below.

Wide differences are observable in the attention given by textbooks to the "clean-up" operations of revision and proofreading, and these differences also have been taken into account in the ratings of column 3. Approximately half of the series devote chapters or extended sections to those problems of disciplining that are necessary for most writers after the first draft of a piece of writing has been completed. In our view, the attention given in such series is adequate and if carefully followed by teachers might be effective in preventing the submission of careless writing. Although it is our intention not to clutter these evaluative summaries with specific titles, one series requires special mention here as far exceeding all others in the amount of pressure put upon students to plan, write, rewrite, rewrite again, proofread, and, indeed, to proceed with caution and care at every detailed step in the preparation of papers. This is the Scott, Foresman series, *Guide to Modern English*. In each of the three volumes of this series, detailed instruction and many exercises precede the actual writing of the first rough draft of a short paper. This particular series is here singled out for special commendation as going far beyond any other in the detailed, specific step-by-step effort it makes to produce, at last, a meticulously finished short paper; the series makes, in brief, the most serious and sustained approach to composition that is offered by any series. Although the question must inevitably be asked whether a student who has been required to grind along in this meticulous fashion toward the completion of one short paper will ever want to undertake a second one during his school career, or after, yet it appears to us that the uniquely serious emphasis placed by this series upon care in the accomplishment of each step in the process of composition is salutary. It will be noted in column 3 of Table IX that this particular series makes fewer than the average writing assignments. Although there is obviously a low number of writing assignments beneath which it would appear inappropriate to go during the four high school years, yet the apparent intent of this series accords entirely with our own basic assumption, that it is best to work at producing somewhat fewer, but better, compositions.

Finally, it is necessary to explain the qualification mentioned above in connection with comments on, respectively, treatments of the paragraph, limitation of topics, and rhetoric. Although it has been stated that treatments of these matters are generally adequate in the series examined, a common reservation has been made about all, namely, that they ignore a basic principle of composition without which, except accidentally, no truly effective work of composition is likely to result. This basic principle is the necessity of *idea* as the directing force in the selection and organization of developmental detail and in the shaping of the whole composition, whether it is paragraph, essay, or research paper.

The word *idea* rarely appears in the textbooks, and when it does appear it is most often used interchangeably with "topic" or "developmental detail." The most obvious place to stress the indispensability of idea to composition is in connection with the topic sentence of the paragraph. One rare example of what we consider appropriate meaning and stress in this connection occurs in the Allyn and Bacon *Effective English* series; any volume of this series will serve to illustrate, and the following abbreviated statements are taken from the volume for grade ten:

Frequently you are assigned just such a general subject or topic as sports to give you opportunity to choose a more specific topic that appeals to you. Here is one way a topic like sports might be narrowed to find an idea for a paragraph.

GENERAL TOPIC: Sports
NARROWER TOPIC: Spring sports
STILL NARROWER TOPIC: Baseball
LIMITED FURTHER BUT STILL TOO LARGE: Central's baseball team.

The last topic is very specific compared to the general topic of sports, but is still too large to handle well in one paragraph. Four different suggestions for further narrowing the topic are given below. Any one of these suggestions could be developed successfully in a one-paragraph theme.

1. Our baseball coach
2. Our baseball record over a period of five years
3. The baseball team's need for equipment
4. Our potential strength this year

You might decide to write a paragraph on the baseball coach. The next step is to form a topic sentence upon which to build the paragraph.

TOPIC SENTENCE

The topic sentence expresses the main idea of the paragraph; all the other sentences in the paragraph help to develop that idea. [Italics added]. . . . If the topic sentence includes your own attitude, or point of view, about the subject, the reader is prepared for what is to follow. . . . The next step is to make a list of points supporting the idea expressed in the topic sentence. Remember that the aim of the paragraph is to develop that one idea; do not include unrelated material in your list. [pp. 29-30]

The above instruction in paragraph writing approaches the concept of composition as the *development of idea*. It stands in signal contrast to the prevailing notions of composition expressed in virtually all textbook series. It must be agreed in fairness, however, that most textbooks, in treating the paragraph, lay heavy stress on the need for a topic sentence, and it is quite true that *topic sentence* is virtually synonymous with *controlling idea*. Yet this very fact is characteristically left unmentioned, and in any event left unstressed, in the textbooks.

The failure to approach composition as the development of ideas is most conspicuous not in treatments of the paragraph, but in discussion of selection of topics for composition, in demonstrations of the processes by which topics are "limited" or "narrowed," in directions for outlining, in approaches to all units of composition longer than single paragraphs, and in treatments of all the varied aspects of "effective writing," including such diverse matters as choice of vivid words, use of figures of speech, the ordering of sentence elements, etc. The basic cause of difficulty may be that textbook writers have neglected to make any clear distinctions between the terms "topic," "subject," and "idea." These are regularly used interchangeably — where, indeed, the word "idea" is used at all. We should like to suggest at this point that a "topic" remains just that and no more, regardless of how skilfully it may be narrowed by mechanical means, until it has been seized upon and converted to "subject" by the application of "idea." Thus to narrow "sports" to "spring sports" to "baseball" to "Central's baseball team" and even to "our baseball coach" is not to convert a *topic* to a *subject* that is ready for writing. Even if the narrowing process were continued until one were left with only "our baseball coach's right index finger," topic would still be only topic, and not subject, ready for writing. While the question, "Well, what *about* it?" remains unanswered, no writable subject has emerged. But when one says, "Our baseball coach's right index finger is his baton," one has converted topic to subject by application of idea. It may turn out to be a bad idea, an inaccurate idea, a stupid idea, but idea has nevertheless been applied, and is ready to direct the selection and order of the details that follow.

The application of an idea to even an enormous topic, such as "sports," may produce a writable subject at one stroke, without necessity for the mechanical narrowing through many steps as advocated by all the textbook series. Thus "sports" is a topic, unwritable, but "Sports develop the physiques of those whose physiques least need developing" is a subject, created by one shaping application of idea — again, perhaps an inaccurate and insupportable idea, yet an idea. The initial problem, of course, is to search out and test ideas that are accurate and hence supportable.

It is similarly our point of view that emphasis on mechanical outlining in rigid form, down to the smallest developmental details, may nevertheless fail to result in clear organization of any "whole" composition unless *idea* directs the entire process; and, conversely, it is our point of view that initial clear statement of idea may make quite unnecessary the elaborate forms of outlines recommended by the textbooks, just as application of idea may make unnecessary the laborious steps involved in the purely mechanical process of narrowing a topic. A brief sketch of developmental items may be quite adequate, at least for short papers, when the *idea* that is to be developed is initially found and kept foremost in the student writer's mind.

In short, we do not find either the mechanical narrowing of topics or the mechanical construction of elaborate outlines to be an adequate substitute for *idea,* though the several series present them as if they were substitutes. The great necessity is to find means of making students themselves see the indispensability of *idea* as guide to the selection of developmental matter and to the shaping of the whole composition, whether paragraph or long paper.

The absence of *idea* is equally conspicuous and, we believe, equally regrettable in the approaches made by all textbooks to "effective writing" — an area in which, we have stated earlier, great energy has been expended by the authors. The contrast between what is and what, we believe, ought to be can be made in the following way. It has been shown earlier that most series devote much space in each volume to such topics as "Writing Effective Sentences," "Variety — the Spice of Sentence Life," "Metaphor Makes Meaning Vivid," "Be Specific: Call a Dog a Beagle," "Vivid Verbs," "Using Significant Modifiers," "Choosing Vivid Language," "Making Colorful and Varied Sentence Patterns," etc. Chapter titles and subsections of the kind, taken from the series collectively, would number in the hundreds. Although no reasonably accurate count of pages for comparative purposes was feasible, since treatment of such matters was found most often to be a part of some other aspect of grammar or composition already counted, the fact is that typical textbook series chosen as examples for spot checks give as many as two hundred pages to these and like attempts at encouraging "effective" as beyond merely "correct" writing. Much of the detail of instruction in these matters is related to descriptive and narrative writing. Discussion, models, examples, sentence exercises requiring rearrangement of order, replacement of general by specific words and direct statements by figures of speech, and, finally, short writing exercises in which students are directed to use all the devices of effective writing that they have studied: these are the items, in brief, included in treatments of these aspects of composition.

From our point of view, these approaches to effective composition are directly opposed to that approach which regards composition as the *development of idea*. The textbooks exhort students to use the devices of effective composition in word and sentence, and they set exercises requiring students to use these devices. *Thus composition becomes an exercise in using devices for effectiveness.* But, in truth, "real" writers do not write in order to use the devices of effectiveness; they write to express ideas, and in the process of expressing these ideas they come upon the need for specific words, all kinds of figures of speech, for sentence patterns that accurately reflect meaning and emphasis, etc. There is all the difference in the world between using the devices of effectiveness because they are needed to express one's ideas fully and sharply, on the one hand, and, on the other, setting out to use the devices of effectiveness merely as an exercise, without having an idea that must be expressed.

To summarize, we find that the textbooks' approach to writing, in terms of instruction in principles and techniques, is made *as an exercise in the mechanics of writing rather than as the development of idea*. Thus students are exhorted to practice all the devices that writers actually *do* use as need arises; but the absence of essential purpose in all this, the development of idea, would appear to reduce the practice of composition to the status of mere exercise. Thus the art of writing, in such circumstances, tends to become an exhibition of a bag of tricks. It is not our intention, certainly, to say that practice in using devices for effectiveness should not be included in the textbooks; much that is potentially best in these books centers on just such practice and its accompanying instruction. The fault, we believe, might be corrected fairly easily by setting such exercises in their proper perspective — by stressing the fact, that is to say, that "real" writers set out with a determination to express their ideas and in the process of doing so find need for figures, specific nouns, action verbs, comparison and contrast, analogies, examples, and all the rest.

Among the principal factors that we have taken into consideration, therefore, in arriving at the ratings of column 3, Table X is the degree to which textbook writers have succeeded in maintaining this "proper perspective."

Appropriateness of Topics and Assignments

Earlier we singled out for special commendation the work of textbook writers in thinking up enormous numbers of "topics to write about." Nevertheless, it will be seen that in both the Comparative and the Survey Evaluations of Table X we have rated all series equal in the matter of *appropriateness* of topics and assignments: in the former case, all are marked "average," and in the latter all are marked "unsatisfactory." What is more, it must be stated frankly here that we consider this matter of appropriateness to be the most important single item on which we have rated the textbooks' treatment of composition — indeed, the most important single point on which we have rated the textbooks as a whole. So crucial do we find this point that, were the textbooks found to be satisfactory with respect to it, though they were indifferent on all other matters, we should be inclined to pronounce them generally satisfactory; and, conversely, because we find them unsatisfactory on this single point, we must find them basically unsatisfactory.

What students write about: this, from our point of view, is the *sine qua non* of courses in English composition, hence also the *sine qua non* of textbooks in grammar and composition.

We consider the appropriate subject matter for composition in high school English courses to be literature, not occasionally but steadily, not in any one year but in all years.

The subject matter for composition in the textbooks examined is not literature. In foregoing pages, under the heading of "Topics and Assignments," we have aimed to represent all series fairly and adequately on this point. It may nevertheless be appropriate once more in this place to set down, at random, a number of topics and writing assignments not from one but from several series; the following are not eccentric but typical examples:

"Tell about a camping trip, a weekend at the beach, a day in the country, a Saturday of fishing."

"Write a personal opinion theme: Dog is man's best friend. My pal is a true friend. My mother is very helpful. Breakfasts are better than dinners."

"Write about one of your unhappy experiences."

"Write a paragraph in which you express some of your thoughts about yourself or a member of the family."

"Write a theme discussing your strengths and weaknesses as they are revealed on your personal inventory chart."

It may be appropriate, again, to repeat here a typical statement on the subject matter of composition. Though this statement is drawn from the Scribner's series, *English at Work,* it fairly represents the point of view of all series:

For subject matter, these composition assignments begin with the student himself and advance by degrees to a consideration of the world about him. . . . It is also worth noting that the subject matter of the oral and written compositions is not confined to so-called English material. Ideas come from any subject because students in the English class are interested in various subject fields. . . . — Preface, v. ix, grade 10.

Essentially, the sources for writing are the same in all series. Briefly, they are the things familiar to students, their personal experiences, all the sorts of things in which students of a given age, as textbook writers have learned from their own educational and adolescent psychology books, are "interested." These include home and family, streets, neighbors, school activities, sports, hobbies, pets, friends, movies, television, etc. Hence a typical list of topics includes such random items as these:

cooking outdoors, a profitable hobby, co-operation at home, how to set a table, how to operate a mangle, how to build a birdhouse, how to polish a pair of shoes, parakeets as pets, stamp collecting, the family takes a trip, birthday party, my dad, sunset on the lake, sports cars, why raising chickens is a tricky business.

Despite the fact that textbook authors repeatedly express confidence in topics such as these as being the ones on which students will write best and most readily, *it is impossible to make even a cursory survey of any series without observing the same authors' underlying misgivings;* indeed, perhaps no single impression left by the textbooks is more enduring than that of these misgivings. Plainly, the authors are all genuinely concerned lest, in spite of all that they can name or suggest, in spite of all their assurances that topics for writing lie about us everywhere, students will in fact find nothing at all about which they have the slightest interest in writing. The signs of these misgivings are conspicuously apparent in three ways: (1) in the very large space given by virtually all series to "motivation" in various forms which will be discussed hereafter under the heading of "Other"; (2) in the truly enormous number of "suggested topics" listed for each writing assignment and in some series appended either to the composition section or to the volume; and (3) in the more or less overt expressions of anxiety by authors that take up paragraphs or pages of many series.

Running through all the textbooks is an underlying tone of futility and mounting desperation, leaving the sense at last of the authors' deep-seated conviction that very likely, in spite of all their efforts, students will *not* find any subject whatsoever on which they would be genuinely interested in writing.

Examples of such anxiety might be multiplied many times over. It will be necessary to confine detail to only one instance. In order to demonstrate, in part, how the textbook authors labor over the great question "What is there to write about?" the following summary is made from the volume for grade ten of Row, Peterson, *Building Better English;* the following series of excerpts and summaries begins on page 192 and continues to page 203:

The excuses that students give oftenest when they fail to turn in an original composition go something like this:
"I couldn't think of anything to write about."
"Nothing exciting ever happens to me."
These statements are not true. Students who make them either are trying to provide a cover for their laziness or have not observed carefully what goes on about them from day to day.

After giving these and other hortatory assurances that theme subjects lie all around us where only lazy students fail to pick them up, the textbook goes on to present four "Guides for Finding Theme Topics," as follows:

1. Look within yourself. You yourself are the best source of writing material. What do you know more about than you know about yourself? You know the experiences that you have had, your likes and dislikes, your ideals, your observations, and so on.
2. Observe what goes on around you. Call on your five senses. Open

your eyes and ears. Train your senses of touch, smell, and taste to be acute. Make use of the scenes that you observe every day, the people whom you see, and the routine actions that are typical of daily life.

3. Tap the newspaper for suggestions. News articles often suggest ideas that can be turned into stories, descriptions, or explanations.
4. *When all else fails, use your imagination.* [Italics added.]

Some seven pages later, in a section headed "Learning Activities in Finding Ideas," the textbook writer is still, with evident mounting desperation, assuring students that they and the world about them are brimming over with things to write about:

B. Think about yourself for a few minutes. List five possible subjects concerned with your life that might be suitable composition material. Go over your lists in class and add to your list as ideas are suggested. File this list in your notebook for later reference.
C. Bring to class several newspaper items that you think could be developed into interesting themes. Tell the class how you would develop one of them. Use your Speech Score Card, page 28.
D. Think about the effect of television on future generations. Let your imagination run freely. Jot down at least three possible effects, serious or humorous, that come to your mind. Go over your lists in class; then suggest other subjects that would allow a writer to use his imagination.

Three pages later the author has evidently given up, for the student is advised:

Choose any subject about which you have a definite feeling. The field is unlimited.

Two pages later are listed thirty-six possible topics, including "My Most Embarrassing Moment," "My Favorite Magazine," "How To Write a Theme," and "An Encounter with a Snake." And yet the textbook author is not done: the student is once more exhorted to:

Add to the preceding list of subjects others from your own ideas and experiences, and from your observation of things and people about you.

Next — and here it appears to us that the textbook writer has become quite frantic:

Bring in two pictures that you think suggest ideas for essays. Post the pictures on the bulletin board.

Finally — and the instruction would seem to mark the author's awareness that, after all, all has been in vain:

Write an essay, developing it in any way that appeals to you.

After this exhausting sequence, which is typical except in the degree of anxiety it exhibits, we can ask only the obvious question: if students truly want to write about themselves, their familiar experiences, families, interests, school activities, hobbies, etc., why should it require such frantic and lengthy beating of the brush to run out, at last, a subject for one disheartening little theme of 300 words? It can only appear to us that this approach is truly "doing it the hard way," for both textbook writer and student. Thus the textbook writer, after giving many exasperated assurances that theme topics lie everywhere about, manages only to suggest his awareness at last that, when these themes come due, some students will have found nothing at all to write, and others will have come through halfheartedly.

The textbooks themselves, thus, offer best proof of our own contention: that students do *not*, in fact, want to write about any of the things that all textbook writers continue to assert over and over again that they *do* want to write about. Though on the face of it, it looks as if students *ought* to want to write about themselves and the things that are nearest and most familiar in the adolescent world around them, yet we are convinced that, like ourselves, most experienced teachers of English have found it all too true that students simply do not want or expect their subject matter for composition in an English class to be made up out of themselves, their personal problems, their classmates, families, neighbors, and the like; and we are further convinced that no amount of motivational activity and exhortation by teacher or textbook can make them really want to write seriously about these things. We believe that all such exhortation must fall essentially upon deaf ears and that the most which can be expected from this approach is perfunctory completion of a written exercise which failed really to engage the writer's mind to the degree that, as all the textbooks make evident, the textbook writers wished it might. Though high school students attend or participate in sports events, go hunting and fishing, have hobbies, have parents, uncles and aunts, brothers and sisters, friends, live on a street in a neighborhood, watch television, go to the movies, and in short, live lives that are filled with all of the things that the textbooks therefore urge them to write about, yet we are convinced that adolescents, like other people, keep the things of their lives rather sharply separated: it does not follow that because high school students like dances they will want to *write* about them, except as an exercise off the top of their heads, to complete an assignment. It does not follow that because they have bigger or littler brothers or sisters, they want to write seriously about them. It does not follow that because high school students may have uncles, they want to write a theme about their favorite uncle. We do not believe that even 300 pages of motivational matter, such as can be counted in one textbook series, can cause students to take a really serious intellectual attitude toward any such subjects or make them want to do more than write a perfunctory exercise to appease a teacher for whom they have already, perhaps, conceived a degree of disrespect for making such assignments.

But another issue also is involved here, and we shall put it frankly. It is this: even if it were an indisputable fact that students want to write about nothing else so much as about themselves and the immediate interests and activities of their adolescent world — as itemized in the hundreds of "suggested topics" listed in the textbooks — we would not consider it appropriate that they do so. We consider these to be unsatisfactory matters with which to occupy their time in English composition. We do not believe that a course has a legitimate excuse for existing that in effect advises the students that *they are themselves to be the subject matter of the course.* Yet it is precisely this that the textbooks, in their approach to composition, do without exception: the student himself, his classmates, his family, street, neighbors, school activities, interests, hobbies, ambitions, personal experiences and personal problems are to furnish the content of composition.

It appears to us an ironic fact that the textbooks are steadily concerned with "growth," advertising, as one series puts it, "experiences to help you grow," and yet present little for students to feed on except themselves. Possibly the English textbooks are the only volumes in the school curriculum that make a determined, four-year long effort to keep the adolescent mind feasting on itself. Though adolescence is undoubtedly a proper study for psychologists, particularly adolescent psychologists, it does not seem a proper or nutritive subject-matter for adolescent youths themselves in an English class. In direct opposition to the point of view that is thus implemented in all the textbooks, we insist that the great necessity is not to keep the adolescent mind forever on itself, but to provide means of getting it *off* itself, and keeping it off. What are these means?

In other subjects, students write, speak, and listen in connection with the proper subject matter of the particular course: in algebra, the adolescent mind feeds on and exercises itself upon algebra; in history, upon history; in biology, upon biology; in chemistry, upon chemistry; in physics, upon physics. But in the textbooks of English composition the authors proceed as if English has no comparable subject matter, or as if they do not know what this subject matter is, or as if they were somehow ashamed of it. English, thus, plays a game of catch-as-catch-can; it is cast in the role of a camp follower, living on such scraps as come in its way. Once again, from our point of view, the truly ironic fact is that there is no necessity for authors of textbooks in English composition to proceed in this fashion, for of course English possesses an enormous subject matter that needs no apologies and deserves no neglect, but is worthy of the steadiest kind of four-year exploitation as the basis of composition.

This subject matter, we have no hesitation to reassert, is literature. It is the appropriate subject matter for composition in English classes, first, because it *is* the subject matter for English, just as history is the subject matter for history classes; second, because it provides a coherent body of material which is essential to the conduct of a coherent course in composition; and third, because it is the one body of matter of which the English teacher can reasonably be expected to be master and, hence, on which the teacher is qualified to guide the preparation of students' paragraphs, "themes," and research papers.

Though authors of the composition textbooks examined are to be commended for the superhuman energies they have all expended in suggesting topics for composition and for their valiant exhortation meant to encourage students to go at writing with genuine interest and vigor, they are at the same time, in our view, to be most severely censured for their universal neglect of that subject matter for composition which is, from every point of view, most appropriate. This is not to say that no series *ever* gives opportunity for students to write in connection with their study of literature. All series do give some instruction and assignments in making book reports, and among the very large number of suggested topics listed occasionally one may be found that relates to literature. Further, most series list "reading" as one of the sources of material and inspiration for composition. But the place of literature among the sources of composition is, in all the series, as foregoing pages of this report make evident, negligible. No series envisages, suggests, or provides for a sustained program of writing in connection with literature; no series examined is so flexible as to allow for inclusion of such a program within its framework, should the teacher prefer.

Therefore we have rated all series examined as "unsatisfactory" in column 4 of the Survey Evaluation, Table X; we repeat that in our estimation this is the most important single item in our total evaluation of the textbooks.

Progression

It will be observed that in column 5, as in column 4, all textbook series are rated "average" on the Comparative Evaluation table.

Within volumes, it is true, several series exhibit a fairly regular progression from shorter to longer forms of writing, most often from the paragraph, through letters, "themes" of various kinds — expository, narrative, and descriptive — to creative writing in the forms of story and poem, and finally to the longer "research report" form.

On the other hand, analysis reveals no significant progression in the treatment of composition from volume to volume within series. Table X shows that approximately the same amount of space is given to composition in each volume of any series, and such forms as are represented in that table are shown to be given generally the same amount of attention from volume to volume.

Three principal concerns have been taken into account in arriving at the ratings of Table X: instruction, forms, and topics. With respect to the first of these, as has already been noted, somewhat fuller instruction is generally given to the preparation of "research" papers in the eleventh and twelfth grades than in the ninth and tenth grades, although the general rule does not hold for all series. On the other hand, with such forms as paragraphs and "themes," no generalization is possible other than that approximately equal space is given to instruction in each volume — again with occasional exceptions that follow no general pattern.

As for assignments to write in the various forms, again no appreciable differences are observable from volume to volume. In short, so far as instruction and practice in the various forms of writing are concerned, any one volume of any series might be exchanged with any other without making any observable difference. The lack of progression that characterizes all series may perhaps best be suggested here by citation from one series of the chapter headings dealing with the paragraph; the following are from American Book Company's *Our English Language:*

grade 9, ch. 5: "Practice in Paragraphs"
grade 10, ch. 15: "Polishing Paragraphs"
grade 11, ch. 5: "For Better Paragraphs"
grade 12, ch. 3: "A Clinic for Paragraphs"

These headings would suggest that the authors themselves are uncertain of the progress that students will make during the four years; further, as has been suggested earlier, the contents of the four chapters are essentially the same. Such examples might be multiplied, not only for paragraph instruction and practice, but, indeed, for all other major forms of writing in the several series for which instruction and practice are given.

From our point of view, however, the most crucial question of all here is that of topics for writing: "What do they write *about* from year to year?" Our analysis shows that only one answer, which admits no qualification, is possible: they *"write about" the very same things from year to year.* Comparison of representative topics listed earlier in this report can leave no doubt on this score, and additional examples demonstrate again what has already been shown. For the purpose of emphasizing what we consider a crucial matter we have chosen to draw not from a "typical" series but from one that on many points of our total analysis we have found to be distinctly superior, in short, from that series which our analysis has shown to be generally outstanding among all series examined. This is the Harcourt, Brace series, *English Grammar and Composition.* Each volume of this series includes, besides many topics suggested at the time that specific assignments for paragraphs, "themes," and other forms are made, a section headed "Topics for Composition." The ninth-grade volume lists 165 topics, classified under the heads of Places, School, Personal, Occasions, People, and Hobbies. The tenth-grade volume lists 230 topics under the heads of People, Personal, Occasions, School, Places, Hobbies, Out of Doors, and Miscellaneous Subjects. The eleventh-grade volume lists 220 topics under the heads of The Arts, Science, Social Studies, School, Sports, Social Life, People, Family Life, Personal Affairs, and General. The twelfth-grade volume lists 220 topics under the heads of The Arts, Family Life, People, Personal, School, Science, Social Life, Social Studies, Sports, and General.

It will be observed here that the eleventh- and twelfth-grade volumes do include certain headings that are not included in the ninth- and tenth-grade volumes and that suggest progression; these are, notably, The Arts, Science, and Social Studies. Actual topics listed under these heads, however, do not appear significantly advanced beyond the general level of topics listed in the volumes for the earlier grades; we shall illustrate simply by naming the first six topics under each of two new heads for grades eleven and twelve:

Grade 11	Grade 12
The Arts	*The Arts*
What to listen for in music	Classical *vs.* popular music
The movies *vs.* the state	Color combinations
My favorite novel (poem, play)	The use of water color
Photography as an art form	What to look for in a painting

Decorating a room

Modern *vs.* traditional houses

How to appreciate good music

How to refinish furniture

Social Studies

Why a two-party system?

Neighborhood gangs

Causes of labor disputes

A workable disarmament plan

Flaws in the UN

A turning point in American history

Social Studies

A threat to international peace

Propaganda techniques

Tolerance in our school

The importance of the minority

If we had no Bill of Rights

Some lessons of history

The lack of progression in even this series, however, is best demonstrated by citing examples of the more prevalent kinds, under headings that are common to all volumes of the series. One such heading is "Personal," from which, again, we list the first six suggestions for each grade:

Grade 9

My Saturday job

My kid brother's hard life

Prejudices

Traits I inherited

Helping out at home

Alibis

Grade 10

My Declaration of Independence

The importance of self-discipline

My reading tastes

I didn't believe it!

No mother is like my mother

Dad knows all the answers

Grade 11

On keeping a diary

A young person's hopes and fears

How to be unpopular

My changing ideas on clothes

An ideal day

A childhood experience

Grade 12

Overcoming an inferiority complex

On being an outsider

My frustrations

Traits I wish I didn't have

On being plain

On being average

A second heading that runs through all volumes is "People," from which, again, we take the first six suggestions for each year:

Grade 9

Characteristics of a popular
  teacher

Grade 10

The man (woman) I admire most

Our school custodian

Portrait of a friend

The way to a girl's heart

Are young people still "going to the dogs"?

Two heads are not better than one

Bad habits of my best friend

A little friend

Our druggist

My crowd

My doctor

Grade 11

My grandfather (or grandmother)

Mr. (or Miss) Know-it-all

My favorite singer

Our doctor

The policeman on our block

A person I'll never forget

Grade 12

My father

The social climber

The school politician

Teachers as they really are

A great sports figure

My little sister

To conclude this section of additional evidence that the textbooks are altogether lacking in even the appearance of progression in the matter of topics on which students are to write from year to year, we present the following random examples of assignments and topics taken from only the *twelfth-grade volumes* of a number of series. It should be readily apparent that if such topics as the following are considered appropriate for the twelfth grade, there can have been *no* progression in composition topics from the ninth grade.

A & B, *Effective English*
"main ideas" for themes:

The heroes (or heroines) in Westerns are all alike

There are several distinct types of daydreamers in our English class

It takes all types of students to make a successful football team

Teachers are not all alike

ABC, *Our English Language*
topic sentences:

I can still remember the old house

Her hat was a miracle of invention

He was just a happy little dog

Ginn, *English Skills*
topics for themes:

Failing to arrive home at the
promised time
My first pay check
On getting up in the morning
My first formal dance
Driving lesson no. 1

Heath, *English in Action*
"theme subjects":

High school fads
Planning a career
Student government in our school
A famous spot in our community
The perfect vacation
The best job I ever had

Lippincott, *English for Today*
topics for a "description":

A cafeteria
A street scene
An airport
A modern filling station
A streamlined train

Macmillan, *The Art of Communicating*
exercises in "critical writing":

1. Choose some performance such
   as a school play, a movie, a
   radio or television performance. Write a critical review.
2. Choose some newly-produced
   object — an automobile, a
   building, a dress of a new style,
   or a new invention, and write
   a critical review of it.

McGraw-Hill, *Your Language*
(11th grade)
suggestions for selecting topics
for writing:

Almost everyone likes to hear
about ideas or events that remind
him of his own experiences. You
will find that most high-school
students enjoy papers on teen-age
problems, on choosing a vocation,
on plans for college or future em-
ployment, or on boy-girl relationships.

Almost everyone also likes to
hear about your personal under-
takings. For instance, you may

take long hikes through the woods, fish, develop your own pictures, study ballet, try out for some athletic event, work at amateur astronomy, tinker with cars, or collect special kinds of records. [p. 48]

Row, Peterson, *Building Better English*
topics for "Personal Reminiscences":

My first date
My first job
My most important decision
My most embarrassing moment
Meet the family
My narrowest escape
Blind date

Scott, Foresman, *Guide to Modern English* (Upper Years)
Main directions for choice of subjects for themes:

After thinking over the many subjects you are familiar with through personal experiences — the people, places, and things you know well, the ideas and opinions you like to discuss and argue about with friends — make a list of ten subjects about which you think you could write a clear, convincing paper that would interest most of your classmates. Make the subjects as specific as you can (for example: "My Father Believes in Discipline," "I Like Living on a Farm," "People Have Strange Ideas About the Value of Old Coins and Stamps," "I'll Never Hitch-hike Again," "Thumbs Down on the New Styles," "Our Town Should Have a University Extension Branch"). [p. 26]

Scribner's, *English at Work*
topics for themes:

The struggle to be well dressed
What my relatives think of me

Singer, *Enjoying English* topics for theme "A Senior and His Problems":

People who find fault with me
The mistakes of umpires
Team jealousies
My family's interest in my dates
Quarrel with my brother
My dad was angry
I wanted to work
Others drink, should I?
Would I make the team?
Making a bad excuse
When I was embarrassed
My mother needed me
Acting like an adult

It is assumed that the above representation of topics suggested as appropriate for high school seniors to write on makes it unnecessary to reproduce here additional topics suggested for the ninth, tenth, and eleventh grades. The topics for the twelfth grade represent neither progression nor retrogression, but continuation at the identical level of preceding years. We should like further to reassert that in the above examples we have sought to represent the textbooks rather favorably than unfavorably: many of these examples are among the most sophisticated, mature, and worthy topics offered to students by the textbooks.

We have not thought it necessary here to exemplify what we find to be perhaps the most intolerable area of repetition, or absence of progression, in the several series, namely, that of instruction and assignments in the writing of letters, personal and business.

Tone

As in the Evaluative Section for Grammar, Usage, and Mechanics, "tone" here embraces much; it refers in general to the level of style and manner with which the textbooks address themselves to the serious task of providing a program of composition. Because "tone" is a characteristic that must be discussed at some length in the section which follows, with implications for both the section on grammar and that on composition, little need be said of it in this place.

Most of those textbooks which have been rated "adequate" or "good" on this item in the Survey Evaluation have been given their rating on the quality of their approach to key units of composition, most notably the paragraph, for it is in this area, as has been stated earlier, that instruction in basic principles of composition has been found to be most satisfactory. It has nevertheless been peculiarly difficult to award satisfactory ratings on "tone" when, after they have presented admirably mature and succinct treatments of the paragraph and other forms, the textbook writers have proceeded to assign or suggest topics for composition that are trivial, irrelevant, or simply childish. These ratings thus pertain strictly to the approach, and not at all to the assigned or suggested practice.

Those textbooks that have been rated "unsatisfactory" on this point have generally failed to compensate, though a few are satisfactory at some stages of their approach to composition, for the prevailing tone of address in which whole volumes are cast. With this, which we consider an unfortunate fault, we are concerned particularly in the treatment of "Other," which follows.

CHAPTER 4

"*Other*"

PRINCIPAL AREAS

FROM THE very great variety of information and activities, other than the materials previously classified under the headings of "Grammar, Usage, and Mechanics" and "Rhetoric and Composition," we have selected for quantitative representation in Table XI of Appendix B only eight principal areas that are covered more or less extensively by virtually all of the textbooks examined. These areas, each of which is represented by a column in Table XI, are as follows: Speech Activities, Listening, Parliamentary Procedure, Motion Pictures, Television and Radio, Newspapers and Magazines, Social Activities, Library, and Spelling.

That these eight principal areas by no means account for *all* matters included in the textbooks, aside from those classified as Grammar and Composition, may readily be seen by totaling the figures for the eight columns and comparing the final figure with that given for "Total Other" in column 2. A few random comparisons will illustrate:

Ginn[1]	total other	817	8-column total	— 606
Heath	" "	863	" " "	— 458
Row, P.	" "	615	" " "	— 410
Singer	" "	698	" " "	— 239

Some of the items that go to make up the differences between these sets of figures will be discussed later.

Computation of the figures given for "Total Other" in column 2 has been carried on with no little difficulty, because the textbooks do not neatly separate and classify according to the main headings of this report all of the matters that they treat. We do not imply that they should do so; the point is stressed only to make evident a basic kind of difficulty that we have encountered in our quantitative analysis. Neither tables of contents nor indices have been sufficient for our purposes, for many varieties of "Other" are found, often in considerable amount, in sections the headings of which primarily suggest either Grammar or Composition — as, indeed, instruction and exercises in Composition are often found in sections primarily devoted to "Other." The task of disentangling the various elements and reclassifying them for tabulation has therefore been an exacting one, and we have accomplished it only as accurately as time and our best judgments would permit.

The considerable but not enormous variation among series in the proportions of total space given to "Other" is readily made apparent by the percentages recorded in column 3. These percentages range from a high of 57 (Lippincott and McGraw-Hill) to lows of 32 (HB[1]) and 34 (Allyn and Bacon, Macmillan, and Scott, Foresman). The average percentage for all series is approximately 42; thus between one-third and one-half of the total pages in the average series is classified as "Other." Percentages for individual volumes have not been recorded in column 3, primarily because they do not vary significantly from the figures given for total series; that is to say, any volume of any series includes approximately the same amount of "Other" as does any other volume of that series. There is thus no appreciably heavier or lighter emphasis upon "Other" in any given high school year.

Speech Activities

The column headed "Speech Activities" records figures that represent a great variety of information, instruction, and practice. As will be noted, figures for this column run substantially higher than those recorded in any of the other seven columns. In many instances these figures include pages counted also in some of the other columns — for example, "Parliamentary Procedure" and "Social Activities" are largely included in the general column of "Speech Activities," since they significantly involve speech instruction and exercises. "Listening" chapters or sections have often also been counted in part in the speech totals. "Speech Activities" is thus, in some measure, a catch-all column, and the fact is reflected in its comparatively high figures.

In most series, prominent speech activities include the following: conversation, class discussion, panel discussion, oral reports, interviewing of class members and others, making announcements, club activities, etc. Some series include rather extensive instruction in the physiological aspects of voice and practice in the use of voice, in pronunciation and enunciation. Instruction and practice in telephoning are included in about half of the series, but total pages involved here do not exceed thirteen in any series.

Practices in the use of speech activities and instruction vary so widely from series to series that it is hardly possible to select a single series to stand adequately for the treatment of all. However, the Row, Peterson series comes as near as any to being typical in both amount of space given and variety of activities; that series will therefore be used here to illustrate typical procedures.

In the volume for grade nine, major speech activities include the following:

Ch. 1. "Becoming a Better Speaker"
(This chapter includes use of the body in speech, use of the voice, improving speech, keeping a score card of speech progress.)

Ch. 2. "Talking with Others"
(This chapter includes conversation, discussion, round-table discussions, and Parliamentary procedure.)

Ch. 3. "Speaking in Special Situations"
(This chapter includes making individual talks, telling stories, making explanations and giving descriptions, giving and following directions, reading aloud, choral reading, making and acknowledging introductions, using the telephone, conducting interviews, and making oral book reports.)

In the volume for grade ten, major speech activities include the following:

Ch. 1. "Talking Together"
(conversation, round-table discussion)

Ch. 2. "Learning the Art of Listening"
(While it primarily emphasizes listening, the chapter includes exercises that involve the class in speech activities such as reading aloud, class discussion, and participation in small groups.)

Ch. 3. "Becoming an Effective Speaker"
(use of the body, use of the voice, judging speech progress)

Ch. 4. "Speaking and Listening Situations"
(reading aloud, choral reading, telling stories, making introductions, introducing speakers, using the telephone, conducting interviews, giving explanations, directions, and descriptions, conducting panel discussions, conducting arguments, parliamentary procedure)

In the volume for grade eleven, major speech activities include the following:

Ch. 1. "Thinking and Speaking"
(This chapter emphasizes thinking, including deductive and inductive reasoning, but includes exercises that involve the class individually and in groups in speech activities.)

Ch. 2. "Are You Listening?"
(This chapter emphasizes the end of listening, but involves the class in speech situations.)

Ch. 3. "What Does Your Speech Reflect?"
(analyzing your speech, finding ways to better speech, acquiring bodily ease, use of voice, improving enunciation and pronunciation habits, analyzing progress)

Ch. 4. "Gaining Skill in Speech"
(asking and answering questions, making explanations, giving directions, reporting experiences and observations, reading aloud, choral reading, meeting and introducing others, making speeches for special occasions, using the telephone, interviewing)

Ch. 5. "Improving Conversational and Discussion Habits"
(courtesy in speech, conversation, parliamentary procedure, special types of discussions)

Ch. 6. "Judging Radio, Television, and Film Entertainment"
(While the chapter emphasizes mass media, it involves the class as individuals and in groups in making announcements and introductions, putting on programs, etc.)

In the volume for grade twelve, major speech activities include the following:

Ch. 11. "Speaking Effectively"
(This chapter repeats most activities covered in the first three volumes: speech as means of communication, use of the body in speech, voice, conversation, telephone, interviewing, radio or television appearance, various types of discussion, making formal speeches, etc.)

Ch. 12. "Reading, Looking, and Listening"
(Though its emphasis is elsewhere, the chapter includes a variety of activities involving speech — discussion of set topics, panel discussion, reports, etc.)

Varieties of speech activities are also covered in a number of other series. Some of these, unlike the Row, Peterson series, distribute these activities fairly widely between the covers of volumes and use less formality in their approach to speech instruction and practice.

This informal method distinguishes the "social" approach to speech activities which opens the volume for grade nine of Allyn and Bacon's *Effective English.* After some preliminary instruction on "Conversation Starters," "Responding to an Introduction," "Rising and Shaking Hands," etc., the following activity is assigned:

Select students to take the roles suggested in the following situations. You need not write out and memorize what to say. Before acting your part, however, imagine that you are in the situation described and think through what you will do and say. Then, without practicing, have the people participating in an introduction stage it before the class. Use classroom furniture to suggest the setting. For example, in the first situation below, arrange desks to resemble a living room. After the dramatization discuss whether the participants remembered what you have learned about making introductions.

Some fifteen "situations" are then listed, of which the following are representative:

1. Sarah Franks has asked two girls in her room at school to come to her home to meet Jill Davis, who is visiting in Reedville. Martha Pearce, one of the girls Sarah has asked, rings the doorbell as Sarah and Jill are seated in the living room.
2. Marjorie Black introduces a friend, Audrey Fulmer, to Nell Curtis. Nell has just transferred from another school. All are freshmen.
3. Estelle Jackson is in the hall of North High and notices Nancy Epps, who attended another school the previous year. Estelle introduces herself.

These will perhaps suffice to show the approach of this volume. It will be observed that the situations assigned for acting out in class are intended to reproduce actual situations that occur on the opening days of the school year; further, the fictionalized students identified in the assigned activity, like the real students who will impersonate them, are all freshmen. Thus the classroom activity rests on the principle of having freshman students impersonate freshman students "just like themselves" in imaginary situations that resemble actual ones; or, in short, real students on the opening days of school are assigned to act the parts of imaginary students just like themselves on the opening days of school. In general, it is on this principle that speech activities — and, indeed, many writing activities — of this volume are based.

Though obviously examples might be multiplied many times over, it is believed that the foregoing summaries of speech instruction and practice from two series adequately represent the approaches of the series examined. One general point remains to be made, namely, that suggested topics for speeches consistently match in kind those earlier listed to illustrate topics suggested for written composition. Like the latter, they are drawn from the student's personal experience and immediate environment. Topics for conversation and informal discussion, as well as those for panel discussion and formal speeches, use content supplied essentially out of the student himself; they do not normally make any use of or reference to literature as a possible source of material or idea. Indeed, in the degree to which they manage to exclude literature from consideration, topics for speech activities exceed even those for written composition.

Listening

As will be seen in column 5 of Table XI, Appendix B, virtually all textbook series devote some space to formal consideration of and practice in listening. High totals of 63 and 57 pages are recorded, respectively, for the Scribner's and Ginn series; lows of 4 and 6 pages are recorded, respectively, for the Scott, Foresman and Singer series, the average for the series as a group being 30 pages. As has been suggested earlier, and as shown in the preceding discussion of speech activities, attention to Listening is very often incorporated in and virtually inseparable from other areas of instruction and practice, most especially Speech Activities and Motion Pictures, Radio, and Television. Nevertheless, several series give individual chapters, or sections of chapters, to the subject. The following representative examples are taken from series which give complete chapters, or clearly defined sections of chapters, to Listening.

Though the amount of space used is relatively modest in comparison to some other series, the treatment of Listening in the Heath series, *English in Action*, so strikingly illustrates typical approaches that it deserves space here as our primary example. The following summarizes main points of the Heath coverage through four volumes.

In the volume for grade nine, Listening is treated in Chapter 6, "Learning by Listening." The chapter begins as follows:

"For your next assignment turn to page 116. Do problems . . ." Miss Coleman's voice became a blur to Len. He was leaning back in his seat gazing out the window at the vapor trail of a jet plane. Just a couple more years, he mused, and I'll be writing my name in vapor trails all the way from here to . . .

"Are there any questions?" Miss Coleman's query brought Len down to earth. Sheepishly he raised his hand.

"I don't think I got the assignment, Miss Coleman. Which problems did you say we're supposed to do?"

The class laughed, and Miss Coleman sighed. "It's no joke," she said. "You've got to learn to listen, Len. Listening is important."

From this beginning the chapter proceeds to Activity 1, Thinking About the Importance of Listening, where six thought and discussion questions are posed, of which the following are examples:

1. What percentage of your school day is spent in listening?
2. Who and what do you listen to at home? Approximately how much time do you spend listening in these various ways?
3. Is listening important in telephoning? How?

Activity 2, Games To Test Listening, includes two exercises of which the first is described as follows:

1. Play "telephone." The first person in each row will start the conversation. He may tell the person behind him: (1) how he gets to school each day, including means of transportation and the time he leaves home; (2) where he will meet this classmate downtown, including the exact time and place; (3) when, where, and how often a particular school club meets; or, (4) any other short, specific directions. Listen sharply so that you will be able to repeat to the pupil behind you exactly what you were told. Try to keep the wording the same. The last person in the row will repeat aloud to the class what he heard; his report will be compared with what the first person said. Try to have the original directions and the final ones identical.

Next are listed six "Listening Hints," of which the first three follow:

1. Stay awake. Get enough sleep each night.
2. Look as if you were listening. Sit up and keep your eyes on the speaker.
3. Force yourself to pay close attention. Don't let your mind wander.

There follows Activity 3, Improving Your Listening:

Listen to one-minute speeches by classmates on the FBI, the uses of hypnotism, television commercials, a spaceship, the Suez Canal, a television program, jet planes, radar, how to brand a steer, how to prune fruit trees, how to study for a test, or other topics. After each speaker has finished, be prepared to answer these questions: (1) What was the main idea of the speech? (2) What important information did the speaker give? (3) What questions would you like to ask him?

Next, in succession, follow four more activities involving listening.

In the volume for grade ten, the principal attention to Listening is presented in Chapter 3, "Listen and Learn." The pattern followed here is essentially the same as that used for grade nine. Activities include keeping a chart of listening activities during a day, analyzing a conversation, taking telephone messages, listening to announcements, following instructions, and listening to radio or television news, music, quiz, and miscellaneous programs.

In the volume for grade eleven, passing attention to Listening is included in Chapter 1, "Talking with Your Friends," but the main activities are included in Chapter 2, "Better Listening and Thinking." Headings in this chapter include The Importance of Listening, Active Listening, Listening Problems, Becoming a Good Listener, Remembering Directions and Explanations, Listening to a Talk, and Listening Critically.

In the volume for grade twelve, principal attention is given to Listening in Chapter 8, "Skillful Listening." Activities in the senior volume include training for better listening, of whch the following instructions are typical:

A. In class discuss the importance of listening in your life. As preparation you may make a record of when you listen and what you listen to during the day.
B. In your English notebook take notes of the main points and supporting details that are brought out in the class discussion of the importance of listening.
C. Organize the class into committees for different listening activities: (1) announcements, assignments, directions; (2) conversations; (3) group discussion and debates; (4) speeches; (5) on the job; (6) radio and television; (7) poetry, drama, and music. In its listening activity each committee will be responsible for instructing the class in appropriate listening habits and for observing and testing listening whenever the class engages in that activity.

Other activities include listening to assembly, radio, or television speeches, reporting on panels and discussions, and listening for enjoyment to radio, television, record, or tape.

A second series that is typical in its coverage of Listening is Row, Peterson's *Building Better English,* whose coverage closely resembles that of the Heath volumes just summarized.

Parliamentary Procedure

As will be seen in column 6 of Table XI, Appendix B, Parliamentary Procedure is represented to varying extents in all series, ranging from a high of forty-one pages (Ginn[1]) to a low of four pages (HB[2]). Five of the series give it attention in each volume; four give it attention in three of four volumes; four more give it space in two volumes. Typical approaches to the subject involve setting up classroom machinery in the form of a club, with chairman and other officers, for the purpose of taking up business, making motions, voting, and taking minutes. In series in which Parliamentary Procedure appears in every year, or approximately, repetition of virtually identical materials and practices is regularly involved; indeed, so greatly do successive treatments resemble one another that it is needless here to take space for more than one sample from a single volume. For this purpose none will serve more fairly than Chapter 21, "Conducting a Club," from American Book Company's *Our English Language,* grade nine.

The treatment begins in the following fashion:

"What a failure *that* was!" Stan said to Al as the meeting adjourned. It was the first meeting of the Hiker's Club since Sam's election as president, and it hadn't gone well.

"It was like football practice, with everyone carrying the ball and no one calling the plays," Al replied.

"Did you ever hear such a jumble? Everyone was making a motion or arguing over inviting the Audubon Club to join us on our next hike," Stan grumbled.

"Poor Sam kept saying, 'Be quiet, everyone,'" Al added.

"I had to laugh when Sam finally asked for the minutes and learned that we voted last time to invite the Audubons. I kept trying to get Sam's attention to remind him, but he wouldn't recognize me," Stan said.

"He didn't recognize anybody. It was a regular free-for-all. You'd think Sam would learn how to conduct a meeting correctly. When I voted for him, I thought he'd be a smooth operator," said Al.

You certainly don't want to be like Sam. This chapter will help *you* to become a "smooth operator" in conducting meetings and in taking part in them.

Thereafter follows instruction in these matters: Understanding the Reasons for Parliamentary Procedure, Learning the Rules of Order, Presiding at Meetings, Making Nominations and Motions, Dealing with Amendments, Learning the Duties of Officers, Learning the Duties of Committees, Writing Minutes, Understanding Parliamentary Terms, and Organizing a Club. Under "Conducting a Meeting" is presented a three-page account of a meeting of the Hiker's Club covering the call to order, reading of minutes, corrections to the minutes, reports of committees, unfinished business, motions and amendments, voting, nominations, and finally, adjournment. After these preliminaries the primary activity of this chapter, the formation of a club, is assigned with directions as follows:

Organize our class as a club. What will you need to do at the first meeting?

Interests such as these may suggest a kind of club:

Hobbies	Music or Poetry
Improving Personality	Original Writing
What's New in the World	Your Book of the Month

You may want to continue meetings throughout the year. So that several may have an opportunity to serve as officers, you may want to hold an election every two or three months.

The chapter closes with a review of parliamentary procedure and parliamentary terms.

Both more elaborate and more condensed treatments of parliamentary procedure are to be found among the several series; the ground covered, however, is common to all, and methods of instruction and practice do not differ enough to require further examples.

Motion Pictures, Television, and Radio

As column 7 of Table XI, Appendix B, shows, all but three of the series examined include chapters or sections of chapters on motion pictures, television, and radio. The sections range from a high of eighty-three pages (Lippincott) to a low of seven pages (Scribner's). Seven of the series include treatment in each volume; three include treatment in three or four volumes. Four series give most attention to the subject in the volume for grade eleven, three in grade ten, two in grade twelve; the least attention is fairly consistently given in grade nine. There is, however, no one year in which attention is concentrated; most series show roughly equal distribution.

To illustrate the general treatment, it will be necessary to summarize sparingly from one representative series. It may first be said that most series make use of motion pictures, television, and radio for a wide variety of activities, some involving home and school projects in listening and evaluating, some leading to oral discussion and individual reports, some leading to writing of a wide variety of kinds, including charts, paragraphs, "themes," and reports. Some series lean toward use of the subject as an end in itself; others tend more toward its use as motivation and source of written and oral expression. The intent of the following summary is to illustrate only one of the variety of activities and approaches found in a few series that, together, best represent the general treatment. From the American Book Company series *Our English Language:*

Grade 9, Ch. 1, "Leisure-time Fun," including relevant sections as follows: "Types of Movies," "How People Choose Movies," "Dial Twisting," "Radio and TV Standards," "The Commercials," "Giving a Newscast," "Radio and TV Reviews."

Activities include: (1) class poll of picture liked best by members in past six months, followed by discussion and justification of choice;

(2) clip and compare newspaper advertisement and newspaper reviews of same film, use for class discussion; (3) class discussion on a film that most have seen, considering director, plot, actors, make-up, sound, lighting, photography, etc.; (4) write a review and share it with others in the class; (5) class discussion on commercials, with poll to decide which the class finds good, which bad; (6) study of newspaper and magazine, radio and TV reviews, followed by student review of a favorite program.

Treatments in the volumes for grades ten, eleven, and twelve of this series use approximately the same approaches, with greatest emphasis in grade ten.

The foregoing abbreviated summary of treatments of motion pictures, radio, and television selected from one textbook series examined is admittedly most inadequate to the purpose of presenting a whole view of the attention given to these topics. It has been possible to extract only a handful of activities from a much larger total. Further, it has been impossible to suggest adequately, by the use of only one source, the detailed instruction that accompanies assignment of activities in most series. The foregoing will nevertheless, it is hoped, give some notion of the attention given by the series to these media.

Newspapers and Magazines

As shown in column 8 of Table X, Appendix B, treatment of newspapers and magazines is included in twelve of the fourteen series examined, with a high of 138 pages (Lippincott) and low figures of 16 pages (Macmillan) and 4 pages (Scott, Foresman). Four series include the topic in all volumes, six in three volumes, and two in two volumes out of three (McGraw-Hill, Scott, Foresman). Six series give most extensive treatment in the volume for grade eleven, four in grade ten, and one in grade nine; at the same time, grade nine is the year in which treatment is most frequently omitted, as it has been in four series.

Like Motion Pictures, Radio, and Television; Newspapers and

Magazines are covered by general instruction, analysis, and evaluation and are made to serve the purposes of a variety of individual and group activities, including writing and speaking. Again, as with Motion Pictures, Radio, and Television, coverage is so extensive and so varied in a majority of series that hardly more than a bare suggestion of the general emphasis can be conveyed by the summaries of representative treatments that follow.

Allyn and Bacon, *Effective English:*

Coverage is included in three of four volumes, the fullest on newspapers being in *grade 10*, which will here serve as the first example.

Coverage of the newspaper is provided in Chapter 9, "We Read and Write the News," with subheadings of "Reading the Newspaper," "Writing the News Story," and "Writing for the Editorial Page." After preliminary instruction follow such activities as the following: (1) oral report including names of newspapers read, time spent daily and Sunday on newspapers, parts of the newspaper regularly read, parts of little or no interest to the student; (2) class discussion on organization of material in newspapers; (3) bulletin board display by committee or committees showing different parts of a newspaper; (4) a group of activities involving comparison of headlines with contents of the news article; (5) writing of a news story from a given lead sentence: e.g., "At the Sophomore Snowball, Friday, January 18, West's Snow King and Queen will be crowned at 8 o'clock in the High School Gymnasium"; (6) "testing" of the foregoing written story by forming groups of 5-7 students in class and passing stories around the circle for comments; (7) similar activities in reading, writing, and discussing editorals.

In the volume for *grade 12*, newspapers and magazines are treated along with movies, radio, and TV in Chapter 8, "Studying the Mass Mediums of Communication." Activities pertaining to magazines include the following: (1) listing and grouping of magazines according to those read regularly, occasionally, seldom, and never; (2) class activity based on preceding activity and intended to rank all periodicals in order of their popularity; (3) class divided into groups, each group to pick a general subject (sports, medicine, the press, education, the theater, TV, or foreign affairs) and carry on a 5-minute conversation about it before the class, using only information found in magazines; (4) detailed analysis of a chosen magazine, including reading at least two issues, writing the publisher for facts such as cost of advertising, history of the magazine, etc., interviewing students, teachers, and parents to get their opinions of the magazine, preparation of a theme (500-1000 words) about the magazine, presentation of 3-5 minute talk telling class what has been learned.

Ginn, *English Skills:*

The most extensive coverage in this series is included in the volume for *grade 11*, Chapter 11, "Making the Best Use of Newspapers and Magazines." After initial instruction on "Purposes of a Newspaper," a newspaper story is printed in full, followed by an editorial concerning the same event, and made the basis of questions for discussion. Eight definitions are given, of "lead," "follow-up," "by-line," etc., followed by seven "Rules for Reading Newspapers." Activities include study of a newspaper by the guidance of ten given directions and questions; writing newspaper stories, features, editorials, and a news column. Magazines are covered similarly: initial instruction in "the nature and kinds of magazines" is followed by activities of the following kinds: (1) division of class into seven groups, to study, respectively, fiction, articles, poetry, news stories, illustrations, advertisements, and general content in two or more issues of a magazine, with all contributing to a general class discussion; (2) study of different magazines by each member of the class; (3) division of class into six groups, each to analyze three magazines to find how they differ in the areas of fiction, articles, poetry, news stories, art work, advertising; (4) writing a theme about a favorite magazine, "Why I Like ————," with reference to Rules for Reading a Magazine Wisely presented earlier in the chapter.

Singer, *Enjoying English:*

The most extensive treatment in this series is presented in the volume for *grade 12*, Part II, Unit 3, "Newspaper Reading: Wise and Otherwise." Principal items covered in this unit include A Newspaper's Task, Judging a Newspaper, Detecting Propaganda, Power of Propaganda, Propaganda Techniques, and Analyzing a Newspaper. Since it has not been covered by summaries of preceding treatments, and since it figures largely in several series, the section of this unit dealing with *Propaganda* is here summarized. The treatment is divided into two main areas, "Detecting Propaganda" and

"Propaganda Techniques." The evident purpose of this treatment is to teach students to be on the alert for propaganda in any of many forms in their daily newspapers. Propaganda techniques are listed as follows: Name Calling, The Glittering Generality, Transfer, Testimonials, Plain Folks, Card Stacking, and The Bandwagon. Definition and illustration of these techniques are presented. The principal activity is suggested at the end of the unit, as follows: Eight committees of four students may each evaluate four newspapers on the basis of the Newspaper Analysis Chart below. The committee may elect a chairman who will make a formal report to the class on their findings. Which of the four newspapers in the opinion of the committee is the best? There follows a "Newspaper Analysis Chart" which includes nine main heads of which examples follow: (1) Are the news reports colored with the prejudices of the editor? (2) How complete and accurate are the reports of foreign news? (3) Does the newspaper publish verbatim accounts of political operations to which it is opposed? etc.

The foregoing three summaries of coverage, instruction, and activities in the general area of Newspapers and Magazines are presented as representative of treatments given this topic by the fourteen series examined; those chosen are neither eccentric nor excessive in any respect.

Social Activities

Like Speech Activities, this area chosen for special attention in Table XI, of Appendix B, is in the nature of a catch-all with uncertain limits and demarcations. It is a fact that the approach of about half of the textbook series examined may be appropriately described as "social." "Approach" in this usage is a general term, with application not only to a single division under "Other," but also to the areas designated in this report as Grammar, Usage, and Mechanics and Rhetoric and Composition as well. That is to say that "social" is the appropriate adjective for the approach taken by approximately half of the series to the subject of English. In this circumstance it will be readily understood that the figures given for "Social Activities" in column 9 of Table XI represent only a fraction of the total fact. For purposes of this column, we have placed a relatively strict interpretation upon the term "social" and have included in pages counted only those that are rather definitely so designated by specific chapters and sections of chapters in the series.

In order to make clear the kind of instruction and activity included in the page counts for column 9, it may be useful first to identify specific chapter headings from a number of different series, as follows:

Allyn and Bacon, *Effective English,* grade 9, Ch. 1, "Let's Start the New Term Right," with subheadings as follows: "Showing Consideration for Others," "Acting in a Friendly Manner," "Introducing One Person to Another," "Reading about Good Manners."

Ginn, *English Skills,* grade 9, Ch. 1, "Getting Along with People," covering topics as follows: "Courteous Behavior and Speech (make friends, practice courtesy at school, show good school spirit, take part in school activities, practice courtesy at home, courtesy in public)." Grade 10, Ch. 3, "Courtesy in Everyday Situations," covering topics as follows: "Be Courteous Sunday through Saturday (consider the rights and feelings of others, how to express and receive thanks, how to extend and receive congratulations and compliments, how to express and receive sympathy, how to make and accept an apology, how to ask and grant a favor, how to refuse a request and accept a refusal, etc.)." Grade 11, Ch. 1, "Considering Others," covering topics similar to those above.

Harcourt, Brace, *English Grammar and Composition,* grade 10, Ch. 16, "Social Conversation," including topics as follows: "Making Social Introductions," "Acknowledging an Introduction," "Topics of Conversation," "Leave Taking," "Expressing Disagreements," "Giving Travel Directions," "Extending Thanks," "Congratulations, Apologies, and Sympathy," "Asking for a Date."

Harcourt, Brace, *Living Language,* grade 9, Ch. 1, "You"; Ch. 3, "You and Your Friends"; Ch. 5, "Language and Social Custom" (Is Your Speech Friendly? Social Courtesies, Making Apologies, How To Disagree Politely, The Sociodrama); Ch. 6, "You and Older People."

Grade 10, Ch. 1, "The Individual and His Groups" (Why People Join Groups, What Makes Groups Successful, Groups Can Be Dangerous, The Leader of the Group); Ch. 5, "Sizing Up Other People" (Clues to Character, Beware of "Types," Gossip, Facts about Human Nature); Ch. 7, "Facing Your Problems" (Finding a Solution, Dealing with Problems, Decisions and Action, Overcoming a Personal Obstacle). Grade 11, Ch. 3, "People Are Interesting"; Ch. 6, "The Individual Faces Society" (Ways of Facing the World, The Individual's Interests and Society's Interests, Facing the Facts); Ch. 9, "What Are Americans Like?" (Who are These Americans? Is There a Typical American? The American Way of Life, American Ideas).

Heath, *English in Action*, grade 9, Ch. 1, "Getting a Good Start" (Meet Your New Friends, Make and Keep Friends, Improve Your Personality, Develop Your Personality in School, Be a Good School Citizen, Develop Good Manners in School, Play Ball on the Family Team, You and Your Community); Grade 10, Ch. 1, "Having Fun with Friends" (Be an Interesting Person, Develop Your Best Qualities, On a Date, If You're a Boy, If You're a Girl, Introducing People, Acknowledging an Introduction, Books on Manners, Being the Ideal Host or Guest, Everyday Manners, Playing Your Part at Home); Grade 11, Ch. 1, "Talking with Your Friends" (Work on Those Weak Points, Be Interested in People, Don't Be a One-Subject Bore, Be Guided by Courtesy, Make Graceful Introductions, Improve Your Telephone Conversations, Be Good Company at Home); Grade 12, Ch. 1, "Learning to Live with Others" (Your Personality Quotient, Making and Keeping Friends, Learning Tact, Dating, Living with Your Family, Just a Big Tease).

The foregoing abbreviated outlines taken from five of the series as a preliminary survey of attention given to the social, or what is identified specifically in some series as "Getting Along With People," must serve to suggest the general nature and scope of matter included in this area. It remains, in very limited space, to exemplify typical activities that implement these outlines. Activities in the "social" area are so extremely numerous in the textbook series that the bare sampling which follows will be highly misleading with respect to actual proportions unless it is clearly understood that what is presented here is truly the barest sampling. The general comment is appropriate here that textbook writers in general have been approximately as liberal in their listing of "Social" activities as they have been, for example, in suggesting topics for composition, the numbers of which have been commented upon and illustrated earlier. Typical activities, from a few series, in the "social" units include the following.

Allyn and Bacon, *Effective English*, grade 9:
1. Let each student stand, give his name, the school he attended last year, and his home address. If your furniture is movable, make the get-acquainted time more informal by arranging the seats in a large circle, or in two circles, one within the other.
2. Select students to take the roles suggested in the following situations. You need not write out and memorize what to say. Before acting your part, however, imagine that you are in the situation described and think through what you will do and say. Then, without practicing, have the people participating in an introduction stage it before the class. Use classroom furniture to suggest the setting. For example, in the first situation below, arrange desks to resemble a living room. After the dramatization, discuss whether the participants remembered what you have learned about making introductions.

Ginn, *English Skills*, grade 10:
1. Recognize courtesy. Study the conversations below. Tell why each does or does not follow one or more of the Directions.
   (10 statements are made; examples: (1) *Glen:* "I'm sorry you sprained that ankle, Mac. I hope it will be well enough so you can play in the game next Friday." *Mac:* "Yeah, I'll bet you're sorry. This is just your chance to get off that bench and play for me, and you know it." (2) *Diana:* "How'd you know about the surprise party for you, Alice?" *Alice:* "Oh, I read your letter to Grandmother, telling all about it. You left your letter right there in plain sight on the desk. Anyone who wasn't blind could have read it." (3) *Grace:* "Congratulations, Joyce, on winning the story contest. I didn't think your story was so good as that, but I'm sure you're glad you won." *Joyce:* "Thanks, Grace. I was surprised that I won, too.")

McGraw-Hill, *Your Language,* grade 11:

1. Pair off. Exchange factual information, such as names, birth-places, previous school attended, current jobs and hobbies, plans after graduation, and favorite forms of entertainment. Write this information on a slip of paper. Then convene in larger groups (about five or six to a group) and elect one member to introduce the others to the class. Each group chairman can then organize the information into a short introduction like this one. [Example given.]

Heath, *English in Action,* grade 12:

1. Answer each of the following personal questions by placing Yes or No on your paper after the number of the question. Be a good sport; play fair. If you have trouble answering some of the questions, ask the advice of your parents or friends.

    (42 questions given under headings of "Your Appearance and Speech," "Your Character Traits," "Your Attitude toward Others," and "Your Range of Abilities." Examples: (1) "Is your weight about right for your age and height?" (2) "Do you take a bath or shower at least every second day?" (3) "Do you form your own opinions?" (4) "Are you punctual?" (5) "Are you an active member of at least one school club?")

Library

As shown in column 10 of Table XI, all series include chapters on the library, with total pages ranging from a high of 131 (HB[1]) to a low of 17 (McGraw-Hill, three volumes) and 24 (HB[2]). In addition, all series include attention to the library in every volume. Six series include most space in grade nine, four in grade ten, one in grade eleven, one in grade twelve; others spread evenly over two or more grades. In most series, attention to the library is included in a special chapter, often with additional information or closely related activities contained in chapters having to do with research papers, use of reference books, newspapers and magazines, etc. There is no agreement among series on the place within volumes at which instruction in the library should be given; thus the principal chapter may be placed early, in the middle, or toward or even at the very end of the volume.

Because both material and activities having to do with the topic represent a common body of subjects, with much similarity of approach in all the series, and because the series follow a common practice in covering essentially the same ground in each volume, it does not appear necessary to present here a wide range of examples. It seems both fair and economical, therefore, to limit ourselves to summarizing with some detail the treatment given by a single representative series. For such a purpose no series will better serve than the American Book Company's *Our English Language*.

Grade 9, Ch. 23, "Using the Library." The chapter opens with the following introduction:
An air of excitement was evident in the class. Tim had a new job as page in the public library and this undertaking had impressed his classmates.
"He surely must have studied the book *75 Ways for Boys to Make Money*," laughed Joe.
"How do you know where to put the books?" inquired Sue.
"Oh, he just arranges them by color and size," Jane chuckled.
Tim, grinning good-naturedly, remarked, "That's an idea, but how would you ever find a book you wanted if you didn't know the color?"
"How do you find a book you want anyway?" retorted Joe.
"That's easy," said Tim. "Every book has a special place on the shelves. Fiction is arranged alphabetically first by author and then by title; and non-fiction, by the numbers printed on the spine of the book. Once you understand those facts, you can find any book in any library anywhere."
"Anywhere?" asked Sue. "Are all libraries the same?"
"Of course," answered Tim. "Almost every library follows the Dewey Decimal System. Come down the hall, and I'll show you in the library what I mean."
There follows, with illustrations of author card, title card, subject

card, and cross-reference card, a brief section on Using the Card Cata-logue. Arrangement of fiction and nonfiction is next explained, and the numbers used in classifying according to the Dewey Decimal System are listed. There follow instruction and exercises in using reference books; for example:

Locate material concerning one of the following subjects in more than one encyclopedia. Summarize your findings. (1) Mushroom Growing. (2) Automobiles. (3) History of Baseball. (4) Stained-glass Windows. (5) Magic. (6) Caves.

Four encyclopedias and four specialized reference books are identi-fied, with an exercise of 15 items; examples:

1. The place of birth of Marian Anderson.
2. The area of the largest desert in the world.
3. Who wrote, "Penny wise, pound foolish"?
4. The location of Rattlesnake Range.

The chapter ends with brief account of the *Readers' Guide;* Word Study, involving use of given words in a sentence; and a true-false test on "Knowing Your Library." Suggested activities are visiting and com-paring the school and the public library, listing the Do's and the Don'ts for dealing with books and people in libraries, organizing a library club, and volunteering services to a library.

Grade 10, Ch. 21, "Consulting Mr. Dewey." The chapter opens with introductory dialogue similar to that in the preceding volume. The four kinds of cards in the Card Catalogue are again illustrated, as in grade 9. The Dewey Decimal System is again presented in full. In-struction and activities in using reference books follow, with a list of encyclopedias and other reference books. Activities include, for ex-ample: (1) use of encyclopedia to find answers to five questions; e.g., "When was the first airship engine made?" (2) use of other reference books to find answers to four questions; e.g., "What are the continents in order of size?" The chapter proceeds with a brief account of the *Readers' Guide,* including an activity as follows:

"Choose one of the following subjects and find three magazine arti-cles about it. If possible, read them and summarize your findings. (1) Automobile racing. (2) Human relations. (3) Jewelry. (4) Fishing boats. (5) Horses. (6) Airplanes, Speed."

The chapter closes with word study, as before, requiring definitions of encyclopedia, almanac, philosophy, essay, atlas, and decimal; and with an objective test of ten questions covering "Library Facts."

Grade 11, Ch. 19, "At the Library." The chapter opens with introductory dialogue similar to that in the preceding two volumes. The four kinds of cards in the Card Catalogue are again illustrated, as in grades nine and ten. The Dewey Decimal System is again presented in full. Instruction and activities in using reference books follow, with a list of encyclopedias and other reference books. Activities include, for example: (1) use of encyclopedia to find information on six topics (parachute jumping, building tunnels, flying saucers, early armor, story of Atlas, forecasting weather); (2) use of other reference books for information on six topics (sports records, Calvin Coolidge, wedding formalities, the poetry of Carl Sandburg, temperature in Pakistan, facts about the President). The chapter proceeds with a brief account of the *Readers' Guide,* including an activity as follows:

Choose a topic in which you are interested. By using the *Readers' Guide,* find how many magazine articles have been written about your topic.

The chapter closes with word study, as before, requiring definitions of card catalogue, Dewey Decimal System, almanac, atlas, drama, and etiquette; and with a true-false test of ten items covering library facts.

Grade 12, Ch. 21, "Library Techniques." The chapter opens with a diagnostic test of ten questions on "library know-how"; examples: (1) What kinds of cards does the card catalogue contain? (2) What is meant by the Dewey Decimal System? Next is presented brief instruction in the Card Catalogue, with illustrations of the four kinds of cards. The Dewey Decimal System is next presented in full. Activities here include the following:

"Consult the card catalogue in your school or public library to find the following: (1) The title of a book on manners. (2) The title of a book on travel in the United States. (3) The name of the author of a biography of Henry Ford. (4) The titles of two cookbooks. (5) The name of an author of a book on philosophy."

Instruction and activities in Using Reference Books follow, with a list of encyclopedias and other reference books. Activities include, for example:

"Which reference books would you consult for these? (1) Maps of England. (2) American Revolution. (3) Edgar Allan Poe. (4) Winston Churchill. (5) Source of a quotation. (6) A chemical term."

The chapter proceeds with a brief account of the *Readers' Guide,* and closes with Word Study (card catalogue, Dewey Decimal System, atlas, almanac, biography, encyclopedia, index) and an objective test of ten questions over Library Facts.

Spelling

As shown by column 11 of Table XI, Appendix B, all series give attention to spelling in each volume. The high total recorded is 106 pages (HB[1]) and the low is 26 (Lippincott). Space given is approximately even in each year of most series, but six series give somewhat greater attention in grade nine and four in grade ten; the generalization is thus accurate that most series give slightly greater attention to spelling in the first two years, but differences are not sufficient to be significant. It is further to be noted that in most cases figures recorded in column 11 represent low rather than high counts, for spelling is often given incidental additional attention, not counted, in connection with units on the dictionary, vocabulary, and the noun, in connection with capitalization, plurals, and possessives. Further, some series (e.g., Scribner's *English at Work*) distribute spelling throughout volumes, sometimes in fractions of pages, making precision in counting most difficult. Finally, besides formal attention given to spelling in a specially designated chapter or section, textbook writers regularly place stress on spelling in connection with composition, especially in subsections on proofreading. It is therefore probable that actual totals including every passing reference to spelling would in most cases run a few pages higher than those recorded.

The virtually universal practice of the textbooks is to include a chapter, or section of a chapter, at some point in the volume, which includes the following items (here represented by HB[1], grade 9): "Spelling Rules, *ie* and *ei*," "Prefixes and Suffixes," "The Final *e*," "The Plural of Nouns," "Words Frequently Confused," "Words Frequently Misspelled." Rules are commonly repeated

from volume to volume, sometimes with emphasis on one special rule, sometimes on another. Lists headed "Spelling Demons" or "Words Frequently Misspelled" vary in length but are
ordinarily of a "standard" kind, with a certain body of words oc-
curring on many such lists; for example, HB[1] includes a list of
300 words in the volume for grade nine; 260 in grade ten; 300 in
grade eleven; 300 in grade twelve. Ginn[1] presents groups of words
representing special "troubles" or "problems" which are treated in
the course of the chapter, the chapter then being concluded
with a "comprehensive test" covering many words from all groups
covered in the chapter; thus at the end of the chapter for grade
nine are listed 148 words; for grade ten, 203; for grade eleven,
334; for grade twelve, 336. It is to be observed that a large number of words included in the Ginn[1] series are repeated from year
to year: indeed, the lists for grades eleven and twelve are identical except that two are added for grade twelve.

Contrasting in distribution with the typical treatments of HB [1]
and Ginn[1], but not contrasting in general coverage, is the practice
of Scribner's *English at Work,* which ends nearly every chapter
of every volume with a brief section on spelling, involving specific rules or particular problems. This series has a number of
"Mastery Tests" at intervals throughout each volume, and in the
final analysis both the words covered and the number of words
covered are approximately equal to those treated in the "typical"
textbooks. Thus the only significant difference is that the Scribner's series places steady emphasis on spelling throughout each
year by the inclusion of formal units regularly spaced, whereas
other series confine main formal emphasis on spelling to single
chapters or sections at a single point in the volume; however,
as has been pointed out earlier, all textbooks lay stress on spelling
in connection with written work of all kinds throughout the year,
and thus the difference between the two styles of treatment is
not so great as may at first appear.

Remaining "Other"

The foregoing pages, relating to page counts shown in columns 4 to 11 in Table XI, Appendix B, are concerned with classifiable topics usually treated by most series in nearly all volumes and often at considerable length. As has already been stated, these varieties of "Other" by no means represent a comprehensive account of materials included in the textbooks aside from those specifically counted as either Grammar, Usage, and Mechanics, or Rhetoric and Composition. We are required, therefore, to summarize and to some extent to classify remaining varieties.

As with the principal kinds already tabulated and discussed, some of the following kinds are more and some are less intimately related to grammar and composition, which the authors of this report think of as the primary business of these textbooks. It would be extremely difficult to draw an exact line between kinds of "Other" included in the textbooks and to assert with any significant authority that on the one side lies all that is *relevant* and on the other all that is *irrelevant;* nor do we intend to draw any such line. Nevertheless, it is quite possible to identify certain topics examined in foregoing pages and to state with reasonable expectation of agreement that these are unquestionably highly relevant; for example, we have no hesitation in so identifying Use of the Library, and Spelling — to take the final items covered in Table XI, Appendix B.

A comparable statement can be made for the varieties of "Other" that remain to be more briefly noted: a few, such as Dictionary, Vocabulary, etc., would appear to be so obviously proper English business that they can be so designated without hesitation; other topics, toward the opposite extreme, would appear less likely to be universally accepted as particularly appropriate subjects for textbooks in grammar and composition.

Some notion of the problems involved in classifying the varieties of "Other" not already accounted for may be had from the following extremely abbreviated survey of miscellaneous headings, not primarily pertaining to grammar or composition; these headings are drawn from a liberal number of series, and they include chapter headings, section headings, and many other subordinate divisions. It is not our purpose here to be comprehensive or to suggest any kind of order, but only to suggest, in brief form, the range in variety of elements included; examples are taken from any or all volumes of series represented:

Allyn and Bacon, *Effective English:*
"Testing Your Reading Abilities," "Reading for Recreation," "Ways of Improving One's Vocabulary," "Using Poetry to Understand People," "Understanding Characteristics of Poetry and Prose," "Analyze Propaganda," "Thinking with Tools of Logic," "How Our Language Has Grown," "Using the Dictionary to Keep Informed," "Reading More Effectively."

Ginn, *English Skills:*
"What Clear Thinking Is," "Learn To Use Clear Thinking in Discussions," "Improving Reading and Study Skills," "The Dictionary and Your Vocabulary," "Reading with Enjoyment and Profit," "Enjoying Poetry," "Better Answers in Examinations."

Harcourt, Brace, *Living Language:*
"What Kind of Person Are You?" "What Has Shaped Your Personality?" "You Can Change," "You Are Now an Older Person," "You and Your Future," "Straight Thinking," "Sizing Up Other People (clues to character, beware of 'types,' gossip, facts about human nature)," "Facing Your Problems," "How We Classify Things and Ideas," "People Are Interesting (beneath the surface, people are preoccupied, behavior is complex)," "Abstractions Are Important," "What Are Americans Like?" ("Who are these Americans?" "Is there a typical American?" "The American Way of Life," "American Ideas"), "What Is Success?" ("Who Is a Success?" "Is Achievement Worth the Price?" "The Successful Life"), "A Place in the World (finding a job, holding a job, continuing your education)."

Lippincott, *English for Today:*
"Knowing Your School (finding your way around, becoming a good

citizen, learning about your school, taking part in extra-class activities, taking inventory, selecting subjects wisely, reading vocational pamphlets and magazines, using other sources of occupational information, learning to study, learning to recite, taking examinations carefully, improving your personality)," "Exploring Your Dictionary," "Improving Your Vocabulary," "Improving Your Reading," "Enjoying Poetry," "Knowing How to Think," "Knowing Your Future."

McGraw-Hill, *Your Language:*
"The Term Begins (the class meets, this book)," "Words," "The Big Book," "The Dictionary," "Languages of the World (how languages are scattered, English among world languages, English and word order)," "Everyone Daydreams," "Words: More Than Meets the Eye (words and feelings, making up words, omitting important words, an advertising game, meanings of words: we study 'old')," "Using Words in Different Ways (metaphor, the magic of words)," "Plays (reading a play, stories of fathers and sons)," "On Guard! (words don't stand alone, English uses us, fun with English)," "Language and Feeling (language conveys feeling, language arouses emotion, language shows membership)," "What Words Really Mean," "Reading and Note Taking," "This Time and This Place (establishing contact, the players, word play, this book)," "Three Important Uses of Language (information and opinion, the language of literature)," "The Words Around Us (the language of sociability, directive language)," "Signals and Structures," "Connecting the Structures," "American English."

Scott, Foresman, *Guide to Modern English:*
"Clear Thinking," "Increasing Your Vocabulary," "Using the Dictionary," "Maps and Language (why inaccurate word maps exist, the importance of checking word maps)," "Taking Tests."

Major recurrent items of "Other" may be discerned in the abbreviated summaries above; these, in general, may be grouped as follows: Dictionary, Vocabulary, Reading and Study, Orientation, Thinking, Propaganda Analysis, College Entrance and Other Examinations, After High School, and Personality. These groups do not, however, account for all items. It should be remarked that the summaries take no note of the repetition of the same items from volume to volume within series, and it should also be pointed out that in virtually all cases each volume of a series gives substantial treatment to each item. Items such as the dictionary, vocabulary development, and reading with great regularity are treated extensively at each grade level. Though not repeated in every grade, and though not, in fact, covered by every series, certain other items such as vocations, thinking, etc., nevertheless are given some impressive total coverages, in terms of page counts.

In addition to the varieties of "Other" listed and summarized above, two additional categories, which will here be identified, very loosely, as "Linguistic" and "Motivational," require comment. The first of these appears in significant quantity in only a single series, that of McGraw-Hill; the second appears in varying but always large quantity in all but two series, HB [1] and Scott, Foresman. Since the first of these is conspicuous in only a single series, it will be dealt with first, and briefly.

This special variety of "Other" may be described in a general way as gratuitous information about language; for, although it is often interesting in its own way, it does not appear to bear directly upon either of two objectives which are, in our view, the primary concerns of textbooks in grammar and composition, namely, correctness and effectiveness of expression, and especially written expression. The presence of a very large and conspicuous quantity of linguistic fringe material in the McGraw-Hill series has prompted the chairman of one high school English department, in a letter to us, to make the following statement: "We find *Your Language* a teacher's rather than a student's instrument." Our view coincides with the general sense of that statement, except that we must reserve great doubt that the series is satisfactory even as a teacher's instrument.

Although some parts dealing with such language information were actually included in the page counts for Grammar, Usage, and Mechanics, we consider the following quantities as being appropriately assigned to the variety of "Other" identified above: Grade nine: 56 pages; Grade ten: 47 pages; Grade eleven: 151 pages. The most striking proportion here is evident in the volume for grade eleven, where the 151 pages make up a conspicuous portion of the total pages (530) in the volume. Although the volume for grade twelve was not yet available for inclusion in the present study, examination of the table of contents for that volume suggests a proportion similar to that for grade eleven.

It is impossible, in limited space, to suggest the range and variety of "talk about language" included in the proportions indicated above. Only a few illustrative quotations can be presented here.

From the volume for *Grade nine,* Chapter 11, "Languages of the World":

Some time ago you discovered how many words the English language has. You also made some investigation of your own vocabulary and of how you use words in your own thinking. There is much more to learn about these questions in the coming months and years. Scientists who study language have been making wonderful discoveries within the past twenty-five years. However, no one knows all there is to know about even his own language, and it is important to realize that our language is only one of many spoken in the world today.

Languages and the Map. For a few minutes think about the people living on the various continents and islands of the world and about the languages they speak. Write a list of the names of fifteen countries, and beside each name, write the name of the language (or languages) spoken in that country. When you have finished your list, look at it to see whether you have listed any of the same languages for more than one country. If you have covered a large part of the world in your list, you will probably find certain languages repeated. . . .

Languages Around You. Begin today your study of the languages of the world by investigating the languages that members of your own class know about.

Your great-grandparents probably thought a trip to another continent was a great event, but today there is scarcely a town in the United

States without some citizens who have been to Africa, Asia, South America, Europe, or Australia. Do you know of people in your community who have visited these parts of the world? Find out, if you do not know. . . .

From the volume for *Grade ten,* Chapter 7, "The Varieties of English":

You have seen that language differs from one century to another. The same language differs, as well, in the way it is spoken from place to place.

Within the United States, there are many regional differences in vocabulary and pronunciation. The kind of language used in a particular part of a country is called a *dialect.* Dialects spoken in different parts of the same country may differ considerably in words, forms, and sounds.

Different Words. The map on the opposite page shows the principal dialect regions in the United States. Only differences in vocabulary are indicated on this map. For example, you can see that people in the South have a different name for *dragonfly* from that of people in the North. (Both may know the standard form, *dragonfly,* but in their everyday speech they are likely to use the dialect word native to their region.) A similar map could be made to show differences in pronunciation.

From the volume for *Grade eleven,* Chapter 5, "The Words Around Us":

The following is a faithful reproduction of one half of a telephone conversation between a distinguished lawyer and a business client. You are listening to the lawyer.

"Jones speaking.
"Sure.
"Of course.
"Uh huh.
"I see.
"Yes.
"Really?
"Uh huh.
"You don't say!

"Yes.
"Uh huh.
"Right.
"Yeah?
"Um-mm . . .
"No-o-o.
"Uh huh.
"Got it.
"So long.
"Yes, tomorrow."

Do these grunts, monosyllables, and short utterances indicate a lack of intelligence on the part of the lawyer? A poverty of language? A failure of courtesy? This lawyer is highly intelligent. He is known for his command of language in the courtroom. Moreover, his friends regard him as an unusually well-bred and courteous person. . . .

The foregoing passages represent in the briefest possible form a limited number of the kinds of attention given to language in this series. Space does not permit us to do full justice to the *extent* as well as to the nature of this particular species of "Other" which consumes a conspicuous portion of the total pages included in the series. In our view, none of this material, and none of the many exercises and activities that accompany the material, can be said to bear directly upon the great central concerns of textbooks in grammar and composition, namely, the improvement of expression in both correctness and effectiveness. Considered with respect to its relevance to those ends, this particular variety of "Other" must be accounted as essentially waste material. Its presence we regard as a liability, for it involves students in unnecessary complication and elaboration and tends to become an end in itself which obscures the essential purposes of instruction in grammar and composition.

Fortunately, material of the kinds represented in the foregoing summary is present only in negligible quantities, except for the series just reviewed, in other series examined. An innocuous chapter of ten pages, which can be readily overlooked by teachers without loss to the students, is included in the Macmillan volume for grade nine (Chapter 9, "New Ways of Looking at Language") and a comparable chapter is included in the volume for grade twelve (Chapter 10, "The Structure of English"). These chapters, which are not represented at all in the volumes for grades ten and eleven, appear to have been rather carefully set apart from the very substantial and relevant coverage of grammatical and mechanical matters included in the handbook portions of the volumes, so that they impair the effectiveness of the main treatment only minimally.

It may thus be said, finally, that to this date, in the great majority of textbooks examined, the contribution of "the new linguistic scientists" has been insignificant; nor does it appear that any additional contributions of the kinds so far apparent are particularly desirable.

Only the second half of the preceding statement is applicable to the final variety of "Other" that remains to be discussed. To this variety the term "Motivational" has earlier been loosely applied, though it is possible that that term is itself not sufficiently loose to accommodate all that is meant here. From this kind of "Other," which in some series occupies more space than any other variety, only three series are virtually free: HB [1], Macmillan, and Scott, Foresman. In no accurate page count has it been feasible to represent this material in tabular form, for it is never confined to any section, chapter, or part, but in many series literally pervades the whole. It should be remarked at this point that among the large number of comments sent us by teachers who use the grammar and composition textbooks the following ranks near the very top in frequency: "We do not use any of the 'motivational' activities of the text and therefore feel that we are paying for material that is useless to us."

Actually, since in most series the "motivational" material is diffused throughout sections on Grammar, Usage, Mechanics,

Composition, and "Other," and is textually inseparable from the instruction and activities in these areas, it must appear that "use" of it is unavoidable unless the teacher would carefully expunge paragraphs and sentences from page one to the end before issuing copies to students.

In the main, the "motivational" passages included in the textbooks appear to us to represent a usurpation by the textbook writer of the teacher's prerogative. These passages may most generally be described as "chats" of the writer with the student, sometimes concerned with topics specifically relevant to instruction in composition and grammar, and sometimes not; they sometimes include general observations on growing up, on getting along with people, and on life itself. They are often little "essays" on things in general; their total effect would appear to be to make the teacher a "fifth wheel." Frequently the "motivational" passages are in the form of a fiction, continued throughout the volume, or the series, representing the doings of individually named fictitious students, John and Mary, or Bill and Agnes, who are always in the same grade as the students to whom the particular volume is assigned. These fictitious students talk, listen, write, and live in situations like those in which the real students find themselves. It should be said at this point that the sharpest dividing line between kinds of series examined in this report is to be drawn between those series that do and those that do not use elaborate "motivational" paraphernalia.

Adequate illustration would require representation of diverse sorts of matter, in considerable quantity, taken from many volumes. Our purpose in the following quotations is to represent this matter as widely as possible in the least possible space.

Allyn and Bacon, *Effective English:*

Grade 9, Chapter 5. "Betty often jokes about her Aunt Lucy's clubs. Aunt Lucy has a sewing circle on Monday, bridge on Wednesday, churchwomen's society meeting on Thursday, and a child welfare committee meeting on Friday. A person may not belong to as many clubs as Aunt Lucy, but almost everyone does belong to at least one organization. Clubs are a popular part of high school life. Even classes may meet as a club for some of their activities.

The following discussion took place in one English class after the teacher had asked whether the students would like to have club meetings during some periods. . . .

Grade 11, Chapter 1. "Our country is based on the principle that every individual has a contribution to make toward an interesting, alive, worthwhile community. Most of you enjoy being with your classmates and participating in the group's activities. You 'belong.' What about those students who for some reason do not feel that security? Ask yourself the following questions concerning each member of the English class:

"Do I really believe —
      that *everyone* is important?
      that *everyone* has something worthwhile to offer to the class?"

"As Betty looked around her English class and asked herself the questions, she found herself quietly musing and evaluating the people with whom she had spent two years in high school — some belonged; some didn't; some she knew well; some she wished to know better; still others she never bothered to know.

"Betty started to think about her own place in the group and to wonder exactly what people thought about her. She liked to analyze herself as well as other people — the strengths and weaknesses in her personality. That night Betty wrote her concept of some of her personality traits. . . ."

inn, *English Skills:*

Grade 9, Chapter 3. "It was late evening at camp. Except for a postcard, Albert had not yet written to his friends Ben and Linda. He knew they would welcome a letter from him because they liked him and he liked them. 'It'll be fun,' he thought, 'to tell Ben and Linda about the good times I'm having. It'll be almost like having a visit with them.' Albert was in the letter-writing mood; he wanted to share his fun with his friends.

"Albert pulled a chair up to the table in his cabin. 'What kind of paper and ink shall I use?' he asked silently. He looked through a box of assorted stationery that his little sister had given him for his birthday. 'This bright blue and pink are not in good taste. White is always good. One of these pastel colors would be all right.' Finally, Albert selected a double sheet of pale grey. He picked up his fountain pen and tested the color of ink. 'Good. It's black,' he thought, showing his good taste. 'Black will look well on this paper. Blueblack would have been good too. I'm glad I don't use gaudy or watery ink any more.' "

Grade 12, Chapter 1. "You'll never be truly independent until you're willing and able to pay for your privileges. As long as you were a child the rights and privileges of home were yours for the asking. They still are, but now you're old enough to pay your way in cooperation, in companionship, and in service.

"Pay your way in cooperation by being willing to talk things over. Listen to the opinions of others and present your facts and reasons as calmly and objectively as possible. Stick to the one point at issue and don't spread the argument over all your real or fancied grievances. Say, 'Let's see if I've got it straight why I can't have the car tonight,' not 'You never let me do anything!' "

"Pay your way in companionship by being good company at home instead of shutting up like a clam or muttering 'Yeah,' 'Maybe,' 'I dunno' when your parents try to talk to you. Take the trouble to do things for your parents, and show your appreciation for what they do for you. Try to eliminate the minor annoyances that cause trouble at home. . . ."

Lippincott, *English for Today:*

Grade 9, Chapter 5. "Another first impression is formed by the way that you answer the door in your home. Perhaps you have had the experience of ringing the doorbell of a stranger's home, only to have it answered in a cool, perhaps even gruff, way. You could not leave quickly enough. Then again you may have had the pleasure of meeting someone whom you have thought you would like to know better because of the friendly manner in which you were greeted.

"If you recognize the person at the door when you answer, be cordial and ask him to come in. If the person is one of your friends, it is your duty to entertain him. If he has come to see another member of your family — your sister, for example — excuse yourself while you call her and tell her who has come. . . ."

The foregoing excerpts from a number of series have been chosen to represent in brief form something of the great variety of "motivational" prose that pervades a majority of the series, taking its place not only in chapters designated "Other" in this report, but also in chapters treating Grammar and Composition. It will be observed from these quotations that such passages are not confined to ninth and tenth grades, but are present in the upper grades as well. No attempt has been made to count actual pages of this material in any series; but that it occupies a very considerable amount of space is amply evident.

EVALUATIVE SUMMARY

It will be evident at once that we have found the treatment of "Other" in the textbooks to be less satisfactory on a greater number of counts than the treatment of either Grammar or Composition. The principal reasons for this judgment are based on figures to be found in Table XII, Appendix B.

First, however, some explanation is necessary for the inclusion on the evaluative sheets of the first three items, Spelling; Vocabulary and Dictionary Study; and Library, since these items obviously differ in kind from the remaining four. These are included as examples of kinds of "Other" that, in our opinion, would ordinarily be accepted as not only appropriate but even indispensable topics to be dealt with by textbooks in Grammar and Composition. Additional examples might, perhaps, have been included here, but these appeared to us sufficient for the purpose of representing unquestionably appropriate kinds of "Other" in the textbooks. It will be observed that on the items in these three columns our ratings are not markedly lower than those assigned to comparably relevant items assessed in the preceding evaluative tables on Grammar and Composition. In most cases, as will be seen, we have found treatments "adequate" or "average," with relatively few deviations either above or below. Foregoing pages of this chapter will suggest major kinds of differences in treatments that we have taken into account in arriving at these ratings.

It is, therefore, with the four remaining items on the evaluative sheets that we shall be primarily concerned here.

Relevance and Appropriateness of Topics and Activities

The two items rated in columns 4 and 5 of Table XII, Appendix B, are related in such a way as to make a joint discussion not only possible but necessary. In the main, relevance here pertains to the question of including in textbooks of grammar and composition a variety of matter — information, instruction, and activities — that does not always appear to have indisputable claim to prominence in such textbooks. On the other hand, appropriateness pertains more specifically to the question of kinds of activity assigned to accompany the many varieties of "Other" included in the textbooks, without special regard to the question of whether the particular varieties themselves "belong" in a textbook of English. Thus a textbook series which is found to give little or no space to kinds of "Other" that from our point of view have questionable claim to space in English textbooks would be rated as satisfactory on the item relevance; but if that same series were found to assign or suggest *inappropriate activities and exercises, in connection with these same legitimate kinds of "Other,"* it would receive an unsatisfactory rating on the item appropriateness. Conversely, a textbook series found to include an appreciable amount of "Other" which we do not consider as having legitimate claim to space in English textbooks would be rated unsatisfactory on the item of relevance; such a series would logically also be rated unsatisfactory on the item of appropriateness, since even "appropriate" exercises attached to inappropriate topics could hardly be judged satisfactory.

To illustrate, all series that have been found to give appreciable space to "motivational" material, to problems of "getting along with people" in the home, at school, on the street, at the theater, in the restaurant, etc., space to movies, radio, and television, to personality assessment and development, to newspapers and magazines, to clubs and parliamentary procedure, and the like, will be found invariably to have been rated as unsatisfactory on the item of relevance. It will be observed that on Part B of Table XII, the Survey Evaluation, we have so rated all but three of the series examined. Though we do not find any of the three rated as satisfactory to be quite flawless in this respect, we recommend it as of great credit to the authors and publishers of these series that they have kept their books relatively free of peripheral or extraneous matter.

Our judgment in this case does not imply that we consider such topics as those summarized above, as well as "Thinking," "Listening," etc., to be simply unworthy matters in themselves. But whatever is given time and space in the English course, as in any other course, is at the expense of something else. Since we assume that the study and practice of grammar and composition are the basic functions which these textbooks must serve, we cannot approve the inclusion of a wide variety of "Other" topics the presence of which inevitably obscures the identity of what is central and competes with its centrality. In the great majority of cases, authors of these textbooks have sought to make their volumes literally all things to all students, to contribute smatterings to a "total education." While it seems quite reasonable that English should bear its fair share of the responsibility to improve students generally — their manners, their ability to think, listen, study, their search for vocation, the development of their personalities, their social adjustment, their orientation to school life, their acquaintance with radio, movies, and television, their parliamentary procedure, etc. — yet to give up so huge a proportion of English time to such matters as is suggested by the tabulated page counts for "Other" must inevitably result in the English teacher's neglect of the primary responsibilities of English as a course. If the textbooks indeed represent true evidence of the actual conduct of courses — as we earnestly hope they do not — their enormous proportion of "Other" makes it painfully apparent that the subject of English has lost its way in a wilderness of things, has become intolerably amorphous, unteachable, and undeserving of anyone's respect as a legitimate and discrete school subject.

It is to be noted at this point that although the figures for "Other" included in Tables I and XI are in most cases so large as to appear startling, even these reveal only a fraction of the whole truth. They tell only the story of *space* usurped from basic matters in the textbooks. They do not tell the story of *time* taken from students' class and study hours. If activities connected with the many varieties of "Other" included in the most typical textbooks were fully carried out by teachers and students — and again we trust that they are not — not only would there be no time for anything else, but months would need to be added to the school year and hours added to the students' waking time. An activity that is counted as half a page in the tabulation of "Other" may, in terms of time, represent whole weeks taken from class hours and preparation time. Examples of the kind are too common in the textbooks examined to merit notation here. The whole may be summarized in this fashion: in the time that would be required for students to perform all of the "Other" activities described in typical textbook series, they could study, discuss, and even write about all of the first-rate literature of the western world. All the works of Shakespeare could be read and discussed in the time that would be required to perform the activities suggested by some series in connection with movies, television, and radio.

It will be observed that although three series have been rated as satisfactory on the item of relevance, *all* series have been rated unsatisfactory on the item of appropriateness; that is to say that even those series which have kept close to the limited varieties of "Other" that we find to have legitimate claim to place in textbooks of English have also assigned or suggested activities and exercises that we consider to be inappropriate. We consider them to be inappropriate for the two general reasons discussed below.

First, and necessarily, we find activities inappropriate which are assigned in connection with matters that are themselves, in our view, not sufficiently relevant to textbooks in English composition and grammar. All but three of the textbook series, as we have indicated in column 4, include a heavy burden of matters that fall into this category. Examples of activities from any one of the eleven other series would serve to illustrate this point; the following, all drawn from the Lippincott series, *English for Today*, will here be used to stand both for all varieties of activities assigned in connection with irrelevant materials and for all series that contain a conspicuous quantity of such materials.

Grade 9

1. Arrange a class period in which the pupils become acquainted with each other and discuss the questions "Where to?" and "How?" Come to class prepared to introduce yourself and to tell what you hope to obtain from high school, what particular courses you plan to take . . . and what extracurricular activities you plan to enter and why.

2. Let us pretend that your class is a Newcomers' Club in your community. Since such a club is usually sponsored by the Chamber of Commerce for new residents in the city, let us say that in this case your Student Council is the school's Chamber of Commerce, which is the sponsoring unit. A series of meetings is ordinarily held in which the city organization, laws, and activities are presented to the Newcomers. Your class sessions are these meetings. For the first one each class member, as a Chamber of Commerce representative, may choose to report on the rules and regulations of the topics given in the list that follows:

   Absence and tardiness procedures

Marking system and report cards
Checking out of studyhall to go to lockers, to lavatories, or to
the library
Fire-drill procedures
Parking-lot regulations
Lost-and-found department
Assembly procedures
Use of the health center
Hall conduct
Use of telephones.

3. On a piece of paper, list as many activities as you can under each of four headings. (See the following form.) In the first column, check those activities in which you participate frequently. In the second column, check those in which you have only slight skill for enjoyment. In the third column, check those that you think you might enjoy but in which you do not now participate or do not have skill.

1. Organizations and clubs. (List as many as you can.)
2. Sports and games. (List as many as you can.)
3. Reading and other intellectual interests. (List as many as you can.)
4. Social activities. (List as many as you can.)

Grade 12

1. To help you further to know yourself, here are two more activities that will prove interesting to you:

1. Appoint several members of your class to interview the director of guidance in your school on aptitude tests and to report to the class. They should find out what kinds of aptitude tests are available, how reliable the results of these tests are, what the procedure for taking these tests is, and how the results of these tests are used. Make a list of any other questions about aptitude tests for which you would like to know the answers. If your school does not have a regular testing service, perhaps you can write to a near-by college or university to obtain this information. In some cities there are commercial testing bureaus from which you can obtain this information.

2. List on the blackboard the 17 aptitudes. Beneath each one list the vocations that require that aptitude. Some

vocations will require more than one aptitude in order that a person may be successful in it. Point out such combinations.

The fact is to be restated here, that the foregoing examples represent but a fraction of the total number of activities assigned in connection with two or three of many varieties of "Other." In the particular (Lippincott) series from which they are taken, approximately six hundred pages are used to treat topics involving such activities. In the total number of series examined, such examples as those cited above might be multiplied hundreds of times over. All together, they leave no choice but the severe ratings we have indicated in Table XII under both relevance and appropriateness.

Secondly, we count as inappropriate those activities that, though used in connection with matters that would appear to have legitimate claim to emphasis in English textbooks, are found to be unsatisfactory for reasons discussed below.

Relatively minor reasons here include a host of details that affect the general level of the activities. A majority of the activities that accompany "Other" topics in the textbooks, particularly those that involve division of the class into groups, have the appearance of being inevitably wasteful of time, productive of confusion in the classroom, and, often, offensively childish. Perhaps it may be said most economically that such activities are inappropriate for the general *tone* that they represent.

The primary reason, however, that we find even those activities inappropriate that accompany treatment of matters which we consider appropriate in textbooks of grammar and composition is that they neglect the subject matter of literature as a center. It should be stated here unequivocally that this neglect of literature as the center of activites is the greatest single fault we find with the textbooks in their inclusion and treatment of "Other," just as it is their greatest single fault in the treatment of

Composition. *It therefore follows also that it is the greatest single fault that we find with the textbooks as a whole.*

We repeat here that we do not disbelieve in or undervalue Thinking, Listening, Speech Activities, including all the varieties from informal conversation to formal debate; and of course we highly value Library, Dictionary, Vocabulary and other topics which appear to us to have indisputable claim to space in the textbooks, as in courses in English. But we must still deplore the wastefulness and sheer perversity of activities which divorce the attention given to these from the attention given to literature.

The most important question to be asked in connection with the textbooks' treatment of composition, we have insisted, is "What do they write about?" In the present case, it appears to us that the most important question to be asked of the varieties of speech activities is "What do they converse about, think about, discuss, have panel discussions on, make speeches about, and listen to?" In the former case, it is our view that the most relevant subject matter to serve as the basis of composition is literature, whereas the textbooks have been found to assign writing on virtually all subjects under the sun except literature. In the present case, it is again our view that the most relevant subject matter to serve as the basis of all speech activities is literature, but again the textbooks leave no question of the fact that students are to converse, speak about, and listen to all subjects under the sun except literature. Such topics, with the accompanying instruction and motivation, take up between 100 and 200 pages in a typical series.

It should be emphasized, then, that we do not find conversing, discussing, and formal speaking as such inappropriate in themselves as classroom activities. But we do find the topics for conversing, discussing, and formal speaking irrelevant and intolerable. Our position may perhaps be defined most succinctly by the following propositions: If there *are* to be simulated telephone

conversations conducted in the English class, let Larry call up
Jill not to ask her to go to the Freshman Party with him, as he
does in a typical assignment, but to argue the meaning of the
"Ode to a Nightingale"; and let David call Bob's mother not to
find out what Bob is doing, but to find out how Bob interprets the
conduct of Brutus in his quarrel with Cassius. If there *are* to be
group conversations, let them concern not whether the members
of the senior class should or should not wear caps and gowns at
graduation, but whether Captain Ahab's pursuit of the white
whale signifies more than one man's search for one whale. If
there *are* to be panel discussions, let them concern not how
students can convince their parents that their judgments in conducting their own social life are trustworthy, but whether Thoreau's motives in going to Walden Pond were reasonable ones. If
there *are* to be speeches to inform, let them concern not the
profitableness of a hobby, but the relevant circumstances in the
age that produced "Dover Beach."

From our point of view it appears no more unreasonable to
suppose that in an English class students should normally converse about, discuss, and give talks about works of literature than
to suppose that in a history class they should converse about,
discuss, and give talks about the men and events of history, or
that in an algebra class they should concern themselves with
problems of algebra, in chemistry class with problems of chemistry, etc.

Turning now to such unquestionably legitimate studies for English courses as Library, Dictionary, and Vocabulary, we reassert
the same principle. We are convinced, in short, that these are
valid and essential accompaniments of the reading and study of
literature and composition. But we have rated the treatments
given these topics as unsatisfactory in every series, for the activities and exercises assigned by the textbooks are in every instance
to be carried on in vacuums without any, unless accidental, rela-

tion to the program of literature and composition. For the purpose of illustration here, we present examples not from any series that we have found generally inferior, or even average, but from that series which we have found to be consistently superior throughout this report, namely, Harcourt, Brace, *English Grammar and Composition:*

Grade 9
2. By using the card catalogue in your library, look up the following information:
   A. Find the cards for each author below, and list the title of one of the books he has written. If there is no card for an author's name, write "not in our library" after the proper number.
      1. Hamlin Garland
      2. Daniel Defoe
      3. Jonathan Swift
   B. By looking up title cards, find out whether or not the following books are in your library. If they are, give the authors; after each name, write the date of his birth and of his death (if given). If you do not find the title in the card catalogue, write "not in our library" after the appropriate number.
      4. *Northwest Passage*
      5. *The House of the Seven Gables*
      6. *Our Town*
   C. By looking for subject cards, find the number of books your library owns on each of these subjects.
      7. metals
      8. hygiene
   D. Give the title, author, call number, and date of publication for:
      9. a favorite novel
      10. a book of nonfiction
   E. Find and list the title and the author of a book about the following:
      11. Benjamin Franklin
      12. William Shakespeare

4. Find in the *Reader's Guide* one article listed under five of the following subjects. For each article, give the title, author, etc.

   1. Boats   6. Petroleum
   2. Comics   7. Thomas Jefferson
   3. Furniture   8. Airplanes
   4. Mexico   9. Painting
   5. Roads   10. Basketball

7. Go to the library and find the shelves of encyclopedias, atlases, and almanacs. After you have looked up each of the following items, write after the appropriate number on your paper the name of the reference book you used. Do not use the same title twice.

   1. a list of national parks
   2. a picture of Michelangelo and pictures of his art
   3. illustrations of Archimedes' principle of specific gravity
   4. a list of points of interest in Kansas
   5. types of face make-up used for motion pictures
   6. the origin and development of polo
   7. a discussion and illustrations of the development of three kinds of mosquitoes
   8. the statistics of baseball last year
   9. the population of Vermont
   10. a map of Sweden

That these examples of exercises in "Use of the Library" are indeed, from our point of view, among the most salutary ones to be found in any series can be seen by the fact that both "A" and "B" under Exercise 2 are directly concerned with authors and books; they are therefore, we believe, more appropriate than are typical exercises found elsewhere in this and other series. But to assume that even these therefore meet our criterion is to miss the main point. *The question is whether or not they are assigned as integral parts of the study of these particular authors and books currently underway in the class;* we must assume that they are not, and that the names of any other authors and books might equally as well have been listed for the purpose of the mere exercise. As for the remaining exercises here listed as examples, it is apparent that except for "D" and "E" they do not concern literature at all; hence it is necessary to conclude that the entire library unit in this volume, as in other volumes of the series and in other series, is unrelated to the main core of study and practice in literature and composition presumably going on in the class and marks a "time out" period from this work.

The same precisely must be said of activities assigned in connection with units on Vocabulary and Dictionary, as well, of course, as with all other units of "Other" that are in nature less intimately related than these to the main core of literature and composition. *All series tend to make everything a mere exercise, without point or relation outside itself.* In our view, this method is literally "doing it the hard way" for everyone concerned — for the textbook author, who must "think up" things to do; for the teacher, who must, if he adheres to the textbook, periodically interrupt the study of literature and practice of composition in order to "get in" these special units; and, above all, for the student, who is obliged to do exercises as exercises only. Although we are convinced of the necessity of exercising techniques, we are also convinced that the operation should be conducted in direct connection with the main study and practice going on, and this opinion holds not only for Library, Dictionary, and Vocabulary, but also for Thinking, Listening, Discussing, etc.

We would, in short, send students to the library to investigate authors and books currently being studied; we would send them to the dictionary when their own limitations in vocabulary became apparent in the course of reading their assigned works of literature; and, of course, we would have them think, discuss, listen, and write in connection with the same central operation.

Progression

It would appear unnecessary here to elaborate on the necessity we have found to rate all series as unsatisfactory on item 6, Part B, of Table XII. The volume-by-volume figures presented for "Other" in Table XI show plainly that most series treat most varieties of "Other" in grade after grade, and the discussion included in foregoing pages of this chapter presents a sufficient number of quotations from the textbooks to show that these varieties are treated in approximately the same ways, with the same details, and to the same depth in each volume of any given series, with rare exceptions that are made apparent by the table itself. The fact is simply that in such areas as speech activities, movies, radio and TV, newspapers and magazines, library, dictionary, etc., there is no sign of progression, but only repetition from year to year. The only discernible difference from volume to volume of the several series, with respect to the varieties of "Other" is that material on "Getting a Job," "Your Future," "Taking College Entrance Examinations," or "Selecting a College," is either treated exclusively or especially emphasized in the volume for grade twelve.

Tone

It will be observed that we have rated only three series as satisfactory, and even commendable, on item 7, Part B, of Table XII. Although we have found "tone" *generally* unsatisfactory also in connection with our ratings of Grammar, Usage, and Mechanics and Composition, we have found it *thoroughly* unsatisfactory with respect to Other. "Tone" is our broadest term of description, representing the most general "image" that we have of the books. It may be said to be the reflection of the *level*, in a wide sense, at which the authors and publishers combined have addressed the subject and the students. It is affected, in our view,

by a variety of features similar to those of the anthologies of literature, such as style and manner of prose, use of "gadgetry" of one
kind or another, copiousness and kind of pictorial devices, as
color pictures, cartoons, use of fictional names and situations to
match "real" students in *their* situations. We believe that unsatisfactory tone in its most unfortunate aspects constitutes a form of
apology for the subject to be studied and for the request being
made of students that they study it. In our view those series have
deserved a satisfactory rating on tone that are devoid of any
devices that look like apologies and indeed of any apologetic
overtones.

Tone, throughout the series examined, is most regularly satisfactory when authors are directly dealing with central, solid matters — when they are explaining the elements of sentences and
how they go together, describing methods of developing and ordering paragraphs, identifying rhetorical principles in the arrangement of parts within sentences and sentences within paragraphs.
At such points, in most series, textbook authors "get on with it"
directly, succinctly, in a businesslike manner, with little or nothing of the manner that elsewhere reeks with apology in the
form of exhortation, childish cajoling, assertions of the "importance of it all," etc.

The most unfortunate extremity of tone is exhibited in those
aspects of books that we loosely identify as "motivational." The
low-density prose of passages presenting fictional Johns and
Marys in fictional situations just like those in which the "real"
students now find themselves as they embark on some new unit,
the "chatty" passages in which authors seem determined to convince students that they, the authors, like the editors of anthologies of literature, are on the same level as the students, sharing
their adolescent interests and tastes — such prose, which abounds
in many series, can, in our view, be counted only as an offense
in tone which loses the respect of even the least able students

and must surely embarrass any teacher who has been exposed to a liberal education. We have earlier reported that the view of many teachers evidently coincides with our own on this matter; perhaps the most frequent comment we have received reads approximately thus: "I have always felt that many of the 'motivational' activities were useless. Also, I object to the fact that over half of the book is taken up with this sort of thing."

In foregoing pages of this chapter, particularly in connection with "motivational material" as one kind of "Other," we have tried to illustrate what is meant by "this sort of thing." Yet one more example, from a series not previously used for the purpose, will indicate the nature of "this sort of thing" in one of its most frequent forms; the following is from McGraw-Hill, *Your Language,* grade 9, chapter 30, "Helps Toward Being at Ease":

Probably there is no one in the world who does not feel embarrassed and uncomfortable at times. Are you sometimes puzzled about what to say to a stranger? Are you embarrassed when introducing friends to your family? Joan, a high school freshman, confided to her mother one evening, "The worst thing happened today. When I was going down the hall at school, I was talking to Mary and almost knocked down the principal." When her mother asked Joan what she did about it, the reply was, "Oh, I felt so terrible I couldn't say anything. I just got out of sight as fast as I could."

Introducing people, apologizing, saying good-bye to a hostess, and asking favors often cause trouble if we have not learned the simple formulas for these occasions. Right now, take out pencil and paper and begin to make a list of such occasions. Are you puzzled about when to rise or to shake hands when being introduced? Do you find it difficult to apologize when you forget an appointment? Are you embarrassed when you enter a room full of people? Do you dislike to go to a school counselor or principal because you are uncertain about how to introduce yourself? You need not sign your name to the list.

Hand the list you have made to the teacher or class chairman, who will appoint a small committee to examine the items and classify them in groups, under three or four headings. When the questions have been sorted and duplicates thrown away, choose as many committees as there are groups of questions. Then each group of questions will be handed to one of the committees. After the class has done the exercises that follow, each committee may lead discussion about the groups of questions assigned to it.

As a general rule, although not invariably, "motivational" prose of this character is used to introduce activities which themselves keep to the same general level, or tone.

Because the tone here presented, together with a typical variety of "Other" that it often accompanies, is so prevalent throughout the series examined, we have found it possible to rate only three series as satisfactory on this particular item.

PART III

Recommendations

CHAPTER 1

The Anthologies

WE HAVE NOT found it possible to generalize about the anthologies to the extent that it is possible in the following chapter to do for the grammar and composition series. As the reader will have noticed, at no point in the preceding analysis and evaluation of the anthologies have we pointed to one volume or to one series as clearly typical. The variations among them are so great in degree and so numerous in kind that instead we have attempted to show by examples the great variety of practices. Hence, too, it is virtually impossible to arrive at an evaluation of their relative merits, to rank them in any kind of qualitative order that would be of use to the readers of this report. If we attempted to rate them on the quality of their editorial apparatus, we should have to say that the ABC series, for example, is to be commended for its restraint in the use of illustrations — and at the same time that its study questions and suggested activities are almost entirely inadequate. Of many volumes intended for the ninth and tenth grades we should have to say that, even if the selections were uniformly acceptable (a conclusion that unfortunately we were unable to reach for any of them), the organization places the selections in inappropriate and misleading contexts. In short, the virtues of particular series and volumes are invariably canceled out by their faults: a good selection of short stories stands alongside a group of trivial and trite poems; an acceptable representation of literary pieces is overshadowed by a large body of nonliterary ephemera; a well-chosen novel or play is emasculated by abridgement and adaptation; a challenging and relevant topic suggested for class discussion is followed by one that requires mindless busy-work or encourages aimless wandering.

If we were compelled to choose one series as superior to the rest, our choice would be HB49; but if we were forced to use it in our own classes, we would ignore most of the questions and activities suggested by the editors, omit from class consideration perhaps as many as half the selections, supplement it very frequently with selections from other sources, including better versions of some that it contains (it has, for example, the most heavily abridged *Julius Caesar* of any of the anthologies we have examined), and in general make so little use of it *as a textbook* that it would hardly seem worth the expense to purchase it in class sets. Indeed, it is not as textbooks but as supplementary or reference books to which one could turn for texts of particular pieces of poetry or prose that the anthologies have their greatest use and perhaps can be ranked in some kind of qualitative order. The following ranking should therefore be regarded in this light: the series and individual volumes in the first group are those to which we would expect to turn most frequently as the source of particular selections not otherwise available to a class; those in the second group would occasionally be used for the same purpose; those in the third group we should expect to find no use for.

Group I: Gn, HB49, HBM, HBO, RM, SF, Sgr; Glb-11, Irq-9, Irq-10.

Group II: ABC, HBL, Hlt, Ldw, McM; MGH-9, RP-9, Scb-9.

Group III: HB2, Lipp, PH; Hth-9, HM-9, SF2-9.

But we should consider ourselves and our students unduly hampered if we had to use any one of them *as the central text-book of literature* in our classes.

Nevertheless, we find some virtues in all or most of the anthologies, about which we can speak in a general way. These are as follows:

1. *Their generally adequate treatment of vocabulary study within the context of the selections.*
2. *Their quantitative sufficiency of reading matter.*
3. *Their physical adequacy: durability of binding, quality of paper, and clarity of letterpress.*

With few exceptions, which have been indicated in the body of this report, all the volumes examined can be praised for each of these points.

Against these virtues we set the following basic faults, all of which, in our view, afflict all volumes, with such occasional exceptions as have been noted in the preceding chapters of this report. Yet the variations among them are so great, as we have previously remarked, that the discussions of the various faults of necessity are often summaries rather than generalized conclusions.

1. *Inadequacy of selections.* There are two varieties of this fault: the inclusion of much nonliterature and the inclusion of much second-rate literature. To the first kind belong the numerous merely factual excerpts from nonfictional books and the many biographical narratives that are more notable for their adventurous content than for their quality as writing. To the second belong not only the ephemeral verse and the formula story but also the lesser works of such distinguished authors as Hawthorne, Whitman, Twain, Wordsworth, Shelley, and Tennyson, which displace their greater and more representative writings.

2. *Alteration of selections.* The alteration to which texts are subjected ranges from slight abridgement to almost complete re-

writing. Lines and stanzas are omitted from poems, characters and dialogue from plays, incidents and chapters from novels, beginnings and endings from essays. Deletions often necessitate alterations in the remaining text to supply transitions that have disappeared. Whole works are "adapted" to avoid difficulties — real or imaginary — in vocabulary, syntax, characterization, or thought. Excerpts are so numerous in some volumes as to make them collections of scraps and snippets. The changes may be so drastic as to make of a piece something other than what it was originally. And any of these changes may be made without indication to teacher or student that he is not reading what he thinks — the work as the author wrote it.

3. *Dominance of organization.* Perhaps three-fourths of the volumes examined appear to have been organized before their content was determined. Thus, selections are included that can be justified only because they fit into a unit, not because they have literary merit. Furthermore, the editorial machinery supporting the scheme of organization is often so great that it overwhelms the selections; in many units more space is used for introductions than for what is introduced. Topically and chronologically arranged anthologies, respectively, are chiefly guilty of these two faults. Most books are overorganized.

4. *Indiscriminate nature of questions and activities.* The questions following the selections and units, intended to aid the student in reading and review or to stimulate discussion, vary widely in their quality and appropriateness. A large number offer no challenge; at least an equally large number lead the student away from, rather than back to, the text. Many of the activities suggested have nothing at all to do with the selections they follow; still worse, others make literature subservient to the social studies or the natural sciences; some seem intended merely to keep idle hands busy; many set group cooperation above individual mastery of subject matter.

5. *Insufficient attention to composition.* In the body of the report we have noted that only 3.2 per cent of the activities specifically ask that students write (this figure includes the permissive assignments: "You may wish to write about . . ."), and an even smaller percentage ask that students write about what they have read. This failure to relate literature and composition is probably the greatest fault to be found in both kinds of series we have examined. Literature offers ideal subject matter for composition — because it is humane and therefore important to all human beings, because it is a definite body of subject matter and therefore can exert a disciplinary force upon the writer, and because it is subject matter possessed in common by students and teacher and therefore available as the basis for full and helpful criticism that can lead to improvement in composition; furthermore, composition based *upon* literature leads to a better understanding *of* literature.

6. *Lack of direction.* There is too much of almost everything in the anthologies — selections, questions, activities, pictures, study guides, introductions, glosses, etc. — so that students are given no help in distinguishing the more from the less important, and teachers who need direction will seek it in vain. There are, of course, any number of things suggested for the teacher to do; he will find no difficulty in filling up the class hour and keeping his students busy. Indeed there is much more than he and his students can do, much of it hardly worth doing. In the meantime the great Anglo-American literary heritage is in danger of perishing through neglect and ignorance.

7. *The dismissal of the past.* Even those volumes which proclaim in their prefaces that they have given "adequate coverage" to literature give relatively little space to anything written before 1900 or even 1930. The chronologically arranged volumes for the eleventh and twelfth grades represent earlier literature more adequately than do the others, but even in the upper years two no-

ticeable trends have developed: earlier literature gets less space as anthologies are revised, and as contemporary literature of the western hemisphere and the world displaces American and English literature, particularly that of earlier periods. The volumes for the first two years often have nothing or almost nothing before the twentieth century. Although we do not object to the inclusion of contemporary literature, we believe that it should have qualities to recommend it in addition to its newness — that it should be at least as distinguished as the earlier pieces it displaces. Furthermore, the classroom provides the opportunity to read what the student may not choose to read on his own — and with the teacher's assistance; he will have a lifetime to read contemporary literature, but he may never again have such a favorable opportunity to read anything else. Finally, since all art relies heavily upon convention, and convention is meaningless without its tradition, even contemporary literature will be more significant if the reader can come to it aware of the common tropes of language that influence authors of all ages, including the most recent. Bulwer-Lytton once wrote: "In science, read by preference the newest works; in literature the oldest. The classics are always modern."

Because the English course is the one place where all high school students will meet the humanities, and because anthologies have been tremendously influential in determining the nature of the English course, the responsibility that the editors have to the humanities, and thus to the greatness of the past, is an awesome one. We wish that it were better borne.

8. *The fear of difficulty.* An analogy that has repeatedly occurred to us as we examined the anthologies is that of "instant" packaged food, the kind that one just "pops into the oven and serves." The emphasis on the "enjoyment" of reading is so great in many of the anthologies as to suggest that editors have become fearful of including selections that require any effort to under-

stand. Yet the real enjoyment of literature is a goal of reading, a goal that is reached by study; it is not a superficial "attractiveness" necessarily apparent at the outset. We have assumed throughout this survey that anthologies are textbooks, *to be studied in and taught from,* not do-it-yourself readers in which the teacher makes assignments but takes little further responsibility. Hence we believe that most anthologies seriously underestimate the ability of students and teachers to cooperate in the thoughtful examination of important and distinguished texts, and that when difficulty exists the importance and distinction of the work at hand are sufficient justification of any effort necessary to overcome it. In the words of the Literature Committee of the School and College Conference, "The books that really need interpretation will work best in the classroom." Literature worth including in the anthologies often will not be "instant" literature to heat and serve.

9. *Editorial tone.* Tone is established in the anthologies both by the choice of selections and by the editorial apparatus that accompanies them. Several of the anthologies stress the deliberate catering to the adolescent mind even to the point of embarrassment. Pieces are chosen because they lie within the narrow boundaries of the teen-age world, and their heroes and heroines are Dick and Jane just a few years older, now dating instead of playing, going to a dance instead of the local fire station, saying "round, round, jump the rut, round, round, round, jump the rut, round, round —" instead of "Jump, Spot, jump," but otherwise hardly different. The "image" of the American Boy that emerges is of a clean-cut, socially poised extrovert, an incurious observer of life rather than a participant, a willing conformer, more eager to get than to give, a bit of a hypocrite but a rather dull companion — a well-adjusted youth not much above a moron. And the "image" of the American Girl? She is one who likes the American Boy. The adolescent should read about adolescents, of course —

but he can and will do so on his own. The constant restriction of the teen-ager's gaze to himself, his friends, his family, his hobbies, his little world of which he is the center, is likely to produce nothing else so quickly as acute narcissism. Unfortunately, it can become a chronic disease, particularly if the editorial context of the selections — questions, activities, illustrations, etc. — directs him to seek answers rather than to raise questions and tends to confirm his prejudices rather than to make him look beyond himself. The final outrage occurs when the editorial machinery is set down in chatty, breezy, affectedly juvenile, permissive prose, for not only is the adolescent kept from reaching toward adulthood but adults have become adolescents and thus have lost their right to be mentors. The conflict between youth and age is a natural condition of man, older than Cicero and Bacon, and as necessary as it is natural; contempt enters the relationship when age pretends to youth. And contempt can transfer itself from apparatus to selection, from selection to teacher, from teacher to subject, from subject to education, from education to the values by which civilized men live. Before the students can grow up, their textbooks must.

We have been severely critical of the anthologies, but we have said nothing that some or many teachers have not said even more harshly; nor have we been as severe as J. Frank Dobie, who said that the textbooks are "stuffed with banal tripe that would bore the brain of a hard-shelled terrapin" (*The New Yorker*, May 6, 1961, p. 90), or as Naomi Bliven, who said, "As long as education serves up the culls of literature, can adults complain if the young don't read?" (*The New Yorker*, July 15, 1961, p. 72.) But we have been severe enough to encourage the question, which has already been asked us several times: "Then do you think that anthologies should be abolished?" Our answer is an emphatic No. A bad program is better than no program at all, particularly for the inexperienced or untrained teacher; and bad programs can be made better. Several of the present series could be vastly im-

proved without undue effort. We have made many recommendations at the ends of the preceding chapters, some of which we
have reiterated here. These, we believe, could make good anthologies out of poor ones and excellent anthologies out of mediocre
ones.

In the meantime, several experiments that look promising will
bear watching. We have earlier mentioned the four-novel volumes published by Harcourt, Brace, to which have recently been
added volumes each containing several biographies. Although
quite uneven in quality, these volumes are equipped with questions that, in general, are much better than those in the anthologies. Some of the works included are abridged. Macmillan's "Literary Heritage" series of texts, including collections by genre,
individual novels, and ten Shakespearean plays appearing two per
volume, offers an "articulated" program that may perhaps be an
adequate substitute for the anthology. This seems to us one of the
most promising experiments outside the anthology format. The
Scholastic Units, several of which have now appeared, seemed at
first to offer something that has long been needed, a thematically
organized program of literature; however, they have two large
faults — thematic arrangement has, in several of the Units, de-
generated into topical organization, which is the bane of the present anthologies for the ninth and tenth grades, and much ephemera and nonliterature have been introduced. Most promising of
all, we believe, is a textbook innovation on the college level that
could be readily adapted for high school use. This kind of book
might be called the "selective anthology," adequately represented so far only by *Trio: A Book of Stories, Plays, and Poems*
(Harper & Brothers), a 487-page paperback that contains twelve
short stories, two novelettes, two plays, and fifty-eight poems by
eighteen different poets. The only editorial apparatus is a biographical appendix. Each selection has a high degree of literary
merit. The flexibility of the arrangement allows the teacher to or-

ganize his own program of reading if he wishes, although the combination of typological and chronological orders used in the volume may itself prove to be all that he requires. The selective anthology may be the best solution to a serious problem, which seems to us to be still unsolved by the textbooks we have examined for this report. Finally, there is an experiment that has now been so widely followed that it can hardly be called an experiment any longer: the use of paperbacks, including "trade" editions, in the high school classroom. We know of English teachers who have seen their classes improve almost overnight as if by magic, simply because their students had in hand books that look like books. But school districts are still hesitant about purchasing paperbacks in class sets, and their relatively short life is an obstacle to their general use.

In spite of these and other experiments, the ideal solution has not yet been found. Although the greater availability of individual titles, inexpensively bound and adequately edited, now makes possible an English course of a scope that was impossible only a few years ago, such a course passes over to the teacher the whole responsibility for two important and difficult processes — the selection and the organization of the material. The ill-prepared or overworked teacher thus is without the help that he needs and has a right to expect. Much of that help must still be provided by the textbooks, particularly by anthologies.

We therefore recommend that editors revise their anthologies, particularly in two ways. (1) *They should be drastically reduced in size*. Instead of offering "something for everybody," they should exert real leadership by presenting a central core of important readings that all members of a class would be expected to study and every teacher would actively teach. The active role of the teacher would reduce the need for much of the machinery; the central core of significant reading could make possible real progression from year to year, since each teacher would know, at least in a general way, what his students had already read. At the same time, because the area of significant literature is vast, there would still be room for variation among books competing in the textbook market. (2) *Every work admitted into the anthologies should be of high literary distinction.* At the outset, certain prevalent but nonsensical equations that have long hampered English studies should be abolished: namely, that what is great is difficult; that what is difficult is uninteresting; that what is uninteresting is unteachable. Neither editors nor teachers should be afraid of giving students "what is good for them." If students knew what was good for them, they would need neither teachers nor textbooks. We must assume that the real basis of education is the assumption that those who know more can give of their knowledge to those who, temporarily, know less. The greatest gift that English teachers and editors of English books have to give is literature. The vapid theories that advocate teaching the "whole child," removing all difficulties from his path, and being permissive at every turn cannot be allowed to put in jeopardy the literacy of a whole nation. The real "wave of the future" was recognized by a committee whose conclusions better deserve our confidence. Although the entire report should be studied by those who prepare textbooks, we shall quote only a sentence from it here:

English can remain genuinely humanistic only by concerning itself clearly and boldly with the great literary tradition. (*Joint Conference Report on Basic Issues in the Teaching of English,* 1958. NCTE, MLA, College English Assn., American Studies Assn.)

CHAPTER 2

Grammar and Composition Series

WE FIND IT appropriate to commend the authors of the grammar and composition series examined upon the following points:

1. *Their generally adequate coverage of details of grammar, usage, and mechanics.*
2. *Their coverage of principles and techniques of writing, particularly with respect to the sentence and the paragraph.*
3. *Their great abundance of exercises, activities, topics for writing, and illustrative material of all kinds.*
4. *Their emphasis on care in writing and care in proofreading and revision.*

With few exceptions, which have been indicated in the foregoing body of this report, all the series examined deserve praise, in our view, upon each of these points.

Against these important virtues we set the following basic faults, all of which, we believe, afflict all series, with such occasional exceptions as have been noted in the body of the report.

1. *Repetition.* Although the volumes of series are clearly marked on the covers with the large numbers 9, 10, 11, and 12, these numerals are the only reliable indicators of the years for which the books are intended. All principal topics are repeated throughout four years, and the many examples cited in the body of the report to illustrate treatment of these topics, in terms of instruction and

activities, plainly evince the fact that virtually all matters included under these main headings are approached and covered with approximately the same thoroughness in successive volumes. New drill sentences, presented in each volume in connection with instruction in grammar, usage, and mechanics, do not vary in kind from volume to volume. New topics for composition, added from year to year, do not differ in kind from volume to volume. Wordings of motivational and explanatory prose are somewhat varied from volume to volume, but the matter covered is essentially the same from volume to volume. In short, all principal matters treated in any given series are treated four times in essentially the same ways. The cumulative effect of this steady repetition can be described only as suffocating.

2. *Irrelevant or waste matter.* Aside from the waste that is implied by steady repetition, typical series contain a high count of pages that are expendable either because they treat topics alien to the primary business of grammar and composition, or because they present an elaborate machinery of "motivational" or purely gratuitous character. Foregoing pages have illustrated the varieties of such waste as richly as space has permitted; but all such illustration as we have been able to provide inevitably falls far short of suggesting how truly large is the bulk of such material in most series. These various forms of waste are not confined to those chapters and sections described as "Other" in this report, but appear also in the parts given to grammar and composition. In our view the presence of gratuitous pages in those parts seriously obscures or negates the principal virtues for which, above, we have commended the authors of the textbooks.

3. *Neglect of literature as source and center of activities.* Universally, the textbooks examined have sought to manufacture a subject matter out of the student himself and his relations with home, friends, school, and community. A statement made in the preface of one series (Lippincott, *English for Today*) may, we

believe, stand accurately for the principle upon which all series examined have been based:

The series is built upon the objectives of English instruction as set forth by the Commission on the English Curriculum of the National Council of Teachers of English; namely, "(1) the cultivation of wholesome personal living, (2) the development of social sensitivity and effective participation in group life, and (3) preparation for vocational competence."

Though we ourselves can hardly fail to cherish such ends, our examination of the actuality that is represented by the textbooks we have analyzed leaves us no choice but to conclude that the adoption of these ends as appropriate aims and purposes for textbooks in grammar and composition has resulted in neglect or burial of that very subject matter through which English courses can most effectively make their contribution to the total education of the generation of students that take these courses. We believe that in literature itself English has the rarest and most glorious of subject matters about which can be wrapped all appropriate activities of conversing, discussing, speaking, listening, thinking, and writing. In neglecting literature as source and center for all these classroom activities, the textbook writers have entered a chaotic wasteland in which their only sign of "progression" is an incessant scrambling after anything and everything that may possibly produce some form of speaking and writing. We believe that foregoing samples, particularly of topics for writing and speaking, give ample and conclusive evidence of this wasteful and futile scrambling, in which the subject of English would appear to have forfeited its dignity, its right to the respect of students, its claim to a central place in the curriculum, and, indeed, to have lost its way. If typical activities recommended by typical series were in fact carried out in full in English classes, we should expect teachers of other subjects to complain about the encroaching practices and disruptive effects of English in the school. We should expect a majority of such activities to call out not the best but the worst that is in students. And, finally, we should expect able English teachers themselves to find their own education in the liberal arts to be a liability rather than an asset in conducting such activities. In contrast, the kind of program which we would substitute for that offered by the textbooks is one in which the teacher's liberal arts preparation is not only an advantage but a necessity.

4. *Catering.* This grossly obvious and unfortunate tendency of the textbooks is intimately bound to the two major faults (2 and 3) characterized above. Catering is evident not only in the form and nature of activities suggested or assigned, but in the manner or tone with which whole enterprises are broached and conducted. Curiously, those textbooks which most insistently base every kind of activity upon the immediate fashion in adolescent interests, tastes, and attitudes are also the very ones that present their material in the most apologetic manner, as though it were an imposition to ask students to indulge themselves in what it is assumed they should be most eager to indulge themselves. Those few series that are virtually free of "motivational" prose are also freest of the most overt signs of catering; but that even these few do not wholly escape is made evident by their choices of topics for speaking and writing, which, like those in all other series, regularly invite the student to exploit himself in the past, present, or future, and his relations with his family, his friends, his streets, and neighbors, his school and community. In the extreme cases of catering, an entire series appears to constitute a kind of apology for the subject of English, or, more precisely, an apology for asking students to do anything other than what they would normally be doing if they were not, at the moment, sitting in an English class.

5. *Artificiality.* Despite the efforts of most textbook writers to simulate "real" situations — a telephone conversation, a club

meeting, an announcement, an introduction, etc. — the reality of the classroom situation makes the "pretend" situation, to use a favorite word of Holden Caulfield's, patently "phony." The plain fact is that the only real situation of students in a classroom is — their situation in the classroom. To put them through exercises prefaced with the demand that they pretend to be elsewhere is surely to invite only foolish, giggling, halfhearted, and self-conscious, or else openly contemptuous performance from normal students who perceive very well that they are only "going through the motions" in an artificial situation; one must suppose that any student who effectively suspended his disbelief and performed as the textbook writer, or teacher, wished would be a case for psychiatric treatment.

But these are only the most extreme and obvious cases of artificiality in the textbooks. Much more frequent, and much more serious, in our view, is the "mere exercise" character of virtually all activities, from the repeated assignments to punctuate given sentences rather than sentences from students' own compositions, to library assignments in looking up assorted details that have no reference to a particular work of literature then being studied in class. An illustration may serve to clarify this important point. If *Hamlet* is being read in class, and students are sent into the library to find an article or a chapter that interprets some problem of character or action, the assignment is not a mere "exercise" that begins and ends as exercise; but if — and this is the method of all the series examined — the reading of *Hamlet* is interrupted for a day or two while students go into the library to "have" some library practice in looking up articles on airplane design, beekeeping, and attempts to climb Mount Everest, the assignment is indeed a mere "exercise" that begins and ends just there. Similarly, to assign students to write a paragraph comparing and contrasting Hamlet and Laertes as avengers, while the study of *Hamlet* is yet going forward, is to do more than "set an exercise" in writing paragraphs that are developed by comparison and contrast. But to assign the writing of "a paragraph to be developed through comparison and contrast," and to offer a list of ten "suggested topics" from which students may choose, is indeed to do no more than "set an exercise" in writing paragraphs developed by comparison and contrast. Again, it is the latter way that is invariably the way of the textbooks.

When the methods illustrated above are multiplied many times and applied to *all* the varied kinds of practice that are represented in the textbooks — practice with sentences, practice with speech, practice with composition, practice in listening, thinking, etc. — it is apparent why the impression created by the textbooks of "going through the motions," of conducting "dry runs," is so overwhelming. We consider the artificiality of the textbooks, in the senses here illustrated, to be a truly formidable obstacle to serious practice and to genuine learning.

6. *Difficulty.* If there is any one aim that the textbook writers have set above all others in their presentation of these volumes, it is patently that of not being difficult. The prose style of any twelfth-grade volume is essentially undifferentiated from that of its corresponding ninth-grade volume. Illustrations and examples of everything are abundant in each volume. Definitions and explanations (with the exception of certain grammatical ones used in a single series and noted in the appropriate chapter of this report) are regularly adequate and clear, and when all definitions and explanations are repeated in four successive years, as is the case, it may even be said that they are somewhat more than adequate. In short, it may be said directly that in these series the ingenious efforts to avoid difficulty are rather overdone than underdone.

It will therefore appear contradictory that we have identified "difficulty" as one of six basic faults of the textbooks. We nevertheless are convinced that the very superfluity of effort to make all "easy" has had the unfortunate effect of making the textbooks more difficult in this special sense, *that though not at all difficult to read in, they are most difficult to learn from.* It is a fact that when 400 to 500 pages are taken to present the salient matter of 100 pages, greater difficulty in mastering this matter results; neither is the likelihood of mastery improved by repetition that brings the total pages to 2000, within which the salient 100 pages are repeated four times. Instead, what is essentially to be *learned* from the treatment of a topic might often be confined to a single, succinct page. Long stretches of low-density, "easy" prose simply make no durable impression on the mind. Though in general we believe the difficulty of *learning* from the books is increased by the presence of the vast amounts of varied material that we have labeled "Other," which tend to obscure the place and significance of more specifically relevant matter, it is also true that the practice of spreading even the essential material widely and thinly contributes to the difficulty of mastering this material. Some textbooks follow the commendable practice of summarizing salient details — for example, the rules of punctuation — on a single page; yet in the same volumes the full treatment of punctuation may be spread over more than thirty pages, and, in the total series, over more than one hundred. We believe that the essential matters of punctuation can be explained, illustrated, and exercised in fewer than ten pages; and, indeed, in some existing handbook treatments we find them to be adequately covered in that space.

RECOMMENDATIONS

We do not wish to lay the blame for the faults we have found in these textbooks at the door of either authors or publishers. We trace the origins of most that we find unfortunate in the textbooks to just two potent conventions: (1) the convention of the four-volume series; (2) the convention of separate series for literature and composition. We shall consider these in order.

We are prepared to agree that textbook writers, confronted

with the gigantic task of somehow filling up four large volumes containing a total of approximately 2000 pages relating to grammar and composition, have succeeded in doing about as well as might reasonably be expected — as well as we ourselves, or others, might do. From the necessity of filling a large amount of space in four successive volumes, two principal faults, already identified, inevitably have resulted: first, *repetition,* which has been a steady and perhaps tedious theme of this report in the chapters on Grammar, Composition, and "Other"; second, the invention and inclusion of a vast quantity and many ingenious varieties of "Other." Repetition is inevitable for a very simple reason: each high school year needs to have available in a textbook the essential information on grammar and composition; since each year needs *all* the basic information, it is unthinkable that it be divided and distributed bit by bit through four volumes — it must all be in all volumes, hence, repetition. But since there is literally not enough that is relevant to be said about the basic matter of grammar and composition to require more than 200 pages at most, and since this, repeated four times, comes only to 800 pages, textbook writers have been left with more than 1000 pages to fill in the entire series. They have done so in two ways: by incorporating in the name of all-embracing "Language Arts" some "Other" into the sections on grammar and composition, thus expanding them; and by adding many entire sections given wholly to "Other." Although we have considered other possibilities, we cannot seriously think that there can be any underlying reason for the inclusion of the vast amounts of "Other" in the textbooks except that of the necessity of somehow expanding the series to conform to the custom of bulk.

The custom of having separate series for literature and composition, *prepared by separate editors and authors,* has, we are convinced, resulted in the largest remaining fault we have found with the textbooks, namely, their neglect of literature as the primary source and center for all activities in conversing, discussing, speaking, listening, thinking, and writing. A few textbook authors have tried valiantly to introduce some use of literature, particularly poetry, into their volumes. They have been unsuccessful simply because the main body of literature is elsewhere — in another book, indeed, we may say, almost literally in another course, although, in practice, composition and literature are in the same course. Such chapters on literature as are included in occasional series appear alien, out of place, and even odd; it has been necessary to count them among the varieties of "Other." The problem, we believe, is not one of incorporating bits and pieces of literary study into the grammar and composition books, but one of incorporating writing and closely related activities into the literature books.

Our recommendations, therefore, are chiefly two:

(1) The abandonment of the four-volume series, and the substitution for this series of a single handbook of approximately two hundred pages treating grammar, usage, mechanics, and the principles of rhetoric and composition; this single volume to be used *as needed* throughout the four years of the senior high school.
(2) The incorporation of speaking and writing activities (necessarily involving also listening and thinking) into the anthologies of literature.

We are convinced that four successive volumes on English grammar and composition are no more needed for the high school years than four successive dictionaries are. We see no virtue in confronting students in each year with "new" sentences for practice in sentence analysis, punctuation, etc., if one set adequately illustrates all the possibilities. And certainly we see no virtue in authors' attempts to vary slightly, from year to year, the wording of definitions, explanations, and other sorts of information; the best possible wording, once presented, we believe, is serviceable for four years. We are pleased to note a number of signs that authors, publishers, and teachers are tending to move away from the four-volume series, as we recommend:

1. Scott, Foresman's *Guide to Modern English* presents a single volume for the "Upper Years."
2. Harcourt, Brace's fourth volume of *English Grammar and Composition* is identified not as "12" but as "Complete Course," and we believe that it might serve four years.
3. The handbook section of Macmillan's series of separate titles is identical in the last three years except for changes in the exercise sentences.
4. Several publishers offer, besides the four-volume series, a handbook that we believe preferable to the series; examples include Harcourt, Brace's *Handbook of English* (two volumes), American Book Company's *English Handbook,* and Heath's *Grammar in Action.*
5. Many teachers have reported to us that they use no series, but turn to either a college or high school handbook or devise their own instruction and drill.

Appendix A

TABLES FOR LITERATURE ANTHOLOGIES

TABLE I

Percentage of Short Stories and
of Pages Devoted to Short Stories

Publisher	Grade 9		Grade 10		Grade 11		Grade 12		Series	
	SS	pp.	SS	pp.	SS	pp.	SS	pp.	SS	pp.
HltD	57	68	54	66	78	87	68	71	66	74
Lipp	47	70	22	33	29	56	8	19	27	46
Hlt	32	51	27	46	18	43	21	42	24	45
PH	28	37	32	45	26	37	29	50	29	42
Ldw	14	29	14	25	18	49	11	14	14	32
HB2	21	35	20	28	12	28	19	34	18	31
McM	24	43	9	18	9	36	7	16	11	28
SF	16	28	21	21	18	39	5	18	14	26
Gn	20	33	22	24	9	32	4	13	12	26
Sgr	22	29	22	28	12	28	6	16	13	25
HBO	18	26	19	24	12	33	5	12	11	24
ABC	15	28	17	30	6	17	6	18	10	23
HBM	19	25	22	25	9	26	5	11	11	22
HB49	16	30	19	24	8	22	4	8	10	21
RM	—	—	23	22	9	26	2	8	8	20
HB-12a	—	—	—	—	—	—	11	24	—	—
Sgr-12a	—	—	—	—	—	—	20	29	—	—
Glb	—	—	—	—	11	24	—	—	—	—
HBL	—	—	20	28	16	26	—	—	—	—
Irq	21	27	15	25	—	—	—	—	—	—
MH	13	21	—	—	—	—	—	—	—	—
SF2	33	42	—	—	—	—	—	—	—	—
HM	14	24	—	—	—	—	—	—	—	—
Hth	21	31	—	—	—	—	—	—	—	—
Scb	14	29	—	—	—	—	—	—	—	—
RP	37	62	—	—	—	—	—	—	—	—
Averages	22	35	22	31	15	36	10	25	16	32

TABLE II

Short Stories Most Frequently Anthologized, and Their Assignment by Grade (Number of Appearances)

Author and Short Story	9	10	11	12	Total
Benét, "The Devil and Daniel Webster"	1	—	10	—	11
Stuart, "The Split Cherry Tree"	5	—	5	—	10
Poe, "The Tell-tale Heart"	3	1	6	—	10
Daly, "Sixteen"	4	—	5	—	9
O. Henry, "The Ransom of Red Chief"	7	1	1	—	9
Saki, "The Open Window"	5	1	—	3	9
Harte, "The Outcasts of Poker Flat"	1	—	8	—	9
Fessier, "That's What Happened to Me"	5	3	—	—	8
Irving, "The Devil and Tom Walker"	—	—	8	—	8
Lagerlöf, "The Silver Mine"	5	2	—	1	8
Galsworthy, "Quality"	1	2	—	4	7
Hawthorne, "Dr. Heidegger's Experiment"	—	1	6	—	7
London, "To Build a Fire"	1	2	4	—	7
Twain, "The Jumping Frog . . ."	4	—	3	—	7
Thurber, "The Secret Life of Walter Mitty"	—	2	4	1	7
Edmonds, "Judge"	5	1	—	—	6
Garland, "Under the Lion's Paw"	—	1	5	—	6
O. Henry, "The Gift of the Magi"	3	1	2	—	6
Maupassant, "The Necklace"	5	1	—	—	6
Brubaker, "The Milk Pitcher"	2	3	—	—	5
Freeman, "The Revolt of Mother"	—	1	4	—	5
Callaghan, "The Snob"	1	2	1	1	5
Conrad, "The Lagoon"	—	—	—	5	5
Connell, "The Most Dangerous Game"	2	2	1	—	5
Faulkner, "Two Soldiers"	—	—	5	—	5
Poe, "The Pit and the Pendulum"	1	—	4	—	5
Saroyan, "Locomotive 38 . . ."	1	1	3	—	5
Steinbeck, "The Leader of the People"	1	—	4	—	5
Stevenson, "Markheim"	—	—	—	5	5

TABLE III

Authors of Short Stories Most Frequently
Anthologized (ten or more appearances)

Author	Short Stories	Appearances
O. Henry	11	33
Poe	6	28
Benét, S. V.	9	26
Stuart, Jesse	13	25
Saroyan	11	20
Saki	7	18
Hawthorne	7	17
London	8	17
West, Jessamyn	11	17
Harte	5	15
Irving	6	14
Thurber	5	14
Mansfield	7	13
Steinbeck	6	13
Lagerlöf	3	12
Maugham	7	12
Twain	3	12
Buck, Pearl	7	11
Jackson, Margaret	8	11
Kipling	6	11
Daly, Maureen	2	10
Fisher, Dorothy C.	6	10
Maupassant	5	10
Schramm, Wilbur	6	10

TABLE IV

Percentage of Pages Devoted to the Novel
by the Anthologies in Group I

Volume	Percentage	Title of novel included
Glb-11	13*	The Voice of Bugle Ann
HB49-10	17	Silas Marner
HBM-9	27	Great Expectations
HBM-10	21	Silas Marner
HBO-9	26	Great Expectations
HBO-10	18	Silas Marner
Hth-9	17*	Winter Thunder
HM-9	13	Johnny Tremaine
Irq-9	43	Ivanhoe
Irq-10	22	Silas Marner
Lipp-10	18*	The Ox-Bow Incident
McM-9	20*	Flamingo Feather
McM-10	14*	The Call of the Wild
McM-11	13*	The Voice of Bugle Ann
McM-12	15*	Dr. Jekyll and Mr. Hyde
SF-9	31*	David Copperfield
SF-10	27*	Silas Marner
SF2-9	20	San Sebastian
Sgr-9	15*	Light in the Forest
Sgr-10	19	Swiftwater

* Includes the pages given to short excerpts of one or more novels in addition to the one listed in the right-hand column. The number of excerpts and the titles of the novels from which they are taken will be found in Tables VIII and X.

TABLE V

Number of Lines* Omitted from Selected Passages in *Silas Marner*

Passage	Irq-10	Number of lines omitted			HBO-10	Number of lines in complete text
		SF-10	HB49-10	HBM-10		
Chap. I, first 14 paragraphs (introduction of Marner, description of Raveloe, superstitious nature of villagers)	13	25	0	0	41.5	159
Chap. IV, last 5 paragraphs (the theft of Marner's gold)	5	1	0	0	0	76
Chap. VI, first half (conversation at the Rainbow)	0	14.5	0	0	105	171
Chap. VII, last half (arrangements to investigate the theft)	0	0	0	0	8	77
Chap. XII, last half (Marner finds Eppie on his hearth)	0	0	0	0	5	101
Chap. XVIII, entire (discovery of the gold; Godfrey's confession)	0	0	0	0	1	135
Total	18	40.5	0	0	160.5	719

* Line count has been adjusted to make comparisons possible.

TABLE VI

Excerpts from Novels in the Anthologies of Group III

Anthology	Number of excerpts	Pages given to excerpts	Range in length of excerpts (pages)
ABC-9	1	4	4
ABC-11	3	10	2-5
ABC-12	4	22	3-7
Gn-10	3	19	5-8
Gn-11	3	18	6
Gn-12	1	13	13
HB49-9	2	16	7-9
HB49-11	2	12	6
HB49-12	3	18	5-13
HBM-11	2	13	6-7
HBM-12	1	5	5
HBO-11	2	12	6
HBO-12	1	5	5
HBL-10	2	24	9-15
HBL-11	6	49	3-25
HB2-10	5	52	6-15
HB2-11	4	38	6-16
Hlt-9	3	23	5-12
Hlt-10	2	8	4
Hlt-11	4	25	2-10
Hlt-12	1	3	3
Ldw-9	3	51	15-20
Ldw-11	2	14	7
Ldw-12	5	35	4-14
Lipp-11	2	27	13-14
Lipp-12	2	24	12
PH-10	1	7	7
RM-10	1	8	8

TABLE VI (*continued*)

Anthology	Number of excerpts	Pages given to excerpts	Range in length of excerpts (pages)
RM-11	4	29	4-9
RM-12	5	35	4-12
RP-9	3	36	7-17
SF-11	2	26	12-14
SF-12	7	51	5-10
Scb-9	2	18	5-13
Sgr-11	3	62	13-27
Sgr-12a	3	52	6-36

TABLE VII

Excerpts from Novels in the Anthologies of Group I

Anthology	Number of excerpts	Pages given to excerpts	Range in length of excerpts (pages)
Glb-11	3	21	7
Hth-9	6	78	5-21
Lipp-10	1	10	10
McM-9	2	18	8-10
McM-10	3	29	9-10
McM-11	4	58	13-18
McM-12	5	54	6-19
SF-9	2	14	4-10
SF-10	2	12	5-7
Sgr-9	1	12	12

TABLE VIII

Attention Given to the Novel in All Anthologies Examined

Grade Level	Percentage of selections	Percentage of pages
Ninth-grade volumes	2.2	12.6
Tenth-grade volumes	2.0	10.6
Eleventh-grade volumes	1.7	4.5
Twelfth-grade volumes	2.2	5.2
All volumes	2.0	8.3

TABLE IX

Excerpts of Novels Included in the Anthologies
(*Number of pages in parentheses*)

Annixter, *Swiftwater* SF-10 (7)

Azuela, *The Under Dogs* Ldw-11 (7)

Barker, *The Plague* ABC-12 (7)

Bennett, *The Old Wives' Tale* Ldw-12 (2)

Bentley, *Inheritance* McM-12 (19)

Bentley, *The Power and the Glory* SF-12 (10)

Brontë, *Wuthering Heights* RM-12 (6)

Butler, *Erewhon* RM-12 (4)

Carlisle, *We Begin* SF-11 (5); HBL-11 (4)

Chase, *Mary Peters* McM-11 (13)

Chute, *The Innocent Wayfaring* SF-12 (5)

Chute, *The Wonderful Winter* Hth-9 (12)

Conrad, *Lord Jim* Ldw-12 (2)

Cooper, *The Deerslayer* Glb-11 (7)

Cooper, *Last of the Mohicans* RM-11 (7)

Crane, *Red Badge of Courage* RM-11 (4)

Daringer, *Debbie of the Green Gate* McM-9 (10)

Defoe, *Robinson Crusoe* Gn-12 (8); Ldw-12 (7)

Dickens, *David Copperfield* Gn-12 (13); McM-12 (12)

Dickens, *Hard Times* RM-12 (5)

Dickens, *Nicholas Nickleby* ABC-12 (6); McM-10 (9)

Dickens, *Pickwick Papers* HB49-12 (5); HBO-12 (5)

Dickens, *Tale of Two Cities* Hlt-10 (8); RM-10 (7)

Dos Passos, *U.S.A.* ABC-11 (4); HB2-11 (6)

Edmonds, *Drums Along the Mohawk* HBL-10 (15)

Eliot, *Middlemarch* RM-12 (8)

Eliot, *Mill on the Floss* SF-12 (9)

Felsen, *Hot Rod* HB2-10 (15)

Ferber, *Cimarron* HB2-11 (6); HBL-11 (6)

Forbes, *A Mirror for Witches* Hlt-11 (4)

TABLE IX (*continued*)

Galsworthy, *The Forsyte Saga* Ldw-12 (2); SF-12 (4)

Gébler, *The Plymouth Adventure* Hlt-11 (14)

Goldsmith, *The Vicar of Wakefield* Ldw-12 (5)

Goudge, *Towers in the Mist* SF-12 (7)

Hardy, *The Mayor of Casterbridge* SF-12 (8)

Hardy, *Tess of the Durbervilles* McM-12 (7)

Harte, *Mliss* Hlt-11 (19)

Hawthorne, *The House of the Seven Gables* RM-11 (8); McM-
    11 (13)

Hémon, *Maria Chapdelaine* Ldw-11 (8)

Hugo, *Les Miserables* Ldw-9 (20); HBO-10 (11)

Johnston, *To Have and To Hold* SF-11 (8)

Komroff, *Coronet* Sgr-12a (36)

Lagerlöf, *Emperor of Portugallia* Hlt-12 (3); ABC-12 (6)

Lewis, E., *Young Fu of the Upper Yangtze* McM-9 (8); Ldw-9
    (14)

Lewis, S., *Arrowsmith* HB2-11 (16); HBL-11 (25)

Lewis, S., *Main Street* Gn-11 (6)

Lincoln, *Mary 'Gusta* Ldw-9 (10)

Maugham, *Of Human Bondage* McM-12 (10)

Melville, *Moby Dick* Gn-11 (6); HB2-11 (10); HBO-11 (6);
    Sgr-11 (27); Hlt-11 (5); Ldw-9 (16); HB2-10 (9); HBM-11
    (6); Glb-11 (7)

Melville, *Redburn* Gn-10 (5)

Melville, *Typee* RM-11 (9)

Meredith, *The Ordeal of Richard Feverel* McM-12 (6)

Nordhoff, *The Pearl Lagoon* Hlt-9 (12)

Nordhoff and Hall, *Men Against the Sea* Gn-10 (8)

Norris, *The Octopus* HB49-11 (6); HBM-11 (6)

Orwell, *Down and Out in Paris and London* HBM-12 (8)

Page, *The Tree of Liberty* Sgr-11 (13); HBL-11 (7)

Paton, *Cry, the Beloved Country* Sgr-12a (10)

TABLE IX (*continued*)

Rawlings, *The Yearling* Scb-9 (13); SF-10 (5)

Rölvaag, *Giants in the Earth* Scb-9 (5); HBO-11 (6); Lipp-10 (10); Hlt-11 (10); Lipp-11 (14); Gn-11 (5); HB49-11 (6)

Saroyan, *The Human Comedy* Sgr-9 (12)

Sinclair, *The Jungle* HBL-11 (4)

Steinbeck, *Grapes of Wrath* ABC-11 (2); Lipp-11 (3); ABC-9 (4)

Stewart, *Storm* Lipp-12 (12)

Struther, *Mrs. Miniver* ABC-12 (3)

Tarkington, *Penrod* McM-10 (10)

Tarkington, *Seventeen* Hlt-9 (5)

Thackeray, *Vanity Fair* RM-12 (12); SF-12 (8); HB49-12 (13)

Tolstoi, *War and Peace* Lipp-12 (12)

Twain, *Huckleberry Finn* Gn-11 (6); Sgr-11 (22); Hlt-9 (6); SF-11 (12); McM-11 (14)

Twain, *Tom Sawyer* Glb-11 (7); Sgr-12a (6)

Ullman, *Banner in the Sky* SF-9 (4)

Wells, *Kipps* Ldw-12 (1)

West, *Cress Delahanty* Ph-10 (7); HBO-9 (13); HBO-10 (11); HM-9 (12)

Wolfe, *Of Time and the River* HB2-12 (3)

Wolfe, *You Can't Go Home Again* Hlt-11 (2); HBL-11 (3)

Wouk, *The Caine Mutiny* SF-9 (10)

TABLE X

Percentage of Selections Altered in Certain Anthologies

Volume	Per Cent Excerpts, etc.	Volume	Per Cent Excerpts, etc.
HB2-10	48.3	PH-10	26.0
Scb-9	40.7	HBO-10	25.0
ABC-10	39.0	Glb-11	24.8
SF-10	37.1	Sgr-9	24.7
Lipp-10	35.0	RP-9	24.7
HB2-11	34.5	Ldw-9	24.0
ABC-9	33.3	Sgr-11	23.6
Gn-10	33.0	HBO-11	22.3
HBL-10	31.2	Sgr-12	21.8
Sgr-10	30.9	PH-9	21.4
SF-9	29.0	Lipp-11	21.1
SF2-9	28.8	Hlt-10	20.9
Irq-10	28.7	HB-12a	20.6
Hth-9	27.9	RM-11	20.4
Gn-9	27.3	ABC-11	20.4
HB49-9	26.9	Hlt-12	20.3
HB2-9	26.5		

TABLE XI

Percentage of Selections Altered in All Anthologies Examined

Grade Level	Per Cent Excerpts, etc.
Ninth	22.7
Tenth	26.1
Eleventh	19.7
Twelfth	17.3
All Anthologies	20.6

TABLE XII

Percentage of Pages Devoted to Miscellaneous Nonfiction

Publisher	Ninth Grade	Tenth Grade	Eleventh Grade	Twelfth Grade	Total
ABC	49.7	32.0	37.8	17.9	33.9
HB2	34.5	34.1	30.4	28.8	31.9
Gn	47.1	48.2	14.2	10.8	29.5
PH	28.6	34.5	25.6	16.7	26.2
HltD	30.5	33.8	23.4	29.4	25.7
HB49	44.5	24.3	24.5	10.1	24.9
HBM	24.0	18.4	33.2	16.3	23.0
Lipp	10.3	35.9	22.7	17.7	21.5
Ldw	28.1	23.2	17.9	15.2	21.4
RM	—	33.5	22.9	8.0	21.1
HBO	20.3	17.8	30.3	16.0	20.8
Hlt	14.3	22.2	22.0	22.8	20.6
Sgr	25.5	19.3	23.6	12.2	20.2
SF	19.9	18.0	26.1	10.1	18.6
McM	7.6	17.7	16.0	8.5	12.4
Sgr-12a	—	—	—	19.1	—
HB-12a	—	—	—	11.5	—
Glb-11	—	—	36.9	—	—
HBL	—	43.9	25.2	—	—
Scb-9	51.9	—	—	—	—
MH-9	47.7	—	—	—	—
HM-9	36.9	—	—	—	—
Hth	29.3	—	—	—	—
RP-9	20.6	—	—	—	—
SF2-9	17.6	—	—	—	—
Irq	1.5	21.0	—	—	—

TABLE XIII

Percentage of Pages Devoted to the Essay

Series or Publisher	Ninth Grade	Tenth Grade	Eleventh Grade	Twelfth Grade	Total
RM	—	8.8	3.4	12.3	7.6
McM	0.7	7.6	10.8	7.0	6.6
Ldw	1.8	8.5	4.4	10.0	6.1
PH	6.1	0.0	11.9	5.7	5.9
Gn	0.0	0.0	5.6	10.7	4.2
Sgr	4.1	3.1	3.0	6.8	4.1
HB49	0.6	0.7	4.7	6.7	3.3
HBO	2.5	5.3	1.0	4.0	3.3
HBM	1.7	2.2	1.2	4.3	2.3
ABC	0.0	1.6	1.4	4.8	2.0
SF	0.4	0.0	1.3	5.9	1.8
Hlt	2.4	1.0	2.0	0.6	1.4
HB2	0.5	0.0	0.9	2.6	1.0
Lipp	0.0	1.0	0.0	1.0	0.4
HltD	0.0	0.0	0.0	0.0	0.0
HB-12a	—	—	—	1.3	—
Sgr-12a	—	—	—	0.9	—
HBL	—	0.9	1.4	—	—
Glb-11	—	—	0.0	—	—
MH	8.9	—	—	—	—
SF2	1.2	—	—	—	—
Irq	1.1	0.0	—	—	—
Scb	0.9	—	—	—	—
Hth	0.0	—	—	—	—
HM	0.0	—	—	—	—
RP	0.0	—	—	—	—
Averages	1.7	2.4	2.9	4.5	2.8

TABLE XIV

Distribution of Miscellaneous Nonfiction (MNF) in the Anthologies

	Ninth Grade	Tenth Grade	Eleventh Grade	Twelfth Grade	Total
Average number of MNF selections per volume	27	23	34	19	25
Percentage of MNF selections in all volumes	24.3	26.2	21.0	11.1	19.3
Average number of pages given to MNF selections per volume	156	155	150	101	141
Percentage of pages given to MNF selections in all volumes	28.6	27.4	25.4	16.5	24.4

TABLE XV

Percentage of MNF Selections in Certain Anthologies

Ninth Grade volume	per cent	Tenth Grade volume	per cent	Eleventh Grade volume	per cent	Twelfth Grade volume	per cent
HltD-9	40.9	Gn-10	51.6	Glb-11	35.2	HltD-12	30.8
Scb-9	40.8	HltD-10	44.2	HB2-11	28.0	HB2-12	25.7
Gn-9	39.1	HB2-10	35.6	ABC-11	26.2	PH-12	16.7
ABC-9	39.0	ABC-10	34.6	SF-11	25.6	Hlt-12	15.2
Hlt-9	13.2	HBM-10	16.3	Hlt-11	18.6	Gn-12	6.5
HBO-9	12.4	Sgr-10	14.7	Sgr-11	14.6	Sgr-12	6.1
Lipp-9	12.1	McM-10	13.5	Ldw-11	11.8	SF-12	5.9
McM-9	8.7	RM-10	12.2	McM-11	11.2	McM-12	5.7
Irq-9	2.4	Ldw-10	11.9	Gn-11	10.6	RM-12	5.4

TABLE XVI

Plays Included in the Anthologies
(*Number of pages in parentheses*)

Abney, *The Beggar*   Ldw-12 (4), radio dramatization of Chekhov's story.

Anderson, *Valley Forge*   Sgr-11 (12), an excerpt.

Ballard and Franklin, *Young America*   McM-9 (10).

Barrie, *The Old Lady Shows Her Medals*   HB49-12 (16); ABC-12 (19); HBM-12 (18); HBO-12 (21).

Barrie, *The Will*   HBM-10 (16).

Battle, *The Outer Limit*   Sgr-10 (24), television adaptation of a short story by Doar.

Benét, *Listen to the People*   HBL-11 (11); SF-11 (8), radio play.

Bennett and Knoblock, *Milestones*   Hlt-12 (45).

Besier, *The Barretts of Wimpole Street*   HBM-12 (56).

Bruckner, *Out of Control*   SF2-9 (16), television play.

Buck, *The Rock*   HB49-9 (4), radio play.

Buck, *Will This Earth Hold?*   HB49-11 (8), radio play.

Capek, *R.U.R.*   Sgr-12a (64).

Chekhov, *The Boor*   ABC-12 (9).

Clarke, *The Ghost Patrol*   HBM-11 (23), television adaptation of a short story by S. Lewis.

Cohan, *Pigeons and People*   Hlt-11 (24).

Corwin, *Ann Rutledge*   HB2-10 (10), radio play.

Corwin, *The Oracle of Philadelphi*   Lipp-9 (8), radio play.

Crutchfield, *A Shipment of Mute Fate*   HB2-9 (13); SF2-9 (16), radio adaptation of Storm's play.

Dillon and Leary, *The Doctor from Dunmore*   PH-12 (14).

Drinkwater, *Bird in Hand*   McM-10 (40).

Duffield, *The Lottery*   HB2-10 (15), dramatization of Jackson's story.

Dunsany, *A Night at an Inn*   RM-10 (8); McM-12 (7).

TABLE XVI (*continued*)

Eastman, *Bread*   HB49-9 (9).

Ferber, *The Eldest*   HBL-10 (10).

Field, *Wisdom Teeth*   Ldw-10 (14).

Fletcher, *The Hitch-hiker*   Sgr-10 (12), radio play.

Fletcher, *Sorry, Wrong Number*   HM-9 (10); ABC-9 (10); RM-11 (9), radio play.

Foote, *The Dancers*   Hth-9 (18); Hlt-10 (18); HBO-9 (16), television play.

Fox, Stephen, *Never Come Monday*   HBO-9 (17), radio adaptation of E. Knight's story.

Fox, Dixon, and Schlesinger, *Elizabeth Blackwell — Pioneer Woman Doctor*   SF-9 (7), radio play.

Fry, *The Boy with a Cart*   SF-12 (21).

Galbraith, *The Brink of Silence*   HB49-9 (5); McM-9 (5).

Gale, *The Neighbors*   HB49-10 (17); SF-9 (14); Irq-10 (19).

Gallico, *The Snow Goose*   HB49-11 (6); HBM-11 (7), radio play.

Galsworthy, *The Skin Game*   McM-12 (45).

Galsworthy, *Strife*   HB49-12 (39).

Geiger, *One Special for Doc*   HB49-10 (8); HB2-9 (6), radio play.

Gilsdorf, *The Ghost of Benjamin Sweet*   Hlt-9 (14); PH-10 (14), radio play.

Glaspell, *Trifles*   ABC-10 (10); Ldw-10 (17); HB2-12 (11); Sgr-11 (11).

Goldsmith, *She Stoops to Conquer*   SF-12 (40).

Gordon, *Years Ago*   Hlt-9 (58).

Gregory, *The Rising of the Moon*   ABC-10 (7); Ldw-12 (9).

Gregory, *Spreading the News*   Ldw-10 (15).

Gregory, *The Workhouse Ward*   McM-12 (6).

Hackett, *A Christmas Carol*   Hth-9 (12), radio adaptation of Dickens's tale.

TABLE XVI (continued)

Hackett, *Rip Van Winkle*   Gn-11 (14), radio adaptation of Irving's tale.

Hall and Middlemass, *The Valiant*   HB49-9 (17); HBM-9 (18); HBO-9 (21); GBC-11 (30); Irq-10 (21).

Helburn, *Enter the Hero*   ABC-9 (11).

Housman, *Victoria Regina*   Gn-12 (8); SF-12 (5), both are excerpts.

Ibsen, *A Doll's House*   Lipp-12 (64).

Kelly, *Finders-Keepers*   Hlt-11 (18); Irq-9 (17); McM-11 (22).

Keppler, *Sixteen*   SF-11 (6), radio adaptation of Daly's story.

Kingsley, *The Patriots*   ABC-11 (5), an excerpt.

Koch, *Invasion from Mars*   SF2-9 (17), radio play.

Lampell, *The Lonesome Train*   HBL-10 (9), radio play.

Law, *The Indomitable Blacksmith*   Hth-9 (11); HB2-10 (13), television play.

Lindsay and Crouse, *Life with Father*   HB2-10 (72), dramatization of Day's book.

Ludwig, "*Interruptions, Interruptions*"   PH-10 (4); Sgr-10 (5), excerpts from motion picture script.

McCarty and McCarty, *Three's a Crowd*   RP-9 (14); Sgr-9 (12).

MacLeish, *The Admiral*   Lipp-11 (10), radio play.

MacLeish, *Ripe Strawberries and Gooseberries and Sweet Single Roses*   Lipp-11 (10), radio play.

McMahon, *The Leader of the People*   HB2-9 (14), dramatization of Steinbeck's story.

Martens, *Blue Beads*   HB2-10 (12).

Medcraft, *The First Dress-Suit*   PH-11 (12).

Miller, Arthur, *Grandpa and the Statue*   SF-9 (9), radio play.

Miller, Arthur, *The Pussycat and the Expert Plumber Who Was a Man*   Sgr-12a (21), radio play.

Miller, Helen, *Thanksgiving à la Carte*   Hth-9 (12).

TABLE XVI (continued)

Mindel, *Benjamin Franklin, American* PH-11 (12), radio play.

Molière, *The Physician in Spite of Himself* Ldw-12 (25).

Monkhouse, *The Grand Cham's Diamond* McM-10 (13).

Monroe, *Coals to Newcastle* Irq-9 (11), radio play.

Mosel, *The Five Dollar Bill* PH-10 (25), television play.

Mosel, *Jinxed* PH-9 (13).

National Broadcasting Company, *Inside Washington* Irq-9 (9), television script.

Niggli, *Sunday Costs Five Pesos* HBM-10 (13).

Niggli, *This Bull Ate Nutmeg* Gn-9 (14).

Niggli, *Tooth or Shave* PH-12 (22).

Nurnberg, *American Names* Gn-9 (3), radio play.

O'Casey, *The End of the Beginning* HB2-12 (15).

Oller and Dawley, *The Apple of Discord* SF-9 (6), dramatization of a Greek myth.

O'Neill, *Ile* HB2-11 (13); SF-11 (10).

O'Neill, *In the Zone* Hlt-10 (14); PH-9 (15); HBO-11 (13); Sgr-11 (12).

O'Neill, *Where the Cross Is Made* HB49-11 (12); Gn-11 (17); ABC-9 (12); Ldw-11 (15).

Orr and Denham, *The Sire de Maletroit's Door* HBM-9 (19), dramatization of Stevenson's story.

Osborn, *Point of No Return* Hlt-11 (50), dramatization of Marquand's novel.

Parker, *The Monkey's Paw* SF-9 (12), dramatization of Jacobs's story.

Pharis, *The Courting of Marie Jenvrin* HBM-9 (20).

Pillot, *Two Crooks and a Lady* Sgr-9 (14).

Quintero, *A Sunny Morning* ABC-12 (7); MH-9 (8).

Rattigan, *The Winslow Boy* Hlt-10 (58); Sgr-12 (56).

Reely and Pettis, *Behold America* RM-11 (6), occasional pastiche based on Whitman's poetry.

TABLE XVI (*continued*)

Reines, *The Man Who Taught Lincoln* Scb-9 (19), radio play.

Richmond, *A Career for Ralph* HB2-10 (6).

Rodgers and Hammerstein, *The King and I* HBO-10 (50); SF-10 (5), an excerpt.

Rodgers and Hammerstein, *Oklahoma* SF-11 (10), an excerpt.

Roos and Mabley, *Borderline of Fear* SF2-9 (12), television play.

Rose, *An Almanac of Liberty* PH-11 (24), television adaptation of a book by Douglas.

Rowan, *Footfalls* Sgr-11 (10), television adaptation of story by Steele.

Saroyan, *The Man with the Heart in the Highlands* ABC-11 (9).

Saroyan, *The Oyster and the Pearl* SF-11 (10), television play.

Saroyan, *The People with Light Coming Out of Them* Sgr-9 (11), radio play.

Schulberg, *The Pharmacist's Mate* HM-9 (21); HB2-9 (24); SF-11 (19), television play.

Seiler, *How To Propose* GBC-11 (26).

Shakespeare, *As You Like It* Ldw-10 (84).

Shakespeare, *Julius Caesar* HB49-10 (62); HBM-10 (73); HBO-10 (82); Gn-10 (83); ABC-10 (50); Ldw-9 (84); RM-10 (60); HBL-10 (65); SF-10 (90); Sgr-10 (90); Irq-10 (36); McM-10 (72).

Shakespeare, *Macbeth* HB49-12 (59); HBM-12 (63); HBO-12 (70); Hlt-12 (69); Gn-12 (98); ABC-12 (62); Ldw-12 (65); RM-12 (56); SF-12 (48); Sgr-12 (77); McM-12 (60).

Shakespeare, *A Midsummer Night's Dream* McM-9 (70); SF-9 (8), an abridged excerpt.

Shakespeare, *The Taming of the Shrew* Scb-9 (9), an excerpt.

Shaw, David, *Zone of Quiet* HB2-11 (12), television adaptation of Lardner's story.

Shaw, G. B., *Caesar and Cleopatra* HB2-12 (68).

TABLE XVI (*continued*)

Shaw, G. B., *The Devil's Disciple*   SF-12 (14), an excerpt.

Shaw, G. B., *Man and Superman*   Sgr-12 (7), an excerpt.

Shaw, G. B., *Pygmalion*   HBO-12 (51).

Shaw, G. B., *Saint Joan*   Hlt-12 (13), an excerpt.

Sheridan, *The Rivals*   McM-12 (7), an excerpt.

Sherriff, *Journey's End*   HB2-12 (63).

Sherriff, *The Kite*   Irq-9 (21), motion picture adaptation of Maugham's story.

Sherwood, *Abe Lincoln in Illinois*   HBL-11 (53); HB2-11 (60); RM-11 (4), an excerpt.

Simon, *Trouble in Tunnel Nine*   HBM-9 (10).

Stirling, *Ins and Outs*   HB2-9 (12), adapted from the play.

Strong, *The Drums of Oude*   HB49-9 (13).

Strong and Osbourne, *The Little Father of the Wilderness*   Ldw-10 (17).

Synge, *Riders to the Sea*   HB49-12 (7); HBM-12 (8); HBO-12 (8); MH-9 (8); McM-12 (8).

Tallman, *The Gentleman from Paris*   McM-11 (10), radio play.

Tallman, *The Man Who Liked Dickens*   HBO-10 (17), television adaptation of Waugh's story.

Tarkington, *The Trysting Place*   ABC-9 (16); RM-10 (16); SF-10 (14); McM-10 (18).

Tompkins, *Sham*   ABC-10 (10).

Totheroh, *Pearls*   HB49-9 (10).

Totheroh, *The Stolen Prince*   HBO-9 (12).

Upson, *The Master Salesman*   Lipp-9 (9).

Valency, *Feathertop*   Gn-11 (13), television adaptation of Hawthorne's story.

Van Druten, *I Remember Mama*   ABC-11 (42), dramatization of Forbes's book.

Vidal, *Visit to a Small Planet*   PH-9 (21); RM-10 (20), television play.

TABLE XVI (*continued*)

Vollmer, *It's Your Business*   Ldw-9 (13), radio play.

Walker, *The Medicine Show*   ABC-10 (5); Ldw-10 (10).

Wilde, Oscar, *The Importance of Being Earnest*   RM-12 (40).

Wilde, Percival, *The Finger of God*   ABC-9 (7), adapted from the play.

Wilde, Percival, *The Hour of Truth*   Gn-10 (13).

Wilder, *The Happy Journey to Trenton and Camden*   HM-9 (10); PH-11 (11); HBL-10 (10); SF-11 (8); Sgr-9 (12); Irq-9 (11).

Wilder, *Our Town*   HB49-11 (34); HBM-11 (38); HBO-11 (38); HBL-11 (44); Gn-11 (49).

Williams, *The Corn Is Green*   Sgr-12 (34).

Wishengrad, *Juliet in Pigtails*   Hth-9 (11), radio play.

Wolff, *Where But in America?*   McM-11 (8).

TABLE XVII

Percentage of Plays and of Total Pages Devoted to the Drama

Series or Publisher	Grade Ninth		Grade Tenth		Grade Eleventh		Grade Twelfth		Averages for Series	
	Selections	pp.	Selections	pp.	Selections	pp.	Selections	pp.	Selections	pp.
HB2	4	13	7	23	2	15	4	26	4	19
McM	3	15	3	24	2	7	3	22	3	17
Ldw	2	17	7	26	1	3	3	21	3	17
SF	4	9	6	21	4	11	2	25	4	17
HBO	4	10	3	21	1	9	2	24	2	16
HBM	4	11	4	16	1	11	2	25	2	16
Hlt	2	13	2	15	2	14	2	19	2	15
Sgr	5	8	6	21	3	6	2	26	3	15
ABC	3	11	4	15	1	10	1	17	2	13
Ginn	2	4	2	16	2	14	1	18	2	13
HB49	5	10	3	12	2	8	2	16	2	12
RM	—	—	4	19	1	3	1	15	1	11
PH	3	10	4	9	5	13	2	7	3	10
Lipp	3	4	0	0	2	4	1	16	2	6
Hlt	0	0	0	0	0	0	0	0	0	0
SF2	8	13	—	—	—	—	—	—	—	—
HB-12a	—	—	—	—	—	—	5	24	—	—
Sgr-12a	—	—	—	—	—	—	3	15	—	—
Globe	—	—	—	—	2	10	—	—	—	—
HBL	—	—	4	16	2	15	—	—	—	—
Irq	6	11	3	12	—	—	—	—	—	—
MH	2	5	—	—	—	—	—	—	—	—
HM	4	10	—	—	—	—	—	—	—	—
Heath	5	10	—	—	—	—	—	—	—	—
Scb	2	5	—	—	—	—	—	—	—	—
RP	1	3	—	—	—	—	—	—	—	—
All Anthol.	3	9	4	16	2	9	2	19	3	13

TABLE XVIII

Number of Lines* Omitted from *Julius Caesar* in the Anthologies

Scene	Lines in full text	HB49-10	HBM-10	HBO-10	HBL-10	Sgr-10	SF-10	RM-10	McM-10	Ldw-9	ABC-10	Gn-10	Irq-10
I, i	80	7	7	7	7	0	9	0	2	0	0	0	
ii	326	0	3	3	0	6.5	26	0	81	0	0	0	
iii	164	81	76	76	81	0	39	0	73.5	0	0	0	
II, i	334	46	46	46	46	0	67	0	47	0	2.5	0	
ii	129	15	12	12	16	0	5.5	0	8	0	0	0	
iii	16	0	0	0	0	0	2[a]	0	0	0	0	0	
iv	46	46	46	46	46	0	1	0	1[b]	0	0	0	
III, i	297	22	22	22	22	0	8.5	0	15	0	0	0	
ii	276	0	0	0	0	0	0	0	9	0	0	0	
iii	43	43	43	43	43	0	43	0	0	0	0	0	
IV, i	51	0	0	0	0	0	11	0	6	0	0	0	
ii	52	0	0	0	0	0	5.5	0	3	0	0	0	
iii	309	41	41	41	41	0	32	0	32[b]	0	0	0	
V, i	126	101	101	101	101	0	92.5	0	66	0	0	0	
ii	6	6	6	6	6	0	0	0	6	0	0	0	
iii	110	45[c]	4[c]	4[c]	4[c]	0	2	0	8[c]	0	0	0	
iv	32	32	32	32	32	0	32	0	32	0	0	0	
v	81	22[d]	22[d]	22[d]	22[d]	0	1.5[e]	0	2[d]	0	0	0	
Total lines omitted		507	461	461	467	6.5	377.5	0	391.5	0	2.5	0	1360
Percentage of play omitted		20.5	18.6	18.6	18.9	0.26	15.2	0	15.8	0	0.1	0	54.9

(Irq-10 column annotation: Rearranged into two acts and eleven scenes)

* Based upon the standard Globe line-numbering; the numbering of prose lines in the anthologies has been adjusted wherever necessary.

[a] This scene is inserted in III, i.
[b] This and the preceding are combined into one scene.
[c] Called scene ii.
[d] Called scene iii.
[e] Called scene iv.

TABLE XIX

Amount of Poetry in the Anthologies

			Appearances of poems	
Grade	*Number of poets*	*Number of poems*	*Total number*	*Average per volume*
Ninth	315	670	890	44.5
Tenth	271	566	697	41.0
Eleventh	227	854	1675	98.5
Twelfth	241	819	1908	127.2
Totals	1054	2909	5170	74.9
Duplicates	377	393	—	—
Net Totals	677	2516	5170	—

TABLE XX

Long Poems in the Anthologies

Author	Title	Length as printed (No. of lines)	Original length
Homer	*The Odyssey*	1505 (HBO-9); 1020 (HB49-9); 705 (Ldw-9); 681 (Hth-9)[b]	—[a]
Tennyson	*Gareth and Lynette*	1394 (HB49-10; Ldw-10); 1195 (Irq-10); 977 (SF-10); 839 (HBM-10, HBO-10)	1394
Tennyson	*Enoch Arden*	907 (RM-10)	907
Arnold	*Sohrab and Rustum*	892 (ABC-10, McM-10); 55 (RM-12)	892
Tennyson	*Lancelot and Elaine*	726 (HBM-10)	1421
Milton	*Paradise Lost*	676 (RM-12); 255 (Gn-12); 245 (HB49-12, HBM-12, HBO-12); 89 (SF-12); 43 (Hlt-12)	798 [c]
Chaucer	Prologue to *The Canterbury Tales*	663 (SF-12); 508 (HB49-12, HBO-12); 499 (HBM-12); 396 (McM-12); 390 (Sgr-12); 332 (Gn-12); 140 (Hlt-12); 54 (ABC-12); 50 (Ldw-12)	858
Coleridge	*Rime of the Ancient Mariner*	625 (HB49-9, Hth-9, Hlt-9, Irq-9, Lipp-9, PH-9, Sgr-9, Gn-10, SF-10, HB49-12, HBM-12, HBO-12, McM-12)	625
Whittier	*Snow-Bound*	562 (Hlt-11); 468 (HB49-11); 449 (HBM-11, HBO-11); 415 (Gn-11); 389 (ABC-11); 364 (SF-11); 329 (HB2-11); 235 (Sgr-11); 28 (Scb-9); 13 (Hlt-10)	759

TABLE XX (*continued*)

Author	Title	Length as printed (No. of lines)	Original length
Tennyson	The Coming of Arthur	518 (HB49-10, McM-10, RM-12); 268 (HBM-10)	518
Wordsworth	Michael	484 (Gn-12)	484
Tennyson	The Passing of Arthur	469 (McM-10); 319 (HBM-10)	507
Anonymous	Beowulf	432 (HB49-12); 346 (HBM-12); 335 (SF-12); 255 (HBO-12); 157 (Gn-12); 135 (RM-12); 132 (Sgr-12); 128 (ABC-12)b	—a
Goldsmith	The Deserted Village	430 (RM-12); 268 (ABC-12); 264 (HB49-12, HBM-12, HBO-12); 183 (Gn-12)	430
Byron	Prisoner of Chillon	392 (ABC-10, RM-10, Gn-12, HB49-12, HBO-12, Hlt-12, Ldw-12, Lipp-12, SF-12)	392
Keats	The Eve of St. Agnes	378 (HB49-12, HBM-12, HBO-12, RM-12)	378
Chaucer	The Pardoner's Tale	340 (RM-12); 232 (SF-12)b	506
Whitman	Salut au Monde	302 (Lipp-12)	302
Pope	Rape of the Lock	266 (HB49-12, HBM-12, HBO-12)	794

a The line length of *The Odyssey* and *Beowulf* does not furnish a usable basis of comparison as the translations do not correspond line-for-line with the originals.

b Besides the volumes listed, there are several others that contain excerpts or abridgements of *prose* translations: of *The Odyssey*, Irq-9, PH-9, Sgr-9, Hlt-10, and SF-10; of *Beowulf*, Hlt-12 and McM-12; of *The Pardoner's Tale*, ABC-12.

c The length of Book I, from which most of the anthologies listed have drawn their selections.

TABLE XXI

Percentages of Poems and of Space Devoted to Poetry in the Anthologies

Series	Ninth Grade		Tenth Grade		Eleventh Grade		Twelfth Grade		Totals	
	No.	pp.	No.	pp.	No.	pp.	No.	pp.	No.	pp.
RM	—	—	53	15	65	41	79	52	69	37
Gn	39	16	22	9	73	31	79	45	60	26
HB49	47	12	53	17	60	20	80	52	59	25
Singer	46	19	47	10	66	30	81	40	65	25
ABC	42	11	38	12	64	32	75	39	60	24
HBO	61	15	54	14	60	26	77	41	65	24
HBM	54	12	52	18	64	24	77	40	65	23
McM	61	15	62	22	60	20	70	28	64	22
Ldw	53	16	54	17	63	23	66	22	60	19
SF	53	12	37	13	49	18	76	28	58	18
Lipp	38	16	45	12	51	14	69	24	51	17
PH	35	19	31	11	33	13	47	19	37	16
Hlt	47	15	48	15	56	15	59	15	53	15
HB2	58	17	32	6	51	17	48	9	48	12
HltD	—	—	2	0.3	—	—	—	—	0.5	0.1
HBL	—	—	38	7	55	24	—	—	—	—
HB-12a	—	—	—	—	—	—	69	31	—	—
Sgr-12a	—	—	—	—	—	—	62	26	—	—
Globe	—	—	—	—	49	15	—	—	—	—
Irq	59	17	54	20	—	—	—	—	—	—
MH	54	17	—	—	—	—	—	—	—	—
HM	46	15	—	—	—	—	—	—	—	—
Hth	44	13	—	—	—	—	—	—	—	—
Scb	41	10	—	—	—	—	—	—	—	—
RP	40	9	—	—	—	—	—	—	—	—
SF2	31	6	—	—	—	—	—	—	—	—
Total	47	14	43	13	58	23	70	29	57	20

TABLE XXII

Qualitative Ranking of Ninth- and Tenth-Grade
Anthologies According to Poetry Content

NINTH GRADE

Group I		Group II		Group III	
Irq-9	215	Scb-9	164	SF-9	133
Sgr-9	187	Lipp-9	162		
Hth-9	183	HBO-9	159	Gn-9	132
		MH-9	159	RP-9	124
		HBM-9	158	SF2-9	106
		HB49-9	157		
		ABC-9	157		
		Ldw-9	156		
		HB2-9	155		
		PH-9	153		
		Hlt-9	151		
		HM-9	149		
		McM-9	145		

TENTH GRADE

Group I		Group II		Group III	
McM-10	253	HBM-10	199	Lipp-10	148
Irq-10	243	ABC-10	195	Sgr-10	143
Ldw-10	220	Hlt-10	195	HBO-10	133
		SF-10	195		
		Gn-10	180		
		HBL-10	180		
		RM-10	180		
		HB2-10	177		
		PH-10	171		
		HB49-10	168		

TABLE XXIII

Most Important Poets Represented in Eleventh-Grade Anthologies
(number of poems; number of excerpts and abridgements in parentheses)

Author	ABC	Gn	Glb	HB49	HBM	HBO	HBL	HB2	Hlt	Ldw	Lipp	McM	PH	RM	SF	Sgr	Total
Benét, S. V.	2	1	0	3(1)	3(1)	2(1)	0	1(1)	1(1)	0	1(1)	0	1	2(1)	4(2)	3(1)	24
Bryant	3	3	2	3	3	3	2	3	0	4	0	3	2(1)	2(1)	2	2	37
Coffin	2	2	0	1	0	0	4	0	1	0	1	1	1	6	0	1	20
Dickinson	9	7	3	11	11	12	5	4	4	5	0	8	3	3	2	7	94
Eliot	0	2(1)	0	3	1	0	0	0	0	0	0	0	0	0	0	0	6
Emerson	5	7(1)	2	6(1)	6(1)	4(1)	0	3(1)	3	4	1	4	0	2	3	5	56
Freneau	2	2	1	0	0	1	1	0	0	0	0	2	1	1	2	2	15
Frost	7	9	1	7	8	9	3	4	5	3	5	3	1	4	3	7	85
Holmes	4	5	4	4	6	4	2	3	1	8	1	2	0	1	1	2	46
Jeffers	1	0	0	3	0	0	0	0	0	4	0	0	0	0	0	0	6
Lanier	2	3	0	5	3	3	2	2	0	3	0	1	0	3	1	1	30
Lindsay	5	3	0	5	4	4	3	0	3	0	1	3	1	2	1	3	37
Longfellow	7	8(2)	2	6(2)	5(1)	6(2)	4(1)	5(2)	4(1)	6	0	6(2)	2	6(2)	2	5(1)	74
Lowell, A.	2	3	2	8	2	0	0	0	4	0	0	2	0	0	0	0	17
Lowell, J.	2(2)	2	1	3(1)	3(1)	5(3)	2(1)	2(1)	0	1(1)	0	2	0	1(1)	0	2(1)	29
MacLeish	1	1	0	3	2	0	0	0	0	0	0	2	0	1	0	1	11
Masters	2	4	1	6	6	5	0	3	2	0	2	4	1	1	3	3	42
Millay	4	5	1	5	5	6	0	1	1	2	4	3	3	1	1	3	43
Poe	5(1)	4	2	6(1)	5(1)	3	1	4	1	4	0	4	0	2	3	3	47
Robinson	3	5	0	5	5	5	1	3	1	5	4	3	0	2	3	2	46
Sandburg	6(1)	6	2	9(1)	9	8(1)	8	1	4	1	7	5	2	5	4	5(1)	81
Teasdale	4	5	0	6	5	0	1	2	2	2	0	3	0	2	1	0	37
Thoreau	2	0	0	0	0	0	0	0	0	0	1	0	0	0	0	0	4
Timrod	1	3(1)	0	1	1	1	0	1	2	0	0	1	0	2	1	1	15
Whitman	8(1)	10	0	10(2)	11(1)	9(3)	8	4	5	10	0	8(3)	1(1)	7(2)	10(3)	12(1)	115
Whittier	4(1)	4(2)	2	4(2)	3(2)	3(2)	2	1(1)	2(1)	5	0	4(1)	0	1	4(1)	3(1)	42
Wylie	2	2	0	5	4	5	0	0	3	0	1	1	0	2	0	0	25
Number of poems	95	106	25	123	111	102	47	47	52	65	29	75	17	62	56	72	1084

Number of excerpts: 6, 7, 0, 11, 8, 13, 2, 6, 3, 1, 1, 6, 2, 7, 6, 8 ... 87

Percentage of all poetry in volume: 66, 72, 48, 85, 81, 76, 55, 68, 63, 73, 58, 62, 61, 84, 70, 69 ... 65

TABLE XXIV

Most Important Poets Represented in Twelfth-Grade Anthologies
(number of poems; number of excerpts and abridgements in parentheses)

Author	ABC	Gn	HB49	HBM	HBO	HB2	Hlt	Ldw	Lipp	McM	PH	RM	SF	Sgr	Total
Arnold	1	3	1	1	1	0	0	0	0	3	0	4(1)	2	1	18
Auden	0	1	1	2(1)	3	3	0	0	0	0	0	1	3(1)	1	15
(The Bible)	4(2)	2	3(1)	2	2	0	2(1)	0	0	3(2)	0	4	4	2	26
Blake	3	3(1)	1	2	3	0	2	0	0	3	0	2	5	3	27
Browning	5	7	11	9	8	0	2	5	1	3	0	7	9(1)	5(1)	72
Burns	5	7	11	8(1)	8(1)	0	3	5(1)	1	8	0	6	10	6	78
Byron	4(1)	6(4)	6(1)	4(1)	5(1)	0	4(1)	7	3	4(1)	0	4(1)	3(1)	3(2)	53
Chaucer	5(4)	2(1)	4(3)	3(3)	5(3)	0	1(1)	2(2)	3	4(2)	0	3(3)	3(3)	3(3)	33
Coleridge	2	1	2	2	2	0	2	4	0	2	0	3(1)	2	1	23
De la Mare	4	5	6	3	3	0	0	0	0	0	0	2	5	3	30
Donne	2(1)	1	0	1	3	0	0	0	0	0	0	1	0	3	11
Dryden	3	1	1(1)	1(1)	1(1)	0	0	2(1)	0	2	0	3	1(1)	0	13
Eliot	1	0	0	0	2	3	0	0	0	0	0	3	2(2)	2(1)	13
Goldsmith	1(1)	1(1)	2(1)	2(1)	2(1)	0	1	1	0	1	0	1	0	0	9
Gray	2	1	1	1	1	0	1	1	1	1	0	1	1(1)	1(1)	13
Hardy	4	5	4	4	4	0	1	4	1	2	0	3	4	2	38
Herbert	1	0	0	0	0	0	0	6	0	0	0	3	0	0	4
Herrick	2	1	1	1	1	0	2	0	1	2	0	3	2	0	23
Hopkins	0	1	0	2	2	0	1	0	1	0	0	0	3	0	9
Housman	4	3	5	3	3	3	2	0	1	1	0	3	6	4	38

TABLE XXIV (continued)

Author	ABC	Gn	HB49	HBM	HBO	HB2	Hlt	Ldw	Lipp	McM	PH	RM	SF	Sgr	Total
Keats	7(2)	5	8	6	6	0	3	9(1)	2	5	0	6(1)	5	3	65
Kipling	6	1	6	4	4	0	0	3	0	2	0	3	3	3	35
Masefield	5	3	4(1)	3	3	3	0	3	1	3	1	2	5	5	39
Milton	3(2)	3(2)	6(3)	6(3)	6(3)	0	2(1)	2	0	3	0	6(1)	3(1)	3(2)	43
Pope	3(3)	1(1)	2(2)	2(2)	2(2)	0	2	1(1)	0	3(1)	0	3(2)	1(1)	2(2)	22
Shakespeare	10(3)	7	13	12	12	0	2	6	3	8(1)	0	8	7	15(5)	103
Shelley	6	5	7	7	7	0	3(1)	9	2	5	0	7	8(1)	4	68
Sidney	1	2	0	0	0	0	0	0	0	1	0	4	2	0	10
Spender	1	2	3	2	3	3	1	0	1	2	0	2	2	1	23
Spenser	2	3(1)	1(1)	1(1)	2	0	0	0	0	2(1)	0	1(1)	1	1(1)	14
Tennyson	12(2)	10(1)	14(1)	14(1)	14(1)	0	1	5	4(1)	8(1)	0	11	12(2)	9	114
Thomas	1	2	0	0	2	3	0	0	0	0	0	0	1	0	9
Wordsworth	8	11	12	13(1)	12(1)	0	4(1)	9	3	5	0	10	12(3)	7(2)	106
Yeats	5	1	7	4	3	3	1	0	0	2	0	3	4	3	36
Number of poems	123	107	143	125	131	21	40	83	26	87	1	123	129	94	1233
Number of excerpts	21	12	15	16	14	0	6	6	1	9	0	11	17	20	148
Percentage of all poetry in volume	62	69	70	70	73	42	50	87	52	61	2	65	75	78	65

TABLE XXV

Poets Most Frequently Represented in
Ninth-Grade Anthologies

Poet	Number of appearances	Poet	Number of appearances
Frost	24	Millay	12
Benét, S. V.	24	Noyes	12
Nash, Ogden	22	Dickinson	11
Kipling	17	Field, Rachel	11
Coffin	14	Service	11
Sandburg	14	Guiterman	10
(The Bible)	13	Hunt, Leigh	10
Longfellow	12	Whitman	10

TABLE XXVI

Poets Most Frequently Represented in
Tenth-Grade Anthologies

Poet	Number of appearances	Poet	Number of appearances
Frost	19	Teasdale	13
Benét, S. V.	17	Dickinson	12
Tennyson	16	Whitman	12
Nash, Ogden	15	Coffin	10
(The Bible)	14	Kipling	10
Masefield	14	Housman	10
Sandburg	13		

TABLE XXVII

Poets Most Frequently Represented in Eleventh-Grade Anthologies

Poet	Number of appearances	Poet	Number of appearances
Whitman	115	Lanier	30
Dickinson	94	Lowell, J. R.	29
Frost	85	Wylie	25
Sandburg	81	Benét, S. V.	23
Longfellow	74	Coffin	20
Emerson	56	Nash, Ogden	19
Poe	47	Lowell, Amy	17
Holmes	46	Freneau	15
Robinson	46	Timrod	15
Millay	43	Markham	13
Masters	42	Parker, Dorothy	12
Whittier	42	Crane, Stephen	11
Bryant	37	Guiterman	11
Lindsay	37	MacLeish	11
Teasdale	37	Riley, J. W.	11

TABLE XXVIII

Poets Most Frequently Represented
in Twelfth-Grade Anthologies

Poet	Number of appearances	Poet	Number of appearances
Tennyson	114	Spender	23
Wordsworth	106	Pope	22
Shakespeare	103	Brooke	21
Burns	78	Browning, E.	20
Browning, R.	72	Arnold	18
Shelley	68	Lovelace	17
Keats	65	Rossetti, C.	17
Byron	53	Rossetti, D. G.	17
Milton	43	Auden	15
Masefield	39	Chesterton	14
Housman	38	Spenser	14
Hardy	38	Suckling	14
Yeats	36	Dryden	13
Kipling	35	Eliot	13
Chaucer	33	Gibson	13
De la Mare	30	Gray	13
(The Bible)	27	Noyes	13
Blake	27	Donne	11
Coleridge	23	*Beowulf* poet	11
Herrick	23	Sandburg	11
Jonson	23	Sidney	10
Scott	23	Stephens	10
		Stevenson	10

TABLE XXIX

Poets Most Frequently Represented in All Anthologies*

Poet	Number of appearances	Poet	Number of appearances
Whitman	138	Masters	46
Frost	136	Milton	44
Tennyson	135	Yeats	43
Sandburg	118	Hardy	42
Shakespeare	117	Lowell, J. R.	41
Dickinson	114	Bryant	39
Wordsworth	111	De la Mare	39
Burns	94	Lanier	34
Longfellow	91	Coleridge	32
Browning, R.	81	Noyes	31
Shelley	70	Scott	31
Emerson	69	Wylie	30
Keats	68	Blake	28
Benét, S. V.	68	Markham	27
Millay	64	Guiterman	26
Kipling	62	Browning, E.	26
Masefield	62	Herrick	26
(The Bible)	61	Rossetti, C.	25
Byron	61	Jonson	24
Nash, Ogden	59	Eliot	23
Holmes	59	Brooke	22
Poe	59	Arnold	21
Teasdale	57	Stevenson	21
Robinson	57	Lowell, Amy	20
Lindsay	50	Auden	19
Whittier	49	Lovelace	19
Houseman	49	Rossetti, D. G.	18

TABLE XXIX (continued)

Poet	Number of appearances	Poet	Number of appearances
Coffin	46	Stephens	18
Chesterton	17	Crane, S.	13
Timrod	17	Marquis, D.	13
Untermeyer	16	Riley, J. W.	13
Garland	16	Service, R. W.	13
Heine	16	Adams, F. P.	12
Suckling	16	Benét, W. R.	12
Hunt, L.	15	Davies, W. H.	12
MacLeish	15	Donne	12
Miller, J.	15	Field, R.	12
Gray	14	Goldsmith	12
Gibson	14	Carman, B.	11
Gilbert, W. S.	14	McGinley, P.	11
Nathan	14	Sill, E.	11
Parker, D.	14	Colum, P.	10
Sarett, L.	14	Field, E.	10

* Poets appearing in anthologies for only a single year have been omitted from this table.

TABLE XXX

Organization of Ninth-Grade Anthologies (Number of divisions)

Volume	Main Divisions							Subdivisions						
	Topical	Typological	Geographical	Mood	Combination	Miscellaneous	Totals	Topical	Typological	Geographical	Thematic Mood	Combination	Miscellaneous	Totals*
ABC	4	4	1	1	0	1	11	13	3	1	5	0	1	24
Gn	4	0	3	0	0	0	7	3	5	6	0	1	1	17
HB49	1	4	0	0	2	1	8	9	6	0	2	3	1	21
HBM	2	4	1	0	2	1	10	7	7	1	2	0	0	17
HBO	1	5	0	0	0	0	6	5	4	1	3	0	0	13
HB2	5	1	1	0	0	0	7	0	0	0	0	0	0	0
Hth	9	2	0	1	0	0	12	0	0	0	0	0	0	0
Hlt	7	0	1	1	0	0	9	0	0	0	0	0	0	0
HltD	7	0	0	0	0	0	7	0	0	0	0	0	0	0
HM	6	1	0	2	0	1	10	6	3	0	3	0	1	14
Irq	0	7	0	0	0	0	7	7	6	2	1	0	1	17
Ldw	5	0	1	0	0	1	7	5	2	1	1	3	0	12
Lipp	6	0	0	0	0	0	6	0	0	0	0	0	0	0
McM	7	3	0	0	0	0	10	0	0	0	0	0	0	0
PH	6	0	0	0	0	0	6	0	0	0	0	0	0	0
RP	7	0	0	0	0	0	7	0	0	0	0	0	0	0
SF	5	2	2	1	0	0	10	10	3	1	1	0	0	15
SF2	7	1	0	0	0	0	8	0	0	0	0	0	0	0
Scb	4	2	1	1	0	1	9	5	4	1	1	1	0	12
Sgr	4	0	0	0	0	0	4	9	1	1	1	0	1	13
Totals	97	36	11	7	4	6	161	79	44	15	20	8	6	175
Average per volume							8							16

* In some volumes having subdivisions not *all* main divisions are subdivided; in these instances undivided main divisions are also counted in with the subdivisions so that their totals in this column represent what most teachers would probably regard as the actual number of teaching units. Where there is no subdivision, the number of units will of course be the same as the total listed under main divisions.

TABLE XXXI

Organization of Tenth-Grade Anthologies (*Number of divisions*)

Volume	Main Divisions						Subdivisions					
	Top-ical	Typo-logical	Geograph-ical	Thematic	Combi-nation	Totals	Top-ical	Typo-logical	Geograph-ical	Thematic	Mood	Totals*
ABC	7	3	0	0	0	10	18	2	1	0	3	24
Gn	5	1	0	1	0	7						0
HB49	0	7	0	0	0	7	10	7	0	1	1	19
HBM	0	6	0	0	0	6	10	7	0	1	3	21
HBO	0	6	0	0	0	6	12	3	0	1	2	18
HBL	8	0	0	0	0	8						0
HB2	6	0	1	1	0	8						0
Hlt	10	0	0	0	0	10						0
HltD	9	0	0	0	0	9						0
Irq	1	5	0	0	0	6	13	2	0	0	0	15
Ldw	0	8	0	0	0	8						0
Lipp	5	0	1	0	0	6						0
McM	1	6	0	0	0	7	5	8	0	0	1	14
PH	6	0	0	0	0	6						0
RM	9	1	0	0	0	10						0
SF	6	2	0	0	1	9						0
Sgr	0	5	0	0	0	5	12	3	1	0	1	17
Totals	73	50	2	2	1	128	80	32	2	3	11	128
Average per volume						7.5						18

* In some volumes having subdivisions not *all* main divisions are subdivided; in these instances undivided main divisions are also counted in with the subdivisions so that their totals in this column represent what most teachers would probably regard as the actual number of teaching units. Where there is no subdivision, the number of units will of course be the same as the total listed under main divisions.

TABLE XXXII

Organization of Eleventh-Grade Anthologies (Number of divisions)

	Main Divisions					Subdivisions						
Volume	Chrono-logical	Top-ical	Typo-logical	Geograph-ical	Totals	Chrono-logical	Top-ical	Typo-logical	Geograph-ical	Mood	Miscel-laneous	Totals*
ABC	2	1	0	0	3	7	4	7	0	0	0	18
Gn	5	1	0	0	6	0	3	20	0	0	1	24
Glb	5	0	0	0	5	4	0	6	0	0	0	10
HB49	2	0	0	0	2	7	0	4	0	0	0	11
HBM	2	0	0	0	2	7	0	4	0	0	0	11
HBO	2	0	0	0	2	7	0	4	0	0	0	11
HBL	0	3	0	0	3	3	6	0	0	0	0	9
HB2	5	0	0	0	5	2	9	2	0	0	0	13
Hlt	0	7	1	1	9							0
HltD	0	9	0	0	9							0
Ldw	6	0	0	2	8							0
Lipp	0	6	0	0	6							0
McM	2	0	1	0	3	4	0	10	1	0	0	15
PH	0	8	0	0	8							0
RM	1	1	0	1	3	6	5	2	7	1	0	21
SF	1	1	1	0	3	6	5	4	0	1	1	17
Sgr	3	0	0	0	3	5	0	6	0	0	0	11
Totals	36	37	3	4	80	58	32	69	8	2	2	171
Average per volume					4.7							14

* In some volumes having subdivisions not *all* main divisions are subdivided; in these instances undivided main divisions are also counted in with the subdivisions so that their totals in this column represent what most teachers would probably regard as the actual number of teaching units. Where there is no subdivision, the number of units will of course be the same as the total listed under main divisions.

TABLE XXXIII

Organization of Twelfth-Grade Anthologies
(Number of divisions)

Volume	Main Divisions						Subdivisions					
	Chrono-logical	Top-ical	Typo-logical	Geograph-ical	Miscel-laneous	Totals	Chrono-logical	Top-ical	Typo-logical	Geograph-ical	Miscel-laneous	Totals*
ABC	2	0	0	1	0	3	7	1	4	1	0	13
Gn	7	0	0	0	1	8	3	0	29	0	1	33
HB49	8	0	0	0	1	9	10	0	4	0	1	15
HBM	8	0	0	0	1	9	6	0	7	0	0	14
HBO	8	0	0	0	0	8	6	0	7	0	0	13
HB2	0	0	5	0	0	5	0	9	3	0	0	12
Hlt	0	8	0	0	0	8	0	0	0	0	0	0
HltD	0	9	0	0	0	9	0	0	0	0	0	0
Ldw	7	0	0	1	0	8	7	0	11	1	0	19
Lipp	0	6	0	0	0	6	0	0	0	0	0	0
McM	1	0	2	0	0	3	5	0	6	0	0	11
PH	0	0	0	6	0	6	9	0	8	0	0	17
RM	10	0	0	0	0	10	9	0	8	0	0	17
SF	11	0	0	0	0	11	7	0	2	0	0	9
Sgr	8	0	0	0	0	8	7	0	2	0	0	9
Sgr-12a	0	8	0	0	1	8	0	0	0	2	3	0
Totals	70	31	7	8	3	119	60	10	81	2	3	156

Average per volume   7.4   15.6

* In some volumes having subdivisions not *all* main divisions are subdivided; in these instances undivided main divisions are also counted in with the subdivisions so that their totals in this column represent what most teachers would probably regard as the actual number of teaching units. Where there is no subdivision, the number of units will of course be the same as the total listed under main divisions.

TABLE XXXIV

Kinds of Units in the Anthologies

Kinds of Units	Ninth Grade	Tenth Grade	Eleventh Grade	Twelfth Grade
Main Divisions				
Topical	60.3	57.1	46.3	26.0
Typological	22.4	38.9	3.7	5.9
Geographical	6.8	1.6	5.0	6.7
Mood	4.3	0.0	0.0	0.0
Chronological	0.0	0.0	45.0	58.9
Thematic	0.0	1.6	0.0	0.0
Combination	2.5	0.8	0.0	0.0
Miscellaneous	3.7	0.0	0.0	2.5
Subdivisions				
Topical	45.2	62.5	18.7	6.4
Typological	25.1	25.0	40.3	51.9
Geographical	8.6	1.6	4.6	1.3
Mood	11.4	8.6	1.2	0.0
Chronological	0.0	0.0	34.0	38.5
Thematic	1.7	2.3	0.0	0.0
Combination	4.6	0.0	0.0	0.0
Miscellaneous	3.4	0.0	1.2	1.9

TABLE XXXV

Number of Pages Devoted to Editorial Apparatus in the Anthologies

	Preliminaries		Body						Appendices					Editorial machinery		Totals		
	Table of contents	Other	Unit introductions	Unit follow-ups	Selection introductions	Selection follow-ups	Pictures in text	Misc.	Indexes	Glossaries	Biographies	General review	Misc.	pages	per cent	Texts of selections pages	per cent	Total number of pages
	(1)	(2)	(3)	(4)	(5)	(6)	(7)	(8)	(9)	(10)	(11)	(12)	(13)	(14)	(15)	(16)	(17)	(18)
ABC-9	18	6	23	24	27	72	0	4	7	6	8	2	2	199	33	409	67	608
ABC-10	22	6	20	25	18	79	0	1	6	8	9	2	4	200	30	473	70	673
ABC-11	24	6	74	39	29	62	0	3	10	6	0	2	4	259	35	476	65	735
ABC-12	26	6	75	39	36	74	0	4	13	8	0	2	6	293	38	472	62	765
ABC Series	90	24	192	127	110	287	0	12	36	28	17	12	16	951	34	1880	66	2781
Gn-9	5	9	19	0	17	70	55	0	5	7	0	0	0	187	34	357	66	544
Gn-10	5	9	15	0	24	67	48	0	5	4	0	0	0	177	26	492	74	669
Gn-11	9	7	52	0	71	38	49	0	6	8	0	0	0	240	33	487	67	727
Gn-12	8	12	102	0	126	72	55	0	5	26	0	0	0	406	50	410	50	816
Gn Series	27	37	188	0	238	247	207	0	21	45	0	0	0	1010	37	1746	63	2756
HB49-9	6	4	11	3	20	42	45	0	3	15	0	0	9	158	24	506	76	663
HB49-10	6	4	22	19	20	61	42	0	8	16	13	0	8	214	28	550	72	763
HB49-11	10	6	102	19	46	48	26	6	5	17	0	0	16	301	36	531	64	832
HB49-12	11	7	111	17	75	86	7	10	7	14	13	0	9	304	38	496	62	800
HB49 Series	33	21	246	58	161	187	120	16	18	62	13	0	42	977	32	2081	68	3058
HBM-9	7	17	20	10	45	40	44	0	2	11	11	0	0	207	29	505	71	712
HBM-10	8	16	24	19	40	44	44	0	1	10	11	0	0	217	30	527	70	744
HBM-11	11	13	80	15	62	44	46	6	5	11	0	0	16	307	38	501	62	808
HBM-12	11	13	107	10	64	41	35	5	5	9	22	0	3	303	38	505	62	808
HBM Series	37	59	231	52	211	169	169	11	13	41	22	0	19	1034	34	2038	66	3072
HBO-9	11	18	22	18	41	44	66	0	4	6	0	0	2	232	32	500	68	732
HBO-10	14	19	30	30	47	41	70	0	2	10	0	0	2	265	35	501	65	766
HBO-11	11	22	119	27	50	48	75	12	5	11	0	0	9	389	45	475	55	864
HBO-12	12	31	82	15	81	38	48	73	5	10	0	0	13	395	47	437	53	832
HBO Series	48	90	253	90	219	171	259	85	16	37	0	0	13	1281	40	1918	60	3194

TABLE XXXV (continued)

	Preliminaries		Unit intro-	Body					Appendices					Editorial machinery		Totals Texts of selections		Total num-
	Table of con- tents	Other	duc- tions	Unit follow- ups	Selec- tion intro- ductions	Selec- tion follow- ups	Pic- tures in text	Misc.	In- dexes	Gloss- aries	Biog- raphies	General re- view	Misc.	pages	per cent	pages	per cent	ber of pages
	(1)	(2)	(3)	(4)	(5)	(6)	(7)	(8)	(9)	(10)	(11)	(12)	(13)	(14)	(15)	(16)	(17)	(18)
HB2-9	9	6	16	14	17	35	79	0	2	15	0	0	0	193	30	447	70	640
HB2-10	6	5	16	15	19	47	68	0	4	14	0	0	0	194	30	446	70	640
HB2-11	10	7	48	7	64	37	59	6	4	9	0	0	0	251	34	485	66	736
HB2-12	7	6	21	21	36	55	52	6	2	9	0	0	2	211	30	493	70	704
HB2 Series	32	24	101	57	136	174	258	6	12	47	0	0	2	849	31	1871	69	2720
Hlt-9	5	9	18	27	6	71	32	0	8	16	0	0	0	192	29	464	71	656
Hlt-10	5	11	20	19	13	92	33	0	10	18	0	0	0	221	31	483	69	704
Hlt-11	5	9	18	17	15	114	42	0	9	12	0	0	0	241	31	527	69	768
Hlt-12	5	9	16	17	21	110	46	0	10	17	0	0	0	251	33	517	67	768
Hlt Series	20	38	72	80	55	387	153	0	37	63	0	0	0	905	31	1991	69	2896
Ldw-9	6	8	16	21	25	39	40	40	5	0	15	0	0	215	31	489	69	704
Ldw-10	6	8	39	19	19	35	21	69	4	0	14	0	0	234	30	534	70	768
Ldw-11	8	8	48	28	100	43	25	57	6	0	10	0	0	333	43	435	57	768
Ldw-12	6	8	68	27	100	37	29	70	6	0	12	0	0	363	45	443	55	806
Ldw Series	26	32	171	95	244	154	115	236	21	0	51	0	0	1145	38	1901	62	3046
Lipp-9	6	6	28	0	7	27	49	0	2	0	0	48	0	173	28	435	72	608
Lipp-10	6	6	28	0	8	46	41	0	1	0	0	48	0	184	33	375	67	559
Lipp-11	8	6	28	0	13	62	29	0	2	0	0	48	0	196	31	440	69	636
Lipp-12	6	6	31	0	9	49	14	0	2	0	0	48	0	165	32	347	68	512
Lipp Series	26	24	115	0	37	184	133	0	7	0	0	192	0	718	31	1597	69	2315
McM-9	4	8	16	24	8	20	31	2	3	0	0	0	0	116	20	466	80	582
McM-10	6	8	21	23	28	22	35	8	3	0	0	0	0	154	23	502	77	656
McM-11	8	8	33	17	33	19	34	1	4	0	0	0	0	157	23	531	77	688
McM-12	7	8	38	9	42	16	27	0	4	0	0	0	0	151	21	554	79	705
McM Series	25	32	108	73	111	77	127	11	14	0	0	0	0	578	22	2053	78	2631

PH-9	3	5	35	12	14	30	49	0	6	0	0	0	0	154	26	438	74	592
PH-10	5	27	12	12	22	33	33	0	4	0	0	0	0	148	26	412	74	560
PH-11	16	11	27	17	26	24	32	0	8	0	0	0	0	161	28	413	62	574
PH-12	12	5	24	12	32	36	37	0	10	0	0	0	0	168	28	440	72	608
PH Series	36	48	98	53	94	123	151	0	28	0	0	0	0	631	27	1703	73	2334
RM-10	4	10	20	32	12	23	41	0	6	0	0	0	16	164	27	444	73	608
RM-11	8	8	76	36	102	49	62	0	7	4	0	0	6	358	44	448	56	806
RM-12	8	8	77	87	52	30	33	0	5	4	0	0	6	310	39	492	61	802
RM Series	20	26	173	155	166	102	136	0	18	8	0	0	28	832	38	1384	62	2216
SF-9	7	3	11	31	16	87	71	0	4	24	0	0	1	205	35	387	65	592
SF-10	7	3	16	32	12	42	73	0	3	35	0	0	1	224	34	432	66	656
SF-11	9	3	36	41	59	44	69	0	6	36	0	0	1	304	41	432	59	736
SF-12	10	5	79	24	63	51	57	0	7	44	0	0	14	354	46	414	54	768
SF Series	33	14	142	128	150	174	270	0	20	139	0	0	17	1087	39	1665	61	2752
Sgr-9	8	6	18	8	18	49	44	0	3	12	13	0	0	179	28	461	72	640
Sgr-10	5	6	16	9	23	52	45	0	2	15	11	0	0	184	26	521	74	705
Sgr-11	11	6	36	20	67	118	41	1	3	11	0	0	0	314	41	455	59	769
Sgr-12	13	6	75	44	83	82	30	0	3	12	0	0	14	362	49	373	51	735
Sgr Series	37	24	145	81	191	301	160	1	11	50	24	0	14	1039	36	1810	64	2849
Totals	490	493	2235	1049	2123	2737	2258	378	272	520	127	204	151	13037	34	25583	66	38620
Averages	9	9	41	19	39	50	41	—	5	—	—	—	—	237	—	465	—	702

Appendix B

TABLES FOR GRAMMAR
AND COMPOSITION TEXTBOOKS

TABLE I

Summary of the Contents of the Grammar and Composition Series

Publisher	Title	Date	Grade	Total pages	Gram., Usage, Mechanics	Writing	Other	No. of Chapt.	No. of Div.	Plan*
Allyn and Bacon	Effective English	1961	9	388	177	104	107	22	2	A&H
			10	422	165	75	182	22	2	A&H
			11	422	212	69	141	21	2	A&H
			12	454	220	80	154	20	2	A&H
			Total	1686	774	328	584	85		
American Book	Our English Language	1957	9	430	192	55	184	30		Alt.
			10	432	200	100	132	31		Alt.
			11	432	141	82	209	31		Alt.
			12	432	153	104	175	30		Alt.
			Total	1726	685	341	700	122		
Ginn¹	English Skills	1959	9	448	172	82	194	25		A&H
			10	468	175	93	200	25		A&H
			11	464	139	76	249	23		A&H
			12	468	191	103	174	18		A&H
			Total	1848	677	354	817	91		
Ginn²	Better English	1955	9	450	175	82	193	29		A&H
			10	478	166	96	216	29		A&H
			11	476	135	85	256	24		A&H
			12	462	125	97	240	23		A&H
			Total	1866	601	360	905	105		A&H

Publisher	Title	Year	Grade							Class*
Harcourt, Brace[1]	English Grammar and Composition	1958	9	546	248	135	163	23	6	H&A
		1957	10	559	273	111	175	27	6	H&A
			11	655	290	121	244	34	8	H&A
			12	691	351	133	207	36	8	H&A
			Total	2451	1162	500	789	120		
Harcourt, Brace[2]	Living Language	1953	9	437	175	36	226	26		A&H
			10	438	213	32	193	24		A&H
			11	437	215	42	180	22		A&H
			12	425	187	69	169	22		A&H
			Total	1737	790	179	768	94		
Heath	English in Action, 7th ed.	1960	9	500	237	70	193	35	2	A&H
			10	500	210	57	233	31	2	A&H
			11	500	210	81	209	33	2	A&H
			12	500	201	71	228	30	2	A&H
			Total	2000	858	279	863	129		
Lippincott	English for Today	1955	9	560	114	112	334	13	2	A&H
			10	560	96	116	348	13	2	A&H
			11	560	110	204	246	10	2	A&H
			12	577	90	128	359	10	2	A&H
			Total	2257	410	560	1287	46		

* A&H Activities followed by Handbook.
H&A Handbok followed by Activities.
AHA Activities, Handbook, Activities.
Int. Integrated A&H.
Alt. Alternating A&H.
Unc. Unclassified.

TABLE I (continued)

Publisher	Title	Date	Grade	Total pages	Gram., Usage, Mechanics	Writing		No. of Chapt.	No. of Div.	Plan*
Macmillan	Our Engl. Lang.	1961	9	451	225	71	155	17	2	H&A
	Essentials of Mod. English	1961	10	470	220	87	163	14	2	A&H
	Language Arts & Skills	1961	11	470	220	102	148	12	2	A&H
	The Art of Communicating	1961	12	470	231	66	173	10	2	A&H
			Total	1861	896	326	639	53		
McGraw-Hill	Your Language (3 volumes)	1956	9	434	121	73	240	23	2	Unc.
		1959	10	530	183	113	234	20	2	Unc.
		1960	11	530	149	45	336	17	2	Unc.
			Total	1494	453	231	810	60		
Row, Peterson	The New Building Better English	1961	9	435	175	122	138	28	4	A&H
			10	438	170	115	153	26	4	A&H
			11	436	130	132	174	27	4	A&H
			12	374	131	93	150	13	2	H&A
			Total	1683	606	462	615	94		
Scott, Foresman	Guide to Modern English	1960	9	484	206	78	200	24	2	A&H
			10	556	254	98	204	25	2	A&H
		1 vol.	11							
			12	544	317	94	133	18	2	Unc.
			Total	1584	777	270	537			

		Year	Grade						Int.	AHA
Scribner's	English at Work	1956	9	526	226	68	232	20		5
			10	522	152	128	242	20		5
			11	518	174	102	242	20		5
			12	526	165	125	236	21		5
			Total	2092	717	423	952	81		
Singer	Enjoying English	1960	9	464	245	34	185	35		
			10	464	215	53	196	36		
			11	464	214	116	134	33		
			12	464	182	99	183	34		
			Total	1856	856	302	698	138		

* A&H Activities followed by Handbook.
H&A Handbook followed by Activities.
AHA Activities, Handbook, Activities.
Int. Integrated A&H.
Alt. Alternating A&H.
Unc. Unclassified.

TABLE II

Number of Pages Devoted to Grammar, Usage, and
Mechanics in Each Volume of the Series

Publisher	Title	Total pages	Total G/U/M*	Grade			
				9	10	11	12
A&B	Effective English	1686	774	177	165	212	220
ABC	Our English Lang.	1726	685	191	200	141	153
Ginn¹	English Skills	1848	677	172	175	139	191
Ginn²	Better English	1866	601	175	166	135	125
HB ¹	Engl. Gr. & Comp.	2451	1162	248	273	290	351
HB ²	Living Language	1737	790	175	213	215	187
Heath	Engl. in Action	2000	858	237	210	210	201
Lipp	English for Today	2257	410	114	96	110	90
Mac	Our Engl. Lang., etc.	1861	896	225	220	220	231
McG-H	Your Lang. (3 vols.)	1494	453	121	183	149	—
Row, P	Bldg. Better Engl.	1683	606	175	170	130	131
ScF	Guide to Mod. Engl. (3 vols.)	1584	777	206	254	—	317
Scrib	English at Work	2092	717	226	152	174	165
Sing	Enjoying English	1856	856	245	215	214	182

* G Grammar
   U Usage
   M Mechanics

TABLE III

Number of Pages Devoted to Various Topics of
Grammar, Usage, and Mechanics

Publisher	Title	Grade	PofS*	Ag	P&C	S&P
A&B	Effective English	9	26	5	16	19
		10	38	9	16	12
		11	16	8	30	6
		12	136	4	24	5
		Total	216	26	86	
ABC	Our English Lang.	9	56	7	17	6
		10	75	7	8	6
		11	54	7	8	6
		12	52	7	8	4
		Total	237	28	41	22
Ginn	English Skills	9	93	4	22	8
		10	81	3	24	5
		11	68	4	23	8
		12	90	3	21	9
		Total	332	14	90	30
Ginn	Better English	9	93	4	26	7
		10	94	4	30	8
		11	83	2	24	9
		12	78	4	20	8
		Total	348	14	100	32
HB [1]	Engl. Gr. & Comp.	9	25	15	76	8
		10	23	16	83	8
		11	19	18	58	5
		12	17	14	53	6
		Total	84	63	270	27

* PofS   Parts of Speech
  Ag   Agreement
  P&C   Punctuation and Capitalization
  S&P   Subject and Predicate

TABLE III (*continued*)

Publisher	Title	Grade	PofS°	Ag	P&C	S&P
HB [2]	Living Language	9	20	13	44	7
		10	20	11	55	9
		11	8	10	33	5
		12	8	9	29	5
		Total	56	43	161	26
Heath	Engl. in Action	9	30	13	23	7
		10	15	10	15	7
		11	10	10	44	4
		12	16	10	47	6
		Total	71	43	129	24
Lipp	Engl. for Today	9	14	6	25	
		10	12	2	12	
		11	16	6	16	
		12	19	3	12	
		Total	61	17	65	
Mac	Our Engl. Lang.	9	99	11	40	15
	Ess. of Mod. Engl.	10	27	10	38	5
	Lang. Arts & Skills	11	27	10	38	5
	The Art of Comm.	12	27	10	38	5
		Total	180	41	154	30
McG-H	Your Language	9	40	5	43	13
		10	63	3	48	15
		11	64	4	52	16
		Total	167	12	143	44
Row, P	Bldg. Better Engl.	9	16	3	30	6
		10	16	6	32	7
		11	18	2	25	6
		12	26	5	17	6
		Total	76	16	104	25

TABLE III (*continued*)

Publisher	Title	Grade	PofS*	Ag	P&C	S&P
ScF	Guide to Mod. Engl.	9	66	14	42	10
		10	60	16	52	9
		11	—	—	—	—
		12	28	4	16	5
		Total	154	34	110	24
Scrib	English at Work	9	11	9	86	8
		10	28	8	27	11
		11	15	7	41	11
		12	12	11	59	5
		Total	66	35	213	35
Sing	Enjoying Engl.	9	50	9	31	7
		10	36	10	22	10
		11	27	10	20	8
		12	22	10	22	7
		Total	135	39	95	32

* PofS   Parts of Speech
  Ag   Agreement
  P&C   Punctuation and Capitalization
  S&P   Subject and Predicate

TABLE IV

Number of Pages Given to Nouns in Each Volume

Publisher	Title	Grade				Total
		9	10	11	12	
A&B	Effective English	21	18	5	24	68 *
ABC	Our English Lang.	12	20	22	12	66 *
Ginn¹	English Skills	8	9	7	5	29
Ginn²	Better English	7	9	7	10	33
HB 1	Engl. Gr. & Comp.	6	6	4	4	20
HB 2	Living Language	11	9	4	5	29
Heath	English in Action	9	6	7	8	30
Lipp	English for Today	4	7	7	8	26
Mac	(separate titles)	8	9	9	9	35
McG-H	Your Lang. (3 vols.)	10	7	7	—	24
Row, P	Bldg. Better Engl.	35	29	24	26	114 *
ScF	Guide to Mod. Engl. (3 vols.)	11	14	—	8	33
Scrib	English at Work	21	10	14	4	49
Sing	Enjoying English	7	7	10	12	36

* Because of different methods of organization these totals are higher. In these volumes all matters pertaining to nouns are brought together in one chapter, in the other totals pages conceived with nouns as subjects, objects, appositives etc. are not included.

TABLE V

Number of Pages Given to Comma Punctuation in Each Volume

Publisher	Title	Grade 9	10	11	12	Total	Organization*
A&B	Effective English	9	7	7	5	28	ch
ABC	Our English Lang.	6	3	3	3	15	d
Ginn¹	English Skills	9	11	12	8	40	ch
Ginn²	Better English	9	10	9	10	38	ch
HB ¹	Engl. Gr. & Comp.	23	24	19	15	81	ch
HB ²	Living Language	15	29	17	16	77	ch
Heath	English in Action	10	11	18	14	43	ch
Lipp	English for Today	7	5	6	4	22	ch&d
Mac	Our English Lang., etc.	10	10	10	10	40	ch
McG-H	Your Lang. (3 vols.)	9	14	15	—	38	ch
Row, P	Bldg. Better English	8	8	8	6	30	ch&d
ScF	Guide to Mod. Engl. (3 vols.)	13	17	—	16	46	ch
Scrib	English at Work	15	15	15	15	60	ch&d
Sing	Enjoying English	11	7	7	8	33	ch&d

* ch   Treated in a single chapter.
  d   Distributed throughout the volume.
  ch&d Handbook section and some material distributed throughout the volume.

TABLE VI

Number of Pages Devoted to Sentence Recognition in Each Volume

Publisher	Title	Grade 9	10	11	12	Total
A&B	Effective English	22	12	6	5	45
ABC	Our English Language	6	6	6	3	21
Ginn¹	English Skills	8	5	8	9	30
Ginn²	Better English	7	8	9	8	32
HB ¹	Engl. Gr. & Comp.	8	8	7	6	24
HB ²	Living Language	7	9	5	5	26
Heath	English in Action	7	7	4	6	24
Lipp	English for Today	6	3	3	3	15
Mac	Our Engl. Lang., etc.	15	5	5	5	30
McG-H	Your Language (3 vols.)	13	15	18	—	46
Row, P	Bldg. Better English	6	7	6	6	25
ScF	Guide to Mod. Engl. (3 vols.)	10	9	—	5	24
Scrib	English at Work	8	11	11	5	35
Sing	Enjoying English	7	10	8	7	32

TABLE VII

Evaluation of Treatment of Grammar, Usage, and Mechanics in the Series

Part A: Comparative Rating

	1	2	3	4	5	6	7	8	9
A&B	av	inf	av	av	av	av	inf	inf	av
ABC	av	inf	inf	av	inf	av	inf	inf	s
Ginn1	av	s	av	av	av	av	av	av	av
Ginn2	av	s	av	av	av	av	av	av	av
HB 1	s	s	s	s	av	av	s	s	av
HB 2	av	av	av	av	av	av	av	av	av
Heath	av	av	av	s	av	av	av	s	s
Lipp	inf	inf	inf	inf	av	av	av	av	s
Mac	s	s	av	av	av	av	s	s	av
McG-H	inf	inf	inf	inf	inf	av	inf	inf	inf
Row, P	av	av	s	av	s	av	av	av	s
ScF	s	inf	inf	av	s	s	inf	av	av
Scrib	av	inf	inf	inf	inf	av	av	av	s
Sing	av	av	av	av	av	av	av	s	av

Part B: Survey Rating
(Direct Estimate without Reference to Comparative Rating)

	1	2	3	4	5	6	7	8	9
A&B	ad	ad	ad	ad	ad	u	u	u	u
ABC	ad	ad	u	ad	ad	u	u	u	g
Ginn1	ad	ad	ad	ad	ad	u	ad	ad	ad
Ginn2	ad	ad	ad	ad	ad	u	ad	ad	ad
HB 1	ad	ad	ad	ad	ad	u	g	g	ad
HB 2	ad	ad	ad	ad	ad	u	ad	ad	ad
Heath	ad	ad	ad	ad	ad	u	ad	ad	ad
Lipp	u	u	u	u	ad	u	ad	ad	ad
Mac	ad	ad	ad	ad	ad	u	ad	g	ad
McG-H	u	u	u	u	u	u	u	u	u
Row, P	ad	ad	g	ad	g	u	ad	ad	g
ScF	g	u	u	ad	ad	u	u	ad	ad
Scrib	ad	u	u	u	u	u	ad	ad	g
Sing	ad	ad	ad	ad	ad	u	ad	ad	ad

Columns for both A and B: (1) Coverage; (2) General Clarity of Presentation; (3) Organization within Volume; (4) Adequacy of Particular Explanations; (5) Progression within Volume; (6) Progression within Series; (7) Relevance of Information and Activities; (8) Tone; (9) Sense of Purpose.

Symbols for A: s-superior; av-average; inf-inferior.
Symbols for B: g-good; ad-adequate; u-unsatisfactory.

TABLE VIII

Treatment of Pronouns in Relation to the Infinitive Phrase

Series	Grade			
	9	10	11	12
A&B, *Effective English*	no*	no	all	s
ABC, *Our English Language*	s	s	so	so
Ginn¹, *English Skills*	no	no	no	s
Ginn², *Better English*	no	no	no	s
HB¹, *English Gram. & Comp.*	no	no	no	no (1)
HB², *Living Language*	no	no	no	no (2)
Heath, *English in Action*	no	no	s	sp
Lipp, *English for Today*	no	no	all	all
Mac (separate titles)	no	sop	sop	sop (3)
McG-H, *Your Language*	no	no	no	—
Row, P, *Building Better English*	no	no	all	all
ScF, *Guide to Modern English*	no	no	—	p (4)
Scrib, *English at Work*	no	no	all	all
Sing, *Enjoying English*	no	no	no	no

(1) "Like a verb, an infinitive may have a subject." No mention of the case form of the pronoun.

(2) Impression is given that in "Let us go" the pronoun is object of verb; no mention of pronoun in relation to infinitive.

(3) Imperfect statement: "The objective form of the pronoun is used as the subject, object, or predicate pronoun of the infinitive."

(4) Omits treatment of subject of infinitive.

* no no uses discussed
  s subject is discussed
  o object is discussed
  p one condition of the predicate pronoun is discussed
 all all uses of predicate pronoun in relation to the infinitive

TABLE IX

Number of Pages Devoted to Composition
in Each Volume of the Series

Publisher	Grade	Total pages	Total Rhet. & comp.	No. of writing assign.	Distribution*	No. of pages	No. of assign.	Pages letters	Personal assign.	Business assign.	Research paper**
A&B	9	388	104	44	M	10	2	36	9	8	R
	10	422	75	26	M	18	5	22	2	2	R
	11	422	69	33	M	3	10	18	1	3	R
	12	454	80	42	M	3	0	16	11	5	Res
	Total	1686	328	145		34	17	92	23	18	
ABC	9	430	55	65	W	17	10	15	2	6	O
	10	432	100	116	W	12	22	11	13	8	R
	11	432	82	100	W	11	11	16	13	8	R
	12	432	104	133	W	12	16	4	11	13	Res
	Total	1726	341	414		62	59	46	39	35	
Ginn¹	9	448	82	60	M	30	4	33	8	4	R
	10	468	93	81	M	30	4	25	6	10	R
	11	464	76	102	M	25	6	28	14	12	R
	12	468	103	64	M	9	3	29	7	9	Res
	Total	1848	354	307		94	17	115	35	35	
Ginn²	9	450	82	48	M	25	6	24	3	3	R
	10	478	96	81	M	24	10	18	6	4	R
	11	476	85	80	M	24	5	35	8	5	R
	12	462	97	91	M	9	2	27	8	10	Res
	Total	1866	360	300		82	23	104	25	22	
HB ¹	9	546	135	61	C	18	6	28	6	5	R
	10	559	111	34	C	29	8	28	5	10	O
	11	655	121	35	C	20	4	34	6	4	Res
	12	691	133	34	C	25	4	30	2	7	Res
	Total	2451	500	164		92	22	120	19	26	
HB ²	9	437	36	25	M	0	0	16	2	0	O
	10	438	32	21	M	20	1	2	0	0	O
	11	437	42	33	M	2	3	3	0	0	Res
	12	425	69	38	W	2	0	15	0	3	Res
	Total	1737	179	117		24	4	36	2	3	

TABLE IX (continued)

Publisher	Grade	Total pages	Total Rhet. & comp.	No. of writing assign.	Distribution*	No. of pages	No. of assign.	Pages letters	Personal assign.	Business assign.	Research Paper**
Heath	9	500	70	63	M	10	13	27	12	28	R
	10	500	57	43	M	11	7	33	13	6	R
	11	500	81	76	M	13	11	30	15	16	Res
	12	500	71	50	M	0	0	32	7	16	Res
	Total	2000	279	232		34	31	122	47	66	
Lipp	9	560	112	74	M	22	6	62	17	10	R
	10	560	116	100	M	20	14	68	9	22	R
	11	560	204	107	M	23	14	64	0	14	Res
	12	577	128	110	M	0	8	20	0	4	O
	Total	2257	560	391		65	42	214	26	50	
Mac	9	451	71	48	C	25	28	10	4	2	R
	10	470	87	49	M	16	10	4	0	0	R
	11	470	102	46	C	19	6	6	0	0	R
	12	470	66	34	M	13	6	6	0	0	Res
	Total	1861	326	177		73	50	26	4	2	
McG-H	9	434	73	34	M	0	0	19	5	3	O
	10	530	113	41	M	23	3	6	0	0	O
	11	530	45	37	M	8	0	7	0	0	Res
	Total	1494	231	112		31	3	32	5	3	
Row, P	9	435	122	55	C	8	4	16	5	6	R
	10	438	115	89	C	9	6	25	21	12	R
	11	436	132	86	C	7	21	23	5	5	Res
	12	374	93	68	C	11	9	25	4	28	Res
	Total	1683	462	298		35	40	89	35	51	
ScF	9	484	78	19	M	28	4	26	3	4	O
	10	556	98	23	M	30	4	38	5	7	O

* M   Moderately distributed
  C   Concentrated
  W   Widely distributed
** O   No material
  R   Report
  Res Research project

TABLE IX (*continued*)

Publisher	Grade	Total pages	Total Rhet. & comp.	No. of writing assign.	Distribution*	No. of pages	No. of assign.	Pages letters	Personal assign.	Business assign.	Research Paper**
	11& 12	544	94	24	M	16	6	16	3	6	Res
	Total	1584	270	66		74	14	80	11	17	
Scrib	9	526	68	15	W	9	4	12	1	1	O
	10	522	128	14	W	25	8	10	0	2	O
	11	518	102	13	W	4	2	3	1	0	Res
	12	526	125	14	W	0	0	7	0	1	Res
	Total	2092	423	56		38	14	32	2	4	
Sing	9	464	34	20	C	5	4	17	1	3	R
	10	464	53	34	W	5	6	15	1	1	Res
	11	464	116	37	W	10	9	16	1	1	Res
	12	464	99	37	W	2	6	20	0	7	Res
	Total	1856	302	128		22	25	68	3	12	

* M   Moderately distributed
    C   Concentrated
    W   Widely distributed
** O   No material
    R   Report
    Res   Research project

TABLE X

Evaluation of Treatment of Rhetoric and Composition
in the Series
Part A: Comparative Evaluation

Series	1	2	3	4	5	6
A&B	av	av	av	av	av	inf
ABC	s	av	av	av	av	inf
Ginn[1]	inf	av	av	av	av	av
Ginn[2]	inf	av	av	av	av	av
HB [1]	av	s	s	av	av	s
HB [2]	inf	inf	inf	av	av	inf
Heath	av	av	av	av	av	av
Lipp	s	av	av	av	av	av
Mac	s	s	s	av	av	s
McG-H	inf	inf	inf	av	av	inf
Row, P	av	av	av	av	av	av
ScF	inf	s	av	av	av	s
Scrib	inf	av	inf	av	av	av
Sing	av	av	av	av	av	av

Symbols: s-superior; av-average; inf-inferior.
Columns: (1) Number and Distribution of Writing Assignments; (2) Emphasis — Forms and Purposes of Writing Assignments; (3) Quality of Instruction — Principles and Techniques of Writing; (4) Appropriateness of Topics for Writing Assignments; (5) Progression within Volumes and within Series; (6) Tone.

TABLE X (*continued*)

Part B: Survey Evaluation (Direct Estimate without Reference to Composition Ratings)

Series	1	2	3	4	5	6
A&B	ad	u	ad	u	u	u
ABC	ad	ad	ad	u	u	u
Ginn[1]	ad	ad	ad	u	u	ad
Ginn[2]	ad	ad	ad	u	u	ad
HB [1]	ad	ad	ad	u	u	g
HB [2]	u	u	u	u	u	ad
Heath	ad	ad	ad	u	u	ad
Lipp	ad	ad	ad	u	u	ad
Mac	ad	g	ad	u	u	ad
McG-H	u	u	u	u	u	u
Row, P	u	ad	ad	u	u	u
ScF	ad	ad	g	u	u	g
Scrib	u	u	u	u	u	u
Sing	ad	ad	ad	u	u	u

Symbols: g-good; ad-adequate; u-unsatisfactory.
Columns: (1) Number and Distribution of Writing Assignments; (2) Emphasis — Forms and Purposes of Writing Assignments; (3) Quality of Instruction — Principles and Techniques of Writing; (4) Appropriateness of Topics for Writing Assignments; (5) Progression within Volumes and within Series; (6) Tone.

TABLE XI

Eight Areas Covered by All Textbooks in the Series

Publisher	Grade	Total pages	Total other	Per cent "other"	Speech activ.	Listening	Parl. proc.	Movies TV-radio	News. Mag.	Social activ.	Library	Spelling
A&B	9	388	107		64	2	8	2	4	16	20	16
	10	422	182		42	0	11	0	22	0	12	14
	11	422	141		24	5	0	0	0	16	2	9
	12	454	154		40	14	0	4	9	5	4	7
	Total	1686	584	34	170	21	19	6	35	37	38	46
ABC	9	430	184		22	8	11	6	6	10	8	24
	10	432	132		30	7	9	10	11	4	17	18
	11	432	209		36	7	7	6	5	4	8	10
	12	432	175		39	8	9	5	9	4	8	11
	Total	1726	700	40	127	30	36	27	31	22	41	63
Ginn1	9	448	194		49	6	6	10	7	14	9	23
	10	468	200		71	8	12	7	10	12	13	21
	11	464	249		72	5	11	19	17	12	24	20
	12	468	174		85	7	12	2	0	0	20	22
	Total	1848	817	44	277	26	41	38	34	38	66	86
Ginn2	9	450	193		29	7	6	4	11	10	15	19
	10	478	216		68	21	9	6	11	15	12	19
	11	476	256		54	6	14	21	29	9	10	14
	12	462	240		68	23	10	0	0	0	9	17
	Total	1866	905	48	219	57	39	31	51	34	46	69
HB 1	9	546	163		29	2	0	0	0	0	18	26
	10	559	175		40	13	8	0	0	16	38	27
	11	655	244		21	0	0	0	0	0	16	28
	12	691	207		17	23	0	0	0	0	59	25
	Total	2451	789	32	107	38	8	0	0	16	131	106
HB 2	9	437	226		48	0	0	0	0	56	13	19
	10	438	193		34	23	0	0	0	38	3	19
	11	437	180		20	0	0	0	0	16	4	19
	12	425	169		5	0	4	0	0	0	4	16
	Total	1737	768	44	107	23	4	0	0	110	24	73
Heath	9	500	193		27	5	6	5	19	40	11	10
	10	500	233		57	6	5	4	8	15	11	19
	11	500	209		29	8	0	18	9	16	9	15
	12	500	228		40	5	13	2	5	20	8	13
	Total	2000	863	43	153	24	24	29	41	91	39	57

TABLE XI (*continued*)

Publisher	Grade	Total pages	Total other	Per cent "other"	Speech activ.	Listen-ing	Parl. proc.	Movies TV-radio	News. Mag.	Social activ.	Library	Spelling
Lipp	9	560	334		52	0	0	30	6	19	25	7
	10	560	348		46	14	0	47	6	32	27	4
	11	560	246		37	12	16	4	92	0	10	5
	12	577	359		54	0	0	2	34	0	1	10
	Total	2257	1287	57	189	26	16	83	138	51	63	26
Mac	9	451	155		26	9	4	0	0	11	12	17
	10	470	163		37	10	9	4	5	0	19	11
	11	470	148		42	8	4	4	6	0	5	7
	12	470	173		25	6	0	4	5	25	2	7
	Total	1861	639	34	130	33	17	12	16	36	38	42
McG-H	9	434	240		53	13	15	8	0	8	4	5
	10	530	234		34	5	6	10	13	14	10	15
	11	530	336		27	20	6	33	29	14	3	13
	Total	1494	810	57	114	38	27	51	42	36	17	33
Row, P	9	435	138		53	9	8	9	7	5	15	7
	10	438	153		28	12	4	12	7	3	10	13
	11	436	174		69	4	8	10	20	5	10	10
	12	374	150		23	10	0	10	10	3	10	6
	Total	1683	615	36	173	35	20	41	44	16	45	36
ScF	9	484	200		30	1	14	0	2	0	16	25
	10	556	204		36	1	0	0	0	0	22	32
	11& 12	544	133		12	2	5	0	2	0	7	5
	Total	1584	537	34	78	4	19	0	4	0	45	62
Scrib	9	526	232		55	12	3	2	0	4	20	31
	10	522	242		43	30	0	2	20	4	6	30
	11	518	242		39	21	2	2	9	4	6	30
	12	526	236		37	0	1	1	2	4	3	13
	Total	2092	952	45	174	63	6	7	31	16	35	104
Sing	9	464	185		4	3	4	2	0	5	10	15
	10	464	196		15	1	7	9	36	5	6	12
	11	464	134		15	2	0	0	2	12	4	6
	12	464	183		10	0	0	15	18	12	5	4
	Total	1856	698	37	44	6	11	26	56	34	25	37

TABLE XII

Treatment of Topics Other Than Grammar and
Composition in the Series

Part A: Comparative Evaluation

Series	Spell.	V&D	Libr.	Rel.	Appr.	Prog.	Tone
	1	2	3	4	5	6	7
A&B	av	av	av	av	av	av	av
ABC	av	av	av	av	av	av	av
Ginn[1]	av	av	av	av	av	av	av
Ginn[2]	av	av	av	av	av	av	av
HB [1]	av	s	s	s	s	av	s
HB [2]	av	inf	inf	av	av	av	av
Heath	av	av	av	inf	av	av	inf
Lipp	inf	inf	av	inf	av	av	av
Mac	av	av	s	s	s	av	s
McG-H	inf	inf	inf	inf	av	av	inf
Row, P	av	av	av	av	av	av	av
ScF	av	s	inf	av	av	av	av
Scrib	s	av	inf	av	av	av	av
Sing	av	av	av	av	av	av	av

Symbols: s-superior; av-average; inf-inferior.
Columns: (1) Spelling; (2) Vocabulary and Dictionary Study; (3) Library; (4) Relevance; (5) Appropriateness of Activities; (6) Progression; (7) Tone.

TABLE XII (*continued*)

Part B: Survey Evaluation

Series	Spell.	V&D	Libr.	Rel.	Appr.	Prog.	Tone
	1	2	3	4	5	6	7
A&B	ad	av	ad	u	u	u	u
ABC	ad	av	ad	u	u	u	u
Ginn[1]	ad	av	ad	u	u	u	u
Ginn[2]	ad	av	ad	u	u	u	u
HB [1]	ad	ad	g	g	u	u	g
HB [2]	ad	u	u	u	u	u	u
Heath	ad	ad	ad	u	u	u	u
Lipp	u	ad	av	u	u	u	u
Mac	ad	ad	g	ad	u	u	g
McG-H	u	u	u	u	u	u	u
Row, P	ad	ad	ad	u	u	u	u
ScF	ad	g	g	g	u	u	g
Scrib	g	ad	u	u	u	u	u
Sing	ad	ad	ad	u	u	u	u

Symbols: g-good; ad-adequate; u-unsatisfactory.
Columns: (1) Spelling; (2) Vocabulary and Dictionary Study; (3) Library; (4) Relevance; (5) Appropriateness of Activities; (6) Progression; (7) Tone.

Appendix C

SECOND-TRACK ANTHOLOGIES

SOME SERIES of anthologies that we have examined are said by the publishers to be intended for what we have called throughout this report the second track; that is, they are deliberately designed to be used with students who are regarded as "terminal" rather than college-preparatory, who are less bright than those in the first track, who are "slow" or "reluctant" readers. Two series of this kind have been included in this survey, HB2 and SF2 (although only the ninth-grade volume of the latter was available in time for our report). At least two other series (Lipp and PH) might also be classified as second-track anthologies, for they differ in no important respects from HB2 and SF2. To these, for the same reason, could be added the third (ninth-grade) volume of some three-volume junior high series, particularly Hth-9 and HM-9. (One series, HltD, included for comparative purposes, is intended for students in a still lower track, commonly called remedial or, euphemistically, "developmental" by teachers and editors, but more often called "bonehead" by the students themselves.)

The second-track anthologies have several distinguishing features: a high percentage of nonliterary and ephemeral prose selections, a relatively small number of poems (other than light and humorous verse), a high ratio of editorial machinery to selections, a consistently chatty kind of editorial prose, and a social orientation. Their unspoken assumption seems to be not only that students in the second track have not profited much from their twelve or fourteen years of living and have read very little, but also that they will profit very little in the future and cannot be interested in reading anything that contains more than factual information and a simple story line.

Even more than the first-track anthologies, these volumes are not textbooks to teach and to study but do-it-yourself readers. They have little in them that is not immediately evident; hence they hardly offer a challenge to their users. They have relatively little teachable substance that falls within the humanistic discipline, but instead are heavily oriented to the "social studies." It is not surprising, therefore, that teachers who must use them are likely to find themselves and their students occupying the class hour more often with "appreciating the mass media," teen-age etiquette, and group activity than with literature. Adolescence itself becomes the principal object of study, and its centripetal, egocentric, exclusive tendencies are strengthened. Even when the activities recommended are acceptable in themselves, they are out of place in the English classroom because they are irrelevant to literature and become a flabby substitute for intellectual exercise. By dwelling so single-mindedly upon social, familial, recreational, and vocational concerns, these anthologies have little room for or interest in the rich heritage of literature. At the same time that they avoid literature as "difficult" they assume that something still more difficult can be directly taught in the classroom — morals. As a result, the selections are likely to be filled with sentimentality or conventional and obvious moralizing, and the immaturity and naïveté of their teen-age heroes and heroines are held up as ideals for readers who are themselves immature. Seldom do these books suggest that man has a soaring, questing spirit; instead, by their concentration upon social activities and transitory processes, they encourage unthinking conformism. Indeed, they seem intended to insure that the second-track student will always remain in the second track. The end-product is a social cog rather than an independent mind.

We can find no justification whatever for such books as these. Why should some students be deprived of an important part of their heritage because of fallacious notions about literature? Literary pieces vary in many ways, including the degree of skill and perception required of the reader. Anthologies can therefore be made less difficult, if that is desired, without abandoning literature altogether. Furthermore, it is the teacher's particular responsibility to bridge the gap for students; he must assist them to read what they cannot yet read for themselves, and he must continue to do so until they can make their own way. Even if they never become able or willing readers of literature after they leave school, they will have had at least a glimpse into a world that otherwise would forever be unknown to them, a world where man ponders and attempts to answer questions of profound importance to everyone — about his identity, his purpose for being, his happiness and his suffering, his conflicting loyalties and responsibilities. These are also matters in which teachers have found their students, even the "slow" and "reluctant," to be interested. A teacher who has two tenth-grade English classes, one college-preparatory and the other second-track, recently told us that she wished she were allowed to use *Julius Caesar* for both classes. She was at the time using *Julius Caesar* with the college-preparatory students and a teen-age novel about drag racing with the second-track students. In one class the students' minds were challenged as they examined Shakespeare's concrete yet universalized presentation of man asking himself such humanly important questions as "Must I place the public welfare above personal friendship?" "Can I be sure that I know what the public welfare requires?" "What are the dangers of mob action?" "Who is a rebel?" In the other class the students were reading an oversimplified story on a topic which many of them knew as much about as the author and which in any case was of value to them only for the moment. The teacher was convinced that even if the second-track students derived from the play only a fraction of what the other class was getting from their study of it they would derive more benefit from it than from the full comprehension of the book they were then reading; at the same time she expected that problems of discipline and class morale would diminish.

This teacher's expectation has been verified by many who were free to make such a substitution in the reading program. The critical element here is of course the teacher himself — the informed, perceptive, enthusiastic teacher who is at home in literature and can convey to his students something of his own perceptiveness and enthusiasm. Unfortunately, the second-track anthologies discourage the development of this kind of teacher. They confront him instead with a collection of pieces whose chief merit is that they are — in the editors' words — "teachable," which evidently means that they do not need to be taught. The minds of the students are deprived of nourishing fare, and the teacher is relegated to a position that makes little use of his talents and training. If it is not a case of the blind leading the blind, it is at least a case of the blind being led by those who are discouraged from seeing.

Appendix D

SUPPLEMENTARY MATERIALS

GRAMMAR AND COMPOSITION SERIES

In the course of preparing this report, we have surveyed, but not analyzed in detail, a total of 67 titles in the field of supplementary materials, including the following categories: Workbooks, laboratory manuals, etc., 38; Business English workbooks and manuals, 3; Spelling books and workbooks, 7; Vocabulary books and booklets, 3; Handbooks, 16. Of the workbooks in grammar and composition, 16 are in series of four volumes each and two are in series of two volumes each; other titles are represented by single volumes. Of the Business English books, one is in a series of two volumes, and of the vocabulary builders, one is in a series of four volumes. All other titles are represented by single volumes.

Although the number of such materials as we have surveyed is substantial, it by no means represents an inclusive list of available materials; many new titles have been announced since we made our original collection. Since our list is thus only partial, it appears hardly appropriate that we identify titles here lest they be mistaken for a complete bibliography of available materials.

Of chief interest to us has been the first category — workbooks designed to accompany textbooks in grammar and composition.

It should first be noted that of the fourteen series in grammar and composition that have been treated in the body of this report, nine are accompanied by workbook series of four volumes each, all of which we have examined. The textbook series so accompanied are as follows: Allyn and Bacon, *Effective English;* Ginn, *English Skills;* Ginn, *Better English;* Harcourt, Brace, *English Grammar and Composition;* Heath, *English in Action;* McGraw-Hill, *Your Language;* Row, Peterson, *Building Better English;* Scott, Foresman, *Guide to Modern English;* and Singer, *Enjoying English.* Titles of these workbook series generally parallel or are identical to the textbook titles.

The contents of the workbooks are truly supplements to the textbooks. Primarily they add exercise material, in the form of many hundreds of new sentences over the four-volume series; but they characteristically repeat also, in abbreviated form, instruction and examples covered in the textbooks. Principal emphasis is upon the many aspects of Grammar, Usage, and Mechanics treated in the textbooks — parts of speech, parts of sentence, punctuation, capitalization, etc., but nearly all workbook series include also, in every volume, additional attention to such matters as letters, library, dictionary, outlining, panels, clubs, reference books, etc. Generally speaking, thus, the workbooks reflect approximately the same proportions given to the varieties of "Other" that are found in the corresponding textbooks.

All workbook series examined include new sentences in each volume to provide exercises on the same matters of Grammar, Usage, and Mechanics that are covered in all other volumes of the series and that are also covered in all volumes of the corresponding textbook series. It may be useful here to report in the following summary some sample figures from three representative workbook series.

Although admittedly our attention to the workbooks has been

Publisher	Grade	Noun	Pages Devoted to Comma punctuation	Subject and verb agreement
Harcourt, Brace,	9	4	10	10
English Workshop	10	3	19	12
Warriner and	11	0	16	7
Blumenthal	Review	3	8	5
Row, Peterson,	9	1	7	5
Building Better	10	1	7	6
English	11	5	7	3
	12	1	7	4
Singer,	9	8	12	2
Enjoying English	10	6	8	3
	11	6	6	5
	12	1	4	2

in the nature rather of survey than of minute examination, we
have seen enough to be aware of their entirely repetitious character, and as we have already severely criticized the repetitious
character of the textbooks which these are designed to accompany,
we are obliged to question the very propriety of the existence
of the workbooks: in our view they merely add repetition to what
is already intolerably repetitious.

Although the convenience of workbooks as devices for keeping students "busy" is well known, we believe that students deserve to be rescued from the endless tedium of incessant drill in
doing things with sentences written by other people for the mere
purpose of drilling. We believe that whatever gains are achieved
by such drill are more than offset by losses in terms of interest,
progress, and genuine learning. In our view the formation of

good habits in the use of language is best accomplished by the steady application and testing of principles in students' own compositions.

We therefore restate and extend one of our former conclusions thus: that, if a single handbook is preferable to a four-volume series in grammar and composition, it is doubly preferable to such a series plus another four-volume series of workbooks.

Appendix E

REPRESENTATIVE PROBLEMS
OF GRAMMAR AND USAGE

As MATTERS of possible interest to readers, we record without comment the following statements from the grammar and composition textbooks on three representative problems of grammar and usage.

"It's I — me," etc.

Allyn and Bacon, *Effective English:*

"It is me" has been accepted by most grammarians as correct in informal English. Even though "It is me" is acceptable, this does not mean that "It is him" is likewise correct.

American Book Company, *Our English Language:*

"It is I" is grammatically correct. However, usage of "It is me" has established the form in informal speech. The choice of the form used will have to depend on the situation. The forms "It is him" and "It is her" are not yet acceptable.

Ginn, *English Skills:*

Pronouns that follow linking verbs are nearly always in the nominative case. The chief exception is the expression "It is me," which is used by many educated persons. It is of course more common in speech than in writing. Most careful speakers avoid saying "It is him" or "It is them."

Harcourt, Brace, *English Grammar and Composition:*

The expression "It's me," which violates Rule 8c, is acceptable in colloquial and standard English. Long-established custom, reflecting the spoken English of educated people, has made this usage part of our language. Following the same principle, you may use or hear such constructions as "That's her," and "If it had been us." These expressions are *becoming* acceptable in colloquial English and are no longer considered serious errors. Up to now, however, only "It's me" has firmly established itself in standard English. Other expressions are best treated in accordance with Rule 8c, which is always safe.

Macmillan (separate titles):

The nominative pronoun form is used as a predicate pronoun.[1] The problem of which form to use in a predicate pronoun occurs primarily after the verb *be.* The rule applies to all verb phrases built around forms of *be:* could have been, can be, should be, etc.

It was I whom they wanted.

Could it have been he who called?

It must have been they that we heard.

Sometimes the nominative form sounds awkward. The awkwardness can be avoided by recasting the sentence.

Awk. The chairmen are she and Tom.

Better. Tom and she are the chairmen.

Awk. It was we who ordered the turkeys.

Better. We are the people who ordered the turkeys.

Scott, Foresman, *Guide to Modern English:*

Formal grammarians explain that the verb *be* should always be followed by the nominative case: *It is I.* But in actual practice *It's me* is so generally used by educated people that it is now

---

[1] Footnote: Standard usage permits the exception in both speech and writing of "It is me."

accepted standard usage (even though some users of formal English still prefer *It is I*).

Though *It's me* is fully acceptable, *It's him, It's her, It's them* are not.

Scribner's, *English at Work:*
Although people are less insistent today than formerly on the strict usage of the predicate nominative, you should understand it. You should be able to use it in formal talk or writing, for many prefer the usage. "It's me" is now considered good collo-quial (informal, conversational) English.

"Different from — than"

Allyn and Bacon, *Effective English:*
While the established American idiom is *different from* the form *different than* is commonly heard. Whenever a clause, rather than a phrase, follows the word *different*, the conjunc-tion *than* is the correct choice.

American Book Company, *Our English Language:*

Wrong	Right
Bill is different than me.	Bill is different from me.

Ginn, *Better English:*
Right: This pencil is different from that one.
Dubious: This pencil is different than that one.

Heath, *English in Action:*
Informal. Election night in America is very different than it was a hundred years ago.
Formal.   Election night in America is very different from what it was a hundred years ago (or from the way it was a hundred years ago).

Lippincott, *English for Today:*
Do not use *different than*. A person or thing always differs

from another person or thing or a person differs *with* another person. Likewise do not use different *than*. Use different *from*.

Macmillan (separate titles):

In most situations *different from* is better usage than *different than*. However, there are some situations in which *than* must be used to avoid awkward expression.

Gil's book is different from ours.

The school is much different than it used to be.

Row, Peterson, *Building Better English:*

Say *different from*, not *different than*. *Than* is a conjunction, not a preposition.

Scott, Foresman, *Guide to Modern English:*

In formal English and in informal writing, *different* is generally followed by *from*.

Colloquial usage is divided; occasionally *from* is used; sometimes *to* (very common in England), and more often *than*.

In both speech and writing, *different than* is becoming common before a clause.

Singer, *Enjoying English:*

Different from is generally preferred. *Different than* is formally acceptable when the attempt to avoid it leads to awkward phrasing.

George is quite *different* from Jerry. (Not *different than*.)

George's appearance is *different than* I had imagined.

"Like — as"

Allyn and Bacon, *Effective English:*

Formal: He acts *as if* he were frightened.

Informal: He acts *like* he is frightened.

At the present time, the use of *like* as a conjunction is increasing so rapidly that it has become accepted as informal English.

American Book Company, *Our English Language:*
Use *as, as if,* and *unless* as conjunctions to introduce clauses.
Use *like* and *without* as prepositions with objects.

Ginn, *English Skills:*
Do not use *like, on account of,* and *without* as conjunctions.
Like may be used as a verb or a preposition, but its use as a
conjunction is avoided by many careful speakers.

Ginn, *Better English:*
Right: Do *as* I say.
Dubious: Do *like* I say.

Harcourt, Brace, *English Grammar and Composition:*
One of the most common violations of standard usage is the
substitution of *like* for *as.* Remember that *like* is followed by a
noun or pronoun *only* — never by a verb.
Wrong: At last your room looks *like* it should.
Right: At last your room looks *as* it should.

Heath, *English in Action:*
Do not substitute *like* for *as if* and *as though. As* is a conjunction; *like* is a preposition. (*Like* may be used as a conjunction
in informal English.)

Row, Peterson, *Building Better English:*
Do not use the preposition *like* for the conjunctions *as* or *as if.*[2]

Scott, Foresman, *Guide to Modern English:*
In writing and in formal speech *as, as if,* and *as though* are used
as conjunctions — to introduce clauses.
In informal speech, *like* is commonly used as a conjunction in
such sentences.
He talks just like I did when I was a child.
It looks like it might rain.

---

[2] Footnote: In informal usage some authorities accept the use of *like* for
as, though not for *as if.*

But this usage is considered inappropriate in writing, except in the South, where it is standard in formal as well as informal usage.

Appendix F

COMMENTS OF TEACHERS

IN the early stages of preparing the report, we invited the comments, both general and specific, of many hundreds of teachers throughout the United States. Most of the replies were received while our own analysis of the textbooks was in its preliminary phases, and long before we were ready to attempt any evaluation. In a majority of instances, teachers were generous, even voluminous, in their comments, and we regret the impossibility of reproducing all of their remarks here. From the vast number we have taken specific comments, in the teachers' own wording, that we consider to be representative of the mass that we have examined. We wish to make only one general statement on the trend of teacher comment as a whole; namely, that our own report tends to be somewhat less severe in its criticism of the textbooks than are the remarks of the teachers who use them.

On the Anthologies of Literature: Content

Tone:

"This is the best edition . . . superior to all the subsequent editions because it assumes students can *think*. The subsequent editions, while 'pretty,' do too much of the work students can be taught to do — and want to do."

". . . [series] seems to make too many concessions to the mentally dull."

Philosophy:

"The anthologies lack 'personality' that the individual books have. There is no remembering their titles; Adventures in this or that! — until you begin to think of them by the colors of their covers."

"There seems to be a policy on the part of . . . to water down the quality, both of the selections and of the understandings which pupils are expected to achieve in the study of literature."

Editing:

"[The editing of texts is] rampant, even sneaky — e.g., Chaucer translations."

"It is possible to ignore such materials [i.e., editorial apparatus] but there is no such easy remedy for the ruthless cutting, editing, and general mangling of materials."

"I find myself frustrated time and time again by abridgements which seriously hamper good teaching practices. I realize that anthologizing limits space, but arbitrary cutting infuriates me. One example of senseless abridgement is the treatment of 'Ode on Intimations of Immortality.' . . . It would have been better to leave it out entirely than to print it as it appears."

"We are dissatisfied with the abridgements, adaptations, and condensations of classic novels, Shakespearean plays, and long poems. . . . We would be willing to sacrifice some of the numbers for a few complete selections. . . . We are especially disappointed in the abridgements of *Julius Caesar* and *Silas Marner.*"

"Our students get nothing from the selection from *Paradise Lost* in our text. It is too brief. . . . I do not like excerpts from novels. . . . I do not believe we need a selection from a current play."

"I do not like adaptations or radical abridgements. . . . The pupil is not informed that the text has been changed. I do not think such deception is right."

"Reading in snatches prevents true learning. The complete piece of work of one author often gives a truer picture of the period than excerpts from the works of many authors. . . . The anthology conditions the pupils to *The Reader's Digest*. They never achieve a sense of style as they never read enough of one author to recognize a style."

Quality:

"Little chance is given to [the student] to read any classical material or any stimulating material."

"The basic philosophies expressed in the stories seem to be very shallow and trite."

"Too many of the stories in the anthologies are, to quote one of my tenth graders, 'driveling and insipid.' Anthologists MUST distinguish carefully between reading for personal adjustment and reading worthy literature for education. The two purposes can't be served by one selection."

". . . selections that seem to be written just for the purpose of interpreting community life to the child."

Scope:

"There seems to be . . . a lack of discrimination among the important and the less important, or trivial, writers. I would prefer to have larger selections from major writers and fewer short selections from the less important writers."

"In the twelfth-grade book there is, as in most twelfth-grade anthologies, an attempt to cover too much material. The old 'sophomore literature' survey course has been pushed back from college into high school."

Contents:

"The tenth-grade book has a weak short story section. I feel that these stories are shallow — that there are others of more value in older editions of the book."

"We would like two longer essays by Emerson, an excerpt from 'Civil Disobedience,' an excerpt from *Bigelow Papers* to relate to introduction, poems of 'O Capt., My Capt.' and 'When

Lilacs . . .' because they are stressed in introduction and yet EXCLUDED!"

"I am dissatisfied with the lack of a portion of *Beowulf* in Anglo-Saxon."

"We are least happy with . . . in upper grades, the teachers protesting that students should not be robbed of Milton, Wordsworth, Chaucer, and Shakespeare."

" 'The Rime of the Ancient Mariner' by Coleridge is sophomore level and should not be included in senior English. 'The Prisoner of Chillon' is also sophomore level and should not be included in the fourth-year anthology."

"I, and the students, *particularly* dislike so many dog stories. They request classics. . . .' "

General:

"I dislike all-purpose anthologies and much prefer paperback single works and collections by genre. This year we have adopted 50 paperback editions, and it is fairly certain that the anthologies will be used less and less."

On the Anthologies of Literature — Editorial Apparatus

Tone:

"I object to the *patronizing, quasi-intellectual tone* of the anthologies, esp. in the 'study' questions."

Apparatus:

"Perhaps the chief criticism we make of editorial appurtenances is that the headnotes tell students the point of the selection — thus, in our opinion, defeating to a considerable extent the purpose of reading the selection."

"I don't believe it matters to youngsters that an author had a bankrupt father as much as it matters to him the purpose of the selection he is reading."

"My constant greatest effort is to make my students hunt for causes or for effects or for methods of gaining success. Since literature is full of good examples, it would be helpful to have this type of thinking emphasized in the teachers' helps and in the study questions. Reading with comprehension is necessary but not enough."

"The questions are too often superficial and do not motivate pupils to read analytically."

"I do not use the editorial apparatus at all."

"Suggested activities concentrate too much on attention-getting 'gimmicks.'"

"Reading tests are poor; they test too minute details instead of meaning."

"Suggestions for expository themes at the end of each long selection would be helpful."

"The editorial apparatus in the anthologies presents a limited point of view that tends to annihilate discussion rather than to stimulate it."

"[The editorial apparatus is] generally weak. Too earnest an attempt is made to make *timely* or to treat as a quaint museum piece."

"The editorial questions and suggestions for activities hamper reading. It is discouraging to see the questions that follow the poem being read."

Illustrations:

"The cover — a picture of square dancing — is a travesty for a literature book."

"Photographs good, but students feel that the sketches are often inaccurate or convey a wrong impression of characters or scenes."

"Publishers seem to be interested in providing beautiful printing examples instead of 'meaty' material. . . . It's like buying a book with upswept fins! Let's concentrate on education instead of putting our material in the trappings of a prostitute."

"Gaudy opening pages, hideous color. The best [of the illustrations] are unobtrusive but of no great import, esthetic or historical."

On the Grammar and Composition Textbooks

General:

"In general most of the grammar books I have used remind me of a loaf of store-bought bread. It's a great big loaf, but by squeezing you can put the whole loaf in your mouth at one bite — the rest is air."

"Although little consensus of opinion can be found, it seems that teachers did agree on a few points. Most seemed to feel that motivational activities were unneeded in the grammar and composition textbooks. Most of our teachers preferred the *Handbook* type of text, although there was some disagreement on what form this should take. Teachers do like definite and complete instruction in helping students to marshal their thoughts to serve the forms of writing. Actual written work of the varied types should be presented in sufficient amount to enable students to know for what they are striving. More material on writing and less or none on activities such as answering a telephone or what to do on a date are definitely in order. The cartoon approach is not favored by teachers in this school. Rather teachers here prefer a tone and approach which suggests to the student he is now a mature individual who can proceed to do his work without the cajolery or sugar-coated method possibly necessary with a child."

"Although the book is termed Handbook of English, it is not what I call a handbook, a text covering much the same general material under chapter headings with a separate section indexed alphabetically, all items that might occasion the necessity of a quickly found, brief explanation. I prefer the kind of handbook I have described."

"The section on reading is remarkable for its nonliterary approach. . . . The series ignores literature; even in the section on verse writing only 16 lines by recognized poets appear."

"The book looks dull and in fact is. The particularly foolish part of it, the front section in general, is very little used. A look at the books in the book-room shows the edges dark and grimy for the grammar sections, the first half on 'language arts' nice and white. A handbook alone would do the job most teachers want done."

"I do not care for this text. I found that the treatment of the material tended to discourage the students. They objected to the small print and long explanations. Also, the illustrations are more for grammar school and junior high school than for high school. The students felt this and resented it."

Progression:
"This book is hopelessly inadequate for college preparatory English. The style, illustrations, and examples are too elementary. The book for grade twelve could be used in an accelerated seventh grade."

"We were especially dismayed that the new edition of our former text for sophomores had gone overboard into pages and pages of trivia in its efforts to entertain the children and catch their eyes with color. They had treated sophomores like small children, made the tenth grade text much too juvenile. Thus while we were told that such a text was sweeping the country, it would not in any degree satisfy our need for a textbook for serious study."

"The books are repetitious; every one in almost every series contains the very same material, presented in exactly the same way, using what seem to be the same sentences for examples."

(Progression of Volumes.) "Not particularly evident. I have had occasion to work with the volume for the seventh grade this semester, and it is alarmingly similar to the tenth-grade volume. A student who had mastered the seventh-grade volume would go out of his mind if he had to plod through the volumes for eighth, ninth, tenth, and eleventh grades. Of course he hasn't mastered this material, and the publisher seems to accept the fact that he never will."

"The book is altogether too childish (so, ineffective) for this grade. This is the consensus of my class, as well as my opinion. They feel insulted at being so lightly challenged. (Of course, I try to make up for the inadequacies of the book.)"

Composition:

"Topics for writing are weak, hackneyed, unliterary."

"Topics are inane. In Book 10 the careful description of paragraph building is followed by a sample composition containing several undeveloped, one-sentence paragraphs."

"The little writing instruction that is presented is good, but it is repeated over and over again to the reader in different ways. The bright student sees this and becomes bored with this repetition."

"Too much emphasis on personal and creative writing — not enough on expository, critical and analytical writing."

"It should emphasize writing to a much greater degree. Only 109 pages from a total of 539 treat of actual composition in any form."

"I personally believe grammar instruction can be just as effective through the actual writing, especially when the most common usage errors are stressed."

"Materials on writing are constantly interrupted by sociology."

Grammar:

". . . is always explaining that there is a formal and informal form which can be used. Often examples are given, and the pupil is left with the feeling that if Dickens split an infinitive it is the thing to do. Since no one ever knows whether his public will prefer the formal or colloquial style, it seems safer to concentrate upon learning the formal one."

"There is hardly anything good I can say about this textbook. Traditional terminology has been abandoned, and infantile new tags substituted for such things as parts of speech and parts of sentences. There is not enough of spelling, either of rules or of lists of words."

"Thorough generally, but the 'simplification' of terms in recent editions causes some confusion, especially in Book 2. The old terms pop up again in Book 3. Many of the drill exercises are made up of inane sentences. Nothing about absolute constructions appears even in the volume designed for juniors."

"Some structural linguistics jargon. Therefore, some confusion in terminology. Mostly traditional material with a little up-to-date frosting."

"I don't think they should use participles as adjectives when they are teaching parts of speech. They should come later after the students study participles. Examples: 'Skulking Indian,' 'battered saucepans.' Also, when you're trying to teach what a noun is, they introduce complicated constructions like nouns as objects of verbals before they teach verbals."

"Less than one half of this book contains any treatment of grammar and usage. Each chapter begins with a diagnostic test, and then it explains the various rules. The diagnostic test approach is good because it introduces the students to what they must learn in order to master the more difficult practices at the end of the chapter. However, not enough illustrations of the rules of grammar and usage are included. Students need a more detailed explanation and examples in their books; their teacher does not have time to compile extra material."

"A principle is half-way introduced, several example sentences follow, and that's it. The organization is awful as far as grammar is concerned."

"The presentation of material is not in a logical arrangement. No mention is made of transitive and intransitive verbs."

"It contradicts itself from grade to grade and even within the same volume, and the exercise material is poorly planned. A typical exercise will devote ¾'s of its sentences to simple constructions which students already know or can learn in a few minutes, and only a fourth to the really crucial constructions which students have difficulty in learning."

"It would seem sensible to have the section on 'Building Sentences' precede the section on writing, the study of the parts of the sentence before punctuation. Such is not the case."

"I object to the word *completer* to describe objects and predicate nominatives. Of course, any teacher can make that correction orally until they see fit to change it."

Relation of Grammar to Writing:

"My chief criticism of this text (and others) is that the functional aspect of the items we include under grammar, usage, and mechanics is not presented clearly. Rules, definitions, and examples of parts of speech, parts of the sentence, phrases, clauses, punctuation and spelling are presented as separate bugaboos, with little effort to give the student insight as to the real necessity for their learning them, that is, the *understanding* of their *function* for effective two-way communication — the ability to handle, or make use of, these items for a command of their language that will enable them to speak and write understandably, and to read and listen understandingly."

"Practice in writing and study of grammar must go together; either one without the other will lead, in my opinion, to mediocrity of written expression."

"The separation of sections on writing and grammar seems to imply to most students that these are entirely separate areas."

"Textbooks need a more functional approach to grammar so

that students will be immediately aware of the relation between their study of grammar and their own speech and writing."

Motivational and Other Activities:

"Many activities concern etiquette, social problems, anthropology; none concerns literature."

"Fair activities except in social, etiquette, and similar material. There is a great deal of material about using the telephone."

"Awfully 'groupy.' Strong semantic emphasis, also strong anti-prejudice slant. What this book needs is less sociology and more English. It probably appeals to teachers of low ability students who have found conventional grammar too difficult to learn."

"The suggested activities are good, that is, for elementary and junior high school students. They seem to insult the intelligence of high school students."

"Little use of motivational material. I prefer to use essays and other literature from the course of study as motivation. I like the handbook type. I do not use a workbook."

"We particularly like this book because it does not go into the field of guidance and does not cover such subjects as boy-girl relationships, interviewing for jobs, and other subjects that are taught in our guidance classes."

"Such things as 'score card for letter writing.' Really grim."

"How to use the library and how to use the dictionary is extraneous and could be omitted."

"I don't use material on conversation, business letters (this is covered in English IV), newspaper work (we have journalism courses). . . ."

"Department policy discourages consideration of 'frill' chapters on subjects such as career guidance, getting along with people, club activities, and social graces."

Appendix G

AUTHORS AND EDITORS

MANY, but regrettably not all, publishers of the two kinds of series reported have generously provided us with detailed information on their authors and editors in response to our request. We had hoped to tabulate information, for example, on the academic preparation of all authors and editors (college major, degrees, etc.), but because we lack complete detail we consider it inappropriate to present the limited data of this kind that we have. It is nevertheless possible to make a few generalizations, and, particularly, to give an account of the present (or immediately past) professional positions of the authors and editors. Even these figures will fall short of the total number involved.

Anthologies of Literature

We have information on the professional status of sixty-two editors of the anthologies of literature, as follows:

High School teachers	26
Professors of English	
(college and university)	9
Professors of English	
(state college)	7

Professors of Education	4
Supervisors (consultants, etc.)	6
Directors Reading Laboratory (clinic, etc.)	3
Principals	3
Director, Division of Library	1
Specialist, U. S. Office of Education	1
Childrens Book Editor	1
Headmaster, Latin school	1

Grammar and Composition

We have information on the professional status of forty-six authors of the grammar and composition series, as follows:

High School teachers	21
Professors of English (college or university)	7
Professors of English (state college)	7
Professors of Education	5
Supervisors, etc.	3
Principal	1
Instructor, junior college	1
Testing specialist	1

Makeup of Author-Editor Teams

In every instance, preparation of a series involves more than one individual as author or editor. Only in rare instances are as few as two responsible for preparation of an entire series; more typical numbers are three and four, with some teams including eight or more. In about half of the cases, whole series are prepared by a single team responsible for all volumes; otherwise, typically, a single author or editor functions for all volumes of a series, with other members of the team functioning on one or two volumes. (These counts do not include persons who have advised, contributed small units, examples, etc., or furnished other assistance; some series list a large number of names in this category.)

In almost no case is a series prepared by a team consisting exclusively of either high school or college people; among the grammar and composition books, for example, only one complete series is edited by just two high school teachers, and in another instance two of the volumes of a series are edited by three high school teachers. More typically, the team combines high school and college teachers, with the occasional addition of others from one or more of the categories identified above.

Professional Activities of Authors and Editors

In virtually every case in which publishers have supplied information, principal authors and editors of the textbooks prove to be individuals who, besides carrying on their teaching or other duties in high school, college, or university, have been notably active in professional organizations, especially those concerned with English, the language arts, reading, etc. As would certainly be expected, most of these have distinguished themselves particularly through work with the National Council of Teachers of English and its regional affiliates. Information supplied us makes it abundantly clear that publishers almost universally have turned for their authors and editors to those who have established their reputations primarily as leaders in the professional organizations concerned with high school "language arts." Hence, again as would certainly be expected, the roll of principal authors and editors of the textbooks on which we have reported reads very much like a *Who's Who* of the NCTE and its affiliates.